Election Journal

Also by Elizabeth Drew

Washington Journal: The Events of 1973–1974
American Journal: The Events of 1976
Senator
Portrait of an Election: The 1980 Presidential Campaign
Politics and Money: The New Road to Corruption
Campaign Journal: The Political Events of 1983–1984

Election Journal

POLITICAL EVENTS OF
1987–1988

Elizabeth Drew

William Morrow and Company, Inc.
New York

bc

Library of Congress Cataloging-in-Publication Data

Drew, Elizabeth.
    Election journal : political events of 1987–1988 / by Elizabeth
Drew.
      p.   cm.
    ISBN 0-688-08332-3
    1. Presidents—United States—Election—1988. 2. United States—
Politics and government—1981-   I. Title.
E880.D74   1988
324.973'0927—dc19   88-8291
                                                                 CIP

Printed in the United States of America

First Edition

1   2   3   4   5   6   7   8   9   10

For David, Daniel, and Alexander

ACKNOWLEDGMENTS

No book of this kind can happen without the help and support of numerous people. Interesting and thoughtful people in and out of the political world had to talk to me—a lot—and share their thinking and insights. Though I have now listened to and dealt with political people for a number of years, they never cease to interest me and surprise me. There are always new ways of looking at things, new approaches tried, new issues (important and relevant or not). These people's generosity with their time is deeply appreciated, and enjoyed. They can't all be named, but they know who they are.

John Bennet, my editor at *The New Yorker,* was once again smart, supportive, and skilled. Kathy Glover, my assistant, was once again able, dedicated, and a critical part of the process of producing this work. Laura Waltz, my former assistant, once again loyally read the proofs of this book. Bob Gottlieb, the editor of *The New Yorker,* gave my work his enthusiastic support, for which I am very grateful. I also remain very grateful to William Shawn, who brought me into *The New Yorker* in the first place, and gave me so much over the years.

E.D.

INTRODUCTION

The Presidential election of 1988 changed Presidential politics, in ways that will be with us for a long time. New techniques, and a new tone, were employed, and since they were successful, they are likely to be emulated—throughout our political system. Future candidates may be less in need of employing these tactics, or, as the case might be, more effective in confronting them, but they now stand as the marker, the point of departure. Virtually unnoticed, television coverage of Presidential campaigns has also undergone important changes—changes far more significant than the much remarked upon shrinking in length of sound-bites. This is only one of the significant effects of the eight-year Presidency of Ronald Reagan, who was in many ways the dominant figure in the 1988 election. The election cannot be understood absent the role Reagan played in our country, and the world. Nor can the situation his successor, George Bush, inherits.

This book grows out of my reporting on the election, and its context, for *The New Yorker*. It reflects what I saw and how I saw it at the time—history as it happened and not tidied up, or distorted, in hindsight to make things seem neater or more inevitable than they were. All judgments (or misjudgments) are left as they were, to give future readers a more immediate sense of what it was like to experience this important piece of history.

—Elizabeth Drew
December, 1988

1987

I

A year from now, we will have elected a new President—a prospect that we can view only hazily at present. One of the many men running for the office will have won it—unless, of course, the victor is not yet in the field—and there will probably be, as there usually is, much analysis that tells us why his victory was inevitable. But nothing seems inevitable at the moment. By this time next year, we will be looking over pictures of the new President and his family, acquainting ourselves with a new set of White House aides and Cabinet officers, and, probably, enjoying a spell, however brief, of innocence and hope once again. We like to start over. The President-elect will be given a line of credit on which to draw support from the public, from other politicians, and from the press. But the next President is likely to face daunting difficulties with the economy. Many people assume that a recession is coming, and the only question is when—the timing of the recession may be the most important factor in the election. After the stock-market crash on October 19th, one prominent Republican economist here quietly moved up the odds on a recession before the election from thirty-seventy to fifty-fifty. A labor leader said to me recently that he didn't think it much mattered who the parties' nominees were, because the most important factor next November would be the rate of growth of the gross national product. This unromantic view of Presidential elections is widely shared among political practitioners. Other than the potential issue of the economy, there is as yet no great issue in this election. Reagan may well have achieved more than one arms-control agreement before he leaves office, and have made his meeting with Soviet leader Mikhail Gorbachev the norm—and thus removed arms control as a political issue. Still, Presidential elections are often affected by exogenous and unpredictable events, and issues, important or otherwise, always develop.

11

Ronald Reagan's legacy will be much debated for a long time. People often talk in terms of what "history" will say about Reagan's Presidency, but there is no such unanimous opinion on Presidencies: as in the case of other Presidencies, opinions on Reagan's will be shaped by the views of those who offer them, and the historical view will change, be subject to revision. Reagan will undoubtedly be seen as a major figure, a President who had a major impact on his country in terms of his policies and his persona. The debate will be over the nature of that impact.

For now, the question is what choice we make as a country for the post-Reagan era, and how the election and the next Presidency will be shaped by the Reagan years. The next President may have already been taken hostage by the incumbent one. Reagan will leave office with a national debt of close to three trillion dollars (having inherited a debt of a trillion dollars), and because of the debt his successor's choices will be limited. The current efforts to reduce the debt, between a reluctant President and bipartisan congressional leaders after the stock-market crash, are aimed only at reducing the rate of growth of the debt, not at reducing the debt itself, and they don't deal with long-run budget realities. The next President will inherit a country that is the largest debtor nation in the world; it was the largest creditor nation when Reagan took office. Reagan gave the American people—or many of them—a whale of a good time; we borrowed and spent our way into the longest peacetime period of economic growth (though the growth was lower than the average during the postwar period), and enjoyed the delusion of prosperity while the debt mounted. The income gap between rich and poor widened, and the poverty rate is higher than it was during the last three Administrations. Americans are facing a lower standard of living; despite tax cuts and the creation of about thirteen million jobs during the Reagan Presidency, real net per-capita income is declining. And though the tax cuts were supposed to spur investment and savings, investment has been minimal, and the savings rate has dropped sharply. Black Monday, the day when the stock market went down five hundred and eight points, may have at long last pierced the bubble, but it is not clear yet that even the crash has brought us back to reality. Meanwhile, conditions in the inner cities are such that we are turning out an increasingly less educated and less trainable work force. There's reason to wonder why anyone would want to be the next President.

Between now and next November, there will be a plenitude of predictions about who will be the parties' nominees and who will ultimately be elected, but they will mostly be guesses. The most obvious fact—that each election is different and has its own dynamic—is largely overlooked each time. The predictions tend to run in fashions, and, like fashions, they change. The essential unpredictability of elections—short of a landslide in the general election, and even that can be late in materializing—stems from many things, but does not inhibit people from predicting. Each contest can be affected not only by unexpected events but also by blunders by some candidate. (In every election, someone makes a fool of himself.) Even the weather on the day of a primary or caucuses can affect the outcome. Polls are temporary and shaky indicators. Most of all, there is the mysterious chemical relationship between a candidate and the public—a relationship that cannot be predicted. That relationship, in turn, does not necessarily foretell the relationship between the new President and the public, which is the most important of all. So as we watch the aspirants it is useful to try to judge as best we can how any one of them would do in office—not at first, when the dew is still on him, but after, say, a year, when the going is likely to have got harder.

Often, this country counterprograms its Presidents. We elected Jimmy Carter because, it is believed, after Richard Nixon we wanted "an outsider" and a man who sounded idealistic about government. After Carter, we turned to Reagan in reaction, it is believed, to Carter's absorption in detail and his worried mien (and a troubled economy). Reagan offered hope, optimism, morale—and a good time. Now, it is widely believed, we are back to wanting a "hands-on" President—we're in the market for competence. This year, no serious candidate is running an anti-Washington campaign. One buzzword in this campaign is "vision": it's stated as a given that a candidate must show us his "vision" for the future. This assumption probably grew out of some successful campaigns for the Presidency that set forth (however vaguely) a "vision": John F. Kennedy, Carter (sort of), Reagan. But maybe what we need is not a spellbinder but someone who can get us through the day.

* * *

Another unromantic truth is that the arithmetic of the electoral college has made it progressively easier for the Republicans—and more difficult for the Democrats—to elect a President. As the population shifts to the South and the Southwest, where, broadly speaking, the voters have tended to vote more conservatively than they have in the Democrats' old stronghold, the New England and Midwestern industrial states, the Democrats' job has become harder. Those states have not had a sufficient number of electoral votes (two hundred and seventy) to elect a President since 1968, when Humphrey failed to carry some of them. In fact, only Minnesota (except in 1972) and the District of Columbia have voted for the Democratic ticket steadfastly since 1964. The Democrats haven't carried California, the most populous state, with seventeen per cent of the electoral-college votes needed to win, since 1964. By contrast, thirty-two states have voted fairly consistently for the Republicans. Since 1932, no Democrat has won the Presidency for the first time without a Southerner on the ticket. Some think that even a Northern liberal's picking a Southerner as his running mate might not necessarily help (barring an economic crisis). Robert Teeter, a Republican pollster (now working for George Bush), says that in recent times the South has consistently voted in the general election for the more conservative candidate, and that it thought Carter was more conservative, at least on social issues, than Gerald Ford. In less than a year, we'll know whether recent patterns still hold true.

The shape of this particular election campaign has many people puzzled—or should have them so. This will be the first election in twenty years when neither party has had an incumbent President for a candidate. (It is also pointed out that the last two incumbent Vice-Presidents who ran for the Presidency—Nixon and Humphrey—were defeated.) No one really knows what will be the effect of so many Southern states' having moved their primaries up, to March 8th, in order to have more of an impact. The Democrats in these various states were behind the move, on the theory that this could break their party's habit of nominating someone who couldn't carry the South in November. The theory went that the change would force candidates for the nomination to spend more time in the South and to shape their positions to appeal to Southerners. We won't know until it's over, but the theory might turn out to have large flaws. It's usually the case that the Democrats who vote in the Southern primaries are more liberal than those who turn out for general elections; the Democratic turnout in the primaries is smaller than it is in the general election, and is more representative of especially interested constituency groups—blacks, labor, and the like. As of now, it is widely expected that the greatest Democratic beneficiary of the "Southern primary" will be Jesse Jackson, but the benefit may not be as great as many think. Not all the states with primaries or caucuses on March 8th are in the South—Washington, Massachusetts, Hawaii, and Idaho, among others, also hold elections on that date—and not all the Southern states are alike. Some Southern Democratic leaders regret the bunching of the contests on March 8th, because they see that it won't give the South a voice later in the contest. Frank Fahrenkopf, the chairman of the Republican National Committee, couldn't be more pleased with what he sees as the fix the Democrats will be in as a result of March 8th. (He hopes to lure conservative Democrats into Republican primaries on that date, to make the Democratic outcome even more liberal.) And it's possible that the bunching of so many contests on March 8th will have the effect of making the Iowa caucuses, on February 8th, and the New Hampshire primary, on February 16th, even more important than they were before—the opposite of what was intended. This would happen if victors in the first two contests get so much free publicity and attention that they are like projectiles shot from those two states, and unstoppable. And the results in Iowa can affect what happens in New Hampshire. Five states have primaries or caucuses between New Hampshire and March 8th, and they can be part of the acceleration—or the slowing down—of various candidates. One can get perfectly reasonable arguments from people who are expert in these matters that the Southern primaries make Iowa and New Hampshire more important and less important than before.

The Democratic candidates are just now starting to come into sharp focus, and to define their differences—and to start slugging. Many Democrats express disappointment with the current field, and one senses among many of them something of an inferiority complex—a feeling that their party has become proficient at blowing it. The term that had been used to describe the field—"the seven dwarfs" (this when Joseph Biden was still in the race)—has begun to recede, but among many Democrats the feeling remains that their party has no giants in the field. That one of the candidates might take off, might acquire "winnerness," which would change the public perception of him, does not yet seem a reality to many Democrats, a large number of whom assume that Robert Dole, or even George Bush (they assume, perhaps incorrectly, that Bush would be the weaker candidate in the general election), will win. Some of the Democrats' discouragement comes from the fact that none of their candidates have played in the major leagues—unlike Bush and Dole—and from embarrassment over the indignities that have befallen some of their potential candidates, forcing them out of the race or keeping them from entering. The fact that some of the Party's stars—Bill Bradley, Mario Cuomo, and Sam Nunn—have for various reasons chosen not to run, and are still pined for by numerous people, casts a doubt over those who are running. Washington has been awash with rumors at various stages about the reasons certain other possible candidates never entered. And the fact that two candidates who were considered quite strong—perhaps incorrectly—had to drop out is taken by many as an embarrassment to the Party (though in this context there is no such thing as "the Party").

Yet there was a certain justice in Gary Hart's and Joseph Biden's having to drop out, because they both faltered on character traits that probably would have knocked them out later on. A great many people knew that Hart seemed incapable of exercising self-control in his sex life, and many believed that his campaign would eventually run into trouble on this score. The only surprises in the whole thing were that Hart took the hit so early in the campaign (last May) and that he was caught, by the Miami *Herald*, in such a reckless adventure. Biden, too, was knocked out by a weakness that was going to catch up with him anyway—a kind of intellectual barrenness. Biden is a nice guy who hasn't demonstrated much depth or mental or verbal discipline. So when he was caught appropriating the biography of the British Labour leader Neil Kinnock—without attribution a couple of times, but that wasn't really the point—and inflating his academic credentials, he was hit in the area of his greatest vulnerability. Biden's campaign hadn't been making a lot of sense anyway: it was based on his reputation as a great orator, but oratorical skills don't count for much in television-era campaigning. And Biden was basing his campaign and his oratory on the odd premise that the election was about a generational change—as if all members of a certain generation think alike. He pulled out graciously, in the midst of the hearings he was presiding over on the doomed nomination of Robert Bork for the Supreme Court.

It is clearly the case that some people have stayed out of the race at least in part because of the ridiculous and brutal demands that it makes on a candidate. It is possible to come out of such a campaign with one's body and soul and dignity intact—but not many do. The demands seem to grow with every election: however long the last nominee spent in Iowa, the next candidates spend longer. This election will be notable for the large number of debates (especially on the Democratic side, where straw polls are out). Having a certain number of debates is good, but things have gone overboard this time, debates being the latest form of self-promotion—and a way to bring pressure on the candidates, with everyone getting into the act. The Democrats are beginning to look like punch-drunk contenders being forced to go too many rounds. Though "pandering" went out of style with the disastrous Mondale campaign in 1984, debates sponsored by various interest groups invite pandering by the candidates, most of whom comply.

The result is long lists of promises. The Democratic candidates heap blame on Reagan for the deficits but for the most part remain vague about their solutions. Most—with the exception of Bruce Babbitt—are loath to talk about raising taxes. The debates tend to enlarge the differences among the candidates, and to force them to find issues that wouldn't otherwise be there. This compounds an old problem for the Democrats. Meanwhile, the six Democrats and the six Republicans offering themselves to us deserve some careful scrutiny, particularly on the matter of how they might hold up as President. One of them might be elected.

Bruce Babbitt is a nice, intelligent man who no one thinks is going to be the Democratic nominee. He has simply been unable to establish himself as a credible candidate: having been governor of a sparsely populated state (Arizona) doesn't help, nor does his remote personality. And the television camera is unkind to him: though Babbitt has been working on his television presence (and shaking his head less than he did in his disastrous appearance in the first Democratic debate, in July), he and the camera don't take to each other, and that's that. Television technology is a ruthless arbiter. In person, Babbitt has considerable charm and a wry, self-deprecating sense of humor. His lack of self-pity and his ability to joke about his situation are attractive. Babbitt is cerebral—perhaps too cerebral for politics—and he sees issues in their complexity, and is not as adept as others at simplifying them. He takes iconoclastic positions (only in part because he can afford to): he is the only Democratic candidate calling for a means test for entitlement programs and increased taxes on upper-income Social Security recipients, and for a national sales tax. There is some speculation that Babbitt will come out of this venture with enhanced standing, and could end up in a Democratic Administration, if there should be such a thing.

The most critical question about Michael Dukakis, since he is a serious contender for the Democratic nomination and considered by many the front-runner at this point, is how he would stand up over time—whether he could lead the people over a sustained period. Without question, Dukakis is a smart, well-motivated, and largely decent man, but he has some traits that present doubts about how successful he would be as President. His personality is not the most engaging one: he is very serious and nearly humorless. There is a certain grimness about him, as if he doesn't quite approve of enjoying himself too much. His campaign, aware of this, has put Dukakis in certain humanizing situations, such as playing the trumpet at a Boston fund-raiser; and it is for the purpose of warming up his image that Dukakis has pointed out in several stump speeches that in September *Playgirl* listed him as one of the ten sexiest men in the country. (A campaign aide told me earlier this fall that this was done to answer complaints from field workers that "Mike doesn't boogie.") It was also for this purpose that in 1983, when he returned to the gubernatorial office, after being defeated for renomination in 1978, he began to have himself called Mike. His Presidential-campaign literature bears the name Mike, while those close to him call him Michael. Similarly, Dukakis's frequent references to his Greek-immigrant parents are new. Dukakis is a notorious tightwad: articles about him point out that he buys his suits in Filene's basement, that he shops for house-brand groceries at Stop & Shop, and that he chides his wife, Kitty, for buying what he considers too many clothes. There is an obsessiveness to his frugality. So it came as something of a surprise when it was learned in September that Dukakis's late father had set up a million-dollar trust, which benefitted Dukakis and his family. (The elder Dukakis left a second million-dollar trust, some of which will also eventually benefit his son.) The disclosure of the trusts arose in a different context: the story broke in Boston papers that until 1986 some of the stocks in the trust held by Dukakis had been invested in companies that did business in South Africa. The problem with this politically was that Dukakis had been boasting about a Massachusetts law that divested the state's holdings in such companies—and that he presents himself as a hands-on administrator. The way Dukakis handled this particular flap led to a Boston *Globe* editorial saying that though Dukakis has admirable qualities, they are "not balanced by humility and concession to error."

I have heard the word "arrogant" as a description of Dukakis in several contexts, and it seems to apply not only to his personal dealings with many people but also to his approach to politics, and even issues—and it is the latter that is the most worrisome. It must be pointed out that many people think highly of Dukakis and are quite loyal to him. Also, he attracts and surrounds himself with able people. His campaign inevitably also draws a number of people who see him more as an opportunity than as their beau ideal. A number of people who know him and are for him are noticeably lukewarm about him. And some people joined the campaign not out of any great attraction to Dukakis but because of their respect and affection for John Sasso, Dukakis's campaign manager, who had to resign at the end of September for having masterminded the distribution to certain media of a tape showing Biden giving the Kinnock speech and Kinnock giving the speech. (A footnote to history: the tape was not, as many supposed, spliced to show Biden's sentence-by-sentence parroting of Kinnock; it showed one speech following the other.)

It was Sasso who was responsible for Dukakis's political resurrection—his return to the governor's office after his renomination defeat. There's something a little troubling about the emphasis Dukakis and some people around him put on that defeat; it's described as having devastated him, and the trauma that he suffered is pointed to as a major fact about him. But politics is a rough business, and entails losing at times, and most people don't go to pieces when they lose. (Though some, particularly those who lose the Presidency, do.) So this raises among other things a question about Dukakis's resilience, his ability to cope when things get tough—as they are sure to do in this campaign and in the next Presidency. Also, the story of his loss is used by Dukakis and people around him to state (even when one hasn't brought the subject up) that it taught him to be less arrogant, to deal with people better. One wonders why they feel they have to say this so much.

Sasso made the Dukakis Presidential campaign into something to be taken seriously by the press by raising a great deal of money and attracting some good people and building an organization—and doing a great deal of talking. Sasso is very persuasive. It was Dukakis's money and organization that won him the early respect of the press. Dukakis has raised more money than any other Democratic candidate—from within the state, from the Greek community, and from, among others, the Hollywood community, which favors his liberalism, especially on arms control and foreign policy. The money, it is hoped, will give Dukakis staying power. When the candidates receive their federal funds in January—matching funds based on how much they have raised—Dukakis stands to be far ahead of any of his rivals; his campaign hopes to use this advantage to wear his competitors down. Despite the public financing of Presidential campaigns, money still counts for a great deal in Presidential elections—and so does organization, which money buys. Dukakis's aides say that he is now ahead of Paul Simon, his strongest competitor at the moment, in every state but Iowa (where the two are close) and that he has the only truly national campaign. Dukakis has won the support of one union in Iowa, and he has changed his position on agriculture to one more favorable to Iowa farmers. The Dukakis people, with an eye to the long hand-to-hand combat with which Mondale won the nomination in 1984, put a lot of emphasis on money and organization—one hears more about that than one does about their candidate. The candidate himself also talks frequently about the size of his campaign, but he still doesn't have a national message. Staying power, of course, is not the same thing as ability to govern.

On the face of it, Sasso didn't have to go because of the tape —it was simply a technologically more advanced form of getting out negative information about a rival—but he had to go because

Dukakis had cornered himself. Dukakis presents himself as a political reformer, and he had been campaigning with more than a touch of righteousness. In fact, last summer he complained in a letter to the other candidates about Richard Gephardt's suggesting that Dukakis's role in Massachusetts' economic revival wasn't as great as Dukakis was claiming, and about Gephardt's criticism of Dukakis's trade policy. After it broke in the press that his campaign was behind the tape affair, Dukakis said that he would be "astonished" and "very angry" to learn that anyone connected with his campaign was responsible. It remains unclear why Dukakis, with his hands-on style, did not know that Sasso was behind the tape affair, especially since the question of who was behind it was the subject of so much speculation for ten days, and why, if after the story broke Sasso gave him an evasive reply, as various press accounts had it, he did not demand the truth. Massachusetts politics is a rough game, and both Sasso and Dukakis know how to play. (The situation was also complicated by the fact that Paul Tully, another important campaign aide, had publicly denied that the campaign was involved in the tape affair; therefore, it would have been awkward for Tully to have to go while Sasso remained on the job.) Many Democrats were angered by the fact that the tape had been distributed just before Biden was about to begin the hearings on the Bork nomination; also, the Dukakis people had helped spread it about that Gephardt's campaign people had distributed the tape, thus causing a temporary crisis in the Gephardt campaign. All this was taking place, of course, while the candidates were spending a great deal of time and effort in Iowa, and Iowans like their politics pure. (In some other states, such a tactic would have been de rigueur.) And Dukakis was running as a reformer, hands on.

The situation was further bollixed by the fact that Dukakis was indecisive: first, he wouldn't accept Sasso's resignation, and then, faced with a continuing clamor from the press and advice from distraught aides that Sasso had to go, Dukakis let him go. This raised a question about Dukakis's competence. It's hard for most people outside a campaign to imagine the panic and paralysis that envelop a campaign when it is faced with a particularly difficult matter: for days, the press will ask about nothing else, and will hear nothing else, and campaign aides are unable to function. So it's decided action must be taken. (This happened to the Hart campaign.) Shortly after Sasso was let go, Dukakis went to Iowa —campaigning in Biden territory, as it happened—and dug himself in further. Sasso, he said, will "play no role, formal or informal, within the campaign." But he and Sasso were an unusually close pair, and Dukakis for some weeks seemed to go through a period of anger and mourning, and didn't function very well. Nevertheless, Dukakis refused to give severance pay to Sasso, who has two small children and had been with him for seven years, or to Tully—and had to be persuaded by other advisers to change his mind. With Sasso gone, the campaign suffered a substantial setback. A lot—much of it intangible—was lost in the weeks following the tape affair. The loss of Tully, an experienced campaign organizer, also hurt, and the Dukakis campaign remains thin at the top. Sasso's successor, Susan Estrich, a Harvard law professor, who had been playing a major role in the campaign, is an exceptionally smart and able person, and was the popular choice within the campaign. She is not likely to withhold from Dukakis what she thinks, but Dukakis is hard to get close to, and through to, and no one other than Kitty Dukakis is as close to him as Sasso was. Dukakis has a stubborn streak, and sometimes seems to have trouble making a decision.

The campaign would have been more difficult for Dukakis at this stage anyway—when he had become a serious candidate and was subject to closer scrutiny. But he seems to have been stalled internally: the anecdotes about the good he did in Massachusetts are wearing thin. (The "Massachusetts miracle" was the result of more than Dukakis's efforts; the entire New England area has been enjoying a recovery, and Massachusetts, with its universities and other technological resources, has won a number of defense contracts.) Unfortunately for Dukakis, General Motors announced in November that it would close an assembly plant in Framingham, throwing nearly four thousand employees out of work—just as his campaign was beginning to run an ad in Iowa saying, "What he did for Massachusetts, he can do for America." Dukakis has given some earnest speeches on other subjects, but they don't seem to lift him or his audience. Several of his appearances have been lacklustre. His speech at a Jefferson-Jackson Day dinner in Iowa in early November—the major event there before next year's caucuses—was a bomb; he didn't seem to give a damn, or to have much to say. (I'm reliably told that Dukakis was miffed that he had drawn the fifth slot to speak.) Lately, his appearances have shown some improvement, but they are uneven.

Dukakis has been substantively shaky all along, and this may be related to arrogance. When I saw him in Washington in February, when it was clear that he was considering running, his response to the question of how he would handle foreign policy was an offhanded "I'd handle it like the last three guys." He went on to say, with assurance, "They all broke the law." (With the exception of the Iran-Contra affair, he could not explain what he meant.) Dukakis has a tendency to be flip. Only when I pressed the matter did he say that he probably would have to spend some time learning about foreign policy—while he ran for the nomination (and remained governor). Wiser heads around him in the campaign realized that foreign policy could be his greatest vulnerability, and some smart people were brought in to brief him. But the fact that he is learning on the run shows; as he talks, in speeches and in debates, one can visualize the briefings going in and coming out. But he seems very assured about what he's saying. Dukakis is comfortable in debates and has good eye contact with the camera—his aides feel that the debate format gives him an advantage because of his experience as a moderator on a PBS program, "The Advocates," in the early nineteen-seventies, and his ability to make his point in a minute and a half. In a speech on Latin-American policy this fall, he had an important fact wrong about the Guatemala peace plan that is now the basis of negotiations. (He said that it would require the removal of Soviet and Cuban troops from Nicaragua, and it wouldn't. In an interview I had with him in mid-September, he repeated this assertion.) In September, he suggested in an interview with David Broder, of the Washington *Post*, that he might favor removing our troops from South Korea because of Korea's human-rights record and stationing them in Japan. Many Democrats were astonished, since Jimmy Carter had got in trouble in 1976 for suggesting that we might remove our troops from South Korea. Moreover, South Korea is going through political change; and many people who know about the area say it is the presence of our troops that keeps South Korea safe from a takeover by North Korea—and that Japan would not welcome our troops. When I saw Dukakis in Boston in mid-September and asked him about this, he said, "I didn't spend six months of my life sitting in rice paddies to have a general deny the Korean people the right to elect their own President." (In July, the South Korean government announced that it would hold an election in December, and it is to be held shortly.) Of course, we fought the war in Korea to keep the North Koreans from overrunning the entire place; human rights was not a consideration. When Albert Gore, in a debate in Iowa in September, pressed Dukakis on what he had said about Korea, he tried to wriggle out of the fact that he had said it. ("Get your facts straight.")

Dukakis deals with the deficit question by saying that great sums of money can be found through enhanced tax collection— a premise that many people question, and that Gephardt has called "hokum." (Dukakis did have such a program in Massachusetts, but the state story doesn't necessarily apply to the federal government—and Congress has already called for enhanced enforcement of tax collection several times, with what many experts say are bogus estimates of the potential results.) Dukakis says that enhanced tax enforcement can bring in a hundred and five billion dollars over five years and thirty-five billion dollars each year thereafter. Intentionally or not, he sometimes scrambles the numbers and makes them seem higher. Representative Byron Dorgan, Democrat of North Dakota (and a Gephardt supporter), who is the sponsor of a report on which Dukakis's figures are based, says that the revenues that could be gained in the first two or three years will be relatively small (increments of seven billion dollars a year), and that therefore additional taxes will also be needed. "You can't pay today's bills with tomorrow's revenues," Dorgan told me. The nonpartisan technical staff of the Joint Committee on Taxation has concluded that Dorgan's report greatly overestimates the overall amount of revenue that is still out there to be collected. Dukakis says he will not propose any other taxes until enhanced enforcement has been tried. He prefers to talk about economic growth as a deficit reducer, and he also espouses a number of new or enlarged federal programs. (In Texas, he promised to cut taxes on oil producers, and to pay premium rates for newly discovered oil reserves.) In my interview with him in September, I asked him what he would do if tax enforcement did not raise sufficient revenues, and he replied, "If you do all this, and put together an economic-development program, and cut spending for programs, and you're still falling short, you have to go to Congress and ask for more money." When I asked him what sort of request for taxes he would make, he replied, "I can't say what, but anybody who knows me knows it has to be progressive and based on ability to pay—no sales tax, no value-added tax." An aide who had sat in on the interview told me as soon as we left Dukakis's office that it was "definitely" not part of Dukakis's plan to ask for taxes if revenues fell short, that he didn't have a two-step plan, but was simply stating what kinds of taxes he would rule out, and felt that as a matter of common sense one could not say there would never have to be more taxes.

Though Sasso tried to present Dukakis as a non-ideological, hands-on manager, he is a liberal, in domestic and foreign policy—his instincts are liberal, though he is careful, and exudes no passion. He has gone further in his arms-control proposals than even some liberal arms-controllers here think is wise (and one so advised him)—but in this he does not differ from any of his rivals except Gore and Babbitt. The new litmus test for Democrats, which all but Gore and Babbitt have met, is to oppose flight-testing of missiles, which could prevent space exploration as well as jeopardize our most effective deterrent. Dukakis opposes the Midgetman missile—a single-warhead mobile missile championed by Gore and also supported by a number of liberals, including Edward Kennedy, as perhaps the most effective deterrent weapon. Dukakis recently gave a speech in which he suggested transferring funds from the strategic arsenal to conventional forces—and appeared to exaggerate the benefit that would accrue to conventional forces from cuts in strategic weapons, which take up only seventeen per cent of the defense budget. (Many politicians, Democratic and Republican, call for more funds for conventional forces.) Recently, after some of Dukakis's advisers became concerned about his leftward tilt in foreign policy, he began to tilt to the right; more recently, he has essentially returned to where he began. In his speech on Latin-American policy, Dukakis talked about debt relief for expanded environmental protection in the Amazon rain forest. It's hard to imagine him putting this over in Chicago, but it's illustrative of the way his mind works: he's a technocrat, something of a mechanic, and believes in the power of example. He likes to talk about examples, and sees no reason that they can't be applied nationally, even internationally. He stresses international coöperation in dealing with foreign-policy questions, and insists that other nations can be brought around to coöperating with us on our various goals. He told me he'd like to see the Europeans and the Japanese help us keep the peace in Central America. His idealism is attractive, but leaves one wondering whether if things didn't turn out the way he wants he'd know what to do. The worrisome thing about Dukakis is his not knowing what he doesn't know—and his total assurance that what he says is right. So a big question is whether Dukakis is seasoned enough to govern. Another is whether he'll be able to move people. When I asked him in September how he would try to move people, he replied, "I don't think you can get anything done these days as a political leader without coalitions—strong coalitions of active people, starting from the beginning. That's a lesson I've learned painfully in my political career, but I've learned it."

Richard Gephardt is trying a strategy that might make it difficult for him to win the nomination, in the hope that, if it works, it could win him the Presidency. He is trying to walk a center line, making himself completely pleasing neither to strong liberals nor to strong conservatives, with the idea that his centrism and his Missouri roots could make him acceptable to a wide swath of the electorate in November. His advisers think that though it is not a good idea to talk about one's "electability," because it's not been something that moves people (viz., John Glenn in 1984), Democrats are in fact looking for someone who can take them to victory. Gephardt's campaign strategy could also do him in—by making him not exciting enough to enough people.

Gephardt's strategy does underscore a question that many people have about him—who is he? Gephardt is a pleasant man with a good mind, but it is hard to know what is at his core. A question some of his colleagues raise about him is whether he has a rudder. This doesn't mean that Gephardt would act outside the bounds of decency; it means that people question whether he has any deep beliefs. Most politicians are opportunists in some form, but Gephardt's opportunism is more noticeable than many others'. His colleagues point out that he seems to seize upon issues that he thinks will help his career, rather than out of any deep belief—and his interest in these issues can be short-lived. Though Gephardt is far from alone in this respect, a lot of people notice it about him—probably because he has been able to ride those issues to prominence. He tends to follow fashion, and was one of the first Atari Democrats—members of Congress who, for a while, saw "high tech" as the answer to our problems, and who consider passion in politics old hat.

Gephardt has had to create himself as a serious Presidential contender. His being a member of the House of Representatives is a handicap, his aides say, because people attribute more importance to senators and governors, and assume that House members don't know much about foreign policy, among other things. Gephardt has tried to deal with this through recent speeches. And even his aides say that Gephardt's looks work against him, since they make him seem even younger than he is—forty-six. "I don't know what to do about it," one aide says. The Gephardt campaign is making much of the fact that he is supported by seventy House members (nearly half of them from the South). This speaks well of the regard many of his colleagues hold him in—he is the fourth-ranking Democratic House leader—and also plays to what the campaign hopes will be an advantage: that Gephardt is a serious and hard-working legislator, and an accomplished one, and therefore can be put forward as someone who could work with Congress and get things done. But it's not clear that a great many people cast their votes with this sort of thing in mind.

Gephardt's style as a House member has been transferred to his campaign for the Presidency, and it is causing him problems. Some of the issues Gephardt has chosen to run on are turning out to be mixed blessings: his championing of trade legislation that many call protectionist but that has won him some labor support in Iowa; his co-sponsorship—with Iowa Democratic Senator Tom Harkin—of a farm bill that calls for large government interference and would raise food prices but that has won him some farmer support in Iowa; his supporting an oil-import fee, which would lower the deficit but which many see as inflationary and a boon to the domestic oil industry. Whether Gephardt's trade proposal is really protectionist can be argued over till the end of time, but he was clearly seeking to exploit workers' anger over the trade imbalance—and enhance his political prospects. (Dukakis, who has attacked Gephardt's trade policy and the oil-import fee, which would particularly hurt New England, since the area is dependent on imported oil, also calls the fee a "regressive tax." Dukakis's own trade policy is vague—intentionally so, to keep both sides in the trade debate mollified.) Gephardt's advocating these issues has colored him as at least a semi-panderer—more of one than his rivals—and put him on the defensive. His response has been to go on the offense. He aggressively champions his trade proposal—some of his advisers have misgivings about it, but it has been proposed, so it might as well be turned into a virtue.

Gephardt has changed some of his views, seemingly with an eye toward running for the Democratic nomination rather than in his largely blue-collar, Catholic congressional district, in south St. Louis. He used to support a constitutional amendment banning abortions, but he dropped it as he got ready to run for the Presidency, and now simply says that he opposes federal funding of abortions, with certain exceptions, and also says that he would not veto a bill to provide such funds. Gephardt has also changed his views on tuition tax credits for private schooling, something important for his largely Catholic congressional constituency but anathema to the teachers' unions; and though he had opposed the establishment of a Department of Education (he was in his more conservative phase), he now says he supports it—the department was a demand on the part of the National Education Association. (That's why the Carter Administration established it.) In a debate before the Iowa State Education Association, Gephardt, when pressed by Gore about these changes, gave a rather lame response.

Gephardt's basic program in his Presidential campaign is to increase economic opportunity. He used to define this as increasing our "competitiveness," but the word was so widely used that it became a cliché (though the concept makes sense), and some Democrats have concluded that the word itself is "downbeat." Gephardt, who has of late become an intense podium pounder, calls for more federal funding for education, training, and research—and a change in the "status quo." Virtually all the candidates, in both parties, are calling for more government help for education (though to varying degrees), because there is a real need, and the subject is uncontroversial. In fact, it scores well in the polls. By placing education under the rubric of "competitiveness," or economic development, or whatever, one might avoid being labelled a spender. Gephardt has thought this through. His campaign is trying to present him as non-ideological (as Dukakis's is doing for him); like Dukakis, Gephardt is cool (despite the

podium pounding and the populist rhetoric) and pragmatic—
which his campaign is also making a political virtue. On arms
control, he champions the ban on missile test flights, but he surrounds this with sentences warning that the Democratic Party must
not appear to be against every weapons system. He is more conservative than most of his rivals on military questions, but slightly
less so than Gore. The differences are less important in terms of
substance than of style. Gephardt is well informed on domestic
issues, and through his experience in the House has been more
exposed to defense and foreign-policy issues than Dukakis. But
his lack of surefootedness showed in the course of one debate
when he suggested that the United States might arm blacks to
fight the white regime in South Africa. (Dukakis said of this, "I
wouldn't rule it out.")

Gephardt has become a polished campaigner, by dint of very
hard work over a long period of time. He is exceptionally disciplined, both in his persona and in his work. Actually and figur-
atively, he never has a hair out of place. He is not humorless, but
he is in all respects tidy, and he's not a lot of laughs. He and his
family even camped around Iowa in the summer of 1985, and
Gephardt has probably worked harder—or longer, at least—at
getting the nomination than any other Democrat. But one has the
inescapable feeling that Gephardt is doing it by the numbers—
that his is a campaign that is designed to get the mechanics just
right, and position him just right, but leaves us looking for the
person. Gephardt's having staked so much on Iowa puts him in
a high-risk situation, but it may have been the only strategy for
such a long-shot candidate. And now that he is in some trouble
he's reaching a bit in the debates—saying too obviously prepared
cutting lines. Still, Gephardt has the wherewithal to be an attractive
and effective candidate.

Since he spent all that time in Iowa, the standard set for him
by the press is that he must win or come close to the top. If he
runs anything less than a very close second, and doesn't do particularly well in New Hampshire—first place there is ceded to the
neighboring Dukakis, and the only argument is over how well
Dukakis "must" do there—the press could well write him off. The
political wisdom about Gephardt has gone in stages: for a while,
he was seen as winning in Iowa; then, as of about a month ago,
it was that his campaign had stalled. For what it's worth, he has

slipped from first to third in the Des Moines *Register* poll—an indication watched closely by "the political community"—and a recent NBC poll had him a distant third there to Simon and Dukakis. His campaign is strained by internal tension—something worth watching for in the case of people who want to be President. Gephardt has in fact chronically had a problem with personnel —he tends to agree with everyone in the room, but doesn't like to hear negative opinions or news, and has gone through a lot of people. And his campaign is running out of funds and borrowing heavily against the federal funds it will receive in January. There is an unforgiving factor in Presidential campaigns: if a candidate doesn't do well, after a certain point the money dries up. (Only a candidate with a passionate following, such as Jesse Jackson's, escapes.) The support Gephardt has in Iowa from union and farm groups is supposed to give him help in organization, but it may cost him in other ways. Gephardt's "national" strategy will be either his triumph or his undoing.

The biggest question about Albert Gore is whether he is ready for the Presidency, even if he could win it. The question does not have to do simply with his age (thirty-nine); it arises about his maturity—something we will learn more about as the campaign progresses. Gore is an almost preternatural figure, in some ways old for his years—perhaps because he expects so much of himself, and his parents expect so much of him. (His father, Albert Gore, Sr., was in the House and then the Senate for many years and once made an unsuccessful effort to be a Vice-Presidential candidate, and spoke to people here last year about his son's possible candidacy.) The younger Gore has always been a super-achiever, and at this point has to be taken seriously as a Presidential candidate. He was considering the race, but, he says, he thought he didn't have a "realistic chance" if Cuomo or Nunn or Dale Bumpers ran. When all three said they wouldn't run (Nunn put off a final decision until late last summer) and when some Democratic money men came to him earlier this year, disappointed that Nunn had said he probably wouldn't run, he decided in April to have a go at it. Southern Democratic leaders, he says, were looking for someone who could take advantage of March 8th, and run as a moderate. As it turns out, the money men haven't raised very much money for him. Gore has shown a lot of development since he entered the race: his delivery in debates is less wooden (but still sometimes wooden), and he shows more confidence. He can come across as cerebral, yet as a Tennessee country politician he can deliver a real stem-winder. His big voice comes booming out of his big body. Appearances notwithstanding, Gore, in private, does not take himself exceptionally seriously, is not pompous, and in fact has a good sense of humor—an ability to poke fun at himself.

Gore is well informed on several matters—and has a tendency to show us how well informed he is, giving long-winded expositions. This may be a question of maturity, of a young man trying too hard. Some of Gore's colleagues inevitably consider him brash—too fond of the spotlight and in too much of a hurry. When he was in the House (he was elected to the Senate in 1984), he had something of a reputation for grabbing press-release issues—issues with more publicity value than real importance. But he has a good, serious mind, and some years ago put it to work on two of the most difficult subjects—arms control and international economics. He has given a lot of thought to the questions of arms control and how to deal with the Soviet Union, and feels strongly that, because of changes in the Soviet leadership, the time has come—and the opportunity may not be available again for a long time—to try to build a different relationship, even if Reagan concludes a long-range-ballistic-missile-reduction treaty, as well as the intermediate-range one. In a speech at Dartmouth this fall, Gore spoke about arms control seamlessly—without notes and with command. He also often shows command in debates, and recently he gave a smart speech about the economy. Some of the people Gore surrounds himself with are neo-conservatives, and some are members of the permanent Washington establishment, with their own agenda, so it will be important to see how intellectually independent Gore really is. In the House, he put himself at the center of the fight over whether to build the MX missile, and was the object of criticism by more liberal House members for, as they saw it, giving the Reagan Administration a victory in return for hollow promises. Gore, of course, doesn't see it this way, and some of his opponents at that time have become more forgiving. One of them, Representative Thomas Downey, Democrat of New York, who is an arms-control liberal, and supports Gore in his Presidential campaign, says that while some of his policy differences with Gore are "difficult things to forget and overlook," he doesn't "spend a lot of time thinking about them, because the differences between Al and the other candidates are really very small." Downey points out that Gore voted for the nuclear freeze when that was all the rage, supports deep reductions in arms, and, Downey says, "understands the question of nuclear stability more than the other candidates." Downey says that Gore "has a more hawkish way of reaching his goals than I do, but the result is the same."

When Gore seemed to be going nowhere in his campaign for the nomination, he struck out against his colleagues in debates, criticizing them for being weak on defense. The problem was not so much that he attempted to set himself apart as that he did it clumsily. Though some Democrats will not forgive him for doing it at all, what he did was not outside the bounds of Presidential politics—which is not for the faint of heart. Yet there was a schoolboyish quality to the way he did it—as if he were trying to show that he was the biggest, toughest boy in the schoolyard. His rivals, inevitably, and especially Gephardt, resent him for—as they see it—talking about bigger differences than exist. He makes a big thing of his support for the invasion of Grenada, which other Democrats would just as soon not point up as a Reagan triumph, and he is more supportive of Reagan's Persian Gulf policy than his rivals are. A number of Democrats didn't think it helped the Party for him to, for example, suggest in a speech to the National Press Club that the other Democratic candidates were offering policies of "retreat, complacency, and doubt" on foreign policy and national security, and in his economic speech he made gibes at his rivals. They don't see why he should be giving material to the Republicans—even though many of them acknowledge that the Party could be vulnerable on the defense issue and the economy.

Yet Gore's tactic worked, at least in the near term: he got people's attention, and he began to be taken more seriously as a candidate. His strategy is to do well in the South and then fight in the industrial states. But first he has to survive until and through March 8th, and the question about how important Iowa and New Hampshire will be comes in here. In the current political parlance, the question is whether Gore can "jump-start" his campaign in the South. He is the second-best-financed Democratic candidate, and his campaign is husbanding resources to run television ads in the South, but it's not clear that that will be enough. Gore's having to disclose that he had smoked marijuana in college and when he was in the Army (in the wake of the disclosure that Douglas Ginsburg, the brief Supreme Court nominee, had smoked pot) was, he says, "painful," and his campaign is praying that as time passes this won't hurt him in the conservative constituency he is going after. (The revelation may have also emphasized Gore's youth.) At the Iowa Jefferson-Jackson Day dinner, Gore gave a stem-winder in which he attacked the Iowa caucus system and the pressure it puts on candidates to play to the liberal Iowa constituency—while the Democrats haven't carried Iowa in November since 1964. Though Gore made it a matter of great principle ("I will not barter my beliefs to win votes here or elsewhere"), he was acting out of necessity. He campaigned in Iowa last summer, but didn't take hold. If Sam Nunn had run, he would have, he told me, done a similar thing—skipped Iowa and New Hampshire and attacked the nominating system. It would be most interesting to see what kind of Presidential candidate Gore would make in eight years—but at the moment that's not an option.

Once again, Jesse Jackson is running for reasons other than to be elected, and once again—only more so—he has other Democrats worried about his potential effect on the Party's chances. In part because of a change in the Party's rules, and in part because there is no white candidate with a claim on the black voters, such as Walter Mondale had in 1984, it is assumed that Jackson will go to the Democratic Convention with more delegates than he had the last time. Also, Jackson did sufficiently well in the 1984 primaries to make it more difficult for black elected officials to not be for him this time, though some are holding out. The big question on other Democrats' minds is what Jackson will do with the power he will have at the Convention. How much power he will actually have obviously depends also on how the other candidates have fared—how badly his delegates, and his blessing, are needed. He could well have more delegates than he did the last time—an estimate by another camp puts the possibility at five hundred and forty delegates (out of a total of 4,160, as opposed to his roughly four hundred and sixty-five of 3,933 in 1984), which may be low. It may also depend on how Jackson is dealt with: if Jackson senses weakness (as he did in the case of the Mondale campaign), he will push hard; if he senses that he is up against strength, someone who won't be pushed around (as he did after Paul Kirk took over as Party chairman), he'll be more reasonable. Trying to predict now what Jackson will want then is pointless. As Ann Lewis, the former national director of Americans for Democratic Action and an adviser to Jackson, puts it, "Jesse doesn't have a blueprint in his pocket. This is a guy who's been on the outside most of his life; he's capable of drawing up a strategy very quickly, based on the people around him." Jackson says that what he wants is "respect," a term that he alone will define; but it is clear that he will also seek some entries in the Party's platform. This could cause problems, since, in an election where most of the Democratic leaders are trying to present the Party as pragmatic and non-ideological, Jackson is over on the left. (Paul Kirk is hoping to avoid a detailed platform.)

It is often said that in this campaign Jackson's approach is less race-based and more populist. But that's what his attempt—essentially futile—to build a "rainbow coalition" in 1984 was all about. Jackson has toned down his style, speaks less (but still some) in rhymes, and displays less anger. Yet he has not completely got away from indications of anti-Semitism, and there is still something intimidating, and hinting of anger, in his style.

Jackson is certainly an enlivening presence in this campaign —a witty man among a sombre crew, and the only one capable of real spontaneity. In Iowa, toward the end of a soporific debate on education, Jackson said, "Whoever can keep your attention tonight during this debate on education deserves to be your next President." When, in another debate, Gore gave a lengthy explanation of chlorofluorocarbons, Jackson remarked, "Senator Gore just showed you why he should be our national chemist. I want to be our next President." Jackson is adept at colorful and funny explications of an issue, and, more than the others, speaks his mind.

The philosophical problem that Jackson's campaign presents, as it did in 1984, is that, despite his effort to broaden his base, his is a cause campaign, a campaign of a faction, while the function of political parties, and candidates, is to mediate among the factions. Most black elected officials deal in coalition politics. Moreover, Jackson's example could lead to candidacies by people representing other factions. (Representative Patricia Schroeder, of Colorado, almost ran this time, as a women's candidate.) A black or a woman or a farmer or a whatever running as a protest representative of a faction, rather than as a politician seeking to govern among many factions, invites further splintering of our politics. The politicians are our mediators. Because Jackson is not expected to win, he is not put to the same tests as other candidates. And because he has a strong following, and is presumed to be able to turn out the black vote in November (his precise effect cannot be known), he is treated gently by the other candidates. One cannot escape the feeling that Jackson is exploiting the nomination process—a thesis to which, to be sure, many people would take strong exception. And they argue, with good reason, that Jackson's presence in the primaries gets some things on the agenda that might not otherwise be there. It's clear that Jackson enjoys the exercise. Ann Lewis says, "Jesse was born to do this. Other candidates complain about being constantly on the road, and consider it hard work. Jesse gets larger crowds and more respect from this than from anything else he's done."

Paul Simon's greatest strength from the outset has been that he comes across as a real person—less posed, less self-conscious, and more comfortable than his rivals. Simon conveys calm and a sort of kindness—and he's widely considered a man of unusual (for politics) integrity. He has a populist program and tells down-to-earth, folksy stories. He enjoys a kind of reverse charisma—the plain features and the long ears setting him apart from his chiselled, almost too perfect competitors. But he is a tough man, often underestimated as a politician. His political career has been one of winning unlikely victories—as a Democrat from downstate Illinois in the state legislature; and in 1984, when he was elected to the Senate after a rough fight with incumbent Senator Charles Percy, in the midst of a Reagan landslide. He's shrewder than he seems. But one also senses a certain naïveté to him, perhaps a certain innocence—an impressionableness. Simon is a very nice man and very thoughtful, and very prolific. He has written eleven books, but even though he has been in combative politics there seems to be a certain academic, ungrounded quality to some of his thought. There is a question of how tough-minded he is.

In one debate, Simon suggested that covert activities be turned over to the military—a truly bad idea. His domestic agenda is vulnerable, because it calls for more spending without spelling out how he would raise the revenues to pay for it. He is programmatic—prone to suggest a federal program for every problem he sees—and this, too, makes him a target. The center-piece, of course, is Simon's program of providing public-sector jobs for at least three million unemployed people, at a cost of eight billion dollars. (Some experts say it would cost more.) He has also called for increased spending on several existing programs (such as health care, college loans, and programs for needy children). When I spoke with him in late October, Simon had a vague pro-gram for paying for this: by cutting defense spending; by lowering unemployment; by persuading the financial markets to lower in-terest rates through giving them confidence that he would get the deficit under control—and, as a last resort, taxes. He says that he would insist on "old-fashioned, Harry Truman, pay-as-you-go government." And his deficit-reduction program is still vague. Simon says that though he opposed last year's tax-reform bill (he argued that it wasn't progressive enough), he's "a political realist" and wouldn't reopen that law. Simon's political "realism" prevents him from suggesting domestic spending cuts—though he tosses in the Postal Rate Commission (which cost just over five million dollars in this year's budget). Simon has long backed a constitu-tional amendment requiring a balanced budget—thus maintain-ing a conservative credential—and he supported passage of the Gramm-Rudman law (as did some other liberal Democrats, in-cluding Edward Kennedy). Simon's jobs program may be not so wrongheaded as it is unfashionable, and he says that it would cost only two and a half billion dollars in the first year. Now that he is doing better politically, he is being pressed to explain how he would pay for what he wants to do, and still balance the budget. In the most recent debate, Simon, though alert to the likelihood that he'd be questioned about this, booted his response. His aides say that he has a better one, and that he will offer it soon—they know he has to.

Simon is making a virtue of his stylistic and ideological differences—it's hard to tell which are more important—from his opponents. He told me that one reason he entered the race was that "what I missed among the candidates was a real gut commitment to use the tools of government to get things done—some real compassion." He says that he entered the race when Dale Bumpers, whom he had announced his support for, said, in March, that he would not run, but in fact Simon was considering in the summer of 1986 whether to enter the race. He is a careful politician. His campaign literature and his speeches refer to Roosevelt, Truman, Hubert Humphrey, and John Kennedy, and the Democratic Party's tradition. Simon presents himself as being out of the same homespun tradition as Truman, bow tie and glasses to boot, and pointedly repeats (perhaps too often) that he refused to let political managers slick him up. He deliberately sets himself apart rhetorically from his cooler competitors. He says, "Isn't it time to believe again?" He says, "I want a government that cares." He was considered a long shot when he entered, and is currently enjoying a surge of popularity in Iowa—his being first in the most recent Des Moines *Register* poll made a lot of people take notice. A more recent poll, by NBC, showed him running neck and neck with Dukakis in Iowa, and anything could happen two months from now, when the Iowans finally vote.

We can't know whether this is simply Simon's brief turn in the spotlight or whether he can make it into something more enduring. (His coming from nearby downstate Illinois, his unpretentiousness, and his liberalism and dovish foreign policy make him a good fit with much of the Iowa Democratic electorate.) Simon insists, of course, that he can parlay a victory in Iowa into a successful drive for the nomination, and in September a few observers began to suggest that he was a sleeper. Simon told me matter-of-factly that he planned to win Iowa, come in second in New Hampshire (which he is now doing in the polls), and then do well in Minnesota, which is liberal in its politics and holds caucuses the week after the New Hampshire primary. (Minnesota is also on Dukakis's map.) Simon figures, he says, that he will have enough "media and momentum" to do "reasonably well" on March 8th, and then go on to Illinois and the other industrial states, and do well in California and the Northwest. A lot of liberal Democrats would like to think that this is the case, and wonder whether, despite the warnings of many that Simon is "unelectable"—an argument made emphatically by other campaigns—they dare go with their emotions again.

* * *

A big question is whether the Democrats might end up nominating someone who is not now in the field. The question arises because the current candidates are not yet seen by many people as major figures (but that can change, as it has before, when someone starts winning); because, though we tend to forget, this question almost always arises at some point in a campaign, in part because of press boredom; and because certain figures have been keeping the subject open. The leading one, of course, has been Mario Cuomo, who has said that while he would not run for the nomination (saying that this would be impossible while he served as governor of New York), he would accept a draft. Instead of lying low, as Bill Bradley is doing (though several people think Bradley would also accept a draft), Cuomo was all over the place and doing a lot of talking—the effect of which has been to keep alive speculation that he might at some point be available. Bradley, like Cuomo, does not flatly rule out a draft; like Cuomo, he says, "That's not what happens." He also told me recently that he "can't conceive of" any circumstances that would get him into the race for the nomination. Cuomo's trip to the Soviet Union this fall was followed by a speech to the Council on Foreign Relations in Washington. He drops the names of foreign-policy experts he talked to before he went. The trip to the Soviet Union included a couple of blunders, and the speech was intelligent but did not, because it could not, convey deep knowledge; yet he drew a big crowd here, of the curious and the ambitious, and he had most of it in his hand. (Bradley, too, has been burnishing his foreign-policy credentials, and has had more time for this—against the day— and is probably better prepared to be President.) What Cuomo actually has in mind is known by almost no one, because he confides in almost no one (except some members of his family). In phone conversations with me and others, he has protested that the current candidates should not be called "dwarfs" by the press, and praised them, the effect of which—perhaps unintended —was to reinforce doubts about them. When, inevitably, his omnipresence drew criticism from the press and from declared candidates, he drew back—at least for a while.

Cuomo is such a large presence on the political scene—magnetic, smart, and even seductive—that he is hard to ignore, and many Democrats pine for him. A large percentage of them remain uncommitted to any candidate. Cuomo, like many strong personalities, is also controversial (he is introverted, and he can be vindictive and hard to deal with). There are questions about how good a Presidential candidate he would be—whether he has enough grasp of defense and foreign policy, whether his thin skin and volatile temperament would get in his way—not to mention what kind of President. While the current nominating process is insane, it does give us a chance to learn important things about candidates. Though it is technically not impossible for a candidate to enter later, Cuomo is running out of time to be a conventional candidate—filing dates are approaching, and he has no organization. He probably should be taken at his word—at least in terms of ruling out a conventional candidacy.

The Democrats could head to their Convention with wounded candidates and no enthusiasm—a situation made for a brushfire, of whatever duration. Democrats could decide by the time of the Convention that they would prefer the spellbinding Cuomo, whatever the questions about him, or someone else, to the candidates they know all too well by then. Technically, the delegates are not bound to the candidate in whose name they were chosen, and there will be more Party officials as delegates at this Convention than there have been since the Party began to change its rules, to make the process more "open," twenty years ago. By far most observers now think that the nominee will come from the current field—that someone will start winning, that the field will be very much narrowed after mid-March, as candidates without victories or money fall by the wayside, and that the Party leaders will start making commitments. But there is a strong likelihood—almost a certainty—that before the Democratic nominee is selected there will be rumors that So-and-So might be available after all, that a move to draft somebody is under way. The prospect of a rumor-swept Convention already gives some Democratic leaders nightmares. Whatever happens, the Democrats' road to the nomination is not likely to be smooth.

II

DECEMBER 13

The Republican nomination for the Presidency is likely to be a
thundering fight. In contrast to the Democrats, the Republicans
have two major, established figures, with substantial resources,
heading for a collision. The fight threatens to get rough, and even
nasty, and it could also end quickly. Even Robert Dole's closest
advisers say that Dole will be on the ropes if he loses to George
Bush in Iowa and New Hampshire. If Dole defeats Bush in those
two states, the Bush campaign will use its superior resources to
try to revive him in the Southern contests that follow—but the
Bush people know that this will be difficult. A mixed result in
Iowa and New Hampshire will place great importance on the
South, where the Bush campaign has invested a great deal—
including the candidate's time. Bush and Dole are both highly
competitive men, and this is probably the ultimate race for both
of them. They have been around for so long, and are so much
better known than their competitors, that it is difficult for the
others to catch up with them. Thus far, Jack Kemp is—surprisingly to many—just limping along, and while it's too early to rule
him out, even his campaign advisers know that he is running out
of time to become a major factor. Kemp is trying to get ruled in
by firing strong blasts at Bush and Dole, and by trying to peel
away evangelical support from Pat Robertson. The Bush, Dole,
and Kemp camps are all watching Robertson's campaign
nervously—they are certain he can't win and almost as certain
that he can cause trouble; they also want his followers. Alexander
Haig and Pierre du Pont aren't even considered factors. Pollsters
say that though Bush starts with a lead among Republicans, the
support for him and also for Dole is "soft," with large numbers
of each one's supporters listing the other as their second choice
—showing an unusual lack of commitment—and therefore there
could be large movements of voters as the race develops.

As of now, most Republicans feel that Bush's loyalty to Ronald Reagan entitles him to the nomination, and a Bush adviser says that Republicans tend to be "authoritarian"—are unlikely to turn down a sitting Vice-President. The other camps say, of course, that this sort of support—based also on Bush's higher name recognition—can easily collapse. A study by the Republican pollster Robert Teeter's firm (which is working for Bush) shows that since 1960, when the modern Presidential-nominating system began, Republicans have always nominated the early front-runner —who in this case is Bush. (Democrats have nominated their early front-runner only three out of seven times.) The Republican race is even more "front-loaded" than the Democratic one, since the Republicans also have a contest in Michigan in January and earlier contests than the Democrats do in some other states as well; as of March 8th, the day of a large number of contests in the South (and several elsewhere), just over fifty per cent of the Republican delegates will have been selected. The idea for the early contest in Michigan was the Bush camp's, but the tactic threatened to backfire—as Kemp forces and Robertson forces teamed up against Bush—and now the Bush forces are fighting back and making some headway. (Dole has stayed away.) The situation there is akin to nineteenth-century Central European politics, and worthy of notice only for its outcome.

As the Republicans position themselves for the post-Reagan era, they pick and choose among items in the Reagan record to identify with—and all of them set themselves apart from it in various ways. Both Bush and Dole say—as the Democrats do— that more must be done for education, and Dole, reflecting his Senate record, says that the Republican Party must be more compassionate. Even Frank Fahrenkopf, the chairman of the Republican National Committee, says, "This party has to stop being the party that just says no"—and says that Republicans must seek to do more for such things as education and child care. But, like the Democrats, the Republicans are limited by the fiscal wreckage they will inherit if elected. Both Bush and Dole also stress their Washington experience—the comparison with the incumbent President is implicit.

Though Reagan's approval rating dropped significantly as a result of the Iran-Contra affair, and remained down until last week's summit meeting with Mikhail Gorbachev, he is still the dominant figure in American politics—and not only because he occupies the White House—and the summit meeting showed his continuing ability to occupy center stage. It also boosted his popularity, at least for a while. And next year, during the Presidential campaign, Reagan will be going to Moscow. His achieving an arms-control agreement and appearing to stabilize relations with the Soviet Union helps his party, and his Administration will use what levers it can to stave off a recession next year. (Treasury Secretary James Baker is an ally of Bush.) Reagan's impact on the Republican Party has been very strong, and shapes the contest to succeed him. He has consolidated, at least for now, the Party's shift to the right. The conservatives who seized power in 1980 now dominate the Party. The 1988 contest doesn't pit, say, a Rockefeller wing against a Goldwater wing: the Rockefeller wing is extinct (except for a few lonely members of Congress), and what was the Goldwater wing is now dominant—is now the conservative center of the Party. It is more conservative than Richard Nixon and Gerald Ford were. (Even Goldwater himself became nearly a centrist.) The takeover was cultural and economic as well as philosophical: it placed the Party in the hands of small-town, small-business, anti-establishment former outs. While big money and Eastern merchants do business with the new Republican Party—and certainly with the Republican Administration—and are still part of it, and contribute money to it, the power to nominate candidates lies with other forces. Bush and Dole are campaigning essentially within the conservative mainstream's parameters. Within those parameters, on domestic policy Bush has adopted some Reaganesque positions, while Dole more closely resembles the traditional Midwestern, Robert A. Taft conservatism. On arms control, Dole is —temporarily and with difficulty—trying to stay slightly to the right. So there is no great ideological struggle going on in the Republican Party this time, as there was in 1980 in the struggle between Reagan and Bush (the pre-Vice-Presidential Bush)— though that struggle was as much cultural as ideological. Bush then seemed to represent moderate conservatism—Gerald Ford and Richard Nixon conservatism—but this was a matter of appearances as much as it was of substance. Since 1980, Reagan has made the Republican Party more conservative, and the conservatives have made Reagan more mainstream—so now there is a conservative mainstream.

Bush has coöpted a large percentage of Reagan's issues, and is seeking the support of Reagan's following, but Bush's cultural apartness from a good proportion of that following remains. His campaign is working on this, but his advisers know that there are limits to what can be done. Some observers believe that it is because Bush and, to a lesser extent, Dole straddle such a wide swath of the Party that Jack Kemp, who is trying to run on their right, has so little room; and Kemp is being crowded on his right by Robertson. Robert Teeter says, "We're running a big-tent campaign—we never let anybody unite a major faction against us." Though all the Republican candidates seek the support of the religious right, several Republican strategists believe that the social issues have faded as "cutting" issues, in part because candidates in the conservative mainstream have assimilated them, and in part because younger voters are heavily libertarian—they don't want the government interfering in their personal lives. Eighteen-to-twenty-four-year-olds still constitute Reagan's largest constituency. This contradiction within the Party requires delicate maneuvering on the part of the candidates—as delicate as that practiced by Reagan during his Presidency. Though Reagan has given voice to the social issues, and has made some speeches that elicited full-throated cheers from evangelical and anti-abortion groups, he didn't do much about them. Reagan's attempts to impose the "new right" view on the social issues on the Supreme Court through his nominees to fill the vacancy left by Justice Lewis Powell last June have thus far been frustrated. His current, and third, nominee, Anthony Kennedy, is considered reliable by the right, but less reliable than Reagan's first two selections. Reagan skillfully danced with his religious-right following and his libertarian constituency.

Though Reagan talked up the social issues, he and his advisers intentionally conveyed the notion that he is a tolerant man. His daughter Maureen, who was engaged in Republican Party activities, was vocal in her support of legalized abortion and the Equal Rights Amendment. One Reagan political adviser says, "There was always a wink." Still, the "gender gap"—the stronger support of the Republican Party by men than by women—widened during Reagan's Presidency. All the candidates will take the correct positions on the social issues, but as they try to attract younger voters in the general election they will have to take care. This is one reason that there is a certain amount of nervousness about Robertson and his following. Also, the other Republican campaigns don't yet know how to gauge the Robertson support—how much trouble he could cause by running strongly in the early contests. Some Dole and some Bush people have said that if Robertson comes in first in Iowa or New Hampshire (Robertson has also been active in New Hampshire recently) this will be less damaging than his coming in second and knocking their candidate into third place. Recently, they have scaled back their public expectations about how Robertson will do in the early states—but essentially they find his movement a mystery.

The fact that there aren't deep philosophical chasms dividing the Republican candidates this time does not mean that there won't be big fights. Bush and Dole, who on the face of it aren't very far apart, already have issues with which they go at each other—the main ones being the question of how to manage the domestic economy (whether there should be more taxes) and the recently signed treaty eliminating intermediate-range and short-range nuclear weapons (I.N.F.). The tax issue, important enough on its own, also stands as a symbol for other differences between traditional conservatives and radicals—albeit radicals we have got used to. The difference over the I.N.F. treaty is more rhetorical than real, but it represents Dole's attempt to mollify the Party's right wing.

George Bush is a decent, likable man with more relevant experience for serving as President than anyone else in the contest—but he has a problem. He lacks definition. He has yet to show us who he is—to define himself beyond his credentials. The credentials will help him, but if he gets in trouble they can't save him. (The Bush campaign has recently begun to run a television ad saying, "No one in this century is better prepared to be President.") Bush has done many things, but usually on behalf of someone else—whoever was President—so the public doesn't know much about him. He is just beginning to define himself, but the picture is still vague—and that might be because he has few deep beliefs, and might be why poring over his statements to determine whether he is a moderate or a conservative is futile. Bush has never been a particularly good candidate, and though it is clear that he has worked hard to overcome some of his liabilities, it's not yet clear how far he can go. He recognizes that he doesn't come across on

television particularly well, and has worked hard, with some success, to improve his television style. He speaks at a lower pitch
and more slowly, cutting down on his usual high-pitched, nasal,
frenetic style—which contributes to the impression that he is weak.

After a great deal of coaching by Roger Ailes, his media
adviser—who told Bush that the faster he talked the higher his
voice went—Bush did show an improved style in the first Republican debate, in Houston in October, and this did him all the more
good because he exceeded the press's expectations. His performance level was about the same in the most recent debate, but as
we become accustomed to this the question of what he has to say
grows. One adviser says that the advice given to Bush for the
debates is "to go out there and look like you're enjoying yourself,
whether you are or not." In the most recent debate, Bush definitely
didn't look happy while he grappled with a well-aimed question
by Haig on the Iran-Contra affair. ("Were you in the cockpit, or
were you on an economy ride in the back of the plane?") Bush
dodged the question—but in an answer to a question on a different matter defended Oliver North and John Poindexter, but
avoided the question, which is prematurely around, of whether
they should be pardoned. Bush may be protecting his right flank
in his talk about the Iran-Contra affair (and he's overestimating
the public's response to North), but it's not clear that he completely
grasps what went wrong. On "Meet the Press" today, Bush said
that North was a hero because "my idea of a national hero is
somebody that believes passionately in a cause" and "captures the
imagination of the American people, cutting through all the sophisticated, inside-the-Beltway chatter about this thing." Bush's
turning, in Houston, on du Pont, who (as the Bush camp expected)
aimed a number of shots at Bush, and who goes by the name
Pete—Bush's saying, "Pierre, let me help you" (thus reminding
the world of du Pont's own blue blood)—seems to be going down
as one of the great moments in political history (alongside Reagan's "I paid for this microphone" in 1980). Bush's going on to
call du Pont's proposal to offer a private alternative to Social
Security "a nutty idea" was designed to establish that Bush is a
mensch.

A Bush aide says that Bush willingly took Ailes' advice, because
he is "very competitive" and because, the aide says, "he really wants
to be President." But he's trying to overcome lifetime habits, and

his campaign appearances aren't consistent—at times the old style
returns. There is a whininess that is not just in Bush's voice, and
when he gets beyond set pieces he sometimes reverts to his old
tendencies to be defensive and to deal in straw men. The question
of how strong Bush is also stems from his cheerleader approach
—beyond the necessary—to the Vice-Presidency, and his seeming
willingness to check his dignity at the door as he sought the support of Reagan's constituency and of certain right-wing groups.
Bush aides say that though he paid a price for appearing to grovel
for the support of these groups, he also gained from it, by showing
that he could get wide support—and by crowding Kemp. Still,
with the criticism in mind, Bush's people had him avoid a candidate parade before a right-to-life group in Iowa earlier this fall.
Bush is thin-skinned as well, and his awkward responses to criticism also raise questions about his strength. As a campaigner, he
can also be awkward physically—making herky-jerky, out-of-sync
motions. (Many people remember his debate with Geraldine Ferraro, in 1984, for this, and for some of his peculiar talk—"Whine
on, harvest moon"). But this year he is calmer, and is often—as
Vice-President—presented in more sedate situations. He seems
more confident at times. But Bush is also somewhat tone-deaf: he
has a propensity for making remarks that come off all wrong.
(His saying after a visit to Poland this fall that Detroit could use
some Soviet mechanics and his comment that he didn't do well in
an Iowa straw poll because a lot of his supporters were at their
daughters' coming-out parties are recent examples.) His aides describe these remarks as jokes that others somehow didn't get, but
they keep a worried eye out for what he might say next. One aide
says that such mistakes are less likely to occur during a debate
than during a long trip abroad or a campaign swing: "The debate
is safer ground, because all the sensitivities are tuned up." These
concerns get not just to Bush's prospects for winning the nomination but also to his capacity for winning, and holding, the people's support, and for leading them—for governing, if he is elected.
If Bush can win the nomination and allay the concerns, he
should—external circumstances being benign—be taken very seriously as possibly the next President.

It's probably a mistake to think that we will learn much more
about Bush in the course of the campaign; it's more likely that

he is the man we've been seeing. His aides say that one of his problems has been that he appeared so often with Reagan, with Reagan inevitably overshadowing him—and, they say, Bush downplaying himself—and that in the campaign we will see the real George Bush. Of course, the other side of it is that the Vice-Presidency gives him a tremendous boost, and may well make the difference in his attempt to be his party's nominee. He was highly visible during the summit meeting last week—even had his own breakfast with Gorbachev, to which Bush invited, among others, a high-school principal and an agricultural expert from Iowa and the governor of New Hampshire. Bush followed his summit activities with a trip to Iowa. One of Bush's problems as a public politician is that he seems to feel the need to prove himself, show us how tough he is, whereas the public, if given a choice and other things being equal, prefers real, unfeigned confidence—like Reagan's. Bush's attempts to show us that he's a tough guy have led to some of his sillier statements. Some Republican observers say that many people who say they are for Bush have trouble stipulating why except that he is Vice-President—and that that won't be enough to hold their support.

One thing we will find out in this campaign is how much Bush has to say. He has made a few proposals, but what he wants to do if he becomes President is essentially unclear. He is basically a cautious politician. His approach to the Vice-Presidency has been that he would keep his own counsel about advice he has given to the President, and he is sticking with this approach in this campaign. His advisers say that he got the highest possible response from a test group during the Republican debate in Houston when he said, "In my family, loyalty is not considered a character defect, it is considered a strength." (The increasingly employed practice of wiring a selected group—in this case to a "Perception Analyzer"—for its responses to lines in a debate is ominous.) The Dole people charge that Bush is using "loyalty" to mask "the wimp factor." (The word "wimp" has been dogging him for some time.) There may be something more than discretion at work here. Bush has a long list of credentials—a member of Congress, ambassador to the United Nations, chairman of the Republican National Committee, ambassador to China, director of the C.I.A.—but a history of not leaving deep footprints. (He was, however, given credit for restoring morale at the C.I.A., and he remains close to the old C.I.A. network.) Bush was also given credit in these jobs as being a decent man with an open mind—and a good listener.

Bush has come out for cutting capital-gains taxes from twenty-eight per cent (as of last year's tax-reform law) to fifteen per cent, but this proposal, whatever its merits—Bush argues that it would spur investment—goes against the basic theory behind the tax-reform law enacted last year. The idea of the law, which Reagan supported, was to treat all income alike in exchange for lower tax rates. Furthermore, though Bush says the capital-gains tax cut will produce revenue for the government, government studies say that Bush's proposal would cost the federal government money. (Tax rates have gone down dramatically during Reagan's Presidency, with the top marginal rate dropping from seventy per cent when he took office to fifty per cent in the tax cuts enacted in 1981 and then to twenty-eight per cent—with some exceptions for the very wealthy—last year.) The capital-gains differential was eliminated last year because it was said to benefit the wealthy disproportionately and distort the proportion of investment that went to certain kinds of activities at the expense of others. The proposed cut in the capital-gains tax is supported within the business community, especially among businesses heavily involved in venture capital— and also by the pure supply-siders. (Jack Kemp also supports this proposal.) Bush is described by an adviser as much more amenable to using the tax code to promote certain businesses than last year's tax bill permitted. In his announcement of his candidacy, in Houston in mid-October, Bush also came out flatly against asking for any new taxes: "I am not going to raise your taxes—period." This put him in an awkward position when, after the stock-market crash a few days later, President Reagan relented somewhat on his own firm stand against more taxes—in fact, Bush at first was repeating his own position while the White House was sending different signals, and he finally resolved this by saying that he supported the Administration's attempts to reduce the deficit but as President he would not raise taxes. One Bush adviser says, "You can't run in the Republican Party today suggesting you'll raise taxes." Another Bush aide says that the no-tax line was taken especially with a view to New Hampshire—where there is adamant opposition to taxes. Bush aides explain that if reality forces him to change his position when President, so be it; and some of Bush's advisers wish that he hadn't added "period" to his statement. Some Party leaders, including House Minority Leader Robert Michel, also have indicated that they wish Bush had not drawn so firm a line. Another proposal Bush has made is for tax-exempt bonds for families to save for college education; after the proposal met with criticism because it would disproportionately help the wealthy, who could put away more, Bush said there would be caps on the program. He also calls for more funds for the Head Start program, which helps poor preschool children with their learning and is a proven success. Like many other candidates, he is for making America more "competitive"—but he has yet to spell out what he means. Nor has he made it clear how he would reduce the deficit.

Bush is clearly trying to signal that the tone of his Administration would be different from Reagan's in several respects. In his announcement speech he said, "The fact is, prosperity is not an end but a beginning," and he also said, "Where is it written that Republicans must act as if they do not care?" Without directly mentioning a certain problem the Reagan Administration has had, Bush says that he wants to attract to government service "people who want to make a contribution, not to make a buck." His advisers say that poll data show that this would be a fruitful thing to talk about, because people are fed up with corruption in government and on Wall Street. He also says that he will offer "hands on" management of the government—again, of course, with no reference to Reagan. But a sitting Vice-President can go only so far in setting himself apart from the President he serves, and this limitation makes it difficult for him to set forth a clear picture of what he would do as President to show independence—even if he wanted to.

Bush is far better informed than Reagan is on foreign policy, and an aide says that he has made it a point to talk to the person who prepares Reagan's daily national-security briefing, and that he makes it a point to call people in and ask them questions—the contrast to Reagan in this respect was left unmentioned. His aides describe him as more curious than Reagan (this would not be difficult) and more involved in what policymaking his office does (nor would this). But someone who has been around Bush for a long time describes him as more oriented to process than to policy, as not delving into issues in any depth (the same could be said of

Dole), and, despite the fact that Bush has been on the public scene
for a long time, we know little about what he thinks. There is
some question about his grasp of domestic issues. And there remains the question of where he was during the Iran-Contra affair:
Bush likes to say that he "expressed reservations" about selling
arms to Iran and that beyond that he won't reveal his advice to
the President—but doesn't suggest that he made much of an issue
of the arms sales. His office was at least on the periphery of the
secret arms aid to the Contras during the period of a congressional
ban on this, and its denials that this matter was ever discussed by
Bush or his staff with one of the major figures in the exercise—
Felix Rodriguez, who became involved with the secret airlift of
supplies to the Contras—have never been convincing. The final
report of the Iran-Contra committees said that Bush attended a
White House meeting where Defense Secretary Caspar Weinberger and Secretary of State George Shultz raised objections to selling arms to Iran in exchange for hostages. Bush says he doesn't
recall being at the meeting and that he would have taken a stronger
position if he had known of their objections, but it has never been
clear why, even if he didn't attend a meeting with them, he didn't
know what they thought. The report also said "there is no evidence" that Bush was involved in the private Contra-aid program,
or knew about the diversion of funds to the Contras from arms
sales to Iran. (This is less than definitive.)

   According to one well-placed source, Bush used his access to
Reagan to play a major role in persuading him to reopen a dialogue with Soviet leaders, and, toward the end of his first term
and in the beginning of the second one, was a key ally of Shultz
and Robert McFarlane, the national-security adviser, in changing
Reagan's thinking about the Soviet Union and directing his energies toward dealing with it, especially on arms control. (McFarlane
is now an informal adviser to Bush.) He is also said to have made
several insightful suggestions about how Reagan should deal with
the Soviet leaders, and bring along the American public—to avoid
the political perils that détente had suffered in the nineteen-
seventies (in part at the hands of Reagan). Bush also, according
to this source, leaned hard on the leaders of El Salvador to curb
the death squads—a position at odds with that of some right-wing
Republicans. But he does not seem to have involved himself much

in intra-Administration arguments. In his campaign appearances, he cites his foreign-policy experience, dropping the names of foreign leaders he is about to meet with or has met with. One of the several benefits of incumbency, beyond flying around in Air Force Two and having autographs and various gewgaws to hand out, is that Bush makes "official" foreign trips—his aides said that the trip to Poland, where he met with Lech Walesa and visited Auschwitz, provided terrific pictures. Camera crews, paid for by his political-action committee and his campaign, have accompanied him on his foreign trips, recording the scenes for further use. But his campaign advisers are divided over how much his foreign-policy credentials will count for in the contest for the nomination.

There is, in fact, some tension among Bush's advisers, some of whom want him to take certain positions to win the nomination, and others who are concerned about the consequences in the general election of his having taken these positions—and also the consequences to his stature as Vice-President. The first group is more inclined to suggest that Bush take a particular position to help him in a certain state or area—oppose taxes for the voters in New Hampshire and be emphatic in his support for the Contras for the South. The second would have him stress issues of more general appeal—such as education and ethics. Bush appears to be accepting everybody's advice. While he points to himself as the only candidate for the nomination giving out-and-out support to the I.N.F. treaty, and it would seem that he has no choice, it is also the case that the treaty is very popular among Republicans in Iowa and New Hampshire as well as nationally, and is considered good politics by the Bush people—one of the very few "cutting" issues, says one campaign adviser. A Teeter poll says that seventy-eight per cent of Iowa Republicans support the treaty, and a recent nationwide Gallup poll had more than seventy per cent of Democrats and Republicans supporting it. As the summit meeting progressed, Bush made many television appearances in which he linked himself with the treaty. Though the Bush people complain about swipes Dole takes at Bush, in a summit-week interview Bush, obviously referring to Dole, said, "I don't have to put my finger in the wind to see where it's going." Bush also says that as President he would press for further arms control. But, perhaps to protect his right flank, Bush also said last week that as President he would seek increased spending for defense and would go forward with the Strategic Defense Initiative (S.D.I.). Recently, while campaigning in Florida, Bush promised never to abandon the Contras: "As President, I will never leave the Contras twisting in the wind." He also said, "I don't care what the liberals say, as President I will strengthen the C.I.A., not weaken it." This is the old Bush style. Leaving aside the fact that the Iran-Contra affair, among other things, raised bipartisan concerns about the role of the C.I.A., it might be useful to find out what Bush has in mind for the agency.

Bush has one of the best campaigns that money can buy. He has some of the best Republican campaign people, and two of Reagan's best speech writers. Both he and Dole will be able to raise all the funds they can legally spend in pursuit of the nomination, but Bush's political-action committee—purportedly to help other Republicans—has spent more than ten million dollars over the past two and a half years, certainly with an eye to Bush's own future. (Dole, too, has a political-action committee, but Bush's is much larger.) Bush has a definite advantage in having a campaign team that has been working together for three years. (Dole is in awful shape in this respect.) The Bush campaign, however, should not be, and is not, complacent. A recent NBC poll said Dole was far ahead of Bush in Iowa; some Bush people explain this away as stemming from Dole's coming from a neighboring farming state—and from Iowa's having had hard economic times, and from Reagan's having been relatively unpopular there. A Bush adviser points out that Bush's state-by-state popularity largely tracks with Reagan's—that Reagan is very popular in the South, which is the region most optimistic about the economy, and so is Bush. Bush's people say they can accept Bush's losing Iowa, but it is clear that they'd rather not. They realize that that would put great pressure on Bush to win in New Hampshire, eight days after Iowa, and as of now the polls have him ahead there. Nationwide polls taken by NBC and the New York *Times*/CBS News in late November put Bush substantially ahead of Dole. But as of now Bush is facing difficulty in several of the eleven other states that hold Republican contests (six more than the Democrats will hold) before March 8th. Robertson's winning a straw poll in Iowa early this fall gave the Bush people a fright and led them to send a top campaign official there. Because of the effort that Bush has recently made in Iowa, and because of the I.N.F. treaty (on which Dole has got himself into a bind), some Bush people think that their candidate is making something of a comeback in the state. Lee Atwater, Bush's campaign manager, says, "Everyone says Iowa is a farm state—Iowa is a peace state." A Republican pollster says that Bush is the second choice of more born-again Christians than Dole is, that they consider Bush one of them—and Bush does nothing to discourage this. In recent appearances, Bush, who never talked this way before, has been telling audiences, "I believe in Jesus Christ as my personal Saviour." A Bush campaign official says that Robertson's presence in the race helps Bush, in that Robertson cuts into support that might have gone to Kemp and keeps Kemp from taking off. As for the contests on March 8th, this adviser also says that over the past seven years Bush has spent more time in Florida—which will have eighty-two delegates at the Convention, second only to Texas of the states holding contests on that date—than any other state. Bush's son Jeb lives in Florida and has been active in Republican politics and among Cuban refugees, who are an important political force in the state (and are very pro-Contra). The aide also points to a poll showing Bush far ahead of Dole in Texas, and says that Bush's superiority in organization will give him an advantage over his rivals on March 8th. Atwater says, "Organization will play a bigger role this year, because of March 8th, when there will be seventeen Republican contests in one day." (The Democrats will have twenty.) Also, the rules governing a number of the Republican contests on that day give Bush a shot at recovering in the South—as Reagan did in 1976, when he was challenging Ford. However, a member of one opposing camp says that Reagan had an ideological base to sustain him in 1976, but Bush has nothing to stave off collapse if he loses the early contests. Recently, Bush told a Florida audience that he would do reasonably well in Iowa and New Hampshire, and then on March 8th he'd "blow 'em away." Should Bush win both Iowa and New Hampshire, he may get interrupted somewhere, as most front-runners do, but he would be hard to stop.

Bush's campaign will stress that he is a unifying candidate, prepared to govern, but whether this will attract voters to him can't be known yet. There is much about Bush that makes him ready to be President; what we don't know yet is whether he can catch on with the people in a way that would make him able to lead them.

Robert Dole is a complex man who, if he can get the Republican nomination, could be a formidable Presidential candidate. If he gets the nomination, this would probably answer the basic question that is also unanswered as yet about him: whether he can attract a mass following and lead. Dole is popular in Washington—because of his wit, his legislative ability, and his mixture of conservative and humane politics. But none of these things give us clues about his capacity for national leadership. His run for the Vice-Presidency in 1976, with Gerald Ford, was less than stellar, and is thought by many to have cost Ford the election, which Carter won narrowly. Dole's run for the nomination in 1980 was so forgettable that it is often forgotten. (He dropped out early, after coming in seventh in New Hampshire, with less than one per cent of the vote.) Dole does seem to have grown in recent years—to have found, in his role as Majority Leader and then Minority Leader of the Senate, a niche for his talents—and he is admired by senators in both parties for his legislative skill, his ability to understand the nature of a problem and work it out. His calling in 1976, in a debate with Walter Mondale, all the wars the United States has fought this century "Democrat wars" gave him a reputation as something of a hatchet man, and though all that is said to be behind him, it still haunts him, and seems to have thrown him and his advisers off. His marriage, in 1975, to his wife, Elizabeth, is said to have taken the harsh edges off him. In fact, Dole has over the years conducted some rough and nasty campaigns, and the current one should tell us the degree to which he has really changed. Dole is one of the funniest people in public life —his humor runs not to jokes and stories but to quick and often spontaneous one-liners (sharper and more spontaneous than Reagan's). It's a contextual humor, with Dole making remarks about the situation he sees around him. Because these remarks are often at someone else's expense, his campaign, at least in the early stages, sought to muzzle him—this accounted in part for Dole's lacklustre performance in the first Republican debate, in October. His advisers at the time (there has been a lot of turmoil and turnover in the Dole camp) also feared resurrecting memories of 1976. But he didn't do much better in the subsequent debate. Between the debates, Bill Brock, the former Secretary of Labor and, earlier, Republican national chairman, who had just taken over the management of the campaign, told me that he rejected the idea that Dole had a "joke problem," and that earlier advisers had gone too far in muzzling him, and that he would not try to limit the humor; Brock thinks that what happened in 1976 isn't relevant now. But his campaign remains nervous about his doing anything that revives the image of Dole as a hatchet man—one that they think could never be shaken if revived. An adviser says that Dole will have to take Bush on soon, and will do so in the next debate, in early January—but only on the basis of issues. Dole has already taken some swipes at Bush for, among other things, approving the I.N.F. treaty right away, and when he was asked by reporters last week whether he thought Bush had gained politically from the summit he replied, "Being endorsed by Gorbachev?" Presidential campaigns aren't gentle, and since Dole needs to overtake the front-runner, he can hardly avoid going at Bush—and risking the revival of an old reputation. But Americans are sometimes excessively dainty about their politics, and accept the notion that criticism of one candidate by another is "mean." One has to look further.

Dole's other problem in the debates has been one that could continue to cause him trouble: he is not an eloquent man. Dole is laconic—Kansas laconic—and he tends to speak in a staccato style, with his eyes blinking rapidly. His tone is flat—Kansas flat —and he doesn't seem to rouse audiences. He sometimes engages in legislative talk, using terms understood on Capitol Hill but not elsewhere. He is impatient with the urgings of some advisers that he must set forth a "vision"—that's not his style. Wrapped up in this is the question of how much Dole has to say. He may be trapped in the mind-set of the legislator—and especially the legislative leader—who sees many sides of an issue and tries to steer between the rocks. The legislator (there are exceptions) is inclined to fuzz issues; as a legislative leader, Dole doesn't often lead but tries to work things out. It's a kind of effectiveness that doesn't easily translate into a run for the Presidency. Howard Baker found that out in his try for the nomination, in 1980. In recent history, the only legislator who became President on his own was John Kennedy, and he wasn't considered much of a legislator.

While Dole is a friendly man, and enjoyable to talk to, he doesn't project warmth, and very few people know him well. He does not come across as particularly kind. There seems to be an impenetrable curtain drawn between him and most of the rest of the world, and he seems to use humor as a deflector. Dole has mastered probably the easiest format for a politician—the talk show, where he doesn't have to develop a thought, and where he is usually talking to people he knows and who appreciate his willingness to make a newsworthy or funny remark. He is a frequent guest on the talk shows. He is also a master at getting himself on the network evening-news programs, usually by making some remark on the Senate floor about the events of the day. But this is a reactive skill, not a creative one. Dole is not much of an initiator. One senses at times that Dole is edgy, and holding in a certain anger, and that he is making an effort to keep his sharp tongue under control. When things become tense on the Senate floor, he can still lash out. Dole has put unprecedented emphasis in this campaign on his humble origins in Russell, Kansas, and on the efforts of the people of that town to help him recover from the severe wounds he suffered in the Second World War. The theory was to "humanize" Dole, and by stressing his humble Midwestern origins draw the contrast with Bush. Dole tells Iowans, "I won't forget where I came from." In September, a campaign adviser said to me, "We're running Russell, Kansas, for President"—but, of course, this won't be enough.

Actually, Dole and his wife are consummate Washington insiders, and Robert Dole is thick with a number of the big lobbyists. The Doles pal around with such other Washington powers as Robert Strauss and David Brinkley. In fact, the Doles, the Strausses, the Brinkleys, the Howard Bakers, and Tip O'Neill all have coöperative apartments in a Bal Harbour, Florida, building that is controlled by Dwayne Andreas, the chairman of Archer-Daniels-Midland, the Illinois-based commodities company. Questions have been raised about the Doles' relationship with Andreas: their apartment was obtained (in the name of Mrs. Dole) apparently at a favorable rate, and Robert Dole has championed legislation of great importance to Andreas's firm (on whose board Strauss sits). The Senator says that his efforts on behalf of ethanol (a significant Archer-Daniels-Midland business) have helped his farm constituency. The Doles are a driven pair—Elizabeth Dole seems even more driven than her husband. A friend says that the Doles are consumed with politics, but beyond that "don't know very much"—and don't read much. Elizabeth Dole is also smart and has an ability to charm people—and the Dole campaign figures that she can be of great help. But the Doles must tread carefully: in a taped segment offered for the first debate, the Doles sat side by side in wing chairs, looking like a royal couple.

By common consent, Dole has taken a big chance in his campaign in calling for additional taxes. The big question is whether by doing the right thing he did himself in. Dole was going to get hit by the tax issue anyway: in the Senate, he had several times called for more taxes to deal with the deficit, and helped get them adopted. But his advisers insist that Dole is not simply trying to turn a liability into an asset: they say he feels very strongly that taxes must be raised. A motif that runs through Dole's campaign appearances is that we must use common sense—to Dole, it is "common sense" that taxes have to be raised. Talking about taxes also fits into the Dole campaign strategy of showing him as someone working at the nation's problems and saying what he would do about them as President—and drawing the contrast with Bush. (Dole takes a shot at Bush by saying, "I offer a record, not a résumé.") Not all of Dole's political advisers were keen on his stressing taxes, of course, and many were concerned over the way he talked about them shortly after his announcement speech. In that speech, Dole emphasized that he would not raise tax rates, which means that he would leave the income-tax levels alone and find the money elsewhere—perhaps through excise taxes, or even a consumption tax. (He also said that he might call for a constitutional convention to adopt an amendment requiring a balanced budget.) The next day, talking off the cuff, Dole said, "The American people are ready for bitter medicine"—but his campaign advisers weren't ready for that. More recently he said, "I'm not the gloom-and-doom candidate, but I hope I'm the candidate of reality." But Dole, resisting the advice of his aides, still talks about the need "to take some medicine." While he calls for reducing the deficit, he doesn't spell out how. Recently, Dole—calling the deficit-reduction package adopted by congressional leaders and the President "a baby step"—picked up on an idea being pushed by Mario Cuomo, for a bipartisan national commission to come up with a plan for reducing the deficit. Commissions are a cop-out,

of course, but that's why they can sometimes work; a similar commission on reforms in Social Security, in 1982, on which Dole
served, was successful for the very reason that it spread the responsibility around. In his campaign, as in the Senate, Dole seeks
to protect the poor from budget cuts, supports health and nutrition programs for poor children, and champions help for the
handicapped. And, of course, he calls for more federal help for
education. He frequently says that the Republican Party (of which
he was once chairman) must "reach out" to the poor, the handicapped, blacks, and Hispanics, and he calls for the expansion of
certain federal programs.

It is in the area of foreign policy that we need to know more
about Dole. He has participated in all kinds of foreign-policy debates in the Senate, but it's not clear what he really thinks. His
campaign advisers are aware that Bush has a lead on foreign
policy, and are thinking about bringing in some people for Dole
to talk to. But time is growing short. In what many took to be a
move to avoid being outflanked on the right by Kemp, Dole in
the past couple of years became a strong partisan of Jonas Savimbi,
the rebel leader in Angola. He took a sort of non-position on the
I.N.F. agreement, saying that it is the role of the Senate to study
the treaty before deciding whether it is adequate and that he
needed to read the treaty before deciding on his position. Dole
was protecting his right side, but this has caused him other political
problems: the treaty is popular, and, in hedging, Dole doesn't
look like a leader. His campaign grew worried about this during
the week of the summit, and began to try to work him out of his
uncomfortable position, but Dole would not move very far. (He
has a stubborn side.) A Dole aide said to me at midweek that he
would come out for the treaty soon—"He can only read it for so
long"—and sponsor non-crippling reservations concerning verification and conventional forces, in which the Soviets have superiority. And Dole, after meeting with Gorbachev last Wednesday,
indicated that he would support the treaty at some point, and said
it would be approved without crippling reservations, but would
go no further—and said, grumpily, that "George Bush had nothing to do with the treaty," but, from the way Bush was campaigning
on it in Iowa, "you'd think he discovered it." At some point, Dole
may have to decide between spending his time being a national
candidate and remaining the Senate Minority Leader—but his

key advisers say that that time hasn't come yet. They realize that the Senate role, for all the strain it puts on Dole in terms of both time and energy, brings him maximum publicity and shows him at work on the major issues of the day. Dole might also be loath to give up the perch he has for a race for one that might elude him.

Brock has his work cut out for him in trying to bring order to the Dole campaign organization. Until he arrived there, in mid-October, the campaign was a hydra-headed thing, with more than the usual infighting and very little organization in the field. However important this is to Dole, it is an important thing about him. Dole is not known for running a good staff or being easy to work for. If he can't get a campaign in order, what will he do with an Administration to manage? Dole is known as a non-delegator, as a candidate who has insisted on doing his own scheduling and making other decisions best left to staff—and also as one who kept his staff guessing what he might go out and do. Brock says that his presence will show that Dole will delegate—and Brock has already carried out an extensive shakeup of the campaign organization. But there are still signs of disorganization. Now we need to see more of what the candidate can do.

Pierre du Pont, the former governor of Delaware, is in this race for reasons best known to himself. Most people figure that du Pont must have figured that with such strong candidates as Bush and Dole, and also Kemp, in the race he would run because "what the hell"—every election has at least one "what the hell" candidate. (This one has more.) Besides, du Pont might have figured, maybe he'd end up as the Vice-Presidential candidate, or, as one friend suggests, build toward another race later on. Most campaigns for the nomination have someone who is actually running for the Vice-Presidency; some candidates run simply to become better known. What with the federal matching funds for candidates who meet certain requirements, there is a fairly low threshold for getting into the Presidential race. Still, the federal-funding laws do more good than harm.

Du Pont is running a very determined campaign. He officially entered earlier than any other Republican—in 1986—and claims to have spent more time in Iowa and New Hampshire than any other Republican candidate. He is affable as a campaigner—but in the Republicans' first debate he showed a certain desperation and came off like a yapping puppy. Du Pont made Bush look good by barking at him so much. Du Pont was calmer in the next debate, but did nothing memorable. Du Pont's patrician demeanor, which his effortful affability cannot hide, almost makes Bush look like one of the boys.

Du Pont is campaigning on proposals no one else offers, or would dare to, and it's hard to tell how much of this attitude stems from courage and how much from a desire to get attention. He calls for phasing out farm subsidies; for mandatory drug testing in high schools and withholding driver's licenses from those who fail; for allowing people to set up a private alternative to Social Security (this is what Bush called "a nutty idea"); for giving parents vouchers with which to send their children to private schools; and for requiring every able-bodied welfare recipient to take a government job at a subminimum wage. Du Pont used to be a moderate, or even a liberal (he also served in the House of Representatives), and the depth of his conversion is in question.

Alexander Haig's motivation for running for the Republican nomination is also best known to him, but people who know him well say that they are certain he thinks he can win. Preposterous as this may seem to others, they say it is not at all preposterous to Haig. Someone who has known Haig for a long time says he is a "true believer"—someone who when he was in the government frequently argued about issues of substance, wrote angry memorandums, and was utterly convinced of the truth of what he was saying. Haig, according to this person, would feel now that only he has the right views about how to deal with the Soviet Union, among other things. A number of people assume that Haig is in the race for the good it might do his speaking fees, but a longtime friend says that though Haig might be aware of this possibility, he is not so cynical. Haig is somewhat odd, of course, but he also has a sense of humor about himself. He will go down as the man who made "caveat" a transitive verb and who announced, in a hyper manner, "I am in control here in the White House" after Reagan was shot, in 1981. But Haig has a substantive grasp of some important questions—mainly having to do with arms control (he opposes the I.N.F. treaty, as some others do, because of the Soviet superiority in conventional forces) and dealing with the

Soviet Union. And he has had valuable—if limited to a few areas—experience. He is wont to point out that he has "served seven Presidencies," and that none of the wars the United States has fought occurred when a general was President. But, like many military men, he does not seem to understand how the political system works, or to have much patience with it. He also has the bearing of a general—or a President. But he's not going to be President.

Jack Kemp had been getting ready for this Presidential race for a long time, and the question now is why he hasn't been doing better. Kemp has been building a following for a long time—his speeches to Republican National Conventions have roused the audiences to fervor. But as of now he hasn't caught on. His campaign is making its major effort in New Hampshire, and has made his having a breakthrough there (coming in first or second) key to his strategy, but thus far—if the polls are to be believed—to little effect; Bush and Dole, in that order, are running far ahead of him there, and Robertson has also been campaigning aggressively there. Kemp is now running a television ad in New Hampshire accusing Bush and Dole of being "Washington insiders" who want to raise taxes. His advisers say that one of his problems is that he has low name recognition, especially compared with Bush or with Dole (who started far behind Bush in name recognition), but a Kemp adviser also says that the importance of the abortion issue in Iowa should not be overlooked, and that Kemp has been very firm on the issue. (So has Robertson, and Bush and Dole don't leave a lot of room for disagreement.) Though it is too early to rule Kemp out in this campaign—and there are some in the other camps who think he could still sneak up on them—his problems seem to be both personal and political.

Kemp is agreeable and attractive, but he seems to lack solidity. This probably stems in part from his youthful looks (Kemp is fifty-two) and in part from his enthusiastic delivery. His advisers have worked hard, and only partially successfully, to get him to shorten his speeches. But there seems to be some confusion about what he should say. His advisers have succeeded in getting him to stop talking about his favoring a return to the gold standard, but that was at the center of his economic thinking; he still blames the Federal Reserve Board for economic ills, and says, as he has been saying for years, that interest rates should be substantially lowered. (Orthodox Republicans—and many Democrats—worry that this could set off inflation and send the value of the dollar still lower.) At a candidates' forum in Iowa in September, and in the recent debate, he attacked "liberal Democrats" for wanting "to spend their time investigating Ollie North," and said, to strong applause, "It's time to stop investigating Ollie North and start investigating the liberal Democratic foreign policy." Kemp, whose hallmark is optimism, misplaced or otherwise, says that "unlike other candidates"—meaning Dole—"I think growth is the only solution to the budget problem," and he calls the budget-reduction package "a hoax." Like Bush, he calls for reducing the capital-gains tax. On foreign policy, he takes the rightmost stands; one of his advisers, Roger Stone, believes that whoever runs furthest to the right on foreign policy wins the Republican nomination. (He cites as examples Goldwater over Rockefeller, Nixon over Rockefeller, Reagan over Bush—and Reagan nearly over Ford, a sitting President.) So Kemp has come out for firing George Shultz and "cleaning out" the State Department (an old right-wing bugaboo), and for immediate deployment of S.D.I. (almost no one thinks it is ready), and he opposes the I.N.F. treaty.

Aides to other candidates suggest that Kemp's problem is that he is out of date. They say that the fight within the Republican Party between center and right is over, and that Kemp—even though he still calls for broadening the Party by attracting labor and blacks—is going after a narrow fringe of the Party. The conservatives are now the nominating wing of the Party, its mainstream—leaving about twenty per cent way over on the right for Kemp to go after. And in doing that he is being crowded by Robertson. (In that sense, the Bush and Dole camps are glad that Robertson is in the race.) The Kemp camp has tried to exploit the differences among evangelicals. Recently, Kemp named as one of his several co-chairmen the Reverend Tim LaHaye, an influential evangelical leader. Five days later, after press reports about anti-Catholic and anti-Jewish writings by LaHaye, he resigned from the Kemp campaign. It might be more than Kemp's strategy that is out of date. Kemp's "new ideas" were much drawn upon by Reagan in 1980, and so now they aren't new. We've tried supply-side economics; we've undertaken a staggering military buildup; we've gone about as far as the country wants to go in foreign and military policy and we're ready for arms-control agreements, which Kemp opposes. So, in a lot of ways, Kemp seems frozen in time.

Pat Robertson is the new unpredictable element on the Republican side, and he has the other camps worried. No one thinks he can win the nomination, but many think he can cause difficulties both for the other candidates and for the Party. If he bumps Bush or Dole into third place in an early state, he causes them trouble. He has shown, in Iowa and in Michigan, that he can summon up and deliver a committed following—people who may not have been practicing Republicans before, or have been involved in politics at all. Robertson is aiming his appeal at people who resent "establishment" politics. His followers are not the same as the fundamentalists who followed Jerry Falwell—who has run into financial and political difficulties and dropped out of politics. On the day that Falwell left politics (November 3rd), he told a radio interviewer, "We're no longer breaking new ground. It's no longer as glamorous to be in the religious right." Robertson's followers are charismatics and Pentecostals—disciplined and highly motivated. The other candidates would like to have those people if they are nominated; so they tread warily and say nice things to Robertson.

Robertson himself is under no compunction to follow form, and the appeal he makes is to deep emotion and fear. He has a babyish, sweet face and smiles a lot, frequently emitting a strange chuckle—and he speaks from the dark side of populism. He has resigned as a minister and given up his management of the Christian Broadcasting Network, which he founded. But he draws on the large audiences his television ministry provided, and is very well funded—second only to Bush. And he employs the terms and the techniques that made him famous. Robertson knows how to lean into the camera better than anyone else in the race, and his delivery rolls and builds. Picking away at anxieties, he tells perfervid followers that he opposes the "cultural relativism of John Dewey," that he is for teaching "the values that made this country great," that he is against the "powerful teachers' unions with leftist tendencies," and that he will "not allow pro-choice to be the rationale for the slaughter of one and a half million babies a year." He told a group of reporters that we must increase the number of babies born in the United States or "die out as a race." He also says that abortions are depriving us of people we'll need to keep Social Security viable. (Such practicality about abortion upsets some evangelicals.) He decries "radical homosexuals" and suggests the quarantining of AIDS victims. (Some Republican strategists say that AIDS will be an issue in this election.) He attacks the Trilateral Commission—which almost makes him the candidate of nostalgia. Robertson speaks of traditional family virtues and calls for tax deductions for women who stay home with their children, and, of course, for prayer in the schools. Citing Reagan, he talks about America as the "city on the hill," and he says, "All of us are unashamed to shed a tear when we see the American flag." He whips his audiences into a frenzy.

Though Robertson won a straw poll in Iowa and has shown strength elsewhere, the other camps don't know how to gauge his strength. Some say that his followers aren't the type of people who will brave the cold Iowa night to go to a stranger's house, or to a community firehouse to cast their vote. Others say that these people are so committed that they will do anything for their candidate, and that because the Republican Party is smaller than the Democratic Party, and because it has more caucuses—and in some states, such as Iowa, one doesn't have to be registered to participate in the caucuses—Robertson could cause all sorts of problems. The real questions are what role he and his followers will play at the National Convention, and how the other candidates can appeal to Robertson's followers without frightening others away.

The wisdom about which party is in a better position to win in November keeps changing, and it will go through several more revolutions. Republicans tend to be confident now, because they have the better-known candidates and because so many people find the Democratic field weak—but that can change. They also know that they start out with an advantage in the electoral college; and they enjoy the prospect of the Democratic Party's nominating someone who is too liberal or having a fractious Convention. Republican leaders feel that if the country is not in a war—or, indeed, seems to be moving toward a better relationship with the Soviet Union—and is in reasonable shape economically they will win. That is why both parties will be watching the economic indicators with increasing interest between now and next November. Certainly, the Republicans can offer a candidate with more experience

than the Democrats can. But no one can say now how much difference that will make to the voters then.

Whatever one thinks of the candidates, the stakes in the coming
elections are high—the stakes in every election are high. There
are both the problems we know and unforeseeable challenges. A
year from now, we will have made a choice. Some time later, we'll
know whether it was a good choice, or at least the best that could
be made under the circumstances.

1988

III

The events of the past year have—or should have—taught us how unpredictable things can be, and made us rethink assumptions. Just as Reagan was widely being written off as irrelevant, as a lame-duck President merely serving out his last days, the recent Washington summit with Mikhail Gorbachev (to be followed by a summit in Moscow by June) demonstrated his continuing importance, and his ability to command center stage—at least on certain subjects. His policies on arms control appear thus far to have turned out to be more successful than many of his critics had thought they would—though the advent of Gorbachev as leader of the Soviet Union in 1985, and the fact that the treaty signed during the summit is good for the Soviets, had something to do with this. Reagan's Persian Gulf policy (as of this date) has also worked better than many expected it to. No great conflagration between us and Iran has occurred—because both countries have sought to avoid one. The two antagonists have reached some implicit understandings. The Administration, to avoid any conflagration with Congress, has put strict limits on the activities of our Persian Gulf forces—allowing them to defend only American-flagged ships, including the eleven Kuwaiti ships that were re-flagged with American flags last year amid much controversy. The Iranians have therefore found still another way to embarrass us—by attacking the ships of other nations while ours stand by. There is still much violence in the Gulf, and Arab nations, whom our stepped-up presence in the Gulf was designed to impress, and whose ships are being hit, wonder why we can't be more helpful to them—and Iranian propaganda is making much of this. But just as the bombing of Libya seems to have curbed Qaddafi, the projection of power in the Persian Gulf, including a measured retaliation (on October 19th, the day of the stock-market crash) for an Iranian attack on an American-flagged tanker, seems to have curbed Iran's appetite for messing with us. The fact that a number of members of Congress thought the retaliation should have been stronger suited the Administration just fine; a State Department official says, "That's where we wanted to be—less hawkish than Congress." The grappling with the enormous budget deficit and the attempt to respond to the stock-market crash also showed that Reagan can still play a big role—for good or ill, or even by inaction. Uncertainty about the economy will be a hallmark of this year—especially given the political implications. And the election is, as of now, entirely unpredictable. Gary Hart's reëntry into the race in mid-December was only one more loop in an already loopy election campaign, and probably not the last one.

Once again, a summit meeting ended with confused statements over what had taken place. This time, the President, in his televised speech the night the summit ended (December 10th), and even more so in a statement the following day, claimed, incorrectly, that the Soviets had yielded on the issue of the Strategic Defense Initiative (S.D.I.), giving us the leeway to do whatever testing we wanted, regardless of the strictures in the anti-ballistic-missile (A.B.M.) treaty, and to deploy the system when it is ready (after a waiting period of an agreed-upon number of years, probably until 1996, or ten years after Reykjavik). What did happen was that the Soviets agreed to compromise wording in a joint statement that finessed the S.D.I. question for now. Not only did the Soviets—as well as Reagan—not wish to have the summit break up in disagreement over S.D.I., as the one in Reykjavik did, but they appear to have adopted a new attitude toward the defensive system that has been Reagan's dream. Increasingly, it appears to informed observers, the Soviets see it as just that—a dream, even a pipe dream, cherished by Reagan. (The Soviet press has been reflecting this.) I'm told by observers that Gorbachev and his colleagues are more relaxed now about S.D.I., seeing it as not likely to work, and not likely to be held in such high regard by whoever succeeds Reagan. Andrei Sakharov, the distinguished physicist, who was brought back to Moscow in December, 1986, after six years of exile in the closed city of Gorki, is said to have become an influential figure in the Soviet debate on S.D.I. He is said to have played a large role, along with other Soviet scientists, in convincing Gorbachev that S.D.I. wouldn't work, and that although Reagan won't make concessions on it, it doesn't matter because of the unlikelihood it will work—and that, if deployed, it could easily be overcome by additional offensive weapons (just as its American critics say). These people are reported to have urged Gorbachev not to make an agreement on S.D.I. a precondition for an agreement to reduce long-range nuclear missiles. At Reykjavik, Gorbachev had made it a precondition for treaties on both long-range and intermediate-range missiles, and had insisted that testing of S.D.I. should be confined to the "laboratory," and the meeting broke up over that. Reagan was advised before the Washington summit by Kenneth Adelman, who has just left the post of director of the Arms Control and Disarmament Agency, to mute his talk of giving S.D.I. to the Soviets, because if it happened it would be the greatest transfer of technology in the history of the world, and if the Soviets were given S.D.I. they could overcome ours—and because the Soviets wouldn't take him seriously. The other thing that could get the summit in trouble, he was advised by Adelman, would be to return to such ideas, discussed at Reykjavik, as removing all nuclear missiles. That, he was told, would frighten Europe and might make it more difficult for him to win Senate approval of the treaty, to be signed at the summit, to reduce intermediate-range nuclear forces, or I.N.F.

The other factor that apparently got the Soviets to back off from their earlier insistence on a ban on extensive testing of S.D.I.—testing that might violate the A.B.M. treaty—was that Congress had recently enacted (and Reagan had signed) a ban on such testing. The ban, sponsored by Senator Sam Nunn, Democrat of Georgia and a relatively conservative man, was attached to a bill authorizing defense funds for the next year—and is likely to be renewed. Last March, Nunn made a study of the negotiating record of the A.B.M. treaty and on three consecutive days made speeches on the Senate floor which demolished the Administration's sudden claim, in 1985, that the treaty permitted the kind of testing needed for S.D.I. Thus, the Soviets are said to have figured, since they had run into a brick wall with Reagan, who was still insisting on deploying S.D.I., it paid to simply outwait him, because no prospective President seems as sold on S.D.I. as he is. An aide to Vice-President George Bush has confirmed to me that Bush takes a more "pragmatic" view of S.D.I. than Reagan does—that he is yet to be convinced that it will work and is there-

fore less definite about his intention to deploy it—and that he
conveyed this to Gorbachev during his meeting with him in the
course of the summit.[1] Also, I am told that Robert Dole, in his
brief meeting with Gorbachev during the summit, conveyed to
him that he is all for researching S.D.I. but that he takes a more
pragmatic, open-minded view than the President does on whether
it should be deployed. Dole, through a spokesman, denied this.

The apparent new Soviet attitude could, if it lasts, provide a
way to get around the S.D.I. issue in connection with a treaty on
long-range missiles, or START (for Strategic Arms Reduction
Talks), on which the two sides are now moving forward. One
possibility is that the Soviets would be willing to continue to fudge
the issue, and reserve the right not to implement START reductions, or to take other "countervailing measures," if they see the
United States going too far on S.D.I. But it's not clear whether
the Administration is prepared to be as relaxed about S.D.I. as
the Soviets now seem to be. Some Administration officials, including Secretary of Defense Frank Carlucci and Secretary of State
George Shultz, do not want to live with the ambiguity, and want
clarified what S.D.I. testing would and would not be permitted—
heading off future wrangles with the Soviet Union over this issue.

The I.N.F. agreement got pride of place at the summit not
because it had priority in our arms-control agenda—that belongs
to a START agreement, which deals with the largest and most
destabilizing weapons—but because the Soviets had "de-linked"
S.D.I. and the I.N.F. treaty. There are a great many knots to untie
before a START agreement can be reached, and though there is
no unanimity on the point, some key officials—who know how
hard it will be—say that the odds are slightly better than fifty-fifty
that an agreement can be worked out by the time Reagan goes to
Moscow. Such an agreement would call for a fifty-per-cent reduction in strategic missiles—and while that sounds good it matters very much how those cuts are allocated among weapons systems.
As things now stand, former national-security adviser Brent Scowcroft and others worry that the proposed agreement gives the
Soviets a dangerous advantage in the ratio of their warheads to
our missile silos. Some moderate-minded people are also disturbed by the picture of a President even going to a summit in

[1]A Bush spokesman later denied this.

his last year in office (where, because of the brief time left in his Presidency, he would have a limited mandate), not to mention pressing for a possibly flawed arms-control agreement that would then be passed on to his successor. It seems inconsistent with a tough negotiating policy to be so public, as the Administration has been, about our desire to reach a START agreement this year.

One of the great ironies of the time is that some strategic thinkers of a centrist stripe worry that Reagan, who began his Presidency saying that the Soviets "reserve unto themselves the right to commit any crime, to lie, to cheat" to further their cause, is now prone, in his enthusiasm for arms reductions, to reach for destabilizing agreements. These people also worry that in pursuing the I.N.F. and START agreements Reagan will deprive us of the weapons we have relied upon for forty years to offset the Soviets' advantage in conventional forces. These thinkers—who include Richard Nixon and Henry Kissinger as well as Scowcroft—believe that the I.N.F. treaty leaves us worse off, because it deprives us of some things we had long sought: a policy, through the presence of our intermediate-range weapons in Europe, of "flexible response," and a confidence on the part of the Europeans that we will defend them against a Soviet attack. Also, it leaves Europe with NATO conventional forces that are inferior to those of the Warsaw Pact—with any prospect of an agreement on conventional forces far off.

A number of Western leaders are concerned about the psychological effects of this on Europe. When Reagan, in 1981, proposed the "zero-zero" option (the removal of all American and Soviet intermediate-range weapons that could hit Europe or the Soviet Union from Europe), the prevailing wisdom in Washington was that the Soviets would never accept it—indeed, that is why Pentagon officials backed the idea, over the objections of the State Department. That the Soviets finally did accept it is now being touted as a victory for Reagan's stubborn negotiating policy. But some say that the reason the Soviets finally accepted it—though it took someone with the imagination of Gorbachev—was that it meets their longtime goal of keeping American missiles out of Europe. (The Soviets also made other unexpected concessions in order to achieve this goal.) Though the treaty does, as Reagan says, eliminate an entire class of weapons, these weapons constitute only four per cent of the world's nuclear weapons. In fact, the buildup of strategic arms, by both sides, since the I.N.F. negotiations began, has been many times the number of nuclear systems that are to be eliminated by the I.N.F. treaty. Moreover, the Soviets can replace their intermediate-range weapons with others not covered by the treaty—and still have missiles targeted on Europe. Therefore, the Soviets didn't really need the weapons they have now agreed to scrap—and while we can reallocate from our strategic forces weapons aimed at the same targets as before, we can't base them in Europe. How much difference this makes politically is a subject of dispute. After the I.N.F. reductions, the United States will still have at least four thousand nuclear weapons stationed in and around Europe—many of them on submarines and bombers, and quite a few of which can hit the Soviet Union—and the British and the French are continuing to increase their nuclear arsenals that can hit Soviet territory.

One critic of the I.N.F. treaty says that the only point of Reagan's hanging tough was to show that he can hang tough—"for a proposal we shouldn't have made in the first place." Richard Perle, a powerful Pentagon official who proposed the zero-zero option and tried to block other arms-control agreements, is now, like his former boss, Defense Secretary Caspar Weinberger, gone from the government. (It is becoming increasingly clear that one reason behind Weinberger's surprise decision to leave, made public in early November, was his awareness that his string was running out—not only on Capitol Hill, which was resisting increases in defense spending, but also within the Pentagon itself, where he lost an argument with the Joint Chiefs of Staff over arms control, and also with the President, who was determined to reach an arms-control agreement and accepted Nunn's restriction on S.D.I. testing.) European leaders are said to be far less enthusiastic about the I.N.F. treaty than they publicly let on. But they and the treaty's critics say that now it would be worse to have it not be approved than to have it approved—after all those negotiations. Even one of the American negotiators said to me recently, "By itself, the treaty isn't much."

By all accounts, the Administration's foreign-policy machinery is working far more smoothly as a result of Weinberger's departure. In fact, one foreign-policy official says, it became progressively smoother with the departure, in 1985, of Jeane Kirkpatrick from her position as ambassador to the United Nations, and the death of former C.I.A. director William Casey, last year. Further, the advent of Lieutenant-General Colin Powell to the job of national-security adviser, succeeding Carlucci when he went to the Pentagon, is said to have assured (as Carlucci did) fair and efficient handling of issues. Though some people, after recent experience, are chary of having military people in the national-security adviser's job (and the Iran-Contra committees' final report said that active military officers should not hold the job), Powell gets high marks from his colleagues—but he is not said to have a particularly creative mind, nor has he yet been put to severe tests. Though institutional differences remain, the absence of personal rancor and of mutual mistrust make the formulation of foreign policy far easier. The role of personal relations in the management of the government is often underestimated. Now, says one official, the key figures "spend their time talking to each other rather than figuring out how to get to the President."

Reagan was obviously much taken with Gorbachev, a modern Soviet leader of great charm, humor, and quickness—as was a high percentage of the American people. Reagan said some things about Gorbachev—for example, he told the network anchormen that Gorbachev may not know what his predecessors had done in Afghanistan—that Jimmy Carter, or even Gerald Ford, would have been run out of town for saying. (Gorbachev was a member of the Politburo in December, 1979, when the Soviets invaded Afghanistan.) And Reagan, showing that he can be simplistic in both directions, told some columnists during the summit that Gorbachev was entirely different from his predecessors, because the current Soviet leaders "no longer" share the goal of world domination. Bush was constrained to take exception to this publicly. Reagan also said after the summit, "I find it's an entirely different relationship than I had with his predecessors," but, of course, Reagan never met any of Gorbachev's predecessors. People had to try to steady themselves in the face of the euphoria that swept Washington during the summit—and of the thought that perhaps the two superpowers were at long last undergoing a profound change in their relationship. Some officials believe that a fundamental change is taking place, because of Gorbachev's attempts to improve the Soviet economy and perhaps to wind down some of the Soviets' expensive international ventures, such as in Afghanistan. (America's arming of "freedom fighters" has made these ventures costly to the Soviets.) In ten years, we'll know.

* * *

The I.N.F. treaty remains an issue in the increasingly heated Republican contest for the Presidential nomination, despite the fact that, on December 17th, Robert Dole ended his public uncertainty over whether he would support the treaty—at a White House briefing, with the President momentarily by his side. (To disavow any idea of partisanship, the President jumped away from the podium as quickly as possible.) There had been no doubt that Dole would eventually back the treaty, but he was also trying to appease the right wing of his party and maintain his options as the Republican Senate leader. The treaty is very popular among Republicans in Iowa, and Dole was on the verge of losing his edge there over Bush—if Dole loses Iowa, that could effectively be the end of the Republican contest. Also, Dole was losing the one real advantage he had over Bush—that he was seen as the stronger leader. Dole's supporters are praying that he switched in time. Bush and his people were furious at White House Chief of Staff Howard Baker for arranging for the Presidential appearance with Dole, questioned Baker's motives (which were to get the treaty approved), and let him know there would be no room for him in a Bush Administration. White House aides say that Bush and his advisers tried just about everything to get the appearance called off—according to an associate of Baker, one important Bush adviser even threatened Baker's former law firm. There was a petulance, even a vindictiveness, in Bush's behavior, and a ruthlessness in that of his associates, that give one pause: Would they behave this way if Bush became President?

Dole, for his part, has been goading Bush to tell more about his role in the Iran-Contra affair, in part hoping to spook him (Bush has been flappable in past campaigns). Dole commenced this tactic in the wake of the release of a newly found memorandum by former national-security adviser John Poindexter suggesting that Bush fully supported (was "solid" for) the arms sales to Iran. Bush explained that the memorandum simply shows that he stood by the President, and one of his aides says that it applied to an early phase of the Iran-Contra affair, before the dealings became arms for hostages—but in fact the memo was written when it was clear that the deal was arms for hostages, and some time after the subject had become highly controversial among the President's top advisers. (Bush has said that he might have opposed the deal if he had known that Weinberger and Shultz opposed it, but the Iran-Contra committees' report puts him at a meeting where they opposed it vehemently. A Bush spokesman says that Bush's logs don't show the meeting and that Bush doesn't remember it.) Another Bush aide says that Bush will have to spell out more clearly his "reservations" about the arms sales to Iran. Bush, who seems to have bought the erroneous idea that Oliver North was a great hero to the American people during the Iran-Contra hearings (the polls all said otherwise), had North and Poindexter to a Christmas party at his Vice-Presidential mansion —setting off speculation as to why he is being so solicitous of them. Among the theories are that he is playing to the Republican right or that he would prefer that North and Poindexter not squeal about his involvement in the Iran-Contra affair—this on the supposition that Bush was more involved than he has let on. Dole, in an interview with David Frost broadcast tonight, said that North is not a hero.

The Democrats are just about finished scraping themselves off the ceiling, where they remained for some time after Gary Hart returned to the race, and are trying to figure out the implications. Democratic Chairman Paul Kirk, a very controlled man, was uncharacteristically, and deliberately, outspoken in his criticism of Hart's latest action. Kirk had done much to make the nomination contest an orderly parade, and this disorderly—and possibly damaging to the Party—intrusion was unwelcome. Hart's reëntry is in retrospect not so surprising, because he had nothing better to do, and was undoubtedly bored and frustrated sitting in his home in the aptly named Troublesome Gulch, outside Denver; because he could convince himself without too much difficulty that he is superior to the other Democratic candidates; because he doesn't understand, and probably never will understand, what the problem was that drove him out of the race last May. The sad thing about Hart—it doesn't rise to the level of tragedy—is that intellectually and by experience he may be one of the best qualified of the candidates, but his character is seriously flawed. Even though his vaunted "new ideas" aren't much to get excited about, and Hart, though intelligent, can't be said to have a great mind, he does have substantial knowledge of important subjects and a relatively good understanding of government—relative, that is, to most of the other candidates. (Hart has always seemed to tout the idea of "new ideas" rather than the ideas themselves, and by now they are not so new.) And Hart, at this point, is the only one in the race who can speak Presidential; that is, can talk about large themes with confidence—in this he is helped by having been around the track before, which is always an advantage.

Even before Hart was caught trysting with Donna Rice, many people who knew him well felt that his character flaws disqualified him from the Presidency. In 1984, he came across as an unsettled person, not the sort of man that people would be comfortable with in the White House. (The Mondale people played on this effectively.) A lot of people, including many in the press, were aware then of his vigorous extracurricular sex life. (Hart took no great pains to conceal it, nor, when he was in full view of the press, was he particularly kind to his wife, Lee.) Hart is not very good at human relations, and has few real friends—fewer, it seems, as time goes on. So even four years ago there was a strong question as to whether Hart could govern. Hart now tries to reduce the question of his behavior to one "mistake"—the dalliance with Rice—but what made it of such great interest and gave it so much salience was that it was part of what is called in civil-rights law a "pattern or practice" of behavior, something so obsessive and flagrant that it raises serious questions about his judgment, and even stability. Hart is trying the old trick of admitting one thing in an effort to persuade people that he has confessed all. The issue is not one "mistake"—in an interview with Marvin Kalb on PBS today he called it "a damn fool mistake"—or the press's invasion of his privacy, and the argument is not over, say, whether he should be ruled out because of one affair carried out discreetly at some point in his life; there is, of course, no plausible explanation for, among other things, a Presidential candidate's having his picture taken with a model in the course of an overnight trip to Bimini (on the Monkey Business, no less). Hart is trying to get us to accept the absurd notion that there is a disconnect between one's "private" behavior—even when there is a pathology involved—and one's public persona and responsibilities. Recklessness, relentless self-indulgence, and blindness to the consequences of one's acts are not traits that can be compartmentalized. In his behavior, he not only jeopardized his party but betrayed some people who had joined his campaign only after extracting from him an explicit promise that this time he wouldn't fool around. Their concern was less moral than political: they understood, if Hart didn't, that his behavior was a potential political disaster.

In 1984, Hart talked mystically about himself—saying that it was his "destiny" to become President. Obviously, he has not shaken that idea. And, for all the amateur psychoanalyzing of Hart that is going on these days, his reëntry in the race has a cool logic in his terms: since his behavior should not have driven him out of the race, the story was unfinished. He means it when he says "Let the people decide." Even if the voters say no, he said on "60 Minutes" recently, "I'll feel better about myself than if I just sat up there on that mountain wondering." Trying to guess how well Hart will do is like playing with quicksilver; it is trying to apply reason to an emotion-laden situation. The polls currently showing Hart doing well are largely discounted as being a reflection of his celebrity, but they should not be so roundly dismissed; they probably also reflect both dissatisfaction with the other candidates and Hart's indisputable star quality. The high "negatives" that also show up in the polling about Hart would disqualify an ordinary mortal. And Hart's entry, at least for a while, distracts attention from the other candidates and slows down their potential catching on. He could damage some by coming in ahead of them in the early contests, when the weeding out begins. Recent polls indicate that Hart's entry may be particularly hurting Paul Simon, who until recently was running first in Iowa (now, according to two polls, Hart is first) and second to Michael Dukakis in New Hampshire (now, according to an NBC-*Wall Street Journal* poll, Hart and Simon are tied for second). On the other hand, if by the time of the voting Hart is considered a strong presence, whoever beat him could gain added stature. Those who thought that Hart would be out of the race in short order (even before the contests began) were probably indulging in wishful thinking—he's at his happiest, and perhaps best, being the guerrilla candidate, the challenger of the powers that be, and he doesn't have anything more interesting to do. For what it's worth, most people don't expect him to last beyond New Hampshire, and he said on "60 Minutes" that he would get out if the votes aren't there for him in the early contests—but, like all his actions, that will be for him to decide.

* * *

Hart's reëntry into the race inevitably set off more speculation about a brokered Convention—a topic that was already in the air, because of the lack of excitement about the declared candidates. While it's usually the case that when some candidate starts winning he takes on new and larger aspects in the eyes of the public, there's no guarantee that will happen this time. Rumors persist that Mario Cuomo, despite his protestations, will get into the race later if the situation seems propitious, and there are also rumors that Bill Bradley is warming up (by having media-performance experts observe some of his appearances)—but perhaps that's for 1992. One theory around is that the next President might end up a Herbert Hoover, and that some Democrats are awaiting the opportunity to be Franklin Roosevelt. If no candidate wins most of the seven contests that precede the twenty-state roundup on March 8th, and virtually puts the nomination away on that date, we may very well discover that the arithmetic of the situation is that no candidate can get the necessary number of delegates (two thousand and eighty-one) to win the nomination on the first ballot. At that point, a few governors and states would still be in a position to offer favorite-son candidacies, or uncommitted slates, and the fun would begin.

Things have changed since John F. Kennedy (having won a few test primaries) was put over by some Party bosses, so the brokering, if there is any, would be different this time, and involve more people. The brokers would be those who would have blocs of votes: some of the candidates; the A.F.L.-C.I.O., which is making an effort to have as many labor delegates at the Convention as possible, without an overall commitment to any one candidate (Lane Kirkland, the president of the A.F.L.-C.I.O., is pleased with the prospects of this strategy); and some individuals, such as Paul Kirk, House Speaker Jim Wright, and perhaps some governors and senators with a strong hold on their state parties. The peripatetic and well-connected Robert Strauss also might get involved. Perhaps, the thinking goes, if no one wraps up the nomination early, many of the six hundred and forty-three officials who will be ex-officio delegates—a larger number than at recent Conventions—will hold back endorsements of anyone. While it is entertaining to fantasize about a brokered Convention, most people who think about it carefully still don't think it's going to happen.

However, if no candidate comes out of the primaries with enough support to win the nomination, Party leaders will try to head off a brokered—and chaotic—Convention and get the nomination settled before the hordes arrive in Atlanta. Some Party leaders have been quietly talking this over. Mark Siegel, a member of the Democratic National Committee and a man who gets around in Party circles, says, "We're not going to have a brokered Convention; we may have a brokered process." (Many recent nominations, including those of Carter and Mondale, were not settled by the primaries and caucuses, and had to be clawed out before the Convention.) If Jesse Jackson has a large bloc of votes, as is likely, he will have to be offered something—perhaps a Cabinet position. In fact, some Party leaders are thinking about having the Party produce not just the Presidential and Vice-Presidential nominees at the Convention but also the Cabinet—with, for example, Sam Nunn as Secretary of Defense—to bind up the wounds. The people who are thinking about these things believe that the nomination will have to go to someone who has been in the race—that there are hazards in picking someone who has not been tested—but that doesn't necessarily mean someone who is in the race now. There will still be time after March 8th to enter a few states—New Jersey and (with difficulty) California among them —to demonstrate one's desirability.

Congress staggered home just before Christmas—over a month later than its planned adjournment—having accomplished little. A divided government, with the Presidency in the hands of one party and the Congress in those of another, is rarely very productive, but a number of things combined to make this session particularly unfruitful. Reagan has been an especially combative President, making coöperation difficult. And the return of the Senate to the Democrats in the 1986 election, plus Jim Wright's succeeding to Speaker of the House, made the Democrats frisky, and difficult as well. (Wright turned out to be even more partisan than his predecessor, Thomas P. O'Neill, whom even the Administration began to miss.) On top of that, after Reagan and the Republicans lost a couple of issues early last year—Reagan's vetoes were overridden on pork-barrel bills left over from the previous Congress and pushed by the Democratic leadership of the House and the Senate—Senate Republicans decided to try to just about shut their chamber down. The House, being large, has rules for floor debate which get the business done; the Senate, being much smaller, operates by rules that require unanimous consent for bringing up bills and for other procedures—and such a motion can be subject to a filibuster, which requires sixty votes to shut off. In a Senate closely divided along party lines, and with the Republicans especially disciplined, the Democrats had difficulty overcoming a filibuster—or the threat of one—to get the Senate's business done. Some legislation was thus held up for weeks. A bill to reform campaign financing, which would get at many current problems, died because the two parties could not agree on its content. The frustrations and strains of being a legislator—in particular, the pain of having to vote on demagogic proposals (and being vulnerable to attack if one votes "wrong") and the constant pressure to raise ever-increasing amounts of money for reëlection—are growing, to the point where some senators, to the surprise of their colleagues, have chosen to retire.

Most of the legislative energy this year was directed at dealing with the budget—even if the outcome was unimpressive. (Legislators realized that because of the deficit there wasn't much room for new or enlarged programs.) "Black Monday," the day of the stock-market crash, led to the President's yielding somewhat in his opposition to taxes, and the result was about nine billion dollars in new taxes. (Because of "Black Monday," we never found out whether the Gramm-Rudman law, requiring that the deficit be lowered by specified amounts or programs would be cut across the board by a certain percentage, would have forced the President's hand on taxes, as many predicted it would.) The deficit-reduction package contains a good bit of funny money and creative accounting, so the numbers are suspect, and the legislation does little to change long-run spending policies. (Of course, it curbs only the growth of the deficit.) In the past two years, Congress has taken to lumping all the appropriations bills into one giant bill—last year appropriating six hundred and four billion dollars for this fiscal year and containing all manner of riders that wouldn't make it on their own. The President is left with the choice of accepting or vetoing the whole thing, and though he can, through veto threats, get Congress to yield to him on certain matters, he has to swallow a lot or let the government be shut down. Though members of Congress themselves complain about these giant "continuing resolutions," they rather like the opportunity to lard them with some bacon. The Democrats oppose the idea, espoused by Reagan and other Republicans, of giving the President the "line-item veto"—the right to veto a particular part of an appropriations bill without vetoing the whole thing—but they are building a case for it.

Reagan will soon get a Supreme Court nominee through the Senate (on his third try), in large part because he was finally persuaded to stop confronting the Senate, as he did in the cases of Robert Bork and Douglas Ginsburg, and get someone on the Court before time ran out. Anthony Kennedy, an apparently moderate-to-conservative circuit-court judge in California, presented himself to the Senate Judiciary Committee, which has completed its hearings on his nomination and is expected to approve him shortly after Congress reconvenes later this month, as balanced and cautious—and he avoided direct answers to many questions. The hearings were used in part to refight the battle over Bork, with Republicans still charging that Bork was defeated by a "lynch mob"—actually, he was defeated by himself—and in part, by both ends of the political spectrum, to "sensitize" Kennedy to their concerns. Conservatives expressed worries that he would be too liberal, and liberals voiced concerns that he is insensitive to civil-rights issues. Some liberal members were concerned about his narrow rulings in civil-rights cases, on three of which he was overruled by the Supreme Court. And Kennedy, in violation of the American Bar Association's Code of Judicial Conduct, remained a member of a San Francisco club that has no black or woman members until the day he was asked to come to Washington to discuss the possibility of his nomination, which at that time went to Ginsburg. Still, Kennedy was greeted mainly with relief; Judiciary Committee members were tired of fighting—and of putting themselves on the line. Members of Congress don't want to be brave too often.

The conviction of Michael Deaver, in mid-December, on three counts of perjury in connection with his lobbying government officials shortly after he left the White House, was one of many personal blows to the Reagans last year. On the day after Deaver's conviction, Whitney North Seymour, the independent counsel who brought the case against him, said—shocking many people by pointing to the obvious—that the problem is "too much 'loose money' and too little concern in Washington about ethics in government." Seymour continued, "Vast sums of money are on call to representatives of major corporations, defense contractors, and foreign governments to buy influence and favors." The White House took exception to this, but the President's people would have been better advised to remain silent, given the Reagan Administration's record and the President's relaxed attitude toward the whole subject. According to the Washington *Post*, more than a hundred and ten senior Administration officials have been accused of illegal or unethical conduct since Reagan took office in January, 1981—not counting those involved in the Iran-Contra affair or the Wedtech scandal. In the latter case, two close associates of Attorney General Edwin Meese were indicted shortly before Christmas; the independent counsel in that case—Meese has now been investigated by three independent counsels, and cleared by one of them—said that there was "insufficient evidence as of this date" to charge Meese with criminal activities but that the matter was not closed. The level of sleaze in Washington seems to have been rising rapidly in recent years. More and more ways are found to in effect bribe members of Congress; more and more people seem to regard government service as an opportunity to cash in as soon as they leave it. Though the Reagans were angry with Deaver over published excerpts from his forthcoming book about them (once again, he did not let discretion get in the way, and he desperately needs the money), Deaver has convinced them for the time being that the excerpts were not meant to be in the book, and his indictment came as a great shock to them. This, on top of Mrs. Reagan's recent surgery for breast cancer, followed closely by the death of her mother, has made it a most difficult year for them, especially for Mrs. Reagan, who is said by friends to be psychologically already back in California. The President is said by aides to have one foot there.

Reagan's Presidency may be winding down, but squabbling among his White House aides is not. No one expects Reagan to be able to get very much done legislatively, especially after the first few months of the year. Still another confrontation with Congress over military assistance to the Contras is scheduled for early February—Reagan wrung some "humanitarian" assistance for them at the close of last year, with the help of the Sandinistas, who once again strengthened his hand, this time with talk of a military buildup despite the peace talks that were under way. Some thought is being given to having Reagan turn, in his final months, to the role of national teacher, giving the nation a series of talks on his ideas about the role of government—bringing his political career full circle. The possibility, much bruited about, that Reagan might pardon Deaver, North, and Poindexter before he leaves office alarms some White House aides; an aide thinks it is likely he will want to pardon Deaver, and that if he does so he cannot avoid pardoning the others—that is, if he didn't already intend to pardon them. One had the feeling during the Iran-Contra hearings last year that we were witnessing "the fall-guy plan," which North said that he and William Casey had discussed: that North would take the rap and then, when it seemed that he was not of sufficient stature, that Poindexter would do so. A logical concomitant of the fall-guy plan would be the pardoning of North and Poindexter. White House aides know that if Reagan does pardon them, all hell will break loose. One aide said to me recently, "The President can still do things that have a positive impact in the first six months, but he can also do some things that undo that impact."

IV

The process by which we choose our Presidential candidates more resembles a demolition derby than a rational procedure. It's an elimination contest, offering us the last man—or men—standing at the end of a long, gruelling, and expensive series of matches, in some strange arenas. Now that it is under way, we watch the candidates carom from state to state, trying to avoid too much damage—or destruction. Observers take a great and ghoulish interest in the question of who will be forced to drop out. Meanwhile, what this is supposed to be about is who is best fit to lead our country. It should be no surprise that people seem to be increasingly unhappy about how we choose our President.

As the survivors struggle in the South, where a large number of contests are to be held shortly, we can try to make sense of what has happened thus far—to the extent that there is any sense in it. The victors in Iowa and New Hampshire still have a lot to prove. The Democrats Richard Gephardt and Michael Dukakis each won only about a third of the votes in those two states respectively; Bob Dole, the victor in Iowa, and George Bush, the victor in New Hampshire, both have serious liabilities as candidates—at this point the liabilities seem more prominent than the strengths. (The contests held this week, in Minnesota and South Dakota, were more important for whatever psychological effect they had than for their impact on the race for delegates to the National Conventions.) There are as yet no big issues in this election. Everyone has declared himself in favor of economic growth and a strong America; everyone is for improving our education system. Gephardt and Pat Robertson are playing on anger and discontent, each of them mining a stream that has long been part of American politics—the politics of resentment. Talk of someone else's entering the Democratic race is diminishing but not gone. Mario Cuomo continues to say that he will not enter, but a conversation with him still reveals a divided soul; he says that the candidate will emerge from the current field, and that he might endorse one after March 8th, when a large number of states vote—and then again he might not—but he is also at least implicitly critical of the current contestants. He said to me recently, "Where are the ideas in this campaign? It needs someone with an idea that rings true, that sounds right. I don't think there have been ideas that are important yet, except trade—but I'm not sure that's enough." And some people are beginning to speculate that both parties might have brokered Conventions, or, at least, fights that go to the end, with some dealmaking before the Conventions. Predictions of how it will all turn out tend to run in fashions, and now it is becoming somewhat more fashionable to say that the Democrats might win. By the time the election is over, everything will have been predicted.

Bush's and Dole's problems as candidates are nothing new. Dole has always had difficulty as a national candidate—in managing himself as well as his own campaign. And ever since Bush entered Presidential politics, in 1980, he has been plagued by the fact that he isn't a very good candidate. But Bush is pluckier and more competitive than he seems. He is presumed—by, among others, his own campaign—to be very strong in the South; as of now, the Dole camp is trying to find where Dole might get votes there. As for the Democrats, luck plays a big role in politics (consider, for example, Ronald Reagan), and Dukakis has thus far been lucky. His coming in third in Iowa—a great disappointment to his staff—was treated by the press (after some sophisticated manipulation by the Dukakis people) largely as a victory of sorts. There is no such unitary thing as "the press" or "the media"— too many people, with disparate views, are covered by these terms—but there are fashions in political reporting. The fate of a candidate can be affected less by how he actually did than by how the press says he did; the press's interpretation can keep a candidacy alive or kill it off. The Dukakis camp had hoped to come in first in Iowa, win nicely in New Hampshire, take on the aura of inevitability, and, with its advantage in money, put the race away early. (There was a period when Dukakis had a shot at coming in first in Iowa, but he couldn't make the sale, and even his own campaign was aware that the Dukakis candidacy was flat—stirring little enthusiasm.) Dukakis's luck held in New Hampshire, where the greater press attention to the Republican race—and the press's misgivings about the kind of race Gephardt was running—kept Gephardt from profiting greatly from his Iowa victory; also, Dukakis had two opponents—Gephardt and Paul Simon—who divided the opposition to him and beat up on each other. Now his principal opponents in the South—Gephardt and Albert Gore—are fighting over many of the same voters. As the Dukakis camp had hoped, Simon, who would have competed for the liberal vote, is effectively out of the March 8th contests. Sometimes a candidate wins a state because of who his opponents happen to be—how many of them there are, and whether they take votes from each other.

As the process goes along, candidates without the stamina, the money, or a built-in following (in the early states, at least) drop by the wayside. Money plays a far larger part in determining the nominees than most people realize: other things being equal, the candidate with the largest resources has a great advantage in the long and expensive process; candidates without the money to withstand early defeats—and without a built-in following—usually don't survive for long. Therefore, observations about the viability of a candidate take as a given that an important measurement—perhaps the most important measurement—is how much money his campaign has on hand. Exceptions this time are Jesse Jackson, who has a built-in constituency—but also needs money—and Gary Hart, who is no longer a serious candidate. (There is a federal limit—about twenty-eight million dollars—on how much can be spent overall by each candidate who accepts federal matching funds, and part of the game is figuring how much to spend or withhold for later fights.)

Candidates have to spend a great deal of their time, and undergo various indignities, in order to have enough cash on hand. Dukakis's bankroll—the largest among the Democrats—was collected early and was self-perpetuating: a candidate who has raised a lot of money is seen as having a greater potential to win and thus has an easier time raising more money. The relationship between the ability to raise money and the Presidency still isn't clear. And the ability to raise money, and stay alive as a candidate, is heavily affected by the ground rules set by the press: it is ruled that a certain candidate "has to" come in second or third in order to stay in the race—even though the difference between second and third, or third and fourth, can be slight.

Because of the elimination contest, voters in some parts of the country are offered less to choose from than those in other parts—which hold their contests earlier. By the time the race gets to the industrial states, many—perhaps most—of the contestants are gone. The nomination process does not honor reflection, or intellectual or substantive achievement. Rewards go to those who are willing to sacrifice most everything else for two years or more, who are quick off the mark, and who (or whose aides) come up with good one-liners, and who offer the most appealing self-portrait, no matter how inventive, or fraudulent, that portrait might be. The candidates are self-selected and self-designed—or redesigned. This election has had more than the usual amount of fraudulence perpetrated on the voters: Dukakis, who didn't talk about these things before, offers himself as the son of Greek immigrants ("I'm part of the American dream") and, through his television advertising, a man of passion on the issues (making up for what even he knows is a "passion gap"); Gephardt, a consummate insider, retooled himself as the angry populist and outsider; Gore is newly portraying himself as having been more of a hawk on foreign policy than he has been; Dole, who never talked about these things before—and who had done his considerable share of wheeling and dealing, has tight relationships with powerful lobbyists, and hangs out with the wealthy and important—presented himself as the plain man from the Kansas prairies, defined by the poverty he grew up in. Bush underwent an overhaul in New Hampshire. Robertson offers himself as a businessman, and throws a little fit, intended to intimidate, when he is referred to as a television evangelist, which he was until recently, and which made him famous.

Among the irrationalities of the nomination contest is the effect of a victory in one state on what happens next—thus the focus on who has "momentum," which can in turn help a candidate's "momentum." The process can be further distorted by the publicity value of winning early. According to recent polls by the Dallas *Morning News*, Gephardt's support in Texas jumped up after the Iowa caucuses, and then Dukakis's rose sharply (overtaking Gephardt) after New Hampshire. (There is a large factor of "name recognition" in these polls.) In every election, the amount of press coverage of the early contests takes a quantum leap, compounding the distortion. In all, about a hundred thousand people voted in each party's precinct caucuses in Iowa. In New Hampshire, 123,360 Democrats and 157,625 Republicans—both all-time highs—ruled on who should be the nominees. If Gore's gambit of largely staying out of the early Democratic contests—where his prospects were poor—and first offering himself later, in more friendly territory, works, the assumptions about the nominating process and the need to get in early will have been shattered.

An increasing number of people are giving thought to how to change the nominating process. The best way of nominating a candidate was probably the way John F. Kennedy was chosen: he participated in seven primaries, to establish his political potential, and then he was put across at the Convention by strong political figures (some governors, and Mayor Richard Daley, of Chicago), who saw him as the Party's best bet to win the election. This system had produced some fine nominees (F.D.R., and even Adlai Stevenson, though he didn't win), but it's gone and irretrievable. The political pros collided with the anti-war movement, which they didn't understand, in Chicago in 1968, and the old system gave way. The bosses are passé, and the process has been opened, and the people are not going to give up their power. (Since the reforms in the Democratic process involved changing state laws, the Republican process was heavily affected.) The new proposals for changing the process leave in place the premise that the people should decide, but seek to change the sequence in which they do so. (In this election and the last, the Democratic Party has sought to give its professionals—members of Congress, governors, and members of the Democratic National Committee—more of a hand on the tiller by making an increasing number of them automatic delegates to the National Convention.)

The main target of efforts to change the calendar is, of course, Iowa, which is widely viewed as having an inordinate impact on the process, through an unrepresentative sample of Democratic voters: they are almost all white, better educated, older, less blue-collar, and also more liberal than the Democratic constituents of many other states. (The same holds true for Iowa's Republican voters.) Because Iowa comes first (by its own law), it receives the candidates' most attention. (Not only did the Gephardt family start camping out there—literally—in 1985 but Gephardt's very determined mother took up residence in an apartment in Des Moines in July, 1987.) Beginning in small states (Iowa and New Hampshire) is supposed to offer lesser-known candidates more of a chance than if the contest started in a larger, industrial state—but the value of giving lesser-known, and often therefore less experienced, candidates an equal shot is not overwhelmingly clear. Dignity suffers as the candidates go "schlepping" (as Cuomo puts it) around Iowa and flipping pancakes, and a large troupe of candidates goes from debate to debate. Obviously, the candidates must be tested, but not to the point of lunacy; we need to have a chance to learn about them and to see if they are resilient, and how well they wear with us, but not to the point of turning them into hollow-eyed robots, which the surviving candidates usually are at the end. We end up testing the wrong things. The current system can give an advantage to whoever has the most time to campaign, which is not necessarily the same thing as having the experience to govern. Yet anything that moved too close to a national primary—including the idea of regional primaries—is not a good idea, because that moves too far in the direction of handing the process over to those with the most money and publicity, and might not give us enough time to take a second look.

Among the ideas floating around for changing the system is the drawing of lots for which state, or group of states, goes first, so that the first contests are rotated among the regions. One important Democrat (who for diplomatic reasons can't speak publicly yet), would like to leave unknown which states will go first until shortly before the contests begin, eliminating the advantage of having the time to camp out in an early state, and perhaps cutting the length of the process. (We'll never know how much Gephardt's camping out in Iowa contributed to his victory there, since there were other factors, but we do know that, per voter, Iowa gets the highest proportion of the candidates' time.) Some Democrats are considering trying to change the Party's rules so that any state can hold its contest at any point in the election year, thus diminishing, or even eliminating, the importance of Iowa and New Hampshire —and they argue that if this causes a bunching of states early, so be it. The greatest barriers to getting any sensible changes made in the system stem from political human nature: a politician who has prospered in the system as it is—particularly if he has been elected President—isn't likely to spend some of his political capital

on changing the system. No would-be candidate wants to make
Iowa or New Hampshire angry.

Some party officials say that the only real way to impose an
orderly system would be through legislation passed by Congress
—the parties are reluctant to create unpleasantness by enforcing
their own rules—but most politicians are loath to let Congress get
into the act. Another inhibiting factor is the knowledge born of
experience that any changes in the system will have unexpected
and unintended consequences. That's what happened in the case
of the current system.

Michael Dukakis has improved as a candidate—he comes across
as less parochial, and his advisers have tried, with some success,
to give his candidacy more focus, and make it more thematic. But
he is still seen as having a "message" problem—though he is not
alone in this. He talks more now about his intention to expand
Americans' economic opportunity, and he paints himself as more
oriented to the future than his most recent rivals—Gephardt and
Simon. Still, toward the end of his Iowa campaign he toned down
his opposition to a farm bill championed by Gephardt (and popular in Iowa), and muted his objections to Gephardt's protectionist
trade policy. Dukakis's tone is usually upbeat and optimistic—can-
do. (Though he is more careful now, he still suggests that there
are more collectible taxes out there than anyone seriously thinks
can be collected.) But Dukakis continues to have characteristics
that raise questions about how well he would wear over time—as
either a nominee or a President. He also has substantive weaknesses that have yet to be thoroughly explored. His campaign still
has to contend with the problem that Dukakis gives off an air of
arrogance, which is apparent in, among other things, the cocksure,
and unreflective—and sometimes also self-righteous—way in which
he speaks. As he answers questions, he nods his head, and has an
any-fool-knows-this, faintly disgusted, expression. In New Hampshire, after some strong advice that he had to give his candidacy
more definition, he deliberately borrowed from Gary Hart's 1984
Presidential campaign, to try to define his candidacy as a cause,
and to draw a future-past contrast with other candidacies, but he
does this fitfully. An adviser says, "He has trouble staying on a
new thing."

Thus far, Dukakis has seemed to be able to get to a certain point

—to appeal to the more cerebral, well-off, good-government-oriented voters—but not, at least as yet, to move large numbers of people, or to greatly expand his constituency. His New Hampshire support ended up about the same size as it was before Hart left the race last May. His victory margin of sixteen per cent has to be viewed in the light of the special factors there: the combat between his main opponents, and his long relationship with the New Hampshire voters. Furthermore, the Dukakis campaign, using Massachusetts state employees "on vacation," had the state wired to get out the vote for him. As governor of a neighboring state, he is often in the news in New Hampshire (whose main television outlets are in Boston), and the lower tier of New Hampshire contains many people who commute to Boston, or who work in the growing number of high-tech companies in New Hampshire and are part of Dukakis's natural constituency. Moreover, Dukakis is a hero among many New Hampshire people for having held up the opening of a nuclear power plant in Seabrook, New Hampshire (by refusing to approve an evacuation plan)—a big issue in New Hampshire. (The columnist Mary McGrory has reported that Dukakis didn't much care about the Seabrook issue at first, and had to be talked into opposing it by Massachusetts Senators Edward Kennedy and John Kerry and Representative Edward Markey.)

Dukakis's Presidential campaign has begun to apply some of the same techniques that have been used in his Massachusetts political career to try to make him appear more interesting and exciting than he is. John Sasso, Dukakis's former top adviser and the man responsible for his political resurrection after a humiliating defeat for reëlection as governor, acted as an impresario, creating excitement around Dukakis, to overcome the fact that Dukakis, although he is smart, well intentioned, and competent, strikes a great many people as a boring man. Sasso also understood that Dukakis is at his political best when he is seen as a fighter against someone (Edward King, the controversial governor who had defeated him and whom he, in turn, defeated) or something (Seabrook). Dukakis's standing for reform in Massachusetts politics provided him with a following. Now, in his Presidential campaign, Dukakis—occasionally but not consistently—says that his first priority as President will be to try to "drastically curtail" the role of political-action committees. (PACs are a problem, but sim-

ply curbing them could leave in place the coördination of supposedly individual contributions, which has the same effect as a
PAC donation.)

Some of Dukakis's ads still argue that his experience in turning
around the economy in his state (the "Massachusetts miracle")
makes him the most qualified candidate to deal with the nation's
economy, and this theme, though vague, is central to his campaign. (Gore pointed out in one debate that unemployment is
lower in New Hampshire than in Massachusetts, and said that he
assumed Dukakis didn't mean that New Hampshire's Republican
governor should be President.) Dukakis's actual success as a
governor—his real role in the "Massachusetts miracle"—continues to be a subject of dispute; some students of governorships
have rated Bruce Babbitt, former governor of Arizona, higher,
and say that other states have better records of encouraging growth.
Dukakis's governorship is marked by a large number of programs,
several of them overlapping, whose national relevance—particularly in encouraging growth—is questionable.

In order to deal with the fact that Dukakis comes across as a
technocrat (people usually come across as what they are), before
the Iowa caucuses his campaign brought in a new ad agency,
known for making emotional ads, to warm up his image and try
to convince the voters that Dukakis has "passion." It began to run
highly emotive and visually striking television ads about Central
America and about the homeless. (Pollsters are finding that homelessness is one of the most salient national issues this year.) Contra
aid is unpopular, and all the Democratic candidates oppose assistance to the Contras, though Gore supports "humanitarian" but
not military assistance; and the House of Representatives recently
rejected the President's proposal for more military and non-
military assistance (which could include helicopters). A vote on
"humanitarian" aid is scheduled soon. Dukakis's anti-Contra and
homeless ads also pitched an appeal to Iowa's liberal Democrats.
But though Dukakis had been making an issue of his opposition
to aiding the Contras and had occasionally mentioned the homeless, the ads seemed grafted onto his campaign, and (unlike Gephardt's) not an integral part of it. (Dukakis's ad that is ostensibly
about Nicaragua has pictures of jackbooted soldiers in mirrored
sunglasses who are actually El Salvadoran—our allies—and have
nothing to do with Nicaragua. The man who made the ad, Ken

Swope, has for years urged Democrats to run ads about Central America, and made a similar one for George McGovern's brief Presidential campaign in 1984. Some of the identical shots in the Dukakis ad appeared in an ad that Swope had made for a Massachusetts candidate for the Senate in 1984, and that was clearly about El Salvador.) And, prior to the voting in Iowa, Dukakis acquired some stardust through the endorsement by Sally Field (who said that she had been torn between him and Simon) and an appearance on his behalf there by Richard Gere. (To loosen up his image, Dukakis is still occasionally shown playing a trumpet, as he did with Gere in Iowa.) His Iowa campaign was also given some oomph by appearances on his behalf by Edward Kennedy (who was fulfilling his obligation as a Massachusetts politician) and former Iowa Senator John Culver—both men impassioned orators.

Dukakis is still on shaky ground on foreign policy, but he has been lucky in this respect, too: if he is asked, as he often is, in a debate or an interview, whether he has sufficient qualifications to deal with foreign policy, he now offers the pat response that George Bush has the best résumé on foreign policy and "he sat next to the President" during the Iran-Contra affair and "did nothing." He adds, "I don't think extended residence in Washington, D.C., necessarily qualifies you to be an international leader." But this is begging the question. Part of Dukakis's problem stems not from just a lack of experience in the field but from a resistance to devoting much time to learning about it, and also from his apparent certainty that whatever he says—about this or any other subject—must be so. His political advisers have always found him difficult to get through to. His tendency to talk about more than he knows is even more troubling than the large gaps in his knowledge. In a debate in New Hampshire, when he was asked what he meant when he said that he wants to make the C.I.A. an intelligence agency, and not "an assassination agency," he replied by talking about the recent, sensational hearings about corruption and drug-dealing on the part of General Manuel Antonio Noriega, the de-facto ruler of Panama—which have nothing to do with assassinations on the part of the C.I.A. (With the exception of one example exposed in a recent book, "Veil," by Bob Woodward— having to do with a failed, and indirect, assassination attempt against a leader of a terrorist group in Beirut—the C.I.A. has not in recent years been seriously charged with assassination attempts, and there is a Presidential order barring such activity.)

Dukakis got himself in a bit of a jam by saying in Iowa that the Monroe Doctrine (which asserts that the United States will not tolerate the establishing of a colony or intervention in this hemisphere by foreign powers) had been "superseded," and, when he was asked about this on "Meet the Press," left the clear impression, in answers to a series of questions about a Soviet "client state," that he would not object to having one in Central America as long as the Soviet Union did not introduce offensive weapons or use that country as a platform for undermining its neighbors. When Gore, predictably, asked him about this in a recent debate in Texas, Dukakis denied that he had said or implied that he would accept a client state—technically, he didn't say those words, but he certainly implied it—just as in a debate last fall he had denied another statement Gore threw back at him, and, as he did then, he snapped at Gore, "Get your facts straight." Shortly before the New Hampshire voting, Dukakis—with a look toward the South —gave a foreign-policy speech in which he referred to "strength" thirty-three times and repeated his formula for when intervention in the hemisphere is warranted, leaving out any reference to a "client state." Afterward, talking to reporters, he added that the United States could use force to oppose the creation of a "satellite of any foreign nation" in the hemisphere but is not justified in "using force to impose our will on others." (He also said that he should have said that the Monroe Doctrine had been "expanded on.") Dukakis did not explain the apparent contradiction in this new formula, but an adviser explained to me later that Dukakis draws a distinction between a "client state" and a "satellite," which he defines as a country under the control of the Soviet Union, but, the adviser explained to me, in either case Dukakis would seek multilateral action through the Rio Treaty or the Organization of American States. Dukakis is in general an advocate of multilateral action. (He has said that he wouldn't have had us go into the Persian Gulf without first getting the coöperation of our European allies—which would have taken quite a while, if it would have been successful at all.)

In giving his foreign-policy speech in New Hampshire, Dukakis began to implement the strategy of taking his campaign national. By stating that he is willing to use force—"to defend our territory, our citizens, and our vital interests, to meet our treaty commitments, and to respond to, or to deter, terrorist attacks"— he is trying to show that, despite a number of past statements, he is no leftie on foreign policy. (This is an impression his advisers have long worried about, and have taken several steps to overcome.) By saying that there are circumstances where he would intervene in this hemisphere, he offers himself as someone not simply against Contra aid, and by saying that he is for building up conventional forces—almost everybody is—he protects himself, it is hoped, from being seen as another anti-defense liberal. When, following the New Hampshire primary, Dukakis arrived in Atlanta, he stood in front of a large American flag and said, "It is absolutely essential to use force against terrorist bases and installations"—which has proved tricky in the past, because of the strong possibility that civilians would also be killed. (That's why the Reagan Administration hasn't conducted more such raids.) In answers to questions from the press, Dukakis got into a tangle over whether he would have approved the raid on Libya, in April, 1986. In response to another question, he said, "I don't yield to Al Gore in toughness in any way, shape, or manner." In the Texas debate, he said, "I'm very tough." He also said he would be tough on terrorists, by "never, ever, making concessions to terrorists. No exceptions." (All Administrations start out saying this, and all of them find certain circumstances that warrant a deal—short of selling arms.) In the Atlanta speech, Dukakis, borrowing from Reagan, talked about the importance of "standing tall."

The Dukakis campaign is proceeding on the correct assumption that the defense issue is far from all that Southerners are interested in, and he continues to stress economic opportunity, saying that Southerners have the same "values, hopes, and dreams" as other Americans. Jackson is generally ceded the black vote, but there are white areas in the South where the Dukakis camp hopes to pick up delegates—and it hopes that Dukakis's facility at speaking Spanish will help him among Hispanics in Texas, but Jackson will be competing with him for those votes. The Dukakis campaign says that it is not trying to win any Southern states (this is an attempt to "lower expectations"), and says that it is focusing for now on winning as many delegates as possible on March 8th—or "Super Tuesday," when twenty states vote, fourteen of them Southern or border states. A total of 1,307 Democratic delegates will be chosen that day—sixty-three per cent of the delegates needed to be nominated. (The Republicans hold seventeen contests that day.) Thus, March 8th approaches the look of a national primary. The Dukakis campaign, says one official, is "trying to exploit the front-loading of this process and let it do a lot of our work for us." Susan Estrich, the Dukakis campaign manager, recently said to me, "The importance of the early contests is demonstrated by the polls today" (showing Dukakis ahead in the South or nationwide). She added, "You can get a real head of steam, and the reality of running in twenty states is it's very difficult to do it without a head of steam." The Dukakis campaign got less steam out of this week's contests than it had hoped. Dukakis easily won the Minnesota caucuses, which his campaign had tightly organized for (and Minnesota is a very liberal state), but lost to Gephardt in South Dakota. At one point, shortly after New Hampshire, Dukakis had South Dakota in the bag, but his campaign let it get away, in part because it was unprepared to counter a negative ad Gephardt ran at the end. The ad pointed out that Dukakis had once suggested to Iowa farmers that they grow Belgian endive and blueberries, as Massachusetts farmers did.

In the South, the Dukakis campaign is focussing mainly on large urban and suburban areas where he is most likely to find his constituency, and which have a lot of delegates. (These areas are mainly in North Carolina, Georgia, Florida, and Texas. The Dukakis camp is also going after the constituency that has elected Bill Clinton, the Democratic governor of Arkansas. It tried, but failed, to get Clinton's endorsement.) It is counting on its superior organization and money to do well on March 8th. There is also a school of thought both within and outside the Dukakis camp that Dukakis must win at least one major Southern state on March 8th (when Massachusetts, Rhode Island, and Washington State, among other non-Southern states, also vote), to show that he might carry some in November, and the Dukakis campaign is devoting large resources to winning Florida, and would also be very happy to carry Texas. (Dukakis has put in time in the condominiums in South Florida, and the fact that his wife, Kitty, is Jewish is being counted on to give him a good break there. Gephardt has the support of Florida Representative Claude Pepper, the patron saint of Social Security, and, at eighty-seven, still an active campaigner, and the Gephardt campaign says it will contest Texas and Florida.)

The Dukakis people hope to come out of March 8th with the most delegates, and sew up the nomination shortly after that—and they have been trying to establish the inexorability of Dukakis's nomination, and to persuade Party leaders to close ranks after March 8th. (Dukakis has been cultivating Cuomo in the hopes he could get his endorsement at that point.) But if Dukakis doesn't carry any important Southern states on March 8th, others will argue that this shows that he wouldn't be able to carry them in November. And there is a long stretch of time (as campaigns go) between now and March 8th.

Gephardt's fraudulent Iowa campaign came under a lot of criticism, but he was able to come in second in New Hampshire and win South Dakota, and other Democrats, though disturbed by some elements of Gephardt's campaign, are beginning to concede that he has a strong message—the clearest message of any of the Democrats. Moreover, some Democrats, hungry for a victory in November, don't feel they can afford to be too fastidious about how that victory comes about. They find highly enticing the fact that Gephardt's message could at last bring back to the Democratic Party the lower-income, blue-collar constituency that voted for both Robert Kennedy and George Wallace. And they see in his message a possible conduit for bringing back to the Democratic column the electoral-college votes in the industrial states—and perhaps even in California—that have eluded them for some time. They see him as the hungriest candidate, and are developing a newfound respect for his political skill. Therefore, though Gephardt is very low in funds (he just got out of debt), William Carrick, Gephardt's campaign manager, says that the campaign will have enough money to buy sufficient advertising for March 8th. Carrick told me recently that Gephardt's current fund-raising "is mostly momentum-driven"—as people decide that Gephardt has a serious chance to be the nominee. (This is why winning South Dakota was so important to Gephardt.) Carrick said, "A fund-raiser in Dallas that three months ago would have got us thirty thousand dollars now gets us a hundred thousand."

Though politicians are by definition opportunistic, exploitative, and manipulative, these are not, in themselves, negative traits. (Gandhi and Martin Luther King, Jr., were manipulative.) What matters is the uses to which these traits are put, and the degree to which they are used. There are many situations in politics in which one cannot draw a line ahead of time but can sense when a line has been crossed. This is what happened in Gephardt's case. His redesign of himself at the end of last year (when his campaign in Iowa seemed stalled, and he was at six per cent in the polls there) as an angry, anti-establishment populist, and his manipulation of anger and prejudices (anti-Oriental), as well as of facts, crossed the line. Moreover, he led people to believe that he was offering more of a solution to their problems than he was—especially when he talked about his trade proposal. His rhetoric and his ads—which were well executed and, unlike Dukakis's emotive ads, totally integrated with his campaign—aroused anti-Japanese and anti-Korean feelings, and sometimes when he talked to Iowa voters he went further. (The Los Angeles *Times* quoted him telling one group that the Japanese political system is inferior to ours, and another group that "we're going to spend ourselves blind if there's another arms race. . . . The only people who are going to benefit are the Japanese.") His famous "Hyundai" ad, denouncing tariffs and quotas placed on American cars by Korea, was misleading. (He is still using it.) A poll taken for another camp last December about what would be most popular with the voters in Iowa, New Hampshire, and the South indicated that the most appealing approaches would be to attack corporations and (by a wide margin) blame foreign nations' unfair trade practices for our economic decline. Gephardt's campaign seems tailored to just such findings, and he has tapped the nativist streak that has long been a component of populism.

Playing also on another old streak of populism, and even radicalism, in Iowa (Henry Wallace), Gephardt assailed grain merchants, "the establishment," and "editorial boards," and called for unspecified "fundamental change in this country." His ads ended with a slogan that appeared on his campaign buttons and with which he often ended his speeches, "It's your fight, too." This line, Gephardt told me recently, is what makes his campaign a "cause." He added, "People want to know it's something they can participate in." So he is onto something larger: his theme is about, as he says, "whether we can regain control of our economic future." He points to the trade imbalance and the drop in real net income, and plays on economic anxieties. The problems, of course, are that his trade proposal can't solve the larger problems, and that, as he sometimes concedes, trade barriers are commonly viewed as representing only a small proportion (about twenty per cent) of our exporting problem. (Gephardt's proposal calls for retaliation against countries—Japan, South Korea, and Taiwan would be among them—whose exports to the United States exceed their imports from us by a large amount, and who have "unfair" trade practices.) Gephardt leaves the impression that more new manufacturing jobs can be created than is probably the case. He knows that other things also have to be done to improve the economy, and, in part to stem the criticism of his campaign, he is beginning to talk about them—about the need to dramatically improve our education system ("I see that as the moon program of the nineties," he told me), for more research, and for pressing corporate America to make better, more competitive, products. He used to talk about these things more, until he decided they weren't getting him very far. His broader message seems to be on call for when Gephardt thinks it's what someone wants to hear. There's no reason to think he doesn't believe these things—it's just that in his campaign, as he is wont to do on issues in Congress, he walks away from them when he doesn't think they are selling.

The objections to what Gephardt was doing went beyond his numerous—more than the average member of Congress's—"flip-flops" on various issues, and had to do with his reinvention of his persona. Aided no doubt by his having majored in speech in college, Gephardt began to turn in a strong—and effective—performance of himself as an angry populist. His presentations had become highly polished and had energy and drive; Gephardt is an exceedingly disciplined politician. But before his transformation he had been a cool politician—one who had in fact placed great value on cool (passion was passé). Gephardt, as a member of the House leadership, had also until then been far from an anti-establishment figure, and is cozy with both corporate and labor lobbies, whose money he continues to take during his Presidential campaign while he denounces corporations and insiders. He even had lobbyists go to Iowa to help him, and also to help finance a trip there by members of the House who support him. Gephardt the fresh-scrubbed Zelig has always had a facility for fitting in: after he came to Congress, in 1977, he simultaneously ingratiated himself with House Speaker Tip O'Neill and also was part of a group of younger House members who complained, publicly (if anonymously) as well as privately, about O'Neill's being "old hat" and insufficiently telegenic. A House member (who doesn't support Gephardt) says that Gephardt became caucus chairman "because he works well with everyone. The conservatives thought he was conservative, and the liberals thought he was liberal. If he's fooling the American people, it isn't because he hasn't had experience—he's fooled the pros." The worry about Gephardt is that since he seems to lack an inner compass opportunism has replaced any governing philosophy, and he won't know when to stop reinventing himself.

The Gephardt people expect his message of economic nationalism, with an overlay of patriotism—his ads show his face superimposed on the American flag—to do well in the South. (In Iowa, he drew the support of lower-income, blue-collar, less educated voters and also of older ones. According to an exit poll, he got the support of more blue-collar voters in New Hampshire than Dukakis did.) Carrick says that the message "is also about 'Stand Up for America.' " Gephardt says his espousal of getting tougher on trade, letting the farmers set crop allotments, and enacting an oil-import fee (good for Texas, Oklahoma, and Louisiana) will do well in the South.

As for the rest of the Democrats, Paul Simon, who came in second in Iowa, third in New Hampshire, and third in Minnesota, which he strongly contested and had once said would decide the fate of his candidacy, is hanging on. (He came in fourth in South Dakota.) Simon had his moment of being the beau ideal of Iowa Democrats, but after Gary Hart reëntered the race the scenery was scrambled, and Simon, who had been first in the polls in Iowa, began to lose altitude—a process that was accelerated by the voters' impression that he was losing altitude. (Hart became first shortly after he reëntered.) Simon was beginning to move out front again by caucus day (probably with the help of an endorsement by the Des Moines *Register*), but didn't quite make it. Whatever strength he had was in his persona: running an old ad about his bow tie (saying that the political professionals told him he should get rid of it), he invited Iowans to trust in his old-fashioned, plain-speaking (as he defined it) personality, to trust him to do the right thing—and that wasn't quite enough, nor, as his advisers understood, would it be enough for a national campaign.

Two of Simon's problems converged in the debates: his campaign style and his inability to explain how he could pay for all the things he was proposing and still balance the budget in three years, as he was promising. One minute—which was all that was usually meted out in the debates (that's a separate problem)—was not conducive to a lucid explanation of anything complicated, even if there was an answer. So Simon would retreat to his slogans— "We can do it"; "We've got to have a government that cares." Further, to the distress of his aides, his shoulders would slump, and so would his voice, dropping at the end of his phrases like a trombone headed for the lower registers. After a long debate within his campaign, Simon began to run negative ads against Gephardt in Iowa (and continued to do so in New Hampshire), showing contradictory positions Gephardt had taken before and during his campaign—with the obvious risk to Simon that this would blur what another camp called his "Uncle Paul" image. Despite the importuning of some of his advisers, he is keeping his candidacy alive until the Illinois primary, on March 15th (but skipping the March 8th contests), in large part because he was under pressure by major Illinois politicians who are on his slate to do so. Some advisers told him that this might hurt him—might even bring him the embarrassment of losing in Illinois. But Simon, who was having trouble letting go anyway, and clung to the idea he could still be a factor, yielded to his impulses and to the powers that be in Illinois.

Jesse Jackson, having muted his rhetoric and spent more time in Iowa than he did four years ago, received nine per cent of votes there, showing that he can attract the votes of whites. Jackson particularly pitched his appeal there to farmers and displaced workers. He got eight per cent of the vote in New Hampshire and came in second in Minnesota; he was sixth in South Dakota. He is still the wittiest man in the Democratic race, and he makes his points with vivid and well-worked images and arguments. After a while, these begin to take on an automaticness. Many of his lines are from four years ago, but he now focusses also on the failure to interdict drugs coming into the country, and on corporations that move jobs overseas. In the Texas debate, he focussed on and spoke eloquently about the condition of poor people in the South—where he is expected, of course, to do very well (estimates vary as to how well in terms of delegates). Jackson also engages in moral blackmail: he says that if you're not for him it's because he's black. But there are a number of reasons many people can't vote for Jackson: among other things, he's far to the left on the political spectrum and he has no real managerial experience. (His management of Operation PUSH, a program to help inner-city black youths, is controversial on grounds of, among other things, financial mismanagement.) Jackson may well be paving the way for a black who might have more of a chance in a Presidential race—if at some point he steps aside.

Bruce Babbitt enjoyed a moment of media chic in Iowa, in part because of his charm, and in part because he was seen as taking unpopular and courageous positions—raising taxes, applying means tests to entitlement programs. Babbitt thus followed in the footsteps of previous candidates who enjoy press affection because of their positions, their sense of humor, and their cerebral style (Morris Udall, John Anderson), and who lose. Toward the end in Iowa, Babbitt in fact began savaging his Democratic opponents, but not much attention was paid to this. Also, when for a brief period in Iowa Babbitt was the focus of attention, his program didn't seem all that attractive to the voters—particularly his proposal for a consumption tax, which Dukakis called regressive and "a Republican tax plan." Babbitt, too, was clearly reluctant to leave the race; candidates—who are often having the most interesting experience of their lives, and like the attention and applause—are often reluctant to give up and go home. After coming in fifth in Iowa and sixth in New Hampshire, Babbitt, out of funds and out of hope—but with a lot of good will toward him—dropped out.

Gary Hart has become a sad case—his face sometimes looks ravaged, and his anger shows. He could not shake the albatross of his extramarital behavior—and he himself, consciously or not, used the words "moral" or "morality" frequently. In some appearances, particularly before college audiences, he talked intelligently and interestingly about his issues—"strategic investment" (in the economy, in education, in energy independence), military reform, and "enlightened engagement" (his concept of foreign policy). But this didn't matter, and he knew it—though he appeared to get pleasure out of connecting with his student audiences, as an affirmation of his substantive worth. On other occasions, he looked forlorn, or even silly—waving his little white pamphlet containing his ideas. Sometimes he and his wife, Lee, wandered through shopping malls in search of an audience, or he spoke before tiny groups—and Hart is smart enough to see what this means, and his pain and embarrassment showed. In the Texas debate, on the other hand, he hit his stride and demonstrated that he is well informed and thoughtful. When, on the night of the New Hampshire primary, it was pointed out to him that he had reëntered the race saying, "Let the people decide"—and that he had got less than one per cent of the vote in Iowa and had come in last in New Hampshire (where he had triumphed four years ago), with four per cent of the vote—Hart replied, "I didn't mean the people of two states, I meant the people of all fifty states."

The period of the Iowa and New Hampshire contests was a tense one for Albert Gore, who has staked everything on doing well on March 8th. After that date, his strategy will be seen as having been either brilliant or wrong—he felt he had little choice but to sit out Iowa, since he had so little chance there. His New Hampshire strategy was on-again, off-again—he didn't want to risk much by fighting a probably hopeless campaign there, but he also yielded to the temptation (to the distress of some of his allies) to try to make a small showing in New Hampshire by some campaigning and running some ads there. He came in fifth, with seven per cent of the vote. (He was a virtual no-show in this week's contests.) While Gore essentially sat out the early contests, his rivals not only received more publicity but also had more opportunity to hone their skills. Fred Martin, Gore's campaign manager, says that the first phase of the campaign, up to the end of New Hampshire, was focussed on raising money and getting endorsements in the South (the Gore strategists believe that endorsements count for more in the South than they do elsewhere), and that the second stage is focussed on winning votes. (The Gore campaign has squirrelled away a fair amount of money, to use on television ads, among other things.) The Gore people had hoped that Gephardt would be all but eliminated before March 8th, leaving Gore the moderates in the South while Dukakis and Simon competed for the white liberals, and that Gore could then pick up enough steam on March 8th to be competitive in the industrial states. But Martin argues that the most important thing is that the early contests were indecisive, and did not give any candidate a big head of steam.

Gore, who has greatly improved his campaign style, is now looser than earlier this year, but still stiff at times—as if he were struggling to be taken seriously despite his youth. He has been going hard at Dukakis on defense and foreign policies, and at Gephardt on the changes in his record—but there is a danger in this strategy. If the first time people focus on Gore they see someone concentrating his energies on attacking others, they might not like what they see. (And Gore got in some trouble of his own last weekend by denying, incorrectly, on "Meet the Press," that he had cast a vote as a House member for the proposition that a fetus is a person from the moment of conception. Though Gore also said he had "never supported restrictions on the ability of a woman to make a choice in having an abortion," his position is that the government should not be involved either way, and he opposes federal funding of any institution that performs abortions.)

Gore has been saying that the other candidates came to the South with the "baggage" (perhaps an allusion to carpetbaggers) of promises made elsewhere, and sets himself apart as the only Democratic candidate who had supported Reagan's policy in the Persian Gulf "to keep the sea-lanes open," or Carter's and Reagan's policy of introducing intermediate-range weapons into Europe in order to get the Soviets to negotiate the removal of their own such weapons targeted on Europe. But he has also cast several "liberal" votes on foreign policy. Gore says that he stands for economic growth, social justice, and an intelligent and internationalist approach to foreign policy. He says that he wants to return the Democratic Party to the "internationalist" outlook of Truman and Kennedy (without overlooking the lessons of the Vietnam War). In the Texas debate, he said Democrats have had a hard time winning in the South in Presidential elections not only because of their perceived weakness on defense but because they have not been consistent in their appeal to working-class families. Gore advocates spending more on certain domestic problems (illiteracy, the homeless, AIDS), and says arms control should be aimed more at reducing or eliminating first-strike weapons. But he supported the giant, multi-warhead MX missile—as a trade for development of a mobile single-warhead missile (the Midgetman), which would be easier to protect and less threatening. (Dukakis opposes the Midgetman, on budgetary grounds.) Of some of the things Dukakis has said, Gore says, "If you don't have a single day's experience in foreign policy and you're naïve about America's role in the world, you're going to make dumb mistakes like that." Gore said to me recently that his rivals "are scared to death that they're going to upset the neo-isolationists in our party." But when Gore was asked, on "Meet the Press," what he would do about a "client state" in Nicaragua, his answer was not very different from Dukakis's. Both Gore and Martin are sensitive to the charge that Gore doesn't have "a message." But if Gore doesn't accentuate the positive more in future debates—if he continues to focus his energies on attacking the others—he risks coming off as someone without positive things to say; being young and large, he risks coming across as an immature bully.

Neither man having managed to knock the props from out of the other early in the race, Bush and Dole—both of them tough, well financed, and determined—will continue to slug it out. Their contest, perhaps inevitably, has taken on a bitter edge: neither man likes the other (a well-placed Republican says, "They hate each other"), and their campaign organizations—particularly Bush's—are playing hard, and rough. There is a difference: Bush affects to stay above it all while some people in his organization, somewhat schoolboyishly, prod and goad Dole in an attempt to get him to lash out—whereupon they say, "See? He's mean." Dole, to the distress of his advisers, sometimes falls into the trap—showing that side of him that lashes out in anger. The activities that Bush condones in his subordinates say something about him—and also raise a question about his Presidency. The whole thing is not an edifying spectacle. Neither man has had very much of substance to say.

Meanwhile, a completely different race is going on on the Republican side—a struggle for the superintendency of the Reagan flame. Try as they might, neither Bush nor Dole has captured the moral force that helped propel Reagan to the Presidency, and which Reagan nurtured—though he didn't fulfill—as President. Reagan was not the first politician to understand—and exploit—

the growing discontent with changing cultural mores in this country; Jimmy Carter also profited by offering himself as a cultural
conservative (and a pious man). Reagan may be the last politician
able to stay atop a rickety coalition of old-fashioned conservatives,
economic radicals, religious zealots, and libertarians. But since he
didn't deliver much on the agenda of the culturally discontent,
their demands have spilled into this election. The culturally discontent also have a non-political agenda that, ultimately, no President can deliver on—and herein may lie seeds of trouble. A
President can cajole and persuade and work at the margins, but
is limited in what he can do about many of the things that bother
this group: drugs, terrible schools, homosexuality, tasteless mass
entertainment, changing family structures and mores. Theirs is
an agenda that mixes understandable and widely shared concerns
with intolerance, and even bigotry—everyone can draw the line
where he wishes—and this country is at the mercy of whoever
grabs hold of that movement. And so are the people who make
it up—and who are ripe for exploitation. In the fight for the
Reagan flame, Jack Kemp has essentially stuck to working the
economic side of Reaganism, but, as expected, Bush and Dole—
and the legacy of "Reaganomics"—don't leave him much room.
Kemp has been plucky and good-humored—and was the target
of smears by the Robertson camp, who spread the word that Kemp
was "pro-pornography" and that one of his daughters had had
an abortion. A Kemp spokesman says that the pornography charge
is a gross distortion, and that the suggestion that one of Kemp's
daughters had an abortion is "the scummiest lie we have ever
heard in politics." (Kemp came in fourth in Iowa, but by coming
in third in New Hampshire he kept his candidacy alive, though
he had spent a great deal of time there and had hoped to do
better. And he didn't do well this week.) Bush and Dole as well
as Kemp espouse the political agenda on abortion and prayer in
the schools. Pat Robertson has captured the force of cultural
discontent—at once giving it voice (he's far and away the most
articulate man on the Republican side) and, like most effective
demagogues, exploiting it and encouraging its intolerant side.

In reaching in there for a victory in New Hampshire, George
Bush showed his own determination (in 1980, he stayed in the
fight for the nomination after even some of his own people thought

Reagan had beat him), and his large and well-financed campaign organization showed the possibilities of its resources. (Almost none of Dole's campaign aides have been through a national campaign before.) Within days of Bush's being humiliated in Iowa (coming in third and losing to Dole two-to-one), he was outfitted with a new speech, a new campaign style (dispensing with the Vice-Presidential limousine and driving trucks and mixing it up with the people), and even a new costume. (Like Gephardt when he was in trouble in Iowa, Bush donned a down jacket. When he hit Texas, Bush sported Western gear.) The new speech was a reflective one that is uncharacteristic of Bush: "Let me tell you, don't take that private side of me for lack of passion and lack of conviction. . . . I don't always articulate but I always do feel." It was also discomfiting. We usually prefer that our leaders do their soul-searching in private. And an ability to articulate things is a pretty basic requirement of leadership. In giving the speech very deliberately, Bush got away from his more frenetic campaign style—where he speaks faster and his voice is higher and his thoughts are jumbled and sentences are nonexistent—which had been on display earlier in the week. (In a perhaps unintentional parody of a line Dole used in Iowa, Bush, who was born in Massachusetts and raised in Connecticut and has a house in Maine, told New Hampshirites shortly after he arrived back in their state, "I'm one of you." Bush uses a hotel suite in Houston to give him a Texas voting address.) Sometimes Bush was downright embarrassing: at another point, he said, "I'd like to see us open up that Alaska refuge, and that's important, because it was said once, remember, when they built the pipeline, 'Don't build the pipeline, you get rid of the caribou.' The caribou love it. They rub up against it and they have babies. There are more caribou in Alaska than you can shake a stick at."

A longtime associate says that Bush is excitable under pressure, prone to braggadocio and saying the wrong thing; at times, when he should most show command, he comes across as weak (and thus perpetuates the "wimp" image that bedevils him). He often seems tone-deaf. Now we have two Bushes: the awkward, frenetic, nasal Bush, and the Bush who squares his shoulders and speaks with painstaking slowness. This will require a lot of management if he's President. But, through making the adjustments, by appealing to his natural constitutency in New Hampshire (he had been about twenty points ahead of Dole there before the Iowa caucuses), and by continuing to ally himself with Reagan (who is far more popular in New Hampshire than in Iowa), Bush arrested the downward slide he had taken in the first few days after Iowa and defeated Dole by nine points. He was also helped by the strong organization of New Hampshire's governor, John Sununu, and probably by last-minute negative advertising against Dole—some of which was misleading. And Dole coöperated.

The Bush camp's efforts in Iowa to poke a stick at Dole were less rewarding but nonetheless disturbing—particularly because of Bush's unwillingness to take responsibility for them. We've just been through something along those lines. For weeks, the Bush people had encouraged the press to point out Dole's current wealth—in light of Dole's poor-boy-from-Kansas routine ("I'm one of you"); it encouraged stories about questionable dealings by a Dole associate in Elizabeth Dole's blind trust. The associate was dismissed, but there was no evidence that the Doles were involved in these transactions. And shortly before the caucuses Bush's Iowa campaign chairman issued a press release charging Dole with a "record of cronyism" and a "history of mean-spiritedness" that "nearly single-handedly brought the Republican national ticket down to defeat" in 1976 (this is a very sensitive point with Dole). Nobody believed Bush's national campaign officials' denials that they had anything to do with this—while Bush was saying, "Frankly, I haven't read the whole statement on it. . . . I didn't know he was making this attack. I don't want to engage in negative campaigning." Dole reacted angrily—he even stagily confronted Bush on the Senate floor—but not so angrily as to do himself in; and the Bush people were seen by many Iowans as having gone too far. (Bush publicly apologized to Elizabeth Dole.) Then Bush's campaign released eight pages of what it said were "mean" things Dole had said about Bush; most of it was pretty tame stuff. And all of this was supposedly about who should hold the highest office in the land.

Bush attributed his New Hampshire victory in part to "my spelling out the issues more clearly than I have before," but this wasn't much of a claim. (In Iowa, he had said little more than that he wanted to be "an education President.") His campaign having caught on to some political weaknesses in a budget proposal Dole had made, Bush, who had until then been noncommittal about what he would do about the deficit, announced that he favored a "flexible freeze"—which sounds self-contradictory, but, as Bush explained it (somewhat murkily), the proposal was to freeze total spending but change allocations for programs (for example, increase spending for education and AIDS). In essence, that's what the budget compromise reached by Congress and the President last year did. Bush explained his proposal further in a debate last week in Texas with Kemp. (Dole and Robertson—probably not coincidentally—stayed away. Dole charged that the debate, being held in Dallas, would amount to "a George Bush pep rally.") Bush said that his proposed freeze (with allowances for inflation) would, given a certain growth rate, lead to a balanced budget in four years. But the budget submitted by Reagan recently was, like Bush's, a freeze-plus-inflation proposal, and, after assuming an even higher rate of growth than Bush does (and thus higher revenues), still showed a considerable deficit (at least fifty billion dollars) at the end of four years. Dole, acting on his own as usual (he still tries to run his own campaign), had already proposed at first a simple, across-the-board freeze for three years (with exceptions for programs for low-income people)—and then, when his advisers came to the horrible realization that this had him proposing to freeze Social Security benefits for three years, he regrouped and talked about a freeze that would allow a two-per-cent increase in certain spending, including Social Security. (His proposal contemplated no increase in taxes.) This still would amount to a reduction in Social Security increases contemplated by law—and Bush pounced, saying that Dole would cut Social Security benefits. Bush also called Dole's proposal "a cop-out" and a product of a congressional way of thinking—which it was, but it would make substantial budget cuts (more than Bush's plan would), and may be the only way to do it, and Bush's proposal was less definitive and brave. Bush, in his speeches and his ads, also said that Dole would probably raise taxes, but his plan does not contemplate that; Bush himself had pledged not to raise taxes, "period"; but he has wavered, too.

The tax issue may matter more in New Hampshire—which has no state income or sales tax—than anywhere. Dole, who had started out his campaign saying that the American people must take their "bitter medicine" (but was moved off that by his advisers), has carefully said that he would not increase "tax rates" —meaning individual and corporate tax rates, but leaving other possibilities open. Both Bush himself and one of his ads also said that Dole would impose an oil-import fee—which Dole angrily denied; Dole had said he would consider such a fee under certain limited circumstances. (New Hampshire depends on imported oil for heating homes.) These charges are what lay behind Dole's snapping to Bush on primary night on NBC, "Stop lying about my record." Kemp, for his part, attacked both Bush and Dole as tax-increasers. Beyond that, Bush and Dole spat over who was more of a leader. A true leader, of course, doesn't have to assert he is one.

Dole's campaign style had improved by the time of the Iowa caucuses—he had become more articulate and effective. His talking about the war wound that left his right hand crippled and about his background as a poor boy seemed to reach his audiences. (At times the bitterness showed: "Nobody gave me anything.") Then, he seemed to have gained confidence from the victory in Iowa—and to have needed an affirmation of his candidacy. (His previous Presidential effort, in 1980, had gone anything but well.) But he isn't consistent—and he is dogged by the fact that his quick and often lacerating wit is sometimes taken for flipness, or even meanness. His problem is that his dark and angry side—which senators who have disagreed with him in floor debate, and his own employees, have experienced—can be neither contained nor compartmentalized. It was clear that his loss in New Hampshire devastated him. Dole's lashing out, on national television, at that moment—however justified—has, with the encouragement of the Bush camp, gone down as a defining event. It may have been understandable, given the Bush campaign's tactics, but he should have known it wouldn't go over well—and Presidents have to exercise self-control. His frustration at losing was also understandable: had he defeated Bush in New Hampshire, Bush would have been in very poor shape. Thus, Dole watched a potential nomination slide away from his grasp. Characteristically, he blamed his staff—a number of mistakes had been made, including some by Dole. (And the quality of staff a candidate picks is one fair measurement of his quality as a leader. The current chaos in Dole's campaign—there was another shakeup today—gives one pause.)

Following his New Hampshire defeat, Dole was in a foul mood and off his feed, and he cancelled some of his campaigning as well as his appearance in the Texas debate. His victories this week in Minnesota and South Dakota (Bush didn't contest either state) gave him something of a lift, but he is in for heavy weather in the South.

The effects of the Iran-Contra affair on Bush's prospects for the nomination are difficult to determine, and aren't separable from other questions about him. In fact, the Iran-Contra affair raises those same questions: about judgment, about strength. The Bush people say that in terms of the nomination contest Bush will not be hurt by the Iran-Contra affair in states where Reagan is popular—that in those states, and especially in the Southern states, his loyalty to Reagan will be seen as a plus. But while that may be true, it is clear they would prefer not to have the Iran-Contra albatross around their candidate's neck. The way Bush has handled the matter may be even more of a problem than his role— or lack of one—in it. He offers explanations that are obviously open to challenge or are contradictory. For example, in his famous interview with Dan Rather, on January 25th, he said that he "went along with" the arms-for-hostages trade because he wanted to rescue William Buckley, the C.I.A. Beirut station chief who had been taken captive and was being tortured by his captors. (In fact, four out of the six arms sales were made after the Administration learned that Buckley had died.) But in the same interview he also said that he did not know that arms were being exchanged for hostages until December, 1986, when David Durenberger, Republican of Minnesota and then chairman of the Senate Intelligence Committee, briefed him. Aside from being contradictory, this last point is bizarre: the world knew about the arms-for-hostages dealings by mid-November, when the Administration couldn't contain it any longer. (The story had broken earlier that month.) And we know that quite a large number of members of the Administration had known about the dealings. To be frank about it, Bush's handling of the matter raises a question about the level of his intelligence. A number of people wonder why he didn't just say that he had supported the President, and maybe some mistakes were made, but the President wanted to take a risk in order to rescue American hostages. A Bush adviser has told me that Bush did not consult any of his political advisers before putting in his campaign autobiography the statement that he might have raised more objections if he had known that George Shultz and Caspar Weinberger had been strongly opposed—another statement that left him open to challenge. Though the Bush people insisted that the encounter with Rather had helped Bush, it was clear that even they weren't so sure. Bush came across as whiny and not Vice-Presidential, and even though Rather crossed the line and hectored him, and though CBS had been less than forthcoming about the nature and circumstances of the interview, Bush still had to live with the lasting impression he had made. He didn't help himself the next day by engaging in his silly talk that is supposed to make him appear macho but does the reverse. ("It's Tension City when you're in there," and "I need combat pay for last night, I'll tell you.") Poll after poll shows that the majority of the public doesn't believe that Bush has come clean on the Iran-Contra affair, and though Dole has to be careful about raising the issue, for fear of alienating Reagan supporters, the Democrats are not likely to show such compunctions next fall.

Robertson's success in the early caucus states—Iowa, where he was second, and before that Hawaii, where he came in first (though hardly anyone noticed)—should not have been a surprise. Robertson also came in second in Minnesota and South Dakota. (Amid extended brawling, Michigan, where the Republicans held a state convention in late January, ended up with one delegation that will be for Bush—thus sparing Bush another humiliation—and one for Robertson, who challenged the legitimacy of the official convention, and the long-running fight over Michigan may well continue into the National Convention.) Anyone who watched the Iowa Republican Party's fund-raiser last September and saw the fervor and organizing power of Robertson's followers—who gave him a victory in the straw poll there—could have seen that this was a force to be taken seriously. A number of people began to predict as of then that Robertson might come in second in Iowa. But since his doing so came as a surprise to many, he suddenly received a great deal of attention. Though Robertson found the ground cold in New Hampshire, where there are few evangelicals, and where he tried for right-wing Republican support and wound up fifth, and last, he is expected to do well in the South, where he has more of a natural constituency.

Robertson's effort to present himself as a businessman and a "religious broadcaster" is an attempt to have it both ways (he objected when Tom Brokaw introduced him as a "former television evangelist," and accused Brokaw of "religious bigotry"), and he likens his situation to that of John F. Kennedy, who had to overcome the misgivings of some about putting a Catholic in the White House—but, of course, there is little similarity between the two situations. Kennedy ran as a secular candidate, while Robertson's religious beliefs and experience as a television minister are at the core of his candidacy. While he has given up his ministry for the Presidential campaign, he has a built-in constituency among the nearly nine million households reached by his "The 700 Club" on his own Christian Broadcasting Network—and his CBN network helped him raise over sixteen million dollars for his campaign. He would prefer that people forget about some of his more perfervid or controversial past pronouncements: he has said that only devout Christians and Jews should be allowed to serve in government, and news programs have dredged up an old tape of Robertson working an audience into a frenzy while he told them that someone was at that moment being cured of a hernia and another one of hemorrhoids. And he recently affirmed his belief that he had prayed Hurricane Gloria out to sea. Moreover, what with the burgeoning sex and financial scandals, this hasn't been a good period for television evangelists. Jim and Tammy Faye Bakker, who not long ago had to relinquish their P.T.L. ministry and many of their splendiferous earthly goods because of scandals over finances and Jim Bakker's sexual wandering, used to work with Robertson. And now Jimmy Swaggart (who had turned Jim Bakker in) is in trouble over sex. Robertson has suggested that the Bush campaign was behind the exposing of Swaggart, in order to embarrass him, but he offered no proof.

Robertson's success thus far has led many analysts to treat him with a certain solemnity, and while many of the issues he is raising are to be taken seriously there is also a part of Robertson that is, to be plain about it, a kook. He drew fire even from the other candidates (who usually treat him solicitously, because of his following) for suggesting, in a debate in New Hampshire, that the Soviet Union had stored SS-4 and SS-5 missiles in Cuba (in caves), in violation of the agreement reached by Kennedy and Nikita Khrushchev following the Cuban missile crisis, in 1962. Pressed on this later, Robertson retreated to saying that he had been told this by a member of the Foreign Relations Committee's staff who works for Jesse Helms—and then that no one had proved that the Russians *hadn't* stored missiles in Cuba. Though he attributed his last-place showing in New Hampshire to the fact that the voters there "might not like what I said about the Cuban missiles," he repeated the charge to a receptive audience of Cuban-Americans in Miami Beach. And now he has said that his CBN had located the whereabouts of hostages taken in Lebanon in 1985—which a CBN employee denied. The charges about Cuban missiles and the hostages were examples of what reporters travelling with Robertson call his "funny facts"—statements for which he offers no proof. Another example was Robertson's saying he knew of a man who gave his wife AIDS by kissing her. Robertson's candidacy threatens the pluralism that is critical to holding our society together, but that doesn't seem to worry him. He is shrewd and clever, and is clearly going to be a factor in this election. He draws on less affluent and blue-collar voters who either used to be or would have been Democrats—he attracts a lot of young voters with children—and while Republican leaders pronounce themselves delighted that Robertson is bringing new people into the political process (and the other Republican candidates treat him gently for fear of alienating his followers), they know that his presence in the race is not without risk to the Party in November.

It was no surprise that Pierre du Pont pulled out of the race two days after the New Hampshire primary; his candidacy had never found traction, and he had come in fifth in Iowa and fourth in New Hampshire. Alexander Haig's pulling out shortly before the New Hampshire primary and throwing his possibly nonexistent support to Dole didn't seem to help Dole much, but it allowed Haig to get in one last shot at Bush, whom he clearly doesn't like. (The Dole people had hoped that at least the coverage of Haig's farewell press conference—on a day when little else was happening in New Hampshire, because of a snowstorm—would be helpful.) Haig had some real knowledge in certain fields, particularly some foreign-policy questions, and brought some real humor to the campaign—showing an admirable gift for self-mockery.

* * *

We're still a long way from choosing our next President, and in the midst of a mysterious process. If it seems that we are in the grip of events that are beyond our control, and of a process that's not rational, it's because we are.

V

As of now, the question of who will govern over the next, probably difficult, four years has, in both parties, come down to matters of arithmetic and mechanics. It is considered all but settled that the Republican nomination will go to the candidate with the best-laid plans and the most money—and the Dukakis campaign is working hard to establish that that's the way it should be in the Democratic contest. As it became clear to Democrats, after the large round of contests on March 8th, that no candidate would be able to win a majority of the delegates through the primaries and caucuses —this was not unexpected—a great deal of maneuvering began, and the Dukakis campaign continued its psychological war of "inevitability." After the contest in Illinois last week, in which Dukakis came in a poor third—far behind Paul Simon and Jesse Jackson—and won no delegates, the question became whether any Democratic candidate would have even forty per cent of the delegates at the end of the contests, and be the clear front-runner. To do even this, Dukakis would have to win nearly seventy per cent of the remaining delegates. He is hoping to recoup in the Michigan caucuses to be held this coming Saturday, March 26th. (He won the Kansas caucuses last Saturday, and came in second to Jackson in Puerto Rico's popularity vote—the delegates remain uncommitted—on Sunday.) But there are several big contests to come, and the matter is far from settled. Oddly, many observers have expressed great perturbation at the fact that the Democrats didn't settle on a clear front-runner some weeks ago—but that's what the nomination contest is for.

The logic of "inevitability" is that whoever starts out best should automatically be the nominee. Nearly half the country's population hasn't had a chance to vote yet. (Thirty-two states, several of them small, have held contests.) Only one industrial state (Illinois) has been heard from, and neither of the two most populous states

(New York and California) has voted. So what's the hurry? The apparent early end of the Republican race is an aberration. The only reason for having a long process is to see how a candidate holds up—to allow people to take another look. The Democratic caucuses coming up in Michigan this weekend may help sort things out further, but the turning point will come later—from mid-April to early May—when the voting will take place in some of the big states (New York, Pennsylvania, and Ohio). At the same time, a large number of the group that may be decisive in the Democratic race—the "super-delegates"—will be chosen. Dukakis has already been relentlessly at work seeking the support of super-delegates and the endorsement of as many political figures as possible—and, for a variety of reasons, not all of them having to do with Dukakis, this is beginning to pay off.

Before Illinois, large theories were already developing around the fact that George Bush and Michael Dukakis were as of then seen as the most likely nominees: that this time the country is turning to competent doers—or what are seen as such—and away from ideological binges. It is becoming fashionable to say that given the fact that neither Bush nor Dukakis is very good at moving people, this will be the year of the bore. But, as is often the case in analyses of elections, fragments were being stretched to create a theory. As is usually the case in elections, the results are brought about by a number of factors—including, of course, who entered in the first place, what kinds of candidates they were, how they played off against each other, and how they divided the vote—and have little to do with the country sitting down and deciding what kind of President it wants. On the Republican side, Robert Dole is no less pragmatic than Bush—and neither of them would win awards for oratory. On the Democratic side, it is hard to imagine great substantive differences between Administrations of Michael Dukakis, Richard Gephardt, or Albert Gore. The fact that Gephardt and Gore are better speakers than Dukakis has no connection with whether they might lose out to him. Dukakis's "Mr. Goodwrench" approach to government is selling somewhat, but it isn't the only reason he may prevail. If he does prevail, it will also be in large part because he had the best campaign plan and the money to implement it and because of the flaws in his opponents' campaigns—and because many key Democrats want to avoid a prolonged nomination fight. It is the money and the planning that have propelled his rather thin message—essentially that he is for "good jobs at good wages." (For all the weakness of Dukakis's message, he has become much better at delivering it. His approach is cheerful and upbeat instead of angry: "The best America is not behind us; the best America is yet to come.") Albert Gore, who might possibly be a stronger nominee if he got a grip on his campaign and gave people more of a reason to follow him, may have started too late to become well enough known or a sufficiently developed candidate to give Dukakis a fight for it in the later contests. Bush's uninspiring argument that he should be elected because he faithfully served Ronald Reagan and has held a number of other important jobs would not have propelled him forward without the daunting campaign machinery behind him, and without unintentional assistance from his chief opponent. Dole's on-again, off-again departure from the scene, his displays of inner turmoil, have been painful to behold. Dole has run a terrible campaign, and has shown characteristics that give even some of his backers pause. Both Dukakis and Bush, in fact, are offering muzzy messages to the voters, being highly unexplicit about what they plan to do if elected. It is probably no accident that the nomination contests, particularly on the Democratic side, are characterized by late decisions by the voters and—with the exception of Jesse Jackson's supporters—little enthusiasm for their choice.

The mood among many elected Democrats and Party officials has gone through three evolutions in the last few weeks. The first, which began to take hold before March 8th, was one of quiet resignation. Not many of these people are very taken with Dukakis—his cool remoteness and lack of charm have long put off other politicians—but they figured that he was likely to be the nominee, and they wanted to avoid bloodshed. They are painfully aware that the Democrats have lost four out of the last five elections, and believe that prolonged bloodletting will give them no chance at all in November. They didn't—and for the most part still don't—see how any candidate in the field can stop Dukakis, given his long and deliberately planned head start and his plentiful resources, and they desperately want to avoid a chaotic Convention. Thus, while the mathematics of the situation before March 8th were that it was likely that at the end of the primaries no

Democrat will have enough delegates to be nominated (2,082), many Party leaders were planning even before that date, when twenty contests were held, many of them in the South, to close ranks around Dukakis—on the assumption that he would be the clear front-runner.

Democratic Party Chairman Paul Kirk, a careful man, began to talk about his idea of holding a meeting with the candidates or their representatives shortly after the final primaries, in New Jersey and California, and within Party circles he had been stressing the importance of reaching a consensus on a ticket before the Convention. When I spoke with Kirk on March 10th, he said that in the remaining big contests—in Michigan, Wisconsin, New York, Pennsylvania, Ohio, New Jersey, California, and others—"we're not likely to have a photo finish. I think you're going to see a consistent pattern of someone ending up first in most of them." He pointed out that the number of super-delegates—Party officials who will automatically go to the Convention—has been raised since 1984 (to 646, amounting to fifteen per cent of the total number of delegates), and this time will include more members of Congress (eighty per cent of them, as opposed to sixty per cent in 1984), and that, unlike 1984, the congressional super-delegates are not to be chosen until late April, and that they are likely to be very pragmatic. (In 1984, most of the super-delegates were chosen in January and most of them signed on with Mondale then. This obviated the idea of having super-delegates—which was to give practical politicians a voice in the selection of a candidate later on.) But Kirk's idea of "brokering" the process is not universally popular: a lot of people will want to "broker," and the delegates won't necessarily be as deliverable as such scenarios contemplate. Also, the other candidates understood that Kirk had Dukakis in mind.

None of these cool calculations anticipated the psychological reality that followed Dukakis's defeat in Illinois, or the degree of Jesse Jackson's success in numerous contests. The Dukakis campaign tried hard to break through in Illinois, and therefore the magnitude of his defeat gave a number of leading Democrats pause. As of now, Dukakis has a lead in delegates: 529 to Jackson's 510.5, and 360.8 for Gore, with the rest further back. Jackson has won more popular votes than any other Democrat. In the wake of Illinois, some of Dukakis's weaknesses as a candidate began to get more attention. But these were easier to see than who it was who could overtake him, since all of his rivals have weaknesses, too. And as Dukakis won more endorsements going into Michigan, the "inevitability" strategy got a lift. Despite the rivalries, and even enmities, among the candidates, the campaign leaders of Dukakis's opponents (except for Jackson) have been meeting and communicating in an effort to hold Dukakis's vote down, and Dukakis's opponents (except for Jackson) are essentially leaving it to only one of them to make a run at him in some states—Simon in Illinois, Gephardt in Michigan. But at least both Simon and Gore will go against him in Wisconsin, on April 5th, and one question is whether more than one of his opponents (in addition to Jackson) will survive, and divide the vote against him in the industrial states.

Political moods change quickly, of course, and if Dukakis gets moving again, and keeps moving, the downdraft of mid-March will have been forgotten. He received a big boost from the endorsement this week by Bill Bradley, and Senator Christopher Dodd and Governor William O'Neill of Connecticut. These endorsements brought about yet another psychological change in the situation, and if Dukakis wins in Michigan on Saturday he will be widely considered on his way to the nomination. (If Gephardt is defeated in Michigan, his campaign will be over and the eighty-odd House members who his campaign says have endorsed him will be set loose.) Now several key Party members are back to where they were before March 8th—figuring that it's time to try to wrap it up for Dukakis. Mark Siegel, a member of the Democratic National Committee and a man who talks to a lot of political figures, had been until just a few days ago praising the virtues and advantages of staying neutral (so as to be "a player"); now he says, "We know the bottom line, so we should get there earlier, rather than have chaos in Atlanta." Therefore, for a pragmatic politician (and most are), if one is to endorse, this is the time—when one can make a difference—to do it. Some Democrats also point out that now—when there are still several candidates in the race—is the time to endorse, to avoid the appearance of a "stop-Jackson" movement. But in fact an unspoken stop-Jackson movement is going on.

Dukakis has often been underestimated, and—some missteps notwithstanding—both he and his campaign organization are skilled. Even as Presidential candidates go, Dukakis is very driven, and knows exactly where he wants to go—and will do what he must to get there. He is an extremely disciplined and tenacious man. After Illinois, some Democrats began to look elsewhere and to entertain all sorts of possibilities. The names of Bill Bradley and Mario Cuomo were back in the air. Even Bradley's endorsement of Dukakis this week didn't convince everyone that Bradley is out of the game for good. (However, it is believed that one reason Bradley endorsed Dukakis was to head off a move to have the New Jersey delegation go to the Convention uncommitted in order to keep the Bradley option alive.) But the prevailing school of thought is that the nominee must come from the candidates in the field. A number of Democrats feel they will have no choice but to end up supporting Dukakis—assuming he does well in the contests to come. Recent polls (for what they're worth now, which isn't much) showing that Dukakis could beat Bush are very helpful to his case, but some Democrats remain troubled that Dukakis's starting to move again doesn't stem from any move on the part of the mass electorate.

The Dukakis camp hopes to complete the elimination contest in short order: to knock off Gephardt in Michigan, Simon in Wisconsin, and Gore in New York—leaving only Dukakis and Jackson standing. But left publicly unsaid by Kirk is what would happen if there isn't a clear pattern of victories in the upcoming contests. (Because the Democratic contests essentially divide up the delegates by proportional representation in congressional districts in each state, it is harder for a victor in a given state to pile up great blocs of delegates.) Kirk and others are said to believe that anyone who has won over half the delegates needed for the nomination has to be considered for it—and, with any luck, only one candidate will have reached that point, but that's not for sure at this point.

Though Dukakis has pressed for a blessing by the A.F.L.-C.I.O., he has not received it because of the constraints on labor's endorsing anyone this year, at least as yet. One person people have been watching is Thomas Donahue, the secretary-treasurer of the A.F.L.-C.I.O. and a very important figure in Democratic politics. The A.F.L.-C.I.O. has not made an endorsement this year (its 1984 endorsement of Mondale turned out to be a mixed blessing for both Mondale and the labor organization) because its constituent unions could reach no consensus on a candidate—though some of their affiliates' local chapters have endorsed candidates. One reason the A.F.L.-C.I.O. has to be careful about endorsing prematurely is that some of its largest and most politically active constituencies are for Jackson. As it turned out, this official neutrality also put labor in a position to be a "broker" if necessary, and spared its appearing, as it did in 1984, to be throwing its weight around. Representatives of some of the campaigns—particularly Dukakis's, Gephardt's, and Jackson's—met with labor officials and, with their own interests in mind, offered to put labor members on their delegate slates. One factor about Dukakis that worries some Democratic leaders is that he has not proved very strong among blue-collar voters thus far. In Illinois, his campaign ran an ad in which a Bostonian official of the New England regional bricklayers' union said, "I've known Mike a long time and I gotta say Dukakis is not your shot-and-beer kind of guy. But working people around here love him. . . . If you want somebody to drink with, call your buddy. If you care about your job, vote for Mike Dukakis." (Some Chicago pols said that this ad raised the question in the minds of many voters, who knew little about him, "What's the matter with Dukakis that he's not a shot-and-beer kind of guy?") Dukakis's foreign-policy views are a bit too far to the left for the comfort of some labor officials, but they, too, have decided that they may have to make a pragmatic judgment, and that, if necessary, they will find Dukakis sound enough.

Donahue said to me recently, "It makes good sense to me that we go into the Convention with a unified body, ready to propel a candidate into the race, and the nation doesn't spend seven days reading about and watching 'the disarray within the Democratic Party.' " He continued, "Our whole role in this turns out to be playing out pretty well. Institutionally, it would have been easier if we had all agreed on one candidate; there's a certain sense of a loss of solidarity. But, on the other hand, we'd have had charges of trying to manipulate the nomination. The result is, we're working in several campaigns and don't have the negative of appearing to dominate a candidate."

Another person being watched is, of course, Mario Cuomo, who still seems to be conflicted—not completely resigned to the prospect of not being the nominee. The Dukakis people had hoped to get Cuomo's endorsement shortly after March 8th. When I talked to him that day, Cuomo told me that he had promised Paul

Simon that he would not endorse anyone until after the Illinois primary, but it seemed likely then that he would not endorse anyone either before the New York primary, on April 19th, or until after all the states have voted. He has perfectly objective reasons, he says, for not endorsing anyone in New York: he has already told his people to support whomever they want, and he runs the risk of looking presumptuous by endorsing one candidate if more than one is still viable. (He did endorse Mondale over Gary Hart in 1984.) But there are some signs that Cuomo might be changing his mind again. The Dukakis people hoped that the Bradley endorsement, from next door in New Jersey, plus those of Connecticut officials, would put pressure on Cuomo and reinforce the idea that if he wants to endorse before the end of the process, and to be relevant, he has to endorse soon. (Bradley and Dukakis deliberately posed against the background of the New York skyline. New Jersey and California hold their primaries on June 7th, the last day.) There is no reason to disbelieve Cuomo when he says, as he did when we talked on March 8th, that he believes that "the Convention should be used to pick the message, not the messenger, or the Party would be very hurt," and that the Party leadership should turn to whoever looks like the consensus winner out of the primaries, and try to rally people around him. But Cuomo has been making a number of appearances around the nation—forswearing any Presidential ambitions, of course. He said to me, "People could say, if I endorse, 'That clever, Machiavellian ruse' "—he would be seen as somehow using his endorsement of someone else to get the nomination for himself.

On the day of our conversation, as the voting in twenty states was taking place, Cuomo, who had been considered by many to favor Dukakis, said to me, "Dukakis will be seen as doing very well today, because he's a Northeasterner and an ethnic getting votes in the South." He continued, sounding less enthusiastic about Dukakis than in previous conversations, "After today, Dukakis is proved the front-runner and he'll be on the hot seat—that's what happened to Gephardt. So Mike will become the target of more scrutiny, and the question is how he handles being the front-runner or being under scrutiny—whether what is turned up about Massachusetts hurts him, what happened in his first term. If he takes credit for the economic recovery, he has to take responsibility for the recession " (When Dukakis first became governor, a recession had already started; the recovery, which occurred throughout New England, actually began before Dukakis's second term—during the period he was out of office—but he helped spread its benefits.)

There are signs that Cuomo is, among other things, still nursing the wound of having been told, before he declared, in February of 1987, that he wouldn't run for the Presidency, that as an ethnic Northeasterner he could not win votes in the South, or be nominated. Dukakis's success must grate—though Cuomo often says that he encouraged Dukakis to make the race. People close to Cuomo (as close as people outside his own family can be) believe that the real reasons he didn't run had less to do with the supposed impossibility of a sitting governor of New York—with one house of the legislature dominated by the other party—making the race than with the fact that his tentative political forays early last year (to Los Angeles and New Orleans) didn't go particularly well, and he didn't want to risk the indignities of running, or rejection by the voters. Cuomo is very different from Dukakis—as flamboyant as Dukakis is contained. Moreover, Cuomo was later reliably reported to have been annoyed with the Dukakis campaign's letting it be known that Cuomo would probably endorse Dukakis after March 8th—its appearing to take him for granted. Yet some think Cuomo is leaning again toward Dukakis, and he now says he will announce within a week or ten days whether he will make an endorsement.

Labor officials are pleased with the personality changes that have gone on among the Democratic candidates, leading Gephardt and then Dukakis and Gore, in their various ways, to run as populists, as champions of the workingman. (Jackson had been there all along.) All of the Democratic candidates have arrived at the conclusion that the most salient issue in this election is economic nationalism—the concern on the part of many Americans that we are slipping, and being overtaken, economically (especially by the Japanese), and are no longer No. 1. Gephardt was the first Democratic candidate to catch on to—and exploit—this concern, and his early success caused Dukakis to sharpen his message, and Gore to change his completely. This theme turns up in the Republican race as well, but Bush, running sycophantically as the true heir to the Reagan legacy, has to be oblique about it—and thus talks about the need to do more about education.

It is a very large irony that at the end of eight years of Reagan's feel-good Presidency majorities of people are telling pollsters that they are anxious about their economic future. The book "The Rise and Fall of the Great Powers" is a best-seller. Yet Reagan himself, characteristically, floats serenely above all this and remains popular (though not as popular as he has been). However, the sharp congressional and public reaction to Reagan's sending of thirty-two hundred troops to Honduras last week, in response to a Sandinista incursion across the border, showed again his weak standing on the issue of Nicaragua. It also showed how much doubt there is about whatever the Administration says about Nicaragua. A great many people didn't believe that the President of Honduras had initiated the request for U.S. military aid, as the Administration said he had. Many did believe that the dispatching of troops had to do with the House's recent turning down of all aid to the Contras—with liberal Democrats and Reagan supporters among Republicans joining to kill the compromise proposal for "humanitarian" aid only. The ceasefire just arrived at by the Contras and the Sandinistas took a great many people—apparently including the Administration—by surprise; nobody is sure what it really means. The guilty plea by former national-security adviser Robert McFarlane for some of his activities in the Iran-Contra affair (not telling Congress the truth) on March 11th was as a bell tolling, and when it was followed five days later by the multiple-count indictments of Oliver North, John Poindexter, Richard Secord, and Albert Hakim the subject came back into prominence. It will come and go for some time to come, and though Republicans insist it won't be a factor in the election, they clearly wish it would disappear.

That part of the nominating process that took place on March 8th ("Super Tuesday") was a travesty. Democrats in twenty states voted—the Republicans had seventeen contests—with only the haziest notion of who the candidates were or what they stood for. (According to one exit poll, only twenty-one per cent knew that Dukakis is a liberal.) It was a tactical battle, not a competition of ideas. The strategists for the various campaigns played a game of poker—trying to dope out where opponents were placing their ads, and to raise them. This seemed to consume most of their time and thought. On the equivalent day four years ago, contests took place in nine states, only three of them in the South. Many of the Southerners who cooked the thing up for this year argue that, because of the emergence of Gore as a serious candidate, they were vindicated, but the outcome of the process has nothing to do with whether it made any sense. Anyway, Jackson and Dukakis were also major victors on March 8th. The idea was to get the candidates to pay more attention to the South, and to tip the scales toward a more conservative nominee than the Democrats had been serving up (with the exception of Jimmy Carter). Instead—and as some Party officials had warned—the candidates spent even less time in the various Southern states, because there were so many of them to cover.

All indications are that most of the people voted on March 8th on the basis of name recognition, and reaction to television advertising. In previous elections, the truism was that the effect of "paid" television was marginal; this time—given the size of the area that the candidates had to cover and the brief period they had to do so—it may have been decisive. (The impact of the ads was enhanced by network news stories about them.) Despite Gore's success—carrying six states (Arkansas, Kentucky, North Carolina, Oklahoma, Tennessee, and Nevada), and coming in second, after Jackson, in five (Alabama, Georgia, Louisiana, Mississippi, and Virginia)—the real story of March 8th was that it made at least the New Hampshire contest (which Dukakis had won) more, rather than less, important than before. The Democratic candidates— with the exception of Jackson—came out in the order of their spending for television advertising. (Jackson carried five Southern states and came in second in eleven, four of which were Southern, and followed this with a victory in South Carolina the following Saturday.) However, Gephardt's complaint that his virtual shutout—he carried only his home state of Missouri—occurred because he was outspent was probably only partly the case. (The Gephardt campaign ran some tough ads against Dukakis and Gore.) Gephardt had already been weakened by the attacks on his change of persona (he had even darkened his eyebrows) and revision of so many of his "beliefs"—and the continuing criticism of him in the press, combined with the ads that both Dukakis and Gore ran against him for the March 8th contests, was enough to finish him off. Even his advisers indicate that if he does not succeed in Michigan this weekend that would be the end. After his poor showing on March 8th, a few people (including former Democratic Chairman Robert Strauss) suggested that he end his candidacy.

A knowledgeable person says that the Dukakis campaign spent far more on negative ads against Gephardt for the March 8th contests than it let on. One of the best and most effective ads run thus far was Dukakis's against Gephardt—showing a red-headed man in a navy-blue suit, such as Gephardt usually wears, doing somersaults and other acrobatics, including jumping through a hoop, while the voice-over told of some of Gephardt's revised positions on issues. Another Dukakis ad listed some of the political-action committees (PACs) Gephardt had taken money from for his Presidential campaign—a direct assault on Gephardt's claim to being "an outsider." Gephardt responded, in person and in an ad, by criticizing Dukakis for accepting money for his campaign from people who do business with Massachusetts. Dukakis, who had self-righteously said that he would insist on running a "positive" campaign, turned aggressive, and even rough, toward Gephardt in the period leading up to the March 8th voting—and his staff described this change as one that Dukakis had most reluctantly made, in light of Gephardt's bombarding of Dukakis with his effective, and successful, "Belgian endive" ad, raising a question about Dukakis's knowledge of agriculture, in the final days of the South Dakota primary, on February 23rd. (The Gephardt campaign ran a Southern version of this ad for March 8th.) These protestations notwithstanding, Dukakis has a history of playing rough in campaigns, and Gephardt's action in South Dakota provided Dukakis with the excuse he had been waiting for. An associate of Dukakis said to me shortly after the South Dakota primary, "Now people will see how good Dukakis is as a counterpuncher; he's the best in the business—it's his special niche." This person added, "Some people are eloquent, some are funny, some are charming, but Dukakis is tough." He said of Dukakis, "He was dying to get at Gephardt, and Gephardt gave him the opening— and he'll rue the day he did." Dukakis was given the opportunity to climb off the moralistic hook that he sometimes places himself on. But his more aggressive debate style—of pushing and pushing a question to Gephardt, and following with a sarcastic remark—

came off to a number of observers as disagreeable, snarly, and not the sort of thing they look for in a President.

Both Dukakis and Gore were anxious to finish Gephardt off —Dukakis because his people thought that Gephardt's strong anti-corporation, anti-foreign-competition message would be a threat in the industrial states, and Gore because he and Gephardt were fighting over the same white, slightly more conservative voters than those going to Dukakis. (There were some second thoughts about this in the Dukakis camp—why not, some realized, let a weakened Gephardt compete with Gore for votes in the subsequent states?) One of the disturbing things about the Democratic contest is the splinterization of the voters that it is causing—into blacks, liberals, and centrists—instead of building coalitions. And it is a reflection on the white Democratic candidates that (unlike Walter Mondale in 1984) none of them has a claim on black voters. (Gore wins blacks in his Senate campaigns, in Tennessee, but in the Presidential race he is no match for Jackson, who won ninety-six per cent of the black vote on March 8th.) Governing, and holding the country together, require the building of coalitions. The Democrats, to win or to govern, will have to do this in the course of the election contest in the fall.

Dukakis was also helped, in the March 8th contests as in others, by his campaign's having more field workers on the ground in key areas—especially Florida—far longer than the other candidates did. (Gephardt had withdrawn his Southern-based workers early in the year to throw everything he had at Iowa.) While the March 8th contests were usually characterized as "Southern," there is little that is Southern in the most populous areas of Florida, and Dukakis didn't win among real Southerners. His victories in Florida and Texas, the states with the most delegates to offer that day—he also carried Massachusetts, Rhode Island, Maryland, Hawaii, and Idaho—came from carefully, methodically, targeting subgroups within each state. Dukakis, who speaks fluent Spanish, carried the Hispanics in southern Texas. He also went after transplanted Northerners and the research, high-tech communities and the upper-income, better-educated voters who form his natural constituency. Kitty Dukakis, who is Jewish, and her father, Harry Ellis Dickson, an associate conductor of the Boston Pops orchestra, helped Dukakis capture the condos in South Florida.

Dukakis's victories on March 8th stopped short—as his victories often do—of being a triumph. For all their success, the Dukakis people were somewhat disappointed with the outcome. They had hoped and tried to win North Carolina as well as Texas and Florida (Gore carried North Carolina, and Jackson came in second), on the theory that that would be the knockout punch. As it turned out, Dukakis's victories in Texas and Florida masked the fact that he came in third in nine states that day. And Jackson ended up later with more delegates in Texas than Dukakis. Dukakis has consistently found his natural constituency and then pretty much stopped there. The political "scouting report" on him is that he finishes flat, and it was because John Sasso, his former top adviser, understood this that he came up with the plan for the Presidential campaign: raise more money than anyone, early, open more field offices, and convince the press that the money and the field offices show that Dukakis—an unlikely nominee, or so it seemed at the outset—was to be taken seriously. When Dukakis entered the race, both Gary Hart and Joseph Biden were in it and were seen as stronger candidates. Sasso, who now works for an advertising firm in Boston, is in touch with Dukakis and with some campaign officials, and feeds in ideas.

Dukakis has had some success in selling himself as someone who brought jobs to Massachusetts, but the national applicability of what Dukakis did do in Massachusetts is still unclear. He is big on getting various participants—labor, business, academia—in a room to work out approaches to projects. When his advisers are asked what he would actually do, nationwide, to promote economic development and create jobs, they talk vaguely about "partnerships," and "leveraging" among government, business, and labor. (Dukakis has proposed federal spending of five hundred million dollars a year for economic development.) An adviser says Dukakis is not more specific because he wants to avoid the trap of saying that what he did for Massachusetts he can do for the country. In the course of a tour of a rubber factory in Texas, televised on C-SPAN, Dukakis, commiserating with the owner about America's loss of the competitive edge (the factory's complicated computer was imported), was asked, "How do we come back?" He replied, "That's a very good question."

On the night of the Illinois primary, Dukakis had a ready explanation for his defeat—that it was understandable that the voters had gone for "two favorite sons," Paul Simon and

Jackson—but in fact the Dukakis campaign was quite disappointed with the outcome. His camp had hoped to catch Simon. Simon, who had almost been forgotten because he passed up the March 8th contests, essentially won for the reason that he stayed in: Chicago machine politicians who were on his delegate slate wanted to go to the Convention. The word was passed by Dukakis allies that a way would be found to get these people to the Convention anyway—but they weren't buying. Simon benefitted from loyalty, but he also became the vehicle for those who didn't want to see Jackson do too well. Simon himself said before the voting, in what many saw as an unmistakable bid for an anti-Jackson vote, "The Dukakis game is to try to take votes away from me, not so that Mike can be in first place, but so that Jesse can be first, and knock me out of the ballgame." A Dukakis ad that tried to counter Simon's calling for support so that he could be a broker made a lot of news in Illinois (and nationally) but little impression on Illinois voters, who don't exactly worship at the altar of pure politics, and some observers say the ad, focussing as it did on process, was precisely the wrong touch. (The ad said, "Some people would like to turn back the clock—to go back to the days when the voters didn't really pick the nominee.") It seemed that Dukakis was temperamentally and politically lost in the emotional Byzantium that is Illinois politics; by comparison, Massachusetts is Walden Pond. Though they have recently begun to wage the separate contest for super-delegates on Capitol Hill, the Dukakis people seem to understand that their candidate must essentially win it on the road. Their money and machinery still count for a lot: shortly after the March 8th contests they dispatched about eighty field workers to Michigan, a caucus state where organization is believed to count for a great deal, and they have long been at work in Wisconsin.

For Michigan, Dukakis won endorsements of sorts—not quite the all-out ones he had hoped for—from Detroit Mayor Coleman Young and Governor James Blanchard. (Blanchard, who will chair the Platform Committee at the Convention, can't be overtly too partisan.) The support of Young—one of the few black elected officials to stray from Jackson, although a number of others stayed neutral—was expected to help Dukakis among the powerful public employees' union in Michigan. Dukakis was also endorsed by some House members, but his announcement a few days ago, upon receiving the endorsement of Senator Donald Riegle, that he now supports Riegle's trade amendment, got him some negative press coverage. Riegle's proposal is less protectionist than Gephardt's, but until then Dukakis had argued vigorously that no new trade legislation was needed. ("You want another law; I will act.") Thus Dukakis blew whatever chance he had to argue that he is consistent, a national candidate who doesn't pander. (Although he had already done a bit of that.) Gephardt had hoped to have strong labor support in Michigan, but almost immediately after his near shutout on March 8th labor officials said that he was likely to receive only token support from the United Auto Workers in Michigan. Politics is not a sentimental trade. But John Dingell, a powerful representative from Michigan, has been in the state rustling up labor support for Gephardt. And the Gephardt campaign is making heavy use of its "Hyundai" ad—which says that if the United States slapped the same kinds of tariffs on a Hyundai that South Korea puts on a Chrysler K car the seven-thousand-dollar Hyundai would cost forty-eight thousand dollars in the United States. (There are some factual problems with this ad, but it makes the point to angry workers.)

The Dukakis campaign had hoped for endorsements by Arkansas's Governor Bill Clinton, Senator Bob Graham, of Florida, former North Carolina Governor James Hunt, and William Winter, the former governor of Mississippi, after, if not before, March 8th—but these have not as yet come through. It had been hoped that these people would say that Dukakis had made the connection between economic needs and the new South, and that that would make him a more credible candidate for the nomination. (Clinton, who wants to be the keynote speaker at the Convention, is in a ticklish spot. And Gore carried Arkansas, with Dukakis coming in second. The Dukakis people reportedly threatened Clinton that if he wasn't coöperative a woman or a Hispanic would be the keynoter.) So even though Dukakis is seen as the front-runner (despite Jackson's success), he still has a long slog ahead of him.

Inevitably, Jackson's success caused the question "What does Jesse want?"—an inherently patronizing question—to be increasingly raised. But, to the extent that the question implies that the answer lies within the framework of conventional politics, it is probably the wrong question. The Jackson of 1984, who demanded and had to be granted some things at the National Convention—particularly changes in the rules—is not the Jackson of 1988. And the Mondale people had, perhaps unconsciously, got off on the wrong foot with Jackson in the course of the 1984 campaign by suggesting that he should not be in the race for the nomination —that he was getting in Mondale's way. (This time, no one's in a position to say that.) This year, argue some people close to Jackson, he has transcended any conventional candidacy and gone way beyond where he was in 1984: he has become, they argue, the voice of and the symbol for the angry and the dispossessed. He speaks with validity when he tells audiences that he has stood at plant gates of companies that were shutting down and forcing people into unemployment, he has been at farm foreclosures, he has (unlike any other candidate) marched with gays and lesbians demanding more rights. Actually, most of the white vote he has been getting comes from the more affluent who share his political viewpoint or are registering their discontent with the other candidates. And the estimates are that Jackson has received at most ten per cent of the white vote—and in some states less. In Illinois, where the voters know him best, he still could not break out of the racial divide—and received only seven per cent of the white vote. Most of the increase in his votes this year, over 1984, stems from the fact that—in part by default—he is winning a much higher per cent of the black vote.

Jackson has the clearest message of any candidate in either party. His overarching theme is "economic violence"—about corporations who take American jobs overseas or suddenly close plants, and the foreclosing of farms. He calls for the government to greatly increase its protection of the economically or politically weak—the fact that his program doesn't come close to adding up is to be overlooked. He aims his appeal straight to the gut. He speaks more eloquently than any other candidate on the subjects of drugs and education. In fact, he speaks more eloquently than any other candidate on anything. Ann Lewis, one of his advisers, says, "This situation is different from 1984," when what the Mondale people wanted was for Jackson to try to persuade blacks to vote for the ticket in November. "Now he has transcended that, to reach broader audiences, and at that level his white opponents are less specific." What he wants, some who know him best say, is simply to be treated as what he is, a political force who has gone out and won a lot of votes—to "be at the table," to be included in. One should not think of it, these people say, as someone playing poker—calling for control over, say, two Cabinet posts—but as someone who is part of the effort to elect a Democratic President. Jackson functions best when he is considered a peer, a friend of his says.

Jackson and some of his top supporters see a connection between his beginning to do very well and Kirk's calling on Democrats to close ranks around the front-runner—and are certain he didn't mean Jackson. (The world of politics being as porous as it is, word got back to Jackson about talk, after Paul Kirk became Party chairman, in 1985, of how Kirk had clipped Jackson's power by standing up to him, and this is said to still rankle Jackson. He was also displeased when the Party put out a now forgotten policy report in 1986 without talking to him about it.) Ann Lewis says that most people who ask "What does Jesse want?" think about this in terms of what they would want, but that Jackson focusses at a different level. She says, "People who ask that have always had a résumé in one pocket and a career ladder in the other, and he hasn't. What he wants is to be made a full partner all the way through." There is much talk on the part of others (also patronizing) to the effect that "Jesse doesn't want to make trouble this year." That misses the point.

On the other hand, Jackson tends to make it up as he goes along, and to be of various minds and moods. Moreover, he is surrounded by a number of people, several of whom have their own ideas—or want to negotiate on his behalf. He has lines both to some radical figures and to some of the icons of the establishment—including the ultimate insider, the Washington attorney Clark Clifford. Some establishment figures, it seems, are trying to get their hooks into Jackson in order to persuade him to be a good fellow and not cause trouble. And Jackson himself recently introduced the issue that had been presumably laid aside—a question about the Party's rules. It was because he was riled by all the talk that the super-delegates should rally around the front-runner—and because he actually had the most popular votes—that he started saying recently that the super-delegates should be apportioned according to the popular vote, "to protect the integrity of the one-person, one-vote democracy." The obvious response to this is that the super-delegates are meant to be independent, to make their own judgments—but the obvious answer to *that* is that calls for them to rally around the front-runner also change their role. How far Jackson plans to push this point is anyone's guess as of now.

This leaves the question of what happens if Jackson himself, as is not totally out of the question, ends up the front-runner, or very close to the front-runner. All his protestations and the insistence of some of his allies notwithstanding, Jackson did not get in this with the idea of being the nominee, and he doesn't expect to be the nominee. The mathematics of the congressional districts of the states to come, say the experts, make it highly unlikely that he will have the most delegates at the end of the contests—but he could well come in a close second. Party leaders, though they can't say so out loud, view Jackson's increased strength with apprehension—even if he won't have a claim on the nomination. Jackson knows that quite a bit of phoning around about how to "stop" him has been going on recently. Should he have the most delegates, or close to that, Ann Lewis says, "we are in uncharted water."

A lot of people have views on how Albert Gore should have run his campaign—so that he would be further along by now. Everyone's an expert on how other people should run their campaigns. Some say he should have run in Iowa and New Hampshire—that he could have done better than his people thought. Actually, Gore had the worst of both worlds in New Hampshire—his campaign spent quite a bit of money there (over four hundred thousand dollars, nearly the legal limit), and he spent some time there, but he was in it without really being in it, and, using money that would have come in handy later, finished fifth. Gore is now paying the price in two ways for not having entered earlier: he has been later than the others in finding his voice and his themes, and he is still barely known outside the South. Running for the Presidency is like any exercise—one has to get in condition. While the others were campaigning flat out—and all of them got better over time—Gore was collecting endorsements, and though he was making appearances, it wasn't the same thing as campaigning. Gore has the potential for being a very powerful candidate—he is knowledgeable, and has more potential "star quality" than anyone, other than Jackson, in the race (in either party). But Gore's absence, or apparent absence, from the first two states denied him the coverage in the press that other candidates were getting—and still are getting. When television-news programs want "reactions" from Democratic candidates, they tend to go to the front-runner—Dukakis.

And then, when the race came to Gore, in the South, he floundered. He had started out his campaign with the rationale that he was more conservative on defense than his competitors—presumably to position himself well in the South. (Many of the architects of March 8th had Sam Nunn in mind. Nunn announced that he had voted for Gore—but that was after the fact.) Gore made the differences between himself and the other candidates greater than they were. And then it occurred to him and his campaign managers that the voters did not consider the defense issue very important—they rarely ever do, and Reagan, through his negotiations and I.N.F. treaty, has neutralized the arms-control issue—and that people were more interested in the economy (as they usually are). So then Gore, too, became a populist, uttering full-throated cries about the need to "put the White House back on the side of working men and women." With the help of a new media adviser, he cut some new ads, wearing a plaid shirt (purchased for him by the media adviser)—rather than his usual navy-blue suit—and talking populist talk with small groups of people. And then Gore appropriated Gary Hart's 1984 theme, saying that the choice is between "the politics of the future and the politics of the past"—Dukakis had tried this one on for a while in New Hampshire. And the other thing that happened to Gore was that he seemed, for a while, to clutch—becoming less loose than he had been before. Close observers of Gore say that this came from his sudden realization of what it meant to be in a Presidential race. After a while, he loosened up again, but he had lost precious time.

It is reliably said that Gore was influenced in going down the military road by some of his early backers—some money men and some of the editors of *The New Republic*, whose judgment he had to respect since they had shown such faith in him. It is also the case that the populism was not new to Gore—that he had run successfully for the House and the Senate on similar themes. Gore also points, with validity, to consumer issues he championed in Congress—and gives them (vis-à-vis Gephardt) a sharper anti-corporate tone than before. His managers also toned down his combativeness in debates, because it was raising questions both about his maturity and about what he was actually for. Until very shortly before the voting on March 8th, Gore was widely written off as all but dead, and the claims from his camp that he was moving were dismissed as so much propaganda. This provided Gore with even more glory when it turned out that he carried six states that day, and came in second to Jackson in five Southern states.

Now Gore is faced with the challenge of doing well somewhere outside the South. His campaign hadn't done much planning for after March 8th, so he and his people had to scramble for both money and a strategy. And they were caught between the need to no longer appear to be picking and choosing among the states, and the reality that he was not prepared to run everywhere. Though he campaigned a bit in Illinois, it was with no real expectation of doing well, and he finished fourth. And, in attempting to do what Fred Martin, Gore's campaign manager, calls "establish a dialogue" with Dukakis, Gore continued to show something of a heavy hand. In Illinois, he said, "We lost four of the last five national elections, twice by a vote of forty-nine to one. Mike Dukakis represents the politics of the past. I represent the politics of the future." He likened Dukakis to Mondale. His campaign is now looking at Wisconsin for his first Northern success, or at least a strong showing (but Dukakis has been at work there, and Simon, having got a new lease from Illinois, is also working in Wisconsin). The Gore people had considered making Connecticut, which holds its primary on March 29th, its target, but then came to the conclusion that it was Dukakis's kind of state. (And now Dukakis has key endorsements there.) The Gore people are hoping that somewhere, before long, Gore can do well enough to be on a roll going into the next industrial states—but Wisconsin, on April 5th, holds the last contest of any significance before New York, on the nineteenth, and it is believed within the Gore camp that in order to have money and "momentum" going into New York, Gore has to do well somewhere before that.

Though Gore is not well known in the industrial states, Martin says, "Time is on our side, because there is a gap of time before we get to New York, Pennsylvania, and Ohio." He points out that three weeks before the March 8th contest most Southerners didn't know that Gore was a Southerner. His strategy is based on Gore's doing very well in the last several states, defeating Dukakis in at least some of them, and then arguing that as the voters saw more of Dukakis they rejected him. Even if Gore doesn't have as many delegates as Dukakis, the argument would be made that he was the "political winner" of the later contests and should be the nominee, and would not have as many vulnerabilities as the liberal Dukakis. Martin, who worked in the Mondale campaign, argues that the "inevitability" strategy of the Dukakis campaign is "the most vulnerable argument a campaign can make." He points out that Gore got more votes than Bush did in eight Southern and border states, whereas Dukakis outpolled Bush in only four, and that on March 8th Gore received the votes of about a third of those who had voted for Reagan in 1984 and also about a third of the independents.

There is much talk—including within Gore's circle—that Gore, if he does well enough, and if he doesn't poison relations with, say, Dukakis too much, could end up with the second slot on the Presidential ticket. Gore, while insisting that he is after the Presidency—and there is no reason not to believe him—is not unaware of the possibility that he could end up as the Vice-Presidential candidate, and that that would not be a bad start. However, if Jackson comes out ahead of Gore in delegates, this would complicate any reaching around Jackson for a running mate— even though there is little reason to believe as of now that Jackson would want that spot. It's not his kind of role.

On March 11th, Gary Hart, facing reality at last, withdrew from the race. He had just about fallen off the map, and was out of money—and hadn't done well enough to qualify for any more federal funds. On the preceding Tuesday, he had drawn a blank, receiving only a handful of votes. His withdrawal statement was a graceful and intelligent one, and underscored the sad story of this smart and thoughtful (in the intellectual sense) man. Hart said, "I got a fair hearing. And the people have decided. Now I clearly should not go forward."

A candidacy that succeeds is believed to be driven by brilliance, and one that fails is written off as managed by hopeless incompetents—and there is no mercy in the field of politics. The interaction of the two is often overlooked—but the brilliant team would be seen as less so if the failing one didn't help. Thus, the

Bush campaign is now widely seen as having done nothing wrong, and the Dole campaign as having done nothing right. While this is closer to the truth than such comparisons often are, there were times when the Bush-Dole race was, or could have been, a closer call—and the whole theory, concentrating on tactics, as it does, overlooks the role of the candidates. Neither Bush nor Dole has been a particularly marvellous candidate, but Bush has shown more resilience and discipline than Dole—and this has made a big difference. Dole has had trouble containing his anger, and even bitterness—which sometimes slips over into self-pity. ("Nobody gave me anything.") When Dole is angry, it shows in his expressive face and in his demeanor. He was so rocked by his loss to Bush in New Hampshire that he lost valuable time. Even Bush people say that the race would have been different if Dole had concentrated on a few states in the March 8th contests—North Carolina, Missouri, and Oklahoma—rather than squandering his time and resources on other states as well. Elizabeth Dole is from North Carolina, and Missouri borders on Dole's home state of Kansas, so the losses there were particularly humiliating. The Bush people, to rub it in, went right at Dole in those states, too. And Bush people agree that if Dole had won New Hampshire the race would have been very different; one Bush strategist says that in that case Dole could have won several states on March 8th—and wouldn't have been completely shut out, as he was, in the races for delegates in Texas and Florida. As it turned out, Bush took sixteen of the seventeen states—Pat Robertson won the caucuses in Washington State—and collected 577 delegates, while Dole won only about a hundred delegates (some of these outside the South). Dole was also at a disadvantage because five of the Republican contests gave all the delegates to whoever won the state (in contrast to the proportional representation in the Democratic contests).

So the battle of New Hampshire continues to be waged—by the Dole people, against each other. There is no question that there were miscalculations: despite the urging of some, the Dole camp didn't prepare an ad to "inoculate" Dole against the predictable charge from the Bush people—in a very tax-conscious state—that Dole might raise taxes, and they failed, for various reasons, to get one on the air toward the end (though the Bush people managed to get a last-minute ad on, probably through string-pulling by the governor of New Hampshire); Richard Wirthlin, Dole's pollster, misinterpreted the fluctuating poll numbers. But all this overlooks the role that Bush and Dole played. And though the Bush campaign is rightly credited with farsightedness, the Bush people had to hurriedly re-create their candidate in New Hampshire. Dole's "mean streak" was showing (even before he said the epochal "Stop lying about my record" on election night). In front of television cameras, he told a du Pont supporter who was badgering him about taxes, "Get back in your cage." In the debate that took place on the Sunday before the voting, Dole was booby-trapped by Pete du Pont's stagy demand that he sign a no-tax pledge that New Hampshire requires of its officials—of such stunts is history made—and he was prone to quips, which don't always go over well with the public. But New Hampshire was Bush's state to begin with.

The fact that Bush has had far better campaign machinery behind him goes back to the personalities and temperaments of Bush and Dole. Dole's lack of a decent, even minimally competent campaign machine was Dole's handling of his Senate staff writ large. (So was his publicly blaming his staff for his New Hampshire defeat; we heard no such sounds out of Bush after Iowa.) The Dole campaign's lack of a strategy mirrored his propensity as a Senate leader to take things as they come—working things out at the moment. In fact, when it seemed, following March 8th, that he was going to pull out of the race either before or after Illinois—Dole, staggered by the magnitude of his defeat on March 8th, was torn, and was receiving conflicting advice, over whether to stay in—some of his theretofore stronger Senate supporters thought that it was for the best that his candidacy was virtually over. (At that point, Dole was facing a humiliating defeat in Illinois, and the gap between him and Bush was widening by the day.) Even senators who had worked closely with Dole in the Senate felt that they had learned some things about him in the course of the campaign. They had thought that talk about his inability to delegate was just gossip among Senate staff people; they were surprised by his weakness on issues; the "mean streak" turned out to be more real than they had thought, as did Dole's propensity for being a loner—they were struck by the narrow range of his human contacts. They feared that if Dole went on in the Presidential race he would undermine his role as a Senate leader—and divide the Party for no real reason. Party leaders who had thought Dole would be the stronger general-election candidate underwent a change of mind in light of the disarray within his organization and what one called his "one-note" and "whiny" campaigning.

But Dole, despite his humiliation in Illinois—Bush beat him fifty-five to thirty-six—decided to stay in the race for a while. His Senate supporters and the Republican National Committee Chairman, Frank Fahrenkopf, had to accept his decision, but publicly as well as privately urged him to keep his campaign "positive." Dole's associates say that he'll make his next stab in Wisconsin— the Republicans have already done Michigan, and Connecticut is one of Bush's home states (he actually grew up there)—and that after that he'll reassess again and wants to make a graceful exit. (At this point, Dole is far behind Bush in Wisconsin.) Even if he stops campaigning actively, it's said, Dole will probably put his campaign on hold rather than withdraw. He believes that the Iran-Contra affair might start hurting Bush, and he wants to be around to catch the fallout. As of now, Bush has 788 (to Dole's 178) of the 1,139 delegates needed for the Republican nomination—and Dole would have to win over ninety per cent of the remaining delegates in order to win the nomination. But he is far from being the first person who is reluctant to give up a candidacy.

The Bush campaign's strength was the mirror image of the Dole campaign's weakness. The Bush group, which contained a number of people who had been through Presidential campaigns before, had been at work for three years, and though it has had the tensions that any campaign has, it has pretty much managed to keep them quiet. For a long time, Dole had almost no one around him with national experience—Wirthlin was the only prominent one, and he didn't join the campaign until last October. When William Brock took over the campaign—and that was not until last November—much of Washington murmured approval: Brock, a former senator from Tennessee and Cabinet officer and a scion of the candy family, is a courtly man of moderate views who takes the time to cultivate good relationships with the press (wise people in Washington do). At last, it was thought, and Brock said, Dole would delegate. But Brock, though he had been chairman of the Republican National Committee in the late seventies, had no direct experience in a Presidential campaign. David Keene, whom Brock publicly fired (along with Donald Devine, another Dole adviser) not long before the March 8th contests, was one of the few people around Dole with such experience. The loss of Keene and Devine, who have good credentials among the right wing, was not especially helpful to Dole at that point. At the heart of it was a power struggle between Brock and the two men, but even Brock's admirers were baffled that he would do something like that so publicly—and, worst of all, blindside his candidate, who didn't know about the firings until after the fact. When Brock took over, he installed a whole new layer of campaign workers— which only increased the chaos—and he failed to solve the problem of Dole's being surrounded by a number of conflicting voices, and going off on his own. Brock is also accused of "bleeding" the Dole campaign—running its expenditures dangerously high. But when he got to the campaign it had already spent a good deal, yet had done virtually no planning or polling. The campaign— and the candidate—continued to display a lack of discipline. And there continued to be a lack of strategy. When, after New Hampshire, Dole joked to reporters, "We get in the plane and say 'Go in that direction,' " he was close to the truth.

The one thing the Dole people hadn't reckoned on, and couldn't overcome, was Reagan's popularity among Republican voters— and they couldn't break the lock that Bush got on Reagan's supporters. The sycophancy worked. The irony is that what was seen as Dole's potential strength in the general election has been part of his weakness in the nomination contests. Dole had consciously set himself somewhat apart from Reagan—he was critical of the Iran-Contra affair, of Reagan's handling of the economy, and even of Reagan. ("When I come to the White House I won't need fifteen staff people to tell me what to say and when to say it.") But this was natural to Dole: he had been of an independent mind throughout the Reagan Administration, and had often let his views be known, often acerbically. In New Hampshire, a solid thirty per cent of the Republicans were strong Reagan supporters, and thought that in voting for Bush they were voting for Reagan. In the Southern states, the Bush-Reagan lock was even stronger.

Both Bush and Dole used other pillars as well. Bush, who got former Arizona Senator Barry Goldwater's endorsement on the day before the New Hampshire primary, trotted the ailing Goldwater around with him in the South. Bush was sometimes also accompanied by Robert Dornan, a hot-tempered right-wing representative from California. Dole—to the surprise and consternation of the Bush people—got Senator Strom Thurmond's endorsement shortly before the primary in Thurmond's home state of South Carolina (on the Saturday before March 8th), but Dole's allowing himself to be drawn into South Carolina, which the Bush people had wired, was a miscalculation. Also shortly before the South Carolina primary, Dole—after a prolonged pursuit—won the endorsement of Jeane Kirkpatrick, who then joined Dole on the circuit. (The theory is that Kirkpatrick threw her support to Dole because everyone assumes that Bush would make James Baker Secretary of State—if that's what Baker wants. Baker, who managed Bush's 1980 Presidential campaign, is advising Bush privately, and doing what he can as Treasury Secretary to make the economy safe for Republicans in the fall.) In South Carolina, as in New Hampshire and Illinois, Bush's fate was put in the hands of a strong governor (Carroll Campbell in South Carolina, John Sununu in New Hampshire, and James Thompson in Illinois), who delivered. Lee Atwater, Bush's campaign manager, says, "I told Bush over a year ago that the three people we most need to get into the campaign were John Sununu, Carroll Campbell, and Jim Thompson, that if we won those three states everything else would fall into place." Bush's strong victory in South Carolina (he got forty-eight per cent to Dole's twenty-one per cent and Pat Robertson's nineteen per cent) gave him an extra push on the following Tuesday. Brock knew that the psychology of the situation was going to make it difficult for Dole to recoup in Illinois. Dole said in Illinois, "I can beat Bush, but beating Reagan is impossible."

Another way the Bush people tried, with success, to secure Bush's position among the Republican voters was to allow no one to get between Bush and the conservative movement. Culturally, Bush is certainly not their kind of guy, and his own views, to the extent he has any, tend to be more moderate. At some risk—it did not help his image as "a wimp"—two years ago, Bush publicly courted Nackey Loeb, the acid publisher of the Manchester *Union Leader* and a fit successor to her late husband, William Loeb, and he also courted Jerry Falwell, who endorsed him. Bush was much derided for these actions—he was called "a lapdog"—but they did the job.

Jack Kemp, who had hoped to persuade Republicans that he was Reagan's true heir, was squeezed out by Bush, and dropped out on March 10th. Kemp, who campaigned in good spirits—no bitterness or self-pity—made it clear he was available to be Bush's running mate, but in any event is giving up his House seat, and plans to try to make himself the next conservative leader.

Pat Robertson, whose plausibility diminished as time went on (he came in third in South Carolina, which he had once said he had to win, and did poorly on March 8th, winning only nine delegates), is now all but out of the race. Robertson, who had built his reputation in the shelter of his own television program, owned by his own company, wasn't ready for the realities of secular politics. Bush even beat him among evangelicals in the South. This had something to do with the divisions within the evangelical movement between the charismatics—who speak in tongues and believe in faith healing, and of whom Robertson is one—and the fundamentalists. In state after state, Robertson got the vote of charismatics but didn't do particularly well among fundamentalists. Also, Bush cultivated fundamentalists, by saying that he accepts Jesus Christ "as my personal Saviour." Robertson didn't succeed in reaching beyond his religious followers to blue-collar workers, as he had hoped. He's keeping his campaign alive, but has acknowledged that only a "miracle" could make him the nominee. Robertson, who has said that he finds the 1984 Republican platform acceptable (and therefore won't start a fight), has told Frank Fahrenkopf that he would like to address the Convention. All of the failed candidates will be accommodated. Robertson says that he will be "positive" for the rest of the campaign and has made it clear that he wants to run for President again.

Throughout all of this, neither Bush nor Dole was saying very much. Dole continued to insist, "I can make a difference," and that he is "a strong leader." In the South, he succumbed to the lure of protectionism on behalf of textile workers, and made himself out to be more of a militarist than he is. He tried to look tough by saying that if the Panamanian ruler, General Manuel

Antonio Noriega, whom the Administration is still trying to dislodge (because of drug-running and corruption), isn't gone soon, the United States should use force. By the time Dole reached Illinois, he was pleading with the voters to keep his candidacy alive. Once again, he was undermined by his and his campaign's ineptitude: five days before the voting it became known that the campaign had cancelled all of the political ads for Illinois—before it was understood that the ads were to be supplanted by a thirty-minute special program on Saturday. (The Bush people appeared to have fanned this; campaigns can easily find out, from television stations, about each other's buys.) At the same time, it became known that Dole was thinking of getting out of the race, and that the campaign had gone through another round of layoffs (reducing its number of workers by eighty per cent over all). Then the thirty-minute program was a technical disaster.

Bush, in the South, returned to the Vice-Presidential cocoon he had briefly shed in New Hampshire—his aides argue, reasonably, that because of all the ground that had to be covered by March 8th Bush couldn't be as spontaneous as he had been in New Hampshire—but they were sufficiently sensitive to the "cocoon" stories that they had Bush all over the neighborhoods of Chicago, as well as the surrounding suburbs. In the South, Bush talked about defense and the deficit. Despite the changes inside the Soviet Union, Bush said in Florida, "There is no change in fundamental direction." He added that Reagan was right to call the Soviet Union an "evil empire," and he said, "Thank God that 'Blame America first' crowd out of that Vietnam thing is silent." In the case of the deficit, he talked about his concept of a "flexible freeze," and argued that Congress should give the President the line-item veto. Even Reagan has not been able to persuade Congress to give him this power. Bush's aides know that his message must be strengthened for the general election. Bush also says, for the obvious reason, that his Administration will be sensitive to the question of ethics.

Bush's aides point to a speech he gave in Chicago about his concept of the Presidency. In the speech, Bush said that on the first day of his Presidency he would initiate negotiations with Congress on the budget, and that he'd head the executive branch's negotiating team. His aides say that the fall campaign will have as a major theme Bush's concern that, overall, the President's powers have been too eroded by Congress: that a President should have a line-item veto and less interference by Congress in foreign affairs. Bush's theme, they say, will be a strong Presidency—he will offer himself as someone who has been there, who has thought about the Presidency and observed it closely. They appear to hope that the more Bush presents himself as the strong executive, the more he will be seen as one. Whether this will move millions is a question. (Of course, all of this rests on the assumption that Bush will be the nominee.) A fact that has not received much attention is that even in Illinois, when the Dole campaign had collapsed, Dole beat Bush among independent voters. This, along with some other things, could mean that if the Democrats settle their nomination amicably, and don't make any major mistakes, they have a real shot at the Presidency.

VI

Having had a big fright, the Democratic Party is now embracing Michael Dukakis with more enthusiasm than it actually feels for him. The momentary spectre of the possibility that Jesse Jackson could end up with the most delegates was all it took; and Dukakis's strong victory over Jackson in Wisconsin this week gave Democrats their opening. Now many Party leaders are more strenuous than even the Dukakis people in arguing Dukakis's inevitability—the Dukakis campaign had learned the perils of doing this—and have joined his side for the last stages of the elimination contest. Though Dukakis in Wisconsin received the votes of more blue-collar workers than he had before, the still unanswered questions about his ability to marshall a large coalition have been set aside. Questions about whether he would be a success at governing aren't even considered; the Democrats have to deal with what is before them—and what is before them, as they see it, is a choice between Dukakis and Jackson. Though many Democrats still hanker for someone else, the desire to wrap the nomination up neatly, and soon, is the prevailing one.

The Democrats of Wisconsin responded to the choice the same way, but, following the pattern in other states, Dukakis's supporters were less enthusiastic about him than supporters of other candidates were about their choices. Jackson was a victim of his own success. When the question arose of taking his candidacy from a symbolic one to a real one, most Wisconsin voters were not ready to take that step. (Dukakis defeated Jackson by ten percentage points in caucuses held in Colorado on Monday.) Albert Gore, who has run at best a distant third in every contest outside the South since March 8th ("Super Tuesday"), is seen by many Democrats not as an option but as an obstacle in the path of getting the thing over. Paul Simon, who came in a poor fourth in Wisconsin, has suspended his candidacy. By suspending, rather than dropping out, he enables his Illinois delegates, who were the reason he stayed alive through that state's contest, to go to the Convention. Simon also wants to use what "leverage" he has left.

If the Party leaders' strategy works, and the voters coöperate —nothing's certain—the Wisconsin primary on Tuesday will be seen as the turning point. Dukakis, by defeating Jackson forty-eight per cent to twenty-eight per cent, not only resuscitated his campaign but even became a giant-killer. His defeat by Jackson in Michigan ten days earlier—Jackson won by an overwhelming fifty-three per cent to twenty-nine per cent—had sent paroxysms of fear throughout much of the Party.

Jackson's victory in Michigan on Saturday, March 26th, was all the more striking because no one saw it coming. Going into the weekend, the polls had Jackson and Dukakis neck and neck, but the reason the polls missed what happened was that Jackson brought out new voters who were not represented in the polls' samples. Jackson, in a triumph of neighborhood-to-neighborhood organizing, got about seventy-five thousand new voters out, and quintupled his own vote over 1984. He won every major city, and carried eleven out of eighteen congressional districts, and he would have won the state even without his overwhelming victory in Detroit. (Dukakis's endorsement by Detroit Mayor Coleman Young, a black, was of little avail.) Richard Gephardt, who came in a weak third in Michigan, winning about thirteen per cent of the votes, gracefully withdrew from the race two days later. The Republicans had already had their fight in Michigan, but Robert Dole, facing a gap of nearly forty percentage points between himself and Bush in Wisconsin, moved up the date of his withdrawal and bowed out, also gracefully, on March 29th. In his farewell, he again urged the Republican Party to reach out, and broaden its base. The Bush campaign was already at work on the general election—attempting to shore up Bush's strength in the states that have been the core of the Republicans' electoral-college majority.

Before Michigan, it had never crossed Democratic leaders'— or very many other people's—minds that Jackson could win the nomination. Now they had to consider that possibility, and they became unglued. Some were highly discomfited when, shortly after Michigan, Democratic National Committee Chairman Paul Kirk, in disavowing any "stop Jackson" effort, said that the Party should rally behind "whoever the person is that's accumulating the most delegates"; earlier, Kirk had taken the position (with Dukakis in mind) that, since no one could win the required majority of the delegates through the primaries, the Party should rally around the front-runner, saying that he did not expect "a photo finish"—and he still hopes to hold the Party together. Some Democrats, disturbed by the thought that Kirk was suggesting that the Party should try to put across whoever has one more delegate at the end of the contests—and that that person might be Jackson—said that there should be other criteria as well, such as who had been most successful in the last, big states, and electability. Last Sunday, on "This Week with David Brinkley," Kirk seemed to modify his position and said that what he meant was that "if there was a very, very substantial plurality of delegates and someone has the nomination virtually within his grasp," the Party should consider rallying behind that person—and he dodged questions about whether he thought Jackson was electable.

After Michigan, panicked Democrats figured that Jackson not only would lose the Presidential race but might also take down with him the Democratic-controlled Senate, and even the Democratic control of the House—which has lasted thirty-four years. A few—very few—leaders kept cool, and pointed out that Jackson hadn't been nominated in Michigan, and that twenty states, including New York, Pennsylvania, Ohio, New Jersey, and California, were still to come. It was also pointed out that, as time went on, Jackson was likely to be facing only one viable opponent— and that unless Jackson won an exceptionally high percentage of the votes of whites his opponent would win. But other Democrats considered it possible that Jackson was on a roll, and that Dukakis, with his limits as a campaigner, couldn't stop him. Some Democrats concluded that the only way to head off what they saw as a calamity was to circle the wagons around Dukakis and try to work it that he would be Jackson's sole opponent as soon as possible. It's not that most of them were wild about Dukakis but they made a pragmatic judgment that he was the strongest of Jackson's opponents—at least of those in the race. On Capitol Hill in particular, where Dukakis leaves many Democratic politicians wondering if that's the best their party can do, there was increased talk of looking beyond the field. By last weekend, when people scattered for the Easter holiday, and Congress (after finally approving humanitarian aid for the Contras, by a large bipartisan vote) took another recess, some of the panic had subsided, and those behind the Dukakis strategy felt that they had made some headway in getting people to regard the Democratic contest as a two-man race—between Dukakis and Jackson—in order to get Jackson more scrutiny and Dukakis more votes.

All of this had to be handled most delicately—for fear of offending Jackson's supporters or of being branded "racist." Any sign that a racial barrier is being broken is positive, but an unpleasant aspect of this period is the racial tension that has also been stirred up. (And other black politicians, in local and state races, have won higher portions of white votes than Jackson has as yet.) Of course some Democrats oppose Jackson—or assume he will lose—because he is black, but the strong opposition to Jackson among Democrats with no racism in them stems from other things: his radicalism in both domestic and foreign policy (Jackson has toned this down, but it's still there), his utter lack of relevant experience, and controversial things he has said and done in the past. Moreover, a number of people simply don't like Jackson—find him unscrupulous and untrustworthy, too much out for himself even as political leaders go. It is no accident that others who were close to Dr. Martin Luther King, Jr.—King's widow, Coretta, and Andrew Young—are among those black leaders who cannot bring themselves to endorse Jackson. (They resent Jackson's claim, which has been strongly challenged, that he cradled the dying King in his arms—Jackson even turned up on television the next day wearing a sweater covered with what he claimed was King's blood.) Mickey Leland, a black congressman from Texas, who did not support Jackson in 1984, said recently that "racist, bigoted" people in the Democratic Party are trying to stop Jackson. While some see Leland's statement as one designed to deter any "stop Jackson" movement, it's poisonous. But it and the fear it is playing upon have had an effect: though there have been movements in the past to stop white candidates, most white Democrats who worried about Jackson's heading the ticket were also scared to death of the possibility of being seen as anti-black. They know that if Jackson's followers are offended there is probably no hope of winning in November.

Overreaction—and overconcluding—has characterized this election. It is as if the political practitioners and the press—dependent upon each other—are living in a cave of winds, and each gust is blown out of proportion. There was an overreaction to Paul Simon's momentary lead in Iowa, to Gary Hart's reëntry into the race and his momentary lead, to Gephardt's Iowa victory, to Pat Robertson's coming in second in Iowa, and, for that matter, to Dole's Iowa victory. (The fact that both Iowa victors are now out of the race will cause some reconsideration of the importance of the caucuses there. But it may not cause any diminution of future candidates' efforts there. This year's caucus process in Iowa is still unfolding—the first test was only at the precinct level, and the state convention is yet to be held—and at this point Dukakis, who came in third in early February, has the lead in delegates.) Too many conclusions were solemnly drawn about these things and also about Dukakis's and Gore's victories on March 8th: it was concluded that Dukakis's nomination was inevitable and that Gore would now be a national figure. Dukakis may very well be the nominee, but it's taking longer than the original "inevitability" theory had it.

Jackson's Michigan victory was dramatic and a triumph—but more was read into it than was there. In a caucus contest, Jackson out-organized Dukakis, but the turnout, though higher than in 1984, was still minuscule. About two hundred and eleven thousand people turned out in a state where there are more than five and a half million registered voters. The caucus was conducted with very loose Democratic Party rules about who was eligible to vote.

Jackson's early strong showing in Wisconsin—the polls had him and Dukakis about even until a few days before the voting —was attributable to the fact that he had identified himself some time back with the two biggest controversies affecting workers, that his campaign organized the state very well, and that he was hot. (Wisconsin has a black population of only four percent.) Moreover, the atmosphere in Wisconsin was relatively free of racial tension. Jackson, in Wisconsin, became a phenomenon, and personified excitement, and drew large crowds. It's been a long time since Democrats have had a candidate who stirred such excitement—not since Robert Kennedy, in 1968. But the excitement was in part extrapolitical: Jackson, a man of undeniable magnetism, took on (for a time) the aspect of a rock star—he was the latest mania. But toward the end there was a defensive note in Jackson's speeches. In an argument over the point that he's never been elected to any office, he said, "I'm glad in 1955 Rosa Parks did not wait until she got elected a public official to lead the Montgomery bus boycott." And his crowds seemed to contain a lot of people who were simply curious. His sending a letter, disclosed on the Sunday before the Wisconsin voting, to Panamanian ruler Manuel Antonio Noriega suggesting that Noriega leave office and offering to help resolve the situation reinforced people's memories of Jackson's other controversial free-lance foreign-policy adventures, and was criticized by Dukakis and Gore, and received a lot of attention in the Wisconsin media.

The swirling around that took place after Jackson's Michigan victory was by a loosely organized and self-nominated group that might be termed the Talkers. The group is made up of past Democratic officials, current members of the Democratic National Committee, chairmen of the state parties, and certain congressional leaders. Gephardt's departure from the race freed up a large number of House Democrats, some of whom, such as House Majority Whip Tony Coelho, were among the Talkers. In the course of any Presidential campaign, a great deal of largely useless conversations and telephoning takes place—among past and present officials, political consultants, and the press. ("What do you hear?" "What does it mean?") A great deal of time and energy is consumed, and a question is whether any of this chatter has any real relevance. Ann Lewis, a former political director of the Democratic National Committee and now an adviser to Jackson, says, "What Jesse has demonstrated again is the irrelevance of the political establishment in the face of a candidate who can communicate directly with voters on the issues they care about. It's because we see this phenomenon so rarely that people sometimes miss it. But once it's under way the best you can do is analyze it honestly and respond appropriately—and don't kid yourself that outsiders can deflect it or divide it or destroy it."

But others in the telephonic daisy chain say that their communications do matter. Mark Siegel, who has a very busy phone, is a member of the D.N.C., and therefore a super-delegate who is in touch with a number of other super-delegates (including state chairmen)—who are, in turn, in touch with still more. Siegel argues that to the extent members of this group are super-delegates, or can influence super-delegates—Party officials and members of Congress whose votes can help put a candidate over—the Talkers do have influence. He says, "We talk to the press, and things take on a life of their own." Paul Maslin, a respected Democratic pollster, says, "The speculating, because it is played in the press, affects the voter." He adds, referring to the New York primary, on April 19th—which many think will be the decisive one—"Whichever wind is blowing after New York will reach gale force."

Thus, in the week following Jackson's Michigan victory many of the Talkers, after recovering from their initial state of shock, made an effort to get people to focus on a two-man race between Jackson and Dukakis, and also to scotch as unrealistic any speculation that the Party would turn to Mario Cuomo or Bill Bradley. (There was also talk of turning to Edward Kennedy—as someone who would not alienate Jackson's supporters.) They urged closer scrutiny of Jackson by the press, arguing, with some validity, that press scrutiny of the weaknesses of what Simon and Gephardt had been saying had helped do them in, while Jackson had virtually been given a free ride. (When, in mid-March, I questioned Jackson, on "Meet the Press," about how he could possibly come up with the funds for the large number of new or expanded federal programs he was urging, his answers were lame and his mood was sulky.) His talk about "slave labor" in foreign countries competing with American workers and what he would do about it is largely gibberish. Jackson had been mostly left alone about his 1984 association with the anti-Semitic Black Muslim leader Louis Farrakhan, and also about his own earlier anti-Semitic statements (referring to Jews as "Hymies" and to New York as "Hymietown"). A number of people have the uneasy feeling that Jackson has not really changed his views but has accepted advice to keep quiet about them. Panicked Democrats pointed out that for now people might feel inclined not to bring up Jackson's earlier, literal, embraces of Fidel Castro and Yasir Arafat, but that there was no reason on earth to believe that if Jackson were on the Democratic ticket Republicans would be reticent about these or a number of other matters.

Jackson was also held to a different standard out of an understanding that he was running by a different standard—not as a serious candidate for the Presidency but as a spokesman for the left-outs and discontented. And there was, and is, a certain respect for Jackson's ability to connect with these people in a way that no other candidate can. He has an obvious knack for coinage ("Reaganism is Robin Hood in reverse: steal from the poor to give to the rich"), and for getting at what's bothering people. Our reverence, however temporary, for demagogues (and there is some demagoguery in what Jackson is saying)—our inclination to feel that anyone (George Wallace, Spiro Agnew, Pat Robertson) who is connecting with a significant slice of the voters, however he is doing it, must be respected for being onto something important —is one of our more naïve traits. Jackson himself has acknowledged his debt for a simple, clear message to George Wallace, who, Jackson told a *Wall Street Journal* reporter, had told him, " 'Keep your message so low the goats can get it.' " (In 1972, Wallace won Michigan and came in second in Wisconsin.) Of course, Jackson is talking about things that matter to people—drugs, the loss of jobs, the need for better education—and there is no reason to doubt his sincerity. He is better briefed and prepared than he was four years ago, but he leaves a lot to be explained. He says he will do so in New York.

Whether Jackson now really considers himself a serious candidate for the Presidency is still in question; it would be inhuman for him not to have been affected by his success in Michigan, but people close to him said as of then that he was prepared to take things as they come, see what happened next. It's just possible that Jackson would not want the responsibility for heading a ticket, or being on a ticket, that lost. His advisers say that for now they are trying to make sure that he has, as one put it, "the widest range of options." It was striking that his campaign chairman, Willie Brown, the Speaker of the California Assembly and the man most likely to negotiate for Jackson, avoided (on the same David Brinkley program that Kirk appeared on) demanding that whoever has the most delegates should be the nominee. For a large portion of Jackson's supporters and would-be supporters, whether his proposals stand up to scrutiny is irrelevant. Their support for him is in a different category—as the leader of a movement. Jackson has become the vehicle for their discontent —with current policies, with the other candidates. He stands in bold, interesting contrast to some fairly dull candidates. He is the anti-politics candidate. Measuring his program is linear, rational, while most of the support for him is based on emotion. What gave some people pause after Michigan was not the details of his program but the reality of the question of whether they really wanted Jackson to be President.

One congressional leader said to me during the week that followed Jackson's Michigan victory, "There's obviously a lot of hand-wringing going on—a sense that Wisconsin could go to Jackson and that conceivably New York and California would, too. If Jesse goes into the Convention with the most votes and delegates, what could we do? We know it's a losing ticket, and we can see the Republicans' delight—they feel this guarantees the election of George Bush." (Republicans made no particular effort to hide their glee over Jackson's success.) He said, "There's a feeling that when this thing gets out of the hothouse of the caucuses and primaries, if Jackson wins, it's over. It would be twice as over as it was for Goldwater in '64 and twice as over as it was for McGovern in '72." He added, "And there's a lot of discomfort—a feeling that we'll be termed racist if we oppose Jackson. So there's a reluctance on the part of anybody to step out and be accused of leading a 'stop Jackson' movement. There's a lot of anxiety." (Like other congressional leaders, this person declined to be quoted by name.) A number of important Democrats were caught: if they endorsed Dukakis right after Michigan—as some had planned to do—they would appear to be trying to stop Jackson, and this they could not afford, even if that's what they were trying to do. Moreover, Coleman Young's fate gave them pause. This particular congressional leader said that there were a lot of doubts about Dukakis on Capitol Hill, and a lot of talk about trying to find someone else—especially Cuomo. Dukakis's victory in Wisconsin gave Democratic politicians an opening to endorse him, but some, such as Coelho, don't plan to do it before New York.

Another House Democrat, who is in touch with a lot of members, said to me during the week after Michigan, "Most people here care more about their own reëlection than about the Presidency, and if Jesse wins Wisconsin that will further the resolve of people around here to stop him." He added, "We may not be able to do it with the current crop of candidates." And all of the people who did run may not be predisposed to helping each other at the end—and might prefer someone who had not run. This House member, like several others, was eying Cuomo, and assumes that, Cuomo's protestations notwithstanding, he is available. But several leading Democrats, and key members of the labor movement, believe that reaching for someone who hadn't been in the race at all would lead to disaster.

The Party establishment has not given up on the idea that Jackson will be coöperative at the end—that, if treated well, he will help put together a "realistic" ticket and support it. At the moment, some Party respectables are using Jackson and Jackson is using them. That's what lay behind the breakfast held in Washington last week between Jackson and a number of Party stalwarts, including Clark Clifford, former Democratic Chairman John White, Bert Lance (who has signed on with Jackson and is one of several who say they'll negotiate for him), and a number of Democrats associated with past failed campaigns. But, outside of Jackson's own supporters, there was only one delegate in the room, and just what these people could deliver to Jackson—other than a smidge of "respectability"—was in question. According to a participant, Jackson wanted the grandees, when talking to the press afterward, to pronounce him electable, but this they declined to do.

Cuomo was seen by some as having got himself in a bind by not deciding, before Michigan, whether to endorse anyone, but he has been leaning against it for some time. There are good reasons. New York is a tinderbox of racial tensions now—what with the Tawana Brawley and Howard Beach cases—and Cuomo has little to gain by alienating Jackson's constituency. (His only conceivable endorsement would be of Dukakis.) Following Jackson's Michigan victory, Cuomo was telling one and all that he thought that a Jackson nomination would be "wonderful" for the Democratic Party, but, fairly or not, few believed that he really meant it. Shortly after the Michigan vote, Cuomo said to me, "I might find that Mike is the better candidate, but I would have to find a way to make sure that that didn't appear to be a 'stop Jesse Jackson.' I'm waiting to see what happens in Connecticut and Wisconsin. I don't make a decision until I have to make a decision." He has again freed up his New York allies and at this point is uncertain about whether he will make any further statement of neutrality—but he feeds ideas to Dukakis.

In the wake of Dukakis's Michigan debacle, he and his campaign knew that they had to retune his candidacy once again. There was recognition of the fact that while Dukakis had been collecting endorsements of established politicians and going to his seemingly endless number of fund-raisers, Jackson was out there talking to the voters. The press was beginning to take note of the fund-raisers. Even Dukakis's aides said that his schedule in Michigan had been too light, but they, and Dukakis, were aware that the problems ran deeper than that. They received a lot of free advice that Dukakis had to strengthen his message, and they tried to strengthen his message—but Dukakis's problems run deeper even than that. Dukakis's message was adequate, if not exciting. Dukakis's liabilities as a politician were catching up with him: his aloofness, the whiff of arrogance he gives off, the sense that he doesn't relate to human experiences. A number of people who have observed him close up know that his personality is not an entirely winning one. Dukakis, to answer the criticism that he is a flat speaker, said, "I am what I am," and in a speech in Wisconsin said, "I don't expect to be known as the Great Communicator; I want to be known as the Great Builder." (If Dukakis is nominated, he will have the good fortune of being up against someone who has admitted a similar failing.)

The other tack taken by the Dukakis campaign was to try once again to sharpen his basic speech, and to have him out there mixing it up with the people—serving food, picking up babies, eating sausages, drinking a beer, and even swearing. Dukakis does particularly well with ethnic crowds by reminding them of his own immigrant roots. He made an obvious effort to convince people that he understands their problems: "I know what you've been going through; I know the pain and anguish." He added, "After seven years of charisma, maybe it's time for some competence in the White House." His campaign cut a new ad, showing laid-off factory workers and some homeless people, with Dukakis saying, "The human cost of seven years of Republican indifference is staggering." He said that he would work hard to try to prevent plant closings—the imminent laying off of thousands of workers at a Chrysler plant in Kenosha was a big issue in Wisconsin, and

Jackson early in the year had joined in the protest against the layoffs. (Legislation to give workers more notice of plant closings is pending in Congress.) All the candidates made pilgrimages to the plant, which Curtis Wilkie, of the Boston *Globe*, called the Lourdes of the Wisconsin primary. (Dukakis won the area.) In his new speech in Wisconsin, Dukakis tried to emphasize the stakes in the election by attacking the Reagan Administration more sharply than before, and, by implication, asked his audience to take seriously the choice between him and Jackson. He also drew a distinction between himself and Jackson by saying in Wisconsin that he is "a doer," that he doesn't "just talk about jobs, I create them." Actually, this distinction was one that Dukakis had tried to draw with other candidates all along, but now, in the new context that he was trying to establish—that it was him or Jackson—these remarks took on new significance.

How, exactly, to deal with Jackson was a topic of some dispute within the Dukakis campaign: Dukakis wants to win the nomination without so alienating Jackson that it would be worthless. Yet some of his responses just after Michigan to questions about Jackson were seen as so lame as to raise a question in some people's minds about whether he would stand up to Jackson on anything. Asked whether he thought he or Jackson was more experienced, Dukakis replied, "I'm not going to answer that question." His advisers, aware that this would not suffice, said that differences would arise in the context of the campaign and of the several debates before the New York voting. But as he campaigned in Wisconsin Dukakis had to start considering the large Jewish vote in New York, and to try to thread his way among the tensions between blacks and Jews in New York, and—with the emergence of the question of what Israel should do about the recent, and continuing, uprising of Palestinians in the West Bank and the Gaza Strip—among Jews themselves.

He didn't start out very well. One related issue is a letter to Secretary of State George Shultz, signed by thirty senators, most of them strong supporters of Israel, in early March, criticizing the Israeli government for intransigence over the Palestinian question and supporting Shultz's plan, envisioning a swap of territory for peace, to try to get the matter resolved. The letter caused a strong reaction from some of the American Jewish community, which is divided—as the Israeli government is—over the Palestinian issue.

When Israeli Prime Minister Yitzhak Shamir visited the United States later in the month, he made an issue of the letter, and helped fan a backlash to it—and even some American Jews who are opposed to the present Israeli policy questioned the wisdom of outsiders' getting involved in delicate negotiations; some of the letter's signers beat a retreat. Meanwhile, Dukakis, on March 6th, said that he would have signed the letter. Gore, making a pitch for the Jewish voters in New York—who constitute nearly a fourth of the Democratic electorate there—met with Shamir and condemned the letter and, without endorsing Shamir's precise views, said that Shamir's objections had been given "short shrift" by the Administration. More recently, in a speech to major Jewish organizations in New York, Gore called Dukakis "naïve" about foreign policy and criticized his saying that he would have signed the letter. Meanwhile, the Dukakis camp was in something of a tizzy over the issue of the letter—with some advisers wanting Dukakis to back off his saying he would have signed it.

But Dukakis was already contributing to his own list of "flip-flops"—the most prominent having been the one over trade, in Michigan—and backing off what he had said about the letter would bring him new problems. So last Saturday, three days before the Wisconsin primary, Dukakis made a speech aimed at New York—and didn't mention the letter at all. (His campaign makes a point of pitching a speech to the next state, so that when he arrives in that state he doesn't seem to all of a sudden be talking about its issues.) He said nothing about the harsh measures Israel has used against Palestinian demonstrators (even the Reagan Administration has been critical) and, no doubt with Jackson in mind as well, was harsh in his criticism of the Palestine Liberation Organization. (Jackson had in the past expressed sympathy with the P.L.O. but this year is trying to be more even-handed.) But some Jewish leaders are not yet satisfied, and think that Dukakis is making a strategic mistake in leaving it to Gore to take on Jackson.

Dukakis's aides, while confident, know that if Dukakis doesn't win New York he'd be in serious trouble. (However, even Jackson's advisers believe that the terrain gets harder for Jackson in the industrial states that follow New York.) In 1984, Jackson got twenty-six per cent of the vote in New York, with eighty-seven per cent of the black vote (Walter Mondale got twelve), and if he does as well as he has been doing lately among whites—he got the votes of twenty-three per cent of them in Wisconsin—he could be very strong. Moreover, the Jewish vote in New York is not monolithic, and some Jews there could go for Jackson. This is why Dukakis's allies are trying to make Gore irrelevant, and the word has been spread in New York that a vote for Gore is a vote for Jackson. Gore is being warned that he won't help his future by attacking the presumptive nominee. But Gore says that he takes his going from four per cent in the polls to seventeen per cent in the result in Wisconsin as an encouraging sign, and that he will go all out in New York. If Dukakis lost New York, he would slug it out with Jackson—and Gore, if need be—state by state, to the end, but a loss in New York could have a strong psychological effect on the remaining contests, and a major effect on the final decision. In the two weeks between April 19th, the day of the New York primary, and May 3rd, over seven hundred delegates will be chosen.

Gore himself is in serious trouble. Before Wisconsin, he had managed to register in only single digits in the Northern states, and he is in danger of losing out on federal matching funds—which are based on getting a certain percentage of votes—if he does not win twenty per cent of the vote in New York or Pennsylvania, the following week. His seventeen per cent in Wisconsin came as a result of making Wisconsin his main target before New York and of spending all the money he could there. (He spent more on television than any of the others.) And Gore, who had sanctimoniously criticized the other candidates for "pandering" to Iowans, came out in Wisconsin for a large increase in the support price for milk. Because whatever votes he gets are presumed to be taken away from Dukakis, some of his supporters are finding it difficult to explain to anxious Democratic politicians why he is still in the race. Susan Estrich, Dukakis's campaign manager, said, after Wisconsin, "Having finished no better than third since 'Super Tuesday' makes it hard for them to make the case that he's anything but a spoiler. We consider this a two-man race." Meanwhile, New York Mayor Ed Koch has sent the signal that he prefers Gore—next to Cuomo. (Koch has also said that Jews would be "crazy" to vote for Jackson.)

Gore is still paying a big price for not getting his campaign legs earlier, and has shown uncertainty about what he wants to be saying. But his problems go beyond that: he has not fulfilled his potential. Even one of his backers says that Gore seems to have problems of his own making: that in continuing to be stiff he doesn't connect with people. And, this person says, "there have been too many discussions of what the message is; you should figure that out before you run." Some attribute Gore's problems to his youth (he just turned forty), saying that he does not yet have a sufficient understanding of who he is and of the world, even arguing that Gore is paying a price for having lived a life of almost no knocks. For all of Gore's braininess and knowledge, there does seem to be something unformed about him, and the campaign has brought this out. Campaigns reveal truths about candidates.

And Gore continues to be heavy-handed. In his first attack on Jackson—and Dukakis—in New York, he said, among other things, "We're not choosing a preacher, we're choosing a President." A number of Gore advisers disavowed having anything to do with this statement, saying that it had the ring of Jackson's scat talk, and that Gore in going after Jackson should stick with issues. In a speech later that day, before the Jewish audience, Gore said of Jackson, "I categorically reject his notion that there's a moral equivalence between Israel and the P.L.O.," and he attacked Jackson's defense policy. Cuomo publicly slapped Gore on the wrist for this, saying he wanted a "positive" campaign in New York; Cuomo had already told David Garth, Gore's media adviser for New York, to avoid negative advertising, especially on the issue of Israel. Garth, known for rough tactics, has said, "It isn't going to be a cutesy-pie campaign." Representations were made by some Jewish leaders to Gore and Garth to not make a big issue of the letter. When I asked Gore this week how much he planned to make of the letter, he said, "I don't see it as much of an issue." Gore complains about the criticism of his attacking the others, and also says he's done it before, so too much is being made of it. But Gore is smart enough to know that, in the current context, such attacks will receive attention—presumably that's why he's making them. Jackson, miffed by Gore's attack, called off a meeting with Gore in Washington, scheduled for two days later. In Wisconsin, Gore said that Dukakis had been "absurdly timid" and was "scared to death" about saying anything negative about Jackson. Gore may be talking himself out of consideration for even the Vice-Presidential spot on the ticket.

The Democrats are more relaxed than they were just a few days ago, but they are still going through a dicey period. A number of them have not abandoned hope that they can arrive at their nominations without too much grief, but they still are less sure of this than they were before. They are waiting to see what happens in New York.

VII

In keeping with this unusual election year, the two parties have in effect decided upon their nominees at an uncommonly early stage of the nominating process, and the general election has begun at an uncommonly early point. Both George Bush and Michael Dukakis, through a combination of superior resources, long-planned campaigns, skill, and luck (and also the failings of their opponents), had their nominations in hand earlier than any non-incumbents since the modern system of nominating candidates began—probably, unfortunately, establishing a model for future campaigns. At no time, under the current system, were the Pennsylvania and Ohio primaries, held in the past two weeks, afterthoughts, as they were this time. Dukakis in effect had the nomination in hand as a result of the New York primary, on April 19th, and Bush, who in effect had his sewed up when Robert Dole dropped out, at the end of March, officially had enough delegates for the nomination as of the Pennsylvania primary, on April 26th. Yesterday, Pat Robertson, the only remaining Republican candidate, said that he would drop out and support Bush, and last night, amid great hoopla at a Republican fund-raising dinner, President Reagan, in what should have been a non-event but had been built up by the Bush people into a big thing, endorsed Bush. The only surprising thing about it was how tepidly he did so. He just may not have relished the idea of moving aside. (Today, Reagan, puzzled by the reaction, put out a more effusive statement.)

Dukakis is still accumulating delegates, but few doubt that he will have enough for the nomination before the Convention. Tad Devine, Dukakis's chief delegate-hunter, says that enough delegates will be in hand "when the voters have spoken on June 7th," when the last major primaries occur. Dukakis, who has used the metaphor of the marathon to describe his effort, has steadily and relentlessly, if unflashily, mowed down the other candidates, until only Jesse Jackson is left. Jackson's continuing fight, in which Dukakis has been defeating him by margins of two to one or more in the major contests, is not for the nomination but for an as yet undefined position in Democratic Party politics. Though the Dukakis people are not completely at ease about what might happen in the California primary, on June 7th, since Jackson is making a major effort there and Californians have a way of registering a protest vote (they have voted against the front-runner in every Democratic contest since 1972), the elimination contest for the Democratic nomination is over. (Jackson will effectively skip New Jersey, which also has a lot of delegates at stake on June 7th, in part because its rules are less advantageous to him.) Talk of the Democrats having a brokered Convention, or a brokered process before the Convention, ceased (with the exception of a few diehards) after New York. Whether or not the public is overjoyed at the choice it is now presented with, the Presidential candidates are the result of the kind of process we have—putting a premium on planning, doggedness, and money—and they won fair and square. Whether any other, "better" nominees could have come out of any other, "better" process is unknowable and academic. Now the nation is embarked on a mystery: despite the certainty with which opinions are rendered, no one can know now which candidate will win. Current polls are meaningless, and predictions are only guesses. Later on, when the outcome is known, there will be a lot of "of course"s, but there is no "of course" now. Hand-wringing over the candidates and the rest of the general election is now fashionable, but those who say, fashionably, that the election will be "dull" understand neither the candidates nor what the fight for the greatest power this nation confers is all about.

There is little question that at the end of the Democratic Convention we will witness a familiar tableau (only the faces will be different), as Dukakis and Jesse Jackson—and Albert Gore and Richard Gephardt and Paul Simon and Bruce Babbitt, and maybe even Gary Hart (who is a bit of a lost soul these days)—stand at the podium, arms raised in unity. Dukakis has to take a number of steps to get there from here, and to be careful, but what is forgotten every four years is that the losing candidates have almost as much need to be there as the winning one does (even if, as in the case of Edward Kennedy in 1980, the loser seeks to avoid the raised, clasped arms). Obviously, for a number of reasons, Dukakis's getting to that point with Jackson is complicated, but it will happen; in the end, Jackson has no choice. As it turned out, Jackson's victory in Michigan, in late March, was also his undoing, as it led Democrats to rally around Dukakis as the most feasible, and available, alternative to Jackson, and to proceed as if it were a two-man race. Michigan set the Dukakis campaign's plans back, but one Dukakis adviser says, "Michigan was the best thing that happened to us." The event not only concentrated the mind of the Democratic Party but taught the Dukakis campaign some lessons. (One measure of a campaign is how quickly it learns from its mistakes.) Gone were the talk of "inevitability" and the numerous appearances of Dukakis with political endorsers (what Dukakis's campaign manager, Susan Estrich, calls "blue suits") while Jackson was out there taking his case to the people. Dukakis literally rolled up his sleeves and tried harder. When Albert Gore was unable to be a viable third candidate in New York, Jackson's hopes of winning that state were destroyed, and Dukakis started rolling up large margins over Jackson, and it was over. After New York, Jackson seemed unprepared for a two-man race.

The New York primary was a nightmare for all three Democratic candidates—all of whom were glad to get out of the place once the contest was over—as well as for a great many citizens of New York. Dukakis's decisive victory—he got fifty-one per cent to Jackson's thirty-seven per cent and Gore's ten per cent (forcing Gore from the race)—may have sealed the nomination for him, but not without considerable discomfort. Dukakis now says he realized that he would be the nominee, and reached what for him was a high, on the beautiful spring Sunday before the voting, when he and his wife, Kitty, marched up Fifth Avenue hand in hand, in a parade marking the fortieth anniversary of the founding of Israel. One could see it in their faces: the recognition that the serious-minded, formerly obscure governor and his equally determined wife were about to realize their dream, become among the most famous people in the world, and could actually contemplate moving into the White House next year. The outcome of the primary was never in as much doubt as the Dukakis people were saying it was in the closing days—to assure a high turnout of Dukakis supporters—and Dukakis could have the satisfaction of having won the state without the support, which he had sought, of either Governor Mario Cuomo or New York Mayor Edward Koch. But the dark nature of the New York primary left a shadow. And the candidates, including the winner, were all but lost in the explosion of racial and religious hatred.

It was another in Dukakis's string of lucky breaks that Koch did not endorse him, though the Dukakis people thought their candidate would receive the Mayor's blessing and were disappointed when Gore received it instead. Koch's manic, running stream of invective against Jackson was a major embarrassment to Gore and made a bad atmosphere in New York still worse. ("Do you want a President who under stress is not capable of telling the truth?" Jackson has "character flaws.") Even without Koch, the story of the New York primary had become blacks versus Jews, and what the candidates were saying on other subjects was drowned out. Cuomo hurt himself by his indecision (accompanied by a string of impenetrable statements) over whether he would endorse a candidate, though it had been clear for some time that his best interests lay in remaining neutral, as he eventually did. Jackson's victory in Michigan may well have been a factor in Cuomo's decision not to endorse Dukakis—after Michigan a number of Democrats held back their endorsements of Dukakis for fear of appearing to be trying to stop Jackson, and thus offending blacks. By the time, shortly before the New York primary, that Cuomo more or less said he would not accept a draft, it appeared all the more that he had actually been hoping for one.

Gore, meanwhile, had got himself into a public argument with Cuomo over his attacks on Dukakis and Jackson, and then even when he toned down the attacks he got into long explanations of why a statement of a difference between him and Dukakis or Jackson was not an attack. Gore's basic problem was, as it had been in most contests outside the South, that people didn't much like him. (New Yorkers do have a way of being more explicit about these things.) Moreover, his campaign still had no rationale. By the end, David Garth, who apparently thought he had signed on with a hot property, and who made mediocre ads for Gore, was publicly dumping on his candidate. Two days after the New York primary, Gore made a graceful withdrawal speech—graceful withdrawal speeches are de rigueur this year—but he did not release his delegates, many of whom want to go to the Convention but not as Jackson delegates. This was acceptable to Jackson, because, as Gore explained to him in an hour-long meeting on the night of the New York primary, many of Gore's delegates would have gone to Dukakis. Also, according to a Jackson associate, Jackson appreciated the fact that Gore had sought him out that night; despite some tensions, Jackson and Gore had maintained frequent contact throughout the primaries. Gore, who was obviously dismayed by Koch's performance, had sent word to Jackson that he was unhappy about it.

Gore's advisers say that, in the end, despite the embarrassment, Koch's endorsement was a net plus, because Gore's campaign was all but dead at that point. For better or for worse, the endorsement got Gore some attention. He came out of the nomination contest with some new problems: a debt of at least $1.8 million; increased unhappiness with him on the part of Senate colleagues (among whom he had never been terrifically popular because of his egocentrism even as senators go), because of his criticism of the letter that thirty of them had signed criticizing the Israeli government; and problems with blacks in Tennessee, who were angered by his attacks on Jackson. The Gore people say that Jackson will make some appearances with Gore. There have been numerous analyses of the tactical mistakes the Gore campaign made: essentially, it had no strategy for what to do after March 8th ("Super Tuesday"), and followed several concurrent strategies, dipping into states it couldn't win and squandering the candidate's time and money—and some of his advisers think he should have got out of the race after Wisconsin; but the problems went deeper than that. (Future tacticians will probably decide that Gore's fate shows that a candidate has to run in every state, starting with Iowa, that "momentum" can be decisive.) Gore never figured out what his candidacy was about, and the persona he presented to the voters was remote and unclear. Some of his associates are already talking about his making another try in four years.

While the Middle East is often a topic in the New York primary, with the candidates bidding for the Jewish vote, it became more of one this time, because of Gore's upping the ante by essentially backing the Israeli government's opposition to the Administration's efforts to get negotiations going, and because of Jackson's past sympathy for the P.L.O. Jackson was all over the lot on this in the course of the primary—at one point saying that as President he would not negotiate with the P.L.O. and at another taking positions more sympathetic to the P.L.O. On this, as on a number of other matters, Jackson (who has Arab-American support) both listened to and acted upon the conflicting advice of his advisers —a trait that continues to cause problems, and that may well make his path to the Convention an unsteady one. Dukakis was extremely fortunate that the great preponderance of Jewish voters in New York were primarily concerned with making sure that Jackson did not win, and understood that a vote for Gore could help Jackson—the message that a vote for Gore was a vote for Jackson was made unmistakably clear—and therefore chose to overlook the fact that Gore was "better" on Israel than Dukakis was. This tendency was disturbing to some Jewish leaders, who felt that it would be a disincentive to future candidates to staunchly take their side, and this concern was believed to be one of the factors that motivated Koch to support Gore. At the same time, many blacks saw the New York primary as the culmination of an effort by the Democratic Party establishment and the media to gang up on Jackson.

The decision of most New York Jews to go with Dukakis was a great relief to his aides, who knew that he had not done particularly well in a critical meeting with Jewish leaders. Though Dukakis, in his speech to the Conference of Presidents of Major American Jewish Organizations, on April 11th, blamed Arab leaders for the impasse in the Middle East, he removed from his speech text a line, urged upon him by his advisers, pledging his opposition to a Palestinian state, and in the question-and-answer session that followed continued to sidestep such a pledge. While his advisers said at the time that this showed that Dukakis is his own man, they were actually very worried. At this meeting, Dukakis also suggested that the status of the city of Jerusalem is negotiable— not only is the possibility of the internationalization of Jerusalem anathema to Israelis but Dukakis's suggesting that the question was negotiable undercut Israel's negotiating position—and shortly after the meeting made himself available to the press to clarify this statement, saying that he had always supported a unified Jerusalem under Israeli rule. But there were also other matters on which Dukakis ruffled the sensibilities of many people in his audience. Several thought that his frequent references—fifteen by some counts—to the fact that his wife is Jewish were heavy-handed, and even condescending; and his telling of his wife's having been called to the Torah upset Orthodox Jews in the room, who forbid such a thing. To some members of his audience, he seemed to have not given his subject serious thought—to be winging it. In her own campaigning in New York, Kitty Dukakis told Jewish audiences that her father, Harry Ellis Dickson, an associate conductor of the Boston Pops orchestra, hoped that his son-in-law would win the Presidency so that he could conduct the Boston Pops in the East Room and conduct the first Seder in the White House. Bush, in New York, pounced on Dukakis's refusal to rule out a Palestinian state, and his advisers say that much will be made of this, but they are also uneasy about the advantage Kitty Dukakis can provide her husband among Jewish voters. Moreover, Dukakis, in a major change in his political persona, has in this campaign made use of his own ethnicity, not only making himself appealing to Greek audiences, who get very excited about him, but also making himself into a sort of generic ethnic—the successful son of immigrants, who talks proudly about his parents and their success. (He was reportedly advised to do this by Cuomo.) His cousin Olympia Dukakis, who had just won an Academy Award for playing an Italian mother in "Moonstruck," was imported to New York to spread the lagniappe. If some voters thought she was Italian, so much the better.

But though Dukakis did not run a particularly wonderful campaign in New York, he stayed steady—his equanimity is an important asset—and his self-righteous insistence on running a "positive" campaign played out well for him amid the maelstrom. (Dukakis took oblique shots at Jackson and Gore when necessary.) By keeping his head down, he got through it, but others dominated the agenda. (Dukakis continued to tell voters, "I am what I am.") Both Dukakis and Gore suddenly started talking a lot about drugs, prompting Jackson, whose anti-drug effort preceded even his 1984 Presidential campaign, and who talks to young people about drugs with great effectiveness, to say that he expected his rivals to echo another of his themes by saying, "I am somebody."

And Dukakis made another mistake in New York that shows a vulnerability his campaign knows must be dealt with. In an interview with the *Daily News*, he insisted, several times, that the position of the Israeli government on negotiating with the P.L.O.

is something other than it is (he said that Israel would negotiate with the P.L.O. if the P.L.O. recognized its right to exist), and eventually had to be corrected by Representative Stephen Solarz, of New York, who had endorsed Dukakis and was accompanying him. This was another sign of Dukakis's arrogance—his relying excessively on the fact that he is a quick study. (It also displayed his stubborn streak.) The vulnerability is the combination of Dukakis's still superficial grasp of foreign policy combined with his firm belief that he knows more than he does. His advisers are hoping to persuade him to spend more time on foreign policy once the nomination is wrapped up, but they have been trying all year to persuade him to spend more time on it. His positions on nuclear weapons don't hang together, and there are other weaknesses in what he has been saying. He has, however, been taking opportunities to say that he would use force in various circumstances—he even presents himself as eager to do so, answering such questions quickly (sometimes too quickly) and affirmatively—and intends to make it difficult for Bush to paint him as a weakling or a naïf. (Some of the things Dukakis says would scare the daylights out of people if they were said by a right-winger.) Besides, some of the things Dukakis gets wrong are details that confuse the public; what will matter more are the impressions the voters have of him and Bush, which man they think is tougher.

Inexorably, the Dukakis campaign is working to roll up the delegate count. Dukakis now has 1,597 delegates (of the 2,081 now needed for the nomination), to 944 for Jackson, with 587 delegates committed to other candidates and 518 as yet uncommitted. The Dukakis people say that, while they want to keep the delegate count growing, they don't want to do it in a way that makes it look as if they are trying to strong-arm their way to the nomination, or that offends Jackson, or that is unattached to what the voters are saying. But there is also a logic in this for elected politicians, who do not want to get too far astray from their followers. And Jackson, in a meeting with House Democrats last week, said that one way to ensure his followers' enthusiasm for the Democratic ticket would be for more super-delegates to vote for him. He is seeking to give pause to elected politicians who might take their black votes for granted and support Dukakis. Jackson, who has

been complaining that his delegate count does not reflect his popular vote, is not expected to mount a challenge to the rules, as he
did in 1984, or at least a successful one, because they have since
been changed in his favor and he accepted those changes. But
Jackson, says a close adviser, doesn't think in terms of ruling
something in or out, and takes things a step at a time. He does
feel, the adviser says, that if the number of his super-delegates is
very at odds with his proportion of the popular vote this would
be a sign of exclusion, and could well affect his enthusiasm for
the Democratic ticket. The Dukakis people say that the rules should
not be changed retroactively. (They may be prepared to discuss
changes for the future.) Just in case, however, they are getting
prepared for challenges of the rules or credentials by Jackson,
and making sure that they have control over the relevant Convention committees. Jackson of course might also mount a fight
over the platform, which Party leaders are trying to keep vague.

Dukakis, consistent with the methodical way he has run his
campaign, has had an operation in Washington for some time,
using a whip system on Capitol Hill and "surrogate advocates"—
all manner of supporters, including former members of Congress
and lobbyists (sometimes these are the same thing)—to win over
members of Congress to the Dukakis candidacy. The Mondale
campaign, in which some of the Dukakis people served, stands as
a model for a number of things that the Dukakis campaign wants
to avoid. One of these is having it appear, as the Mondale people
did, that the delegate accumulation toward the end came simply
as a result of political machinations, which, in combination with
some other things—such as the appearance of pandering to interest groups, and the parading of Vice-President potentials (including two women, a black, and a Hispanic) before the press—
contributed to an impression of Mondale as a political hack. But
some politicians are holding back from endorsing Dukakis for
their own reasons. Some who didn't endorse Dukakis early, when
it counted more, see no great reward in endorsing him now. Some
are still loath to offend Jackson's followers among their constituents, and a number of members of Congress, particularly from
the South and Southwest, think that Dukakis will lose the general
election, at least in their territory, and that supporting him would
be a liability.

Paul Simon, who also did not release his delegates—though

the Dukakis people are at work to take them from him—says he still contemplates the possibility that Dukakis might stumble and the Party might still turn to someone else (not him, he says), who might generate more enthusiasm (Mario Cuomo, Bill Bradley, Dale Bumpers), and that he might still play a role. But his position also has to do with the desire of other Illinois politicians, as it has all along, to go to the Convention. He says that some senators are holding back on endorsing Dukakis less because they have strong negative feelings about him than because they want to remain free to turn elsewhere. Though Gephardt has released his delegates, he has asked his congressional supporters to stick with him until the Convention—this would give Gephardt leverage for who knows what, and some of his congressional supporters entertain the idea of his being tapped for the Vice-Presidential slot. Releasing whatever power one might have is unnatural for a politician, especially if he has made great exertions to obtain it. An influential Southwestern congressman whom the Dukakis forces had especially hoped to win over says that he is staying with Gephardt "because that's the safest place to be." Staying with Gephardt gives some members of Congress a place to park rather than risk their political necks with conservative whites by backing Dukakis or offend their black constituents. Moreover, Representative Les Aspin, Democrat of Wisconsin and, as chairman of the House Armed Services Committee, a centrist on defense matters, has been privately telling his Democratic colleagues that Dukakis's defense program makes no sense. (Aspin says he is hopeful that Dukakis will sort this out.)

Some senators and congressmen feel that they are in for another Jimmy Carter—another President who would have to be educated, another President from an alien culture. The frequent likening of Dukakis to Carter is facile, but understandable: both men ran for the Presidency from a governorship, both are technocratic, humorless, and confident of the power of their brains to overcome obstacles. The Dukakis people have recently taken additional steps to soothe and woo Washington politicians: Dukakis and top campaign people have made trips to the capital to seek support and assuage worried members of Congress (with the Dukakis headquarters in Boston, the two worlds seldom meet), and some respected Washington figures have been added to the campaign roster, though their roles are for the moment undefined. One close observer of the campaign says, "They need to be seen to be reaching out." The Dukakis people also emphasize that Dukakis is listening to certain respected members of Congress on foreign policy, which unwittingly underscores the need for him to do so. (The Dukakis campaign wants to get away from the impression that the candidate is surrounded by Harvard.) Some people, in Washington and elsewhere, having missed the boat by advising other candidates, are now trying to hustle, even muscle, their way into the Dukakis campaign. The Dukakis people talk quite a bit about their attempts at "outreach," and their intention to work with national Democrats on issues, and also to begin to build alliances for the time when Dukakis may be President and have to govern. While there is no reason to doubt that they have these sincere intentions, what the exercise really seems to be about is playing to large egos, bridging a culture gap, making people more comfortable with Dukakis.

Then, there is the relationship with Jackson to be worked out. On one level, Dukakis is working out the relationship simply by beating him soundly. (He defeated him in Pennsylvania sixty-seven per cent to twenty-seven per cent, and, the following week, in Ohio sixty-three per cent to twenty-eight per cent and Indiana seventy per cent to twenty-two per cent, and, on Tuesday, by large margins in West Virginia and Nebraska.) At the same time, shortly after New York the Dukakis campaign started to send the message to Jackson that if he wanted to face large defeats on several Tuesdays, so be it, and if he wanted to fold 'em Dukakis was ready to talk. Dukakis and Jackson have actually spoken weekly, the morning after primaries, and chat in the course of joint appearances. But Dukakis, according to his advisers, has taken care not to give the appearance of thinking that he has the nomination sewed up, not only to avoid riling Jackson but also to eschew "inevitability" and avoid a political backlash (for instance, in California).

Jackson has been buffeted by conflicting political advice, exhausted, and was for some time after New York in a bad mood (the latter two were connected). He felt battered by the events surrounding the New York primary and, having believed some of the predictions that the race was tight there, and even that he might win, was disappointed in the result. After New York, Jackson congratulated Dukakis for his "splendid" campaign, and for a while was almost playful with him. But then, at the instigation of some of his more ideological advisers, he began to press Dukakis to make more of a commitment to spending for certain domestic programs and pressuring South Africa, and also to pledge to send arms to the Marxist government of Mozambique, which is under attack by forces backed by South Africa. Jackson is surrounded by a free-floating group of advisers, any part of which gets his ear at a given time, and some of whom take pride in showing how muscular they can be on his behalf. His less ideological advisers feel that Jackson's pushing Dukakis toward more leftish positions has simply resulted in helping Dukakis, who didn't give, come across as a moderate, and got Jackson away from what his campaign was about.

Dukakis, meanwhile, ran in Pennsylvania and Ohio as "a full-employment Democrat"—he said, "I'm a dyed-in-the-wool, true-blue, full-employment Democrat"—but it is clear that he is not to be confused with Hubert Humphrey, because he is not offering the full-employment programs of old, nor is he espousing old Democratic redistribution policies. Dukakis talked, for example, of bringing to western Pennsylvania, where a number of steel mills have been shut down and unemployment is relatively high, the recovery and high employment that Massachusetts has experienced. But the parallel is questionable. No candidate has a solution for the laid-off steelworkers, because there may not be one: a revival of the steel industry would involve new techniques, using fewer workers. (Dukakis did tell workers in Pennsylvania that he won't be able to get back to the same employment levels of eight or ten years ago, but this was not a prominent part of his speeches.) Dukakis proposes a "Fund to Rebuild America," of a half-billion dollars, which would be used as "leverage" to restore prosperity across the country, through "teamwork" among business, labor, and government. This is something approaching an industrial policy, of which Gary Hart spoke in 1984, and which some Democratic economists champion, but how and whether it could bring prosperity to the land is unclear. And Dukakis is as yet unformed, and apparently still to be tutored, about macro-economics and monetary policy. Jackson, seeming more resentful as time went on, complained that while he had submitted a budget Dukakis had not—any proposed budget, of course, raises questions, and Dukakis is seeking to avoid such questions and commitments. In

response to Jackson, Dukakis says, in his snappish way, that anyone who says that you should submit a budget now "doesn't know
what budgeting is all about." Dukakis is said to be haunted by his
having had to raise taxes when he first became governor, after
campaigning on a pledge not to do so, and to believe this was one
of the things that led to his defeat for reëlection in 1978. Jackson
complains that Dukakis "would manage Reaganomics, I want to
change Reaganomics."

Some of the Jackson people's tendency to go off on their own
hasn't been particularly helpful to their candidate. Shortly after
New York, Gerald Austin, his campaign manager, and Willie Brown,
the Speaker of the California Assembly and his campaign chairman, started saying that Jackson should be considered for the
Vice-Presidential slot on the Democratic ticket. Jackson, annoyed
at such public suggestions that the nomination fight was over,
publicly told them to cut it out. (Jackson was also unhappy that
his national campaign had lost control of his schedule in New
York and Pennsylvania, and had him essentially appearing before
black audiences, which left him little opportunity to broaden his
base. For a variety of reasons, he received less of the white vote
in these states and Ohio than he had in some earlier contests.)
Recently, Brown, in a talk with *Wall Street Journal* editors and
reporters, issued a series of demands on Jackson's behalf—which
other Jackson advisers didn't find helpful. A number of people
have been trying to set themselves forth as the ones to be nego-
tiated with on Jackson's behalf, but the Dukakis people are going
on the assumption that the person to negotiate for Jackson will
be Jackson, when he is ready.

Jackson appears to be aware that Dukakis does not plan to
offer him the Vice-Presidential slot (Dukakis has already sent that
signal), and to have the self-knowledge to understand that it is
not a role he would be well suited for; he is also said to understand
that if he were on a ticket that lost he would be blamed. But he
also has the problem of coming away from his highly successful
—in its own terms—Presidential campaign with enough to satisfy
his followers. The press has helped to get his followers' expectations up by continually raising the question of whether Jackson
will, or should, be on the ticket; polls that "show" that a ticket
with Jackson on it would win are, like many polls, the result of
people's telling pollsters what they think is the right thing to say.

The Dukakis people understand that Jackson must be treated with sensitivity and—to use a word he used four years ago—respect. Jackson himself has indicated that he might like the position for which he is perhaps ideally suited—as the leader of a Democratic Administration's anti-drug crusade. There are a number of possibilities. Since Jackson in the end has no choice but to try to help the ticket (his standing would be significantly diminished if he didn't), what it will all come down to in the end is how Jackson chooses to play it. He is likely to give off conflicting signals before he finally decides.

In keeping with the displacement theory of political speculation, now that the question of who the nominees will be is all but officially settled, the speculation that went into that question now goes into the question of who the running mates will be. Both candidates will keep the answer as close to the chest as possible —it's the one surprise they have left for the Conventions, or shortly before—and it is probable that neither has made up his mind. But that doesn't discourage the speculation. Since Dukakis feels that he can't appear to be assuming that the nomination is in hand, his campaign says that he has sworn not to talk about a running mate until later. But there have been discussions within the Dukakis camp, and Dukakis himself has already sent some public signals.

Shortly after New York, in an interview with Thomas Oliphant, of the Boston *Globe*, Dukakis transmitted the thought that he would not ask Jackson—by laying out his criteria for the person to be on his ticket: that the person has to be credible as a potential President; that experience in foreign and defense policy is important (thus filling a Dukakis gap); and that consideration of other political factors, such as what region the person would presumably be helpful in (it doesn't always work out that way), would come only after the other criteria had been met. Of course, a Presidential candidate is not likely to admit that political factors would be paramount, and, in fact, all of Dukakis's criteria are political.

People close to Dukakis think that he may well have one or two names in mind, and that one of them most likely is Senator Sam Nunn, of Georgia, who is the consensus choice of a number of Democratic politicians. The argument for Nunn is that his stature on defense issues, on which he is a sort of conservative centrist, and his politically moderate record would make him the most helpful. Even those who think that even with Nunn as a running mate Dukakis can't carry most Southern states believe that Nunn would be helpful in numerous other states because he might bring moderate and conservative whites across the country back to the Democratic Party. Some even see him as potentially the factor that could seal California, with its conservative swing areas, for the Democratic ticket. The combination of Nunn's relative conservatism and Dukakis's fluency in Spanish leads some Democrats to dream of capturing Florida, Texas, or California. A lot of people with nothing better to do have argued that Dukakis should also offer Nunn the role of Secretary of Defense, which is a terrible idea (among other things, a President has to be able to fire his Cabinet officers, and if a Vice-President has any important role it is as a dispassionate adviser to the President about the competing claims of the Cabinet departments), or that Dukakis should offer Nunn the role of coördinator of foreign and defense policy. (This presents problems' as well.) The idea is to come up with something substantial enough to tempt Nunn to give up his current position, which he had long hankered for, as chairman of the Senate Armed Services Committee. While Nunn has not publicly or privately ruled out accepting the Vice-Presidential nomination—if it is offered—he also expresses a desire to stay where he is. Nunn is a proud man, as well as a cautious one, and is aware of the demeaning aspects of the Vice-Presidency, even with a well-intentioned President. He is also aware of the fact that if he accepted he might have to spend a good deal of time during the campaign explaining the many differences of view between him and Dukakis; this would cover domestic policy as well, where Nunn has a fairly conservative voting record, including on civil rights. (Some of Nunn's allies say that, because of this record, running as Vice-President might be the only way for him to get considered for the Presidency. Nunn, on the other hand, has to consider the impact on his stature if he ran and lost.) Lane Kirkland, the president of the A.F.L.-C.I.O., is enthusiastic about Nunn as the running mate because Nunn's views on foreign policy are closer to his than Dukakis's are and because labor, like most of the Democratic constituency groups, wants to win this time. Some liberal Democrats in Congress are willing to swallow Nunn's voting record in the interest of regaining the White House—and making the next Supreme Court appointments. One leading congressional Democrat told me that, while he is not enthusiastic about Dukakis, and doesn't much like Nunn, the Supreme Court's recent five-to-four vote to reopen a 1976 civil-rights decision jarred him into enthusiasm for a Dukakis-Nunn ticket. But Dukakis is described by associates as most disinclined to bargain away, or appear to bargain away, the Vice-Presidential slot.

The current thinking at the top of the Dukakis campaign is that if the Nunn idea does not work out Dukakis should go for the strongest national figure he can get, rather than pick someone because he might carry a certain state. Therefore, other names on the list the Dukakis hierarchy is preparing for him to consider are Bill Bradley (if he is available, which is doubted), John Glenn (a hero, military weight, plus Ohio), Daniel Inouye (Senate stature, a war hero, service on the Intelligence Committee, an appeal to minorities), House Majority Leader Thomas Foley (from the state of Washington and therefore possibly helpful in the West, highly popular, but considered unlikely to give up his place in line for the Speakership), and Dale Bumpers (another popular senator, a strong speaker, a Southerner, but has balked at running for the Presidency for what he said were family reasons). And then again Dukakis and his people might come up with an entirely new idea.

Bush has the luxury of spending longer on his decision, and waiting until after the Democratic Convention, in mid-July (the Republican Convention begins in mid-August), to weigh all the factors, including the Democratic ticket. A number of Republican Vice-Presidential names are floating around, and two criteria, aside from the usual high-minded ones, appear to be Bush's feeling of compatibility with his choice and the political exigencies of the Bush effort. In other words, a decision will be taken as to whether Bush most needs to mollify the moderates (which could lead him to a number of names) or the conservatives (which could lead him to Jack Kemp). The name of California Governor George Deukmejian has been floating around, but recently it has sunk in upon the Bush people that Deukmejian would be replaced by a Democrat and that this would not sit at all well with California Republicans. (The current political thinking is that Dukakis cannot win without California but that Bush can. Still, Lee Atwater, Bush's campaign manager, says, "I can see three, four ways we could win without California, but it would be no fun, so the easiest thing for us is to win California." When we spoke, a couple of days ago, Atwater was planning to go to California to scout the situation. Bush people say that because of Reagan's dominance Bush has had little exposure there.) Others said to be under serious consideration are Supreme Court Justice Sandra Day O'Connor and Kansas Senator Nancy Kassebaum (these may be names floated for political effect), Senate Minority Whip Alan Simpson (popular, from Wyoming, and perhaps helpful in the West), another Western senator or two, and a number of governors or ex-governors: Thomas Kean, of New Jersey (but an aristocratic preppie, like Bush); Lamar Alexander, (ex) of Tennessee; Richard Thornburgh, (ex) of Pennsylvania; James Thompson, of Illinois (his name always seems to be on the Vice-Presidential list); and even White House Chief of Staff Howard Baker (who has tried to be a Vice-Presidential nominee as well as a Presidential one, but hasn't shown much national political appeal). By the time the choices are made, some other names will probably be floated, some for political effect. That no one knows who the choices will be, and that sometimes the decision doesn't make any difference, does not discourage the speculation.

Though the outlines of the general election are already clear, something always happens, and some issue or other always develops, that no one can foresee. No one should doubt that this will be a tough, hard-fought election. Bush has shown himself to be tenacious, and his campaign staff has shown that it can play very rough; Dukakis is about as determined as a person can be, a tough cookie, and he has shown that he can play rough. The Bush people have been saying that they expect the election to be very close, and some people solemnly accept this as inside information, but what else can the Bush people say? They can't say that they expect to win, for fear of fostering lethargy in the troops; and they can't exactly say that they expect to lose. Some Bush people have been confident—overconfident, in the eyes of some Republicans—but others believe that Dukakis will not be easy to defeat. Atwater says, "He has shown that he's formidable, durable, and knows how to follow a plan." One Bush adviser said to me recently that among Dukakis's advantages are that he is a new face, that the public might decide after eight years of a Republican

Administration that it is time for a change, that Dukakis is very smart and has run a good campaign, he has largely avoided the traps set by the special interests, he speaks Spanish, has an ethnic appeal, and has a Jewish wife.

The Dukakis people themselves argue that their campaign has navigated through the special interests and avoided looking like Mondale four years ago, but Dukakis has made a few promises, including a very expensive one demanded by certain Social Security recipients, who feel that they didn't get as large a windfall from a change in the law as other retirees got. In New York, he also made a little-noticed statement, to a senior-citizens forum, that he favored ending the taxation of half of Social Security benefits of those with an income over twenty-five thousand dollars. (This was imposed in the 1983 reforms of Social Security for budgetary and equity reasons; it brings in about three and a half billion dollars a year. A number of Democrats think the tax should, if anything, be increased.) Dukakis has also told certain peace groups what they wanted to hear, including that he supports a ban on the flight-testing of new missiles—a position that some other Democrats think is unwise. Dukakis has also stated at various times that various objectives would be his first priority: he would introduce legislation to reform campaign financing (he hasn't talked about that for a while), and more recently he said, "If I'm elected President, there will be an agenda ready to go that already has a congressional majority: minimum wage, welfare reform, plant closings, health care, housing." At other times, he has said that his priorities will be job creation and education. In New York, he told the audience of Jewish leaders that the first thing he would do as President would be to go into round-the-clock negotiations on the Middle East. But Dukakis has shown in his campaign for the nomination a fleetness of foot, an elusiveness, that makes him hard to pin down and doesn't leave him on the defensive for long. Peter Teeley, Bush's press secretary, says, "I think Dukakis will be like a moving target; he adds up to a candidate that is a greased pig."

Dukakis's response to questions about whether he has sufficient foreign-policy credentials (a dumb question to ask him, since he has a pat response) continues to be that Bush may have a long résumé but he was sitting in the room when Reagan made decisions to sell arms to the Iranians. His response to questions about whether his claim to have created the "Massachusetts miracle" is valid (it is only in part) is to smile at the question and cite statistics about Massachusetts' low unemployment rate, and Dukakis's people feel that the public won't want to get bogged down in the minutiae of what, exactly, Dukakis did and did not do for the state. Dukakis was recently hit with a substantial revenue shortfall, due to slower growth in Massachusetts, causing the cutting back of various social programs, and the Bush people will undoubtedly make as much of this as they can. Dukakis's response is that he'll deal with the matter by making the "hard decisions" Reagan has avoided to balance the budget. (Massachusetts' constitution requires a balanced budget, and, of course, the state has no Pentagon.) Dukakis's people know, with some unease, that another target for Bush will be Massachusetts' program, supported by Dukakis, allowing convicts, including first-degree murderers, brief furloughs after ten years in jail. (This was changed after a convicted murderer on furlough escaped and committed rape.) Challenged on this by Gore, in New York, Dukakis gave a rather lame response, and can be expected to respond by asserting that Massachusetts has a tough criminal-justice system. The Dukakis people know that Bush will also campaign against Dukakis as an opponent of the death penalty for drug pushers—which a large majority of the public supports.

Bush and his campaign people have already been working to depict Dukakis as a Northern Jimmy Carter and a Kennedy-style Massachusetts liberal all rolled into one. Not all Bush advisers are happy with this negative strategy, especially at a time when it is also important to start painting a positive picture of Bush and take him out of Reagan's shadow. Also, it bespeaks worry. Bush talks about Dukakis's probably taking us back to the "malaise" of the Carter period, but this point about a misused quote of Carter's has become a bit tired, and Dukakis will argue that the campaign is about the future. Bush also says that the issue is the future, but he is having a harder time defining what he means by that. His advisers say that he has been spending a lot of time with experts, in Washington and on the road, on such subjects as education and drugs and health care (why is he just now learning about these things?), and that he will shortly give a series of speeches about where he wants to take the country. Thus far, Bush has had trouble enunciating a message, and in his attacks on Dukakis he often appears on the defensive. Bush charges that Dukakis says that "it's midnight in America" and that he talks about "pink slips" and gloom, but though it is true that Dukakis talks about laid-off workers he campaigns as an optimist to whom nothing is impossible (even if he is hazy about how he will do it). Some Bush people (and perhaps Bush) are dismayed by Reagan's announcement that he will veto the trade bill because of a provision requiring companies to give employees sixty days' notice of plant closings. The issue is largely political on both sides: the Democrats, prodded by labor unions, saw a good issue in the plant-closings provision, and put it in the trade bill, which had been worked on for three years, in the view that, whether or not Reagan accepted the provision, the Democrats couldn't lose. Reagan was responding to the U.S. Chamber of Commerce and probably his own instincts. Most companies already announce closings well in advance.

Dukakis has begun to show how he will handle the "liberal" issue. In the recent primaries, he has told voters that it's not conservative to pile up the kind of deficit that Reagan has, and that he has cut taxes and balanced budgets. (He also does not rule out raising taxes.) The Dukakis people have not had as much time as the Bush people to develop the general-election issues (and the Republicans boast about their formidable research effort on Dukakis's record), because they still have the nomination to wrap up. But an adviser says that the Dukakis side will counter the Dukakis-as-Carter argument with challenges to Bush on whether he is attached to Reagan completely or is his own man, and say that either answer will cause Bush problems.

And the Democrats will have fun trying to stick Bush with Edwin Meese and the "sleaze" issue, whether or not Meese remains Attorney General through this fall. A report by an independent counsel on Meese's role in the Wedtech scandal is due soon, but even if Meese is not charged with an indictable offense (the independent counsel, James McKay, has already said he probably would not be) he would still be in a lot of trouble as a result of his numerous ethical lapses—more come out each day. Presumably, there is a higher standard for an Attorney General than that he hasn't been indicted. The sudden resignation, in late March, of two high Justice Department officials, along with four assistants (followed by three more resignations later), had the desired effect of getting Washington's attention on the fact that something was very wrong at the Justice Department, and Meese has had an embarrassingly hard time getting respectable people to fill the high-level slots. Morale at the Justice Department is terrible; officials there don't want to push new policies now, for fear that Meese's name on them would doom them. The country has recently been treated to what has become the standard libretto for these matters: word is leaked that Mrs. Reagan, high White House officials, and old friends of the President want the offender to leave office, but the President stands by his man. After the leaks, there is a round of statements that, perish the thought, no one is trying to get So-and-So out of office. The story usually ends with So-and-So leaving, and though both Reagan and Meese are stubborn and prideful men, a number of people think that Meese will be gone before the election. The Bush people desperately want him gone, and know that Bush will be taunted to criticize Meese or be seen as a "wimp." A previous victim of the ouster strategy, Donald Regan, who is still hopping mad over having been pushed out unceremoniously, got his revenge by writing in his new book that Mrs. Reagan determined the President's schedule according to the advice of an astrologer. The White House says that the astrologer didn't affect substance, but a President's schedule is substance. The book is shallow and spiteful, and overlooks Regan's own considerable shortcomings, but it has the ring of authenticity. It shows Mrs. Reagan as a powerful and difficult force, and the President as passive and largely uninterested in what is going on around him. He is content, in Regan's picture of him, to speak to his advisers in generalities and to manipulate the symbols of the Presidency—which he does superbly.

Reagan has been plagued by ungrateful memoirs—by David Stockman; by his daughter Patti; by his adopted son, Michael; and, recently, by his former spokesman Larry Speakes, who wrote that he had made up some quotes that he had attributed to Reagan. The everyone-out-for-himself ethos of the Reagan Administration has come back to bite its leader. The book market and the speaking circuit are overloaded by former Reagan Administration officials, who have shown an unprecedented propensity for cashing in on government service. The lack of discipline within the Administration, another consequence of Reagan's passivity, continues to cause him damage; his inability to establish close relationships with anyone other than his wife left a loyalty gap.

The oddest thing about the Speakes story is that Reagan didn't notice the manufactured quotes—or, perhaps, as a former actor, he thought they went with the job.

Though Bush is vulnerable on the Iran-Contra issue—his explanations don't hold water, and there are more questions about his role, and trials could be under way this fall—Dukakis will have to come up with more than that on foreign policy. He criticizes Bush for his florid toast to Ferdinand Marcos during a trip to the Philippines in 1981. ("We love your adherence to democratic principles.") He will argue that the Reagan Administration has been delinquent on the Middle East and should have got involved sooner, and he will remain critical of the Nicaragua policy as "illegal." (There is a temporary truce in Nicaragua, and ceasefire talks between the Sandinistas and the Contras are limping along; both sides needed a respite.) But Dukakis does not grant that U.S. aid to the Contras got the Sandinistas to negotiate, just as he does not concede that the U.S. arms buildup got the Soviets to the table. He opposed the United States' initial taking of military steps to protect shipping in the Persian Gulf (so did Nunn and Henry Kissinger), and when, during the New York primary, there was a clash between U.S. and Iranian forces in the Gulf, he first said that he approved of the President's retaliation, and then, as the conflict grew, said he needed more information before he could comment. This was a reasonable position under the circumstances, but the Bush campaign plans to make much of it. Meanwhile, the United States has broadened its commitment to protect shipping in the Gulf.

Dukakis has already weighed in against Bush on the issue of drugs, arguing that he accomplished little as head of a Reagan Administration task force on drugs, and against the Reagan Administration for having done business with Panamanian leader Manuel Antonio Noriega, a known drug dealer. Dukakis (like Dole before him) raises the question of whether Bush, as a former director of the C.I.A., or as Vice-President, knew about Noriega's involvement in the drug trade. (Noriega is said to have received money from the C.I.A., and he was helpful in aiding the Contras.) Bush had said he didn't know about Noriega's drug activities until Noriega was indicted by Florida grand juries, in early February; more recently, he said that he didn't have "evidence" of them until the indictments. It's not clear that this is a question on which the

Presidency should be decided, but though Republicans will argue that the Carter Administration did business with Noriega, too, and also knew about drug activities in Panama, the issue does, as Bush's closest advisers know, present Bush with problems: "drugs" is a hot word, and Bush himself has said that he was Reagan's "co-pilot," so where was he on this (especially as head of the drug task force) as well as on the Iran-Contra matter? Is he telling the truth?

The Reagan Administration is now suffering acute embarrassment over the difficulty it ran into in trying to get Noriega to leave office, especially since, early this year, the President called for "democracy" in Panama and Secretary of State George Shultz said that Noriega had to go, and for some time Shultz and other officials publicly predicted that Noriega would be leaving the country soon. The policy was essentially initiated by Assistant Secretary of State Elliott Abrams, who, other Administration officials believe, was trying to find something that would divert attention from Nicaragua and demonstrate that we still have clout in Central America, show that he was against dictators of the right as well as the left, and put himself in better odor on Capitol Hill, where his having misled Congress on the Iran-Contra affair had earned him substantial enmity. Abrams talked Shultz into going along, and so the United States embarked on a public policy of overthrowing a head of government—and for a long time hasn't been able to pull it off. The policy was begun without clear thought being given to how to make it work. Other officials, reportedly including Treasury Secretary James Baker, Defense Secretary Frank Carlucci, and national-security adviser Colin Powell had serious reservations about the policy—Baker opposed the imposition of economic sanctions, which have had the effect of ruining the Panamanian economy and alienating Panamanians from the United States. But the combination of Congress's agitation (from left to right) about drugs and Noreiga, and the indictments (which weren't coördinated with other officials), eroded the position of officials who thought the policy was going too far too fast. Some of Abrams' more harebrained ideas, such as kidnapping Noriega or using United States troops to overthrow him, were scotched (and leaked) by others in the government. A number of deals with Noriega, including our dropping the indictments (this idea met with outrage on Capitol Hill), have been rumored in recent days, and most people think that he will be gone before long—but not on the terms the Reagan Administration had publicly stated, and long after the Administration said this would happen. Some officials say that our meddling strengthened Noriega's hand. The whole thing has taken on the aspect of comic opera.

Dukakis, of course, has his own vulnerabilities from things he has said about foreign and defense policy. Bush has already begun to attack his lack of experience in foreign policy, and to question his toughness. ("Can you imagine the Democrats standing up to Qaddafi and liberating Grenada?") The Dukakis campaign has begun to stage some foreign-policy events to make Dukakis appear "Presidential."

Those who think that the campaign for the Presidency will be "dull" haven't been watching the candidates. The coming campaign may not be inspiring, there may not be many lines that lift our hearts, but two determined politicians, each with a large number of determined people behind him, will be fighting over very large stakes. Neither man may be a rock star, or a spellbinder, but both are tough campaigners. If Dukakis is not the most compelling speaker, neither, certainly, is Bush. Bush, moreover, is an awkward campaigner, has a tin ear, and can panic, leading him to sound squeaky and say something silly. Dukakis has developed a way of speaking that has urgency and energy to it, while Bush has developed more self-control. (And his campaign keeps him largely cocooned from the press.) Neither man is very good at humor, but Dukakis every once in a while comes up with a line that seems to work; it seems to stem less from natural humor than from a knowledge that humor is part of the job. More efforts have been made to loosen up Dukakis's image: having him talk to children, toss a football, dance the Lindy (as well as Greek dances). Dukakis will be scrappy, but even he is aware that he sometimes goes overboard in debates, going from being scrappy to being unpleasant. While Bush is still developing his general-election message, Dukakis clearly will run as a can-do man, a doer; he argues that he can create jobs, points to a recently enacted universal-health-care program for Massachusetts (this had been worked up with the Presidential campaign in mind), argues that more should be done for the homeless. Both men say they are for doing more for education, but neither is proposing anything that will bring about the reformation that our school system desperately needs. Both candidates will use the economic facts that best suit their purposes: though there has been an unprecedentedly long period of economic growth, and unemployment is, at 5.4 per cent, the lowest it has been since 1974, the growth has been neither great nor even, and a number of polls continue to show that most Americans are worried about their economic future. Recent exit polls in large industrial states showed that blue-collar workers and independents were more inclined toward Dukakis than toward Bush. People close to Bush know that it is difficult for a party that has been in power for eight years to appear fresh and energetic. The Democrats, for all their own problems, do project an energy and a pragmatic desire to win.

While Dukakis comes across to many as a competent, can-do man, he also has characteristics that aren't particularly likable. The public may grow tired of them—before, or after, the election (if he is elected). Bush comes across as a likable man, who has had important experience, but who lacks definition and may be weak. Barring some event or the emergence of some issue that tips the scales, and barring any great mistake on the part of either campaign, the election may well be decided, as elections often are, not on arguments about policy but on the visceral sense of the voters—how they actually feel about the two candidates. And that's a decision that may well be made late in the game.

VIII

JUNE 23

Inexorably, Ronald Reagan is leaving the stage, and the two men who are fighting to succeed him are coming into more national focus. But Reagan, as he showed in the recent summit meeting in Moscow, can still command the spotlight. The exodus of officials continues. Though Chief of Staff Howard Baker, who announced last week that he would leave at the end of June, said that he wanted to spend more time with his ailing wife, one also senses that he, like the Administration, was running out of steam, and that he had grown tired from the many battles, several of which he had lost. Meanwhile, widely held, if ungrounded, assumptions about who will succeed Reagan have switched around. Despite the fact that nobody knows how the election will turn out, a large number of people who until a few weeks ago assumed that it was, as the phrase went, "George Bush's to lose," are now equally certain that Michael Dukakis will win. The same Bush campaign aides who were widely seen as geniuses when Bush quickly put away the Republican nomination are now viewed as floundering. If the polls change, so will this latest set of certainties. And other events, such as the growing Pentagon procurement scandal, which broke just last week and could well give Dukakis a "mess in Washington" issue, or something we don't yet know about, could also whang into the campaign at any moment, and shift assumptions some more.

What turned much of the thinking around recently was a set of polls, in mid-May, which showed Dukakis defeating Bush by a substantial margin. (The Gallup poll, which in mid-March had Bush defeating Dukakis fifty-two per cent to forty per cent, two months later had Dukakis defeating Bush fifty-four per cent to thirty-eight per cent; a New York *Times*/CBS News poll had Dukakis leading Bush forty-nine to thirty-nine; and a poll taken in California, which both sides say Dukakis must win in November

189

if he is to be elected, had Dukakis beating Bush by thirteen points.)
A *Wall Street Journal*/NBC News poll published last week also gave
Dukakis a big lead—forty-nine to thirty-six among most-likely
voters—and showed Dukakis running ahead of Bush in every
region in the country, including the South. And a Washington
Post poll published a couple of days ago had Dukakis leading Bush
by twelve points. The alarming—even enraging—thing for Republicans is that polls also show that a majority of people think
the Democrats would be better at dealing with the economy. Moreover, the *Wall Street Journal*/NBC News poll said that Bush trails
Dukakis by a two-to-one margin among blue-collar voters, and by
three to one among Democrats who say they voted for Reagan in
1984. To some extent, these various data are connected with the
voters' views of the two men, and to some extent with the desire
for change which usually comes after a party has been in power
for eight years. Lee Atwater, Bush's campaign manager, says,
"The worst problem we have is that we're fighting against the
cycle."

Though polls this far in advance of an election are usually
meaningless, a question as we now enter more deeply into our
national mystery is whether they might be predictive this time.
More than one Republican strategist thinks that they could well
be, at least as to the outcome if not the magnitude; even some
Republicans believe that Bush's problems as a candidate are so
serious as to be insurmountable. Bush aides, though privately
shaken and dismayed by the polls, insist that this trough will be
climbed out of; they point to the fact that in 1976 Gerald Ford
made up nearly all of a thirty-three-point deficit against Jimmy
Carter, after the Democratic Convention, and lost by only two
points. Dukakis and his aides, though obviously exhilarated by
the polls, have been preparing for a tough fight. The Bush people
say that Dukakis's lead is attributable to his having had a string
of victories over Jesse Jackson, who, they argue, is unpopular with
the nation as a whole, while Bush was largely on the sidelines. At
the same time, they say that the public doesn't know Dukakis very
well—and polls for the Dukakis camp confirm this. A number of
people, including some in the Bush camp, think that the Bush
people miscalculated by having their candidate relatively inactive
during the spring, while Dukakis was out there slugging—mainly
against Bush. And the Bush people threw such large resources

into putting the nomination away that the campaign had neared the legal spending limit at a time when Bush needed to be out and around more (though there are ways to get around the limit). The Dukakis campaign, by contrast, husbanded its resources carefully. One by-product of this difference in planning is that in the final weeks of the primary season Dukakis spent more time than Bush did in California, and the Dukakis campaign began to build a large organization there. The Bush people have one paid campaign worker in the state. Because the Republican Convention comes a month later than the Democratic one, the Bush campaign will have to wait longer for its federal funds for the general election. (Candidates don't receive the funds until they have been formally nominated by their parties.) A Bush campaign official says, "When we get the federal money in August for the general election, we'll throw everything, including the kitchen sink, at California." Bush might have benefitted from a longer nomination campaign, one that would have tested him more, sharpened his skills. There is little question that Dukakis has benefitted from having been tested longer.

Dukakis has his own vulnerabilities. One of them, as his campaign people know, has to do with his inexperience in foreign and defense policy, and the fact that his left-of-center defense policy has him outside the mainstream. The one bright spot for Bush in the recent *Wall Street Journal*/NBC News poll was that, by large margins, people felt that Bush would be better at dealing with the Soviet Union and maintaining a strong defense, and nearly half felt that Dukakis is too "inexperienced" in foreign policy. Dukakis's recent speech on these matters, in Washington, before the Atlantic Council, may not have helped much.

For all the talk about issues and themes, what we are in for is a tough fight for a majority (two hundred and seventy votes) in the electoral college, and both sides agree that Bush still has an advantage here, because of the historical voting patterns of a number of states in the South (including Florida) and the West. But the Dukakis people say that their polling shows Dukakis competitive in many states the Democrats usually lose, and for now they are talking about challenging Bush everywhere, in part to make him disperse his resources in defensive actions. Both sides will battle hard over Texas as well as California, and over some of the usually hard-fought big industrial states. The Vice-Presidential selections by both candidates will be made with the electoral-college math in mind. A rising prospect for Bush, at least in the speculation, is Robert Dole, who has been energetically campaigning for Bush and gives every sign of being interested. (Politicians can be marvelously flexible.) Dole could help in the Middle West and among Independents; he was the Republican Presidential candidate most Democrats least wanted to run against. As Dukakis comes more into focus, so will some of his less attractive personal traits: his touch of arrogance, his inclination to be flip. Reports of people who have been to see him to discuss issues are that he still isn't much of a listener. Dukakis is an acquired taste, and some, even if they have no particular predisposition against him, never acquire it. On the other hand, large numbers of people saw him in the course of the primaries as a steady, straight, down-to-earth, no-nonsense guy, a take-charge type of the sort they feel the country needs now. And with his success Dukakis acquired "winnerness": an almost mystical process in which a winning candidate, interacting with his public, takes on a kind of glow, gains more confidence, and seems to be of a larger dimension.

Any remaining doubts that this will be a rough campaign should be gone by now. While a large number of observers, and some Bush advisers, say that Bush must define himself, and what he is for, before he attacks Dukakis, other Bush advisers, and clearly Republican officials, believe that there is no time to be lost in tearing up Dukakis, in trying to "define" him before a positive definition of him settles in the public's mind. Bush, in attacking Dukakis himself, is taking a risk that this will not go over well with the voters he needs to attract, and will, in the parlance, "drive up his negatives"—which are, as the Dukakis people like to point out, unusually high for a Presidential candidate at this stage. (The May Gallup poll said that forty-one per cent of the respondents had a negative view of Bush, the highest for any major candidate at this point in an election since 1960, the first election year for which Gallup has comparable figures. Dukakis had a seventy-one-per-cent positive rating and only a fifteen-per-cent negative one.) The Dukakis people also point out that Albert Gore's attacks on Dukakis backfired. But for all Dukakis's pious talk about running a "positive" campaign, he will be, as he has been for some months, very tough in his own way. Increasingly, despite all its consideration of themes and "message," the Dukakis campaign is putting the emphasis on the contest between the persons Dukakis and Bush. Susan Estrich, Dukakis's campaign manager, says, "Ultimately, most Presidential campaigns are about character, broadly defined; they are a choice between two men, and which one the voters decide they trust with their future." The Bush people understand this point.

Issues, then, are for the most part symbols—code for what we are to feel about one man or the other. The symbols the Dukakis people draw upon range from issues to class, as they try to paint Bush—with some help from Bush—as a patrician who is out of touch with mainstream America. One Dukakis aide said, following Bush's Memorial Day retreat with advisers and experts at his family estate in Kennebunkport, Maine, "Every time they put that house on TV I thought it was worth a point or so." The Bush people are trying to establish that it is Dukakis who is out of step with the majority of the voters. The symbols the Bush people draw upon are Jimmy Carter, George McGovern, "tax and spend" Democrats who are "soft" on crime and a little short on patriotism. Bush said recently, "It'll be like the Nixon-McGovern race in '72 as far as the breadth of differences on issues."

When Dukakis, in California, wrapped up the nomination on the night of June 7th, his remarks signalled what is to come. He raised a series of questions on which he wants to draw the contrast between himself and Bush: "Every day between now and November, working Americans will be deciding whether we"—meaning himself and Bush—"understand their frustrations and dreams." Alluding to the President's veto (which has been sustained by the Senate) of the trade bill because of its provision on plant closings, he asked, "When people are shut out of factories with no warning, will we fight for their future?" He raised questions about the two candidates' independence. Dukakis's California victory was a substantial one (he defeated Jackson sixty-one per cent to thirty-five per cent), and his victories that night there and in New Jersey (where he defeated Jackson sixty-three to thirty-three), plus victories in Montana and New Mexico, plus the other delegates his campaign had collected, gave him more than enough delegates for the nomination, as his aides had predicted. (As of June 7th, Dukakis had 2,251.2 delegates to Jackson's 1,122.6 delegates.) On the day after the final primaries, Bruce Babbitt, Richard Gephardt, Paul Simon, and Mario Cuomo endorsed Dukakis, and last week Albert Gore, after doing some mending with his black constituency, endorsed Dukakis warmly, and Joseph Biden, who is recovering from surgery for aneurysms, endorsed him yesterday. That leaves Jackson and Gary Hart. The Dukakis campaign is going for a lot more than the required number of delegates, shooting for at least two thousand six hundred so as to have firm control of the Convention. And Dukakis is continuing to campaign—last week he went South, where he stressed being tough on drugs and crime, posing with policemen and the like, and next week he'll go to the Midwest—because he and his campaign think that both Jimmy Carter and Walter Mondale wasted valuable time and momentum by going to ground once they had their nominations wrapped up. And, the thinking goes, by their sitting in Plains, Georgia, and North Oaks, Minnesota, respectively, the last two Democratic Presidential candidates let the story become their search for a running mate and whatever Convention disputes might be developing. Dukakis hoped his travels could deflect some attention from those stories, but he was only partially successful.

Befevered attention hops from topic to topic in any election year, and recently the hot topics became whether Dukakis would put Jackson on the ticket, which he has no intention of doing, and whether there would be bloody fights over the platform. Like the question of who will be the candidates' running mates, the platform story is a quadrennial, and one that is soon forgotten. Dukakis's Vice-Presidential search has officially begun, with Paul Brountas, his close friend and campaign chairman, in charge; Dukakis and his people had been saying that the subject was verboten until after he had the nomination wrapped up, but of course they were considering it. Brountas, covering his tracks, saw, he says, over forty people in Washington last week, including some possible running mates—among them were Bill Bradley (who has publicly said he doesn't want it), John Glenn (who does want it), Sam Nunn (who has expressed strong misgivings), House Majority Leader Thomas Foley (who wants to become Speaker some day), and Senators Lloyd Bentsen, of Texas, and Bob Graham, of Florida, and Representative Lee Hamilton, of Indiana (who has risen in the speculation). Others are possible, and there's been speculation about Gore and Gephardt—but, among other things, it would be awkward to bypass Jackson for one of them. Brountas solicited a wide range of opinions as well as saw more people than were seriously being considered, but simple prudence was at work here: if the "short list" is too short, there is the danger of running low on options, and whoever is picked should have wide support. (After Graham's office let it be known this week that Graham had been sent a detailed questionnaire by Dukakis, the game became finding out who else had been sent one.) Bentsen and Graham are from key states, of course, but the Dukakis people used to talk about picking national figures, of being above such a consideration as whose presence on the ticket might guarantee them a key state (it doesn't always work out that way), and Dukakis himself has stipulated that experience in Washington and specific experience in defense and foreign policy would be requirements. Bentsen serves on the Intelligence Committee, but Graham, who was elected to the Senate in 1986, does not have the credentials that Dukakis has set forth. Their expressions of caution notwithstanding, Dukakis and his people are said to feel freer, as a result of the polls, to make what choice they want—that is, under less pressure to pick Nunn, who had been all the talk in political circles around the time of the New York primary, in mid-April. Though Nunn would bring formidable credentials to the ticket, there is the problem of his conservative voting record on domestic issues, and neither Dukakis nor Nunn may want the hassle (and Nunn likes being chairman of the Senate Armed Services Committee). Since the Dukakis people want to avoid the kind of parade of Vice-Presidential possibilities that was staged by both Carter and Mondale, they have sought to work out logistics by which Dukakis can clandestinely spend time with a potential running mate he barely knows. Meanwhile, there is the relationship with Jackson to be dealt with.

Jackson, constantly reminded that he has done something historic (no one expected him to do as well as he has done), subject to conflicting advice, possessor of a very large ego, and moody, has seemed confused lately. For all the speculation about what Jackson wants now, Jackson himself does not seem to know. His advisers, who can be roughly categorized as the Ideologues and the Sensibles, are in a continual struggle, and his actions proceed on a day-by-day, sometimes hour-by-hour, basis. Jackson is having even more trouble than the runners-up usually have in letting go. Despite the strain, campaigning for the Presidency, if one has enough success, is intoxicating, and it's difficult to walk away from the crowds, the cheers, the acclaim, and even the comforts of limousines and Secret Service protection. Like addicts, candidates come to need a regular shot of adulation. Candidates don't have to get airline tickets, or wait at gates; they don't even stop at stoplights. At the end of the primaries, Jackson was faced with the fact that he didn't have anything else nearly so interesting or exciting to do. He was constantly reinforced in the view that he had built a following and that he owes that following continuing leadership, which is in fact what most runners-up for the nomination come to believe. So, like Gary Hart four years ago and Edward Kennedy eight years ago, he will carry the fight to the Convention, even if it is unclear what he is to fight for. The trick is in knowing when and where to stop. On the night of the California primary, Jackson said his campaign would continue. Actually, Jackson did not do as well at the end of the contests as Hart (who won California) and Kennedy (who won both California and New Jersey) had done: he had only done well in a crowded field, and after New York, when it became a two-man race, he was routinely beaten by about two to one. (Contrary to earlier intentions, he campaigned in New Jersey despite its unfavorable rules, and the Dukakis people have agreed to give him more delegates.) His showing in California was not nearly as strong as many had expected it to be. As one way to keep going as the leader of a cause, Jackson also announced on the day after the last primaries that he would form a political-action committee, called Jackson Action, to back progressive candidates. As another way, he began to toy with the Vice-Presidency.

Though some people close to Jackson have never believed that he wants the job (he has told some he doesn't), and though Dukakis had said publicly that in effect Jackson doesn't have the qualifications he's looking for, and though polls show Dukakis winning with various people on the ticket but losing with Jackson, Jackson began demanding that he be given "serious consideration" for the Vice-Presidential slot. Then he stepped up the heat and seemed to be demanding that he be chosen; and then, some of the Sensibles having weighed in, he backed off a bit. Asked on "Meet the Press" a couple of Sundays ago whether he was insisting that

Dukakis ask him to be on the ticket, Jackson replied, "I do not want to push Mike Dukakis to that point." But he continued to push to some point. Following their meeting in Los Angeles on Tuesday night, Dukakis said that Jackson is under "serious consideration." Today Jackson said that he has made up his mind on whether he wanted to join the ticket but that he wouldn't divulge his decision. An adviser says that this was "inadvertent," that though Jackson doesn't want the job, even if it were offered, more has to happen before he makes his intentions known. (However, Jackson's receipt of the detailed questionnaire, the first step of a rigorous examination, is believed to have focussed his mind.) Some close to Jackson think he has known all along that the Vice-Presidential slot is not in the cards but have said that he won't publicly drop the idea until he sees what all the options are. Recently Jackson said, "If the Vice-Presidency agenda were not a matter of real discussion now, some of the other items of substance would have less meaning." Some Jackson advisers say that Jackson pushed for "serious consideration," or whatever, because he was becoming "invisible"—that is, other names were getting attention, and he was getting less, and that he merited at least serious consideration because of what he had done; other advisers tried to convince Jackson he should go on the ticket because of the precedent that would shatter, and the importance he would assume, and at times Jackson seemed to lean this way. He said, "The Vice-Presidency is not quite the top, but it's a long way from where I started."

It is nowhere written that the runner-up gets to be on the ticket; neither Kennedy nor Hart made such a claim, and each of them came in closer to the top than Jackson. It should be understood by now that the most important thing a Vice-President does is be ready to become President at any moment. Jackson has never held public office, and his record as a manager is not stellar. Considerable thought has been given by people in the Jackson and Dukakis camps to how to get both candidates out of this thicket, though these people know that Jackson is not easily programmed. Dukakis's saying that Jackson was under "serious consideration" was a move toward such a resolution. The next step would be for Jackson to thank Dukakis for his consideration, claim victory for himself and his constituency in the proceedings of the platform and rules committees, which are to meet this weekend, and decline further consideration. The situation was not made easier last week by several members of the Congressional Black Caucus (few of them natural allies of Jackson), who, after meeting with Jackson, made statements that he should be considered, or should be on the ticket, and that if he were not, said one, it would be for "racist" reasons. The Dukakis people, aware that expectations about Jackson's possibly being picked were being raised by Jackson and others (and that if Jackson allowed it his name could be put in nomination at the Convention for the Vice-Presidential slot), and also aware that the speculation and political pressures over Dukakis's choice could get out of hand, will try to have his running mate selected and announced in advance of the Convention.

Dukakis's approach thus far has been to meet with Jackson, listen to him, but not engage in protracted public negotiations, lest Jackson prove insatiable and Dukakis look weak. Dukakis campaign people have been saying for some time that they will compromise with Jackson on Party rules (for the future) and the platform where they can, and where they can't the issue will go to the floor of the Convention; they would not mind being seen defeating a Jackson proposal or two at the Convention. (The idea that the platform would be short and vague this year has been overtaken by political reality, but it might still be briefer than the forty-thousand-word document of four years ago.) The Sensibles around Jackson are essentially (but not entirely) in charge of his Convention planning. There has been a lot of talk between the Dukakis and Jackson camps about the platform, and the hope is that there can be disagreements without causing Armageddon. Thus far, the Dukakis people have acceded to Jackson's proposal that South Africa be labelled a terrorist state—figuring that was no big deal—but have made it clear that they will fight any proposals for higher taxes or a reduction in the defense budget. (Jackson is calling for a five-year freeze in defense spending, with no allowance for inflation.) It's not hard to see why the Dukakis people would not at all mind being seen on nationwide television defeating Jackson on the tax and defense proposals. They say they would also oppose calls for specific large increases in spending. At the heart of a comprehensive budget plan Jackson offered in California in late May were increased taxes on the wealthy, a cut in the defense budget, and more spending for various domestic programs. The Dukakis people are understandably loath to have any talk of tax increases in the platform. Dukakis continues to say that at least a hundred billion in unpaid taxes can be collected, which is doubtful, and that tax increases should only be a "last resort," and levied "on the basis of the ability to pay." Thus he is leaving himself some room for raising taxes.

Another issue the Dukakis people have said they will not compromise on, if Jackson pursues it, is a pledge that the United States would not be the first to use nuclear weapons. The big trouble might come if Jackson pursues a proposal that the platform call for the establishment of a Palestinian state. Some of Jackson's advisers and supporters are trying to dissuade him from pushing this proposal on the ground that it would once again stir tensions between blacks and Jews and cause a serious division within the Party; others around him, who encourage his emphasis on the Third World and who have helped him win the support of Arab-Americans, have been egging him on. Jackson, who is said to remain bitter about the New York primary, has been torn, but might compromise.

Dukakis has stood firm against putting out his own budget, saying that since we can't know all of the economic factors now, it would be "irresponsible" to do so; but no budget—even the ones put out by a President—can anticipate all of the economic factors. Bush, too, is declining to put out a budget, though even the broad-brush one he talks about (a "flexible freeze") counts on optimistic assumptions. Neither man wants to propose anything unpleasant, or anything that might divide the coalition each is trying to put and hold together. Specificity is something the press calls for, but both Dukakis and Bush know that with specificity come trouble and further questions; besides, Reagan ran the ultimate in unspecific campaigns in 1984 and got away with it. Yet Dukakis has stated a number of things he is for: "good jobs at good wages," "decent, affordable housing," a larger federal effort in anti-drug enforcement (including more money for the Coast Guard), more drug treatment, more aid to education, more health care and child care—and he often says of each of these things that it is "more important than MX missiles running around on railroad cars," or than "Star Wars." But his defense program also calls for improvements in conventional weaponry, which is very expensive. At the same time, he calls for holding defense spending to the current

real level (that is, the current level plus inflation). Some of the
things are to be paid for, Dukakis's people say, through the public-
private "partnerships" Dukakis vaguely refers to. But someone,
somewhere, has to pay for them.

The Dukakis people have long counted on his personal style
to convey various political messages. It is hoped that the fact that
he is himself a skinflint will ward off any idea that he would be a
"big spender," and he has been careful not to make explicitly
expensive promises. If he wins, the reckoning would come later.
His conservative personal habits are counted on to deflect any
concern that he might push upsetting social policies. To underscore this, the Dukakis campaign deliberately had him appear
before an audience of gays and lesbians in California, where, as
expected, he got a negative reaction when he repeated a position
he had taken in Massachusetts which assigns a lower priority to
gay and lesbian couples than to heterosexual couples who want
to be foster parents. Some Republican analysts were awed by this
Dukakis campaign tactic.

Dukakis is also supple, and can reverse field when necessary.
In California he said, in contradiction to what he had said in New
York, that Jerusalem should be the capital of Israel (in New York
he had said, to the distress of some Jewish leaders, that the subject
was negotiable). And he recently reversed an opinion he had offered in New York that Social Security income of the better-off
should not be taxed. The Dukakis campaign has put a fair amount
of time into anticipating the attacks that would come from Bush.
If Bush criticizes Dukakis for inexperience in foreign policy, Susan
Estrich says, "Every time he mentions foreign-policy experience,
I guarantee you we or someone on the Dukakis side will say, 'Oh,
really? What about Iran-Contra? What about Noriega?' " Dukakis
works in references to the Administration's dealings with Panamanian leader Manuel Antonio Noriega whenever he can, sometimes reaching pretty far to make the connection. When he is
asked about his opposition to the death penalty for drug "kingpins," which is now all the rage in Congress and which Bush
supports (Dukakis is against the death penalty altogether), he refers to the Administration's past dealings with Noriega. The Dukakis people say, and obviously hope, that foreign and defense
policy will have a lower priority in the coming election than domestic questions. Estrich says, "We'll ask who best understands

our lives, our problems, sees things the way we do: is it a Greek-immigrant son who is himself the product of the American dream, or is it the Kennebunkport Republicans?"

George Bush's challenge is to prevent that from being the question on which the election turns. A Republican strategist said to me recently, "Couldn't he have spent the Memorial Day weekend in Houston?" He went on, "The thing to watch in this election, the real point of difference, will not be over issues, but who owns what perceptual territory when the people go to the polls in November." Bush's mannerisms as well as some of the things he says underscore the fact that he is the child of privilege. Some of Bush's people have understood for some time that his largest political problem might be a cultural one. Life is unfair in many ways, and while a Democrat—a Roosevelt or a Kennedy—can get away with being the product of wealth, especially if he has the common touch, it's more difficult for a Republican to do so, especially if he doesn't have it. A Democratic strategist says, "If our soft underbelly is that we are the party of blacks and poor people, their soft underbelly is that they are the party of country-club Republicans." Reagan is wealthy, but he had been through hard times and was able to convince people that he understood their problems. Neither Richard Nixon nor Barry Goldwater came from the Wasp aristocracy. Bush does, and it shows. His good manners make him the subject of ridicule: he said recently that Dukakis was saying "naughty" things about him, he says "heck" and refers to "deep doo-doo." His efforts to counter his breeding by trying to be one of the boys often come a cropper. A Republican strategist says, "The worst thing you can do in politics is try to be something you aren't." Bush says things that reinforce an impression that he might be out of touch with Americans from a less privileged background. In California, in the course of a speech to the students of Garfield High School, a predominantly Hispanic School in East Los Angeles that is famous for sending seventy per cent of its graduates to college and for specializing in calculus (it was featured in the movie "Stand and Deliver"), Bush told the students that "you don't have to go to college to be a success." He continued, "We need those people who build our buildings. . . . We need the people who run the offices, the people who do the hard physical work of our society." The Dukakis campaign charges that Bush's proposed cut in the capital-gains tax would benefit the rich. Bush, understandably, bridles at the "class" argument, saying that it is "absurd."

Bush quite validly points out that he has spent years in honorable public service, but that may be part of his problem now. Years of public service, no matter how honorable, can blunt one's thinking as well as one's political instincts. The trappings of the Vice-Presidency can easily become a cocoon. A Republican senator who likes Bush says that Bush may have had a clearer set of beliefs some time ago, but that as he has watched Reagan succeed by championing things he himself never would have espoused, it has become harder for him to know what he thinks. Someone who has worked closely with Bush says, "George Bush's thought process is that you go through the chairs—serve as this and that— and then run for the Presidency, and, if elected, you go out and get like-minded people and run the government." This explains, the person said, why Bush "has no vision" (Bush refers puzzledly to "the vision thing") and doesn't seem to know what he wants to do as President. In 1980, Reagan came across as quite clear about what he wanted to do.

Bush shows his awkwardness as a candidate in other ways as well. When he speaks off the cuff, he fights a continuing, and often losing, battle with the English language; he seems unable to resist critiquing his own performances ("Somewhere between going ballistic with Dan Rather and being benign and pleasant with Ted Koppel is the real me"). Recently, after making a strong speech at the Texas Republican State Convention attacking Dukakis, Bush made an appearance on "Nightline" that didn't go at all well. A number of people, including Republicans, questioned the wisdom of this scheduling: of having him step on the story of his speech by making another attention-getting appearance, or of having him appear on the program at all. In appearing on "Nightline" for an hour, Bush guaranteed that the topics would not be those he was stressing in his campaign. For most of the program, he was on the defensive about Noriega and the Iran-Contra affair. In the pressure of the moment, he several times confused Koppel with Rather ("It's Freudian. Hey, listen, it's Freudian"), with whom he had had a famously unfortunate interview earlier this year.

This gets to another piece of "perceptual territory" both candidates are fighting over: the question of who is tougher. The

Dukakis people are confident that their man will win this one, because of his aggressive style (which not everyone will find attractive) and his avoidance of a bleeding-heart image. By questioning Bush's independence from Reagan, Dukakis and his people are raising questions about Bush's strength. Bush has a style problem here, too. Bush is a man of dignity and poise, and he is, as he points out, a war hero, but when he tries to show that he is tough (which may be his mistake) he often gets it wrong, and too often the dignity goes. It is then that Bush's voice goes to the higher registers, as he speaks faster, and that he looks frantic. (In a piece of self-revelation, Bush said to reporters at Kennebunkport, "When I get up here . . . I don't feel frantic.") What Bush doesn't seem to understand, or perhaps understands but hasn't assimilated, is that in most cases tough equals calm: Clint Eastwood, Gary Cooper, Ronald Reagan. In battling over who is tougher on drugs and crime, Bush and Dukakis are actually battling over who is tougher.

It has been Bush's misfortune thus far that the failures of the Reagan Administration attach to him, because he has been so loyal, while the successes do not, because they are so strongly identified with Reagan's persona. (This is what has given rise to the expression "Velcro candidate" to describe Bush, as opposed to Reagan as the "Teflon President.") Bush has taken several steps to separate himself from Reagan, as he has done in urging that the Administration not drop indictments against Noriega, in indicating that he would like Edwin Meese to resign, in calling for a postponement of certain drilling for oil off the California coast, in calling for stronger environmental protection. Republicans are, of course, delighted with the opportunity that House Speaker Jim Wright's current difficulties give them to try to blunt the "sleaze" issue; thus far, the charges against Wright do not seem very serious, except for some odoriferous arrangements by which friends and lobbyists were apparently able to help him out financially by publishing and purchasing a slim volume of his writings and sayings. An independent counsel's report on Meese is due any day now. When Bush does separate himself from Reagan, it is often a belabored exercise, one that draws attention to the fact that he is taking some steps, however small, out of the larger man's shadow. Some of this problem has to do not with Bush but with the institutional fix he is in. He is far from the first man who has found it difficult to run for the Presidency from the Vice-Presidency, which gives every appearance of being a soul-crushing job.

Robert Teeter, Bush's pollster, says that the way the Bush campaign can win is "by keeping the election focussed on the issues that are usually the most important issues of an election—the economy and foreign policy." Thus, Bush stresses peace and prosperity under Reagan. But Teeter adds, "You also stress experience and qualifications and the kinds of values that people want to have in a President now." The Bush people obviously feel that by attacking Dukakis on certain "values" issues they can show that he is the one who is not in tune with most Americans' values. In his Texas speech, Bush argued that it is Dukakis who is the élitist. Bush said, "When I wanted to learn the ways of the world, I didn't go to the Kennedy School, I came to Texas." (Dukakis went to the John F. Kennedy School of Government after he lost his bid for reëlection as governor.) Bush said, "I didn't study a monograph on the effects of economic growth, I started a business." He said, "Governor Dukakis, his foreign-policy views born in Harvard Yard's boutique, would cut the muscle of our defense." In an attempt to undermine Dukakis's efforts to paint himself as a moderate (in which Jackson helped him), Bush painted him as a liberal who imposed tax increases in Massachusetts, despite a campaign pledge that he would not do so, and might do so as President; he says that under Dukakis's governorship "Massachusetts has raised its spending far faster than has the nation as a whole." Bush and other Republicans point out that Dukakis opposes the death penalty, had a state program that granted furloughs to convicted murderers (the Dukakis people say many states have furlough programs), and vetoed a bill to require that schoolchildren recite the Pledge of Allegiance (the Dukakis people say that the bill was unconstitutional). The Bush campaign has test-marketed these issues, and also Dukakis's opposition to major weapons systems, and found them to be effective in trying to depict Bush as closer to the views of most of the American people. Though the Dukakis people say that the public won't focus on this or that weapons system, the Bush people say that the issue of Dukakis's wanting to cut major weapons systems will be the easiest of all, because it will be seen as part of a pattern. They are trying to portray Bush as generally tougher on law enforcement, including against drug users. In his Texas speech, Bush played to people's dislike of the Internal Revenue Service, which Dukakis vows to use more forcefully, by allying himself with a proposal for a Tax-payers' Bill of Rights, which has been floating around on Capitol Hill. A big effort is going into trying to undermine Dukakis's reputation as an effective governor; much will be made of Du-kakis's now having to raise taxes to meet his state's revenue short-fall. Bush's approach is not only one of attack: he has also made a speech recently on his education proposals, which were modest, and addressed urban policy, about which he said that a task force should be appointed, and called for more assistance for certain programs, and, like his opponent, called for "initiative involving federal/state/private partnerships."

The many analyses of Reagan's visit to the Soviet Union which largely write off the meeting as a substanceless, "photo oppor-tunity" summit miss the point. The very symbolism of the summit was substance: the meeting was an important political, even his-toric, event—and Reagan, a few missteps notwithstanding, played his part well. He oversimplified, of course, but in doing so, as is often the case, he got a powerful message across: The relationship between the United States and the Soviet Union has changed. Summit meetings are now the norm. By throwing in with Mikhail Gorbachev and endorsing his attempt at economic and social re-forms (*perestroika* and *glasnost*), he sent the clear signal to the world that Gorbachev is a different kind of Soviet leader, one with whom, Margaret Thatcher said over three years ago, to many guffaws, "We can do business." In putting his arm around Gorbachev in the course of a walk in Red Square, in calling him his friend, he validated him. Asked by reporters for the umpteenth time whether he still considered the Soviet Union an "evil empire" (Reagan: 1983), Reagan said, "I was talking about another time, another era." In fact, the Reagan Administration is treading warily, and without a road map, into its new relationship with the Soviet Union. In part, this is because it doesn't know how long Gorbachev will last or what would come after him; in part, because it must tread carefully around the land mines of domestic politics, not appear to have gone all soft; and in part because it has not undertaken the serious analysis that such a dramatic change in policy would presumably warrant.

One official described the changing policy toward the Soviet

Union as "a very big thing that the government has not been able
to argue out and decide how to deal with." The "optics" provided
by the President in Moscow, he said, while going a long way to
give Gorbachev encouragement, are not backed by any settled
economic policy toward the Soviet Union. "There has been no
internal debate in the Administration about how to greet this,"
he said. The reason, it appears, is that there is still a wariness
among people inside the government about even engaging in such
a debate; "everyone's afraid of looking too soft," said one official.
While many of the ideologues who populated the Reagan Administration are gone, there are still enough of them around, and
the atmosphere even outside the Administration is still sufficiently
militant that officials are wary of getting too far beyond what is
deemed acceptable. A number of careers have been destroyed in
the past eight years for ideological incorrectness. The debate on
the outside is also constrained. Even George Bush, after the summit, took issue with Reagan's generous new view of the Soviet
Union. So officials deal with the dilemma, and displace serious
debate, and substitute for a policy, by saying they don't know how
long Gorbachev will last. They also raise the obvious question of
whether Gorbachev's attempts to improve the Soviet economy will
turn the Soviet Union more inward and be accompanied by a
reduction of external adventurism, or whether an improved economy would be used to back increasingly aggressive behavior. My
sense is that most top officials, looking at the current Soviet withdrawal from Afghanistan and involved in discussions with the
Soviets about using their influence with the Cubans and Angolans
to work out a settlement in southern Africa, and listening to Gorbachev, are inclined to believe that he does consider such adventurism passé and the possibility of a military conflict with the
United States out of the question. (Gorbachev said, "It is the fate
of our two countries, two peoples, whether we want it or not, to
live together and to coöperate.") But they are covering their bases,
and when Defense Secretary Frank Carlucci, in what appeared to
be a dissent from the chummy atmosphere of the summit, said in
a recent speech that helping the Soviet Union modernize may be
"an enormous miscalculation," and warned against emulating the
détente of the nineteen-seventies (the word never crosses Administration officials' lips), White House officials said that this was
consistent with their views. Quietly, trade and investment policy

toward the Soviet Union has been loosened, though Administration officials are quick to say that of course this will not violate our ban on giving the Soviet Union sensitive technology. But even a very conservative official said to me recently that he wondered whether the Administration was doing enough to help Gorbachev, or whether it might miss a historic opportunity.

Despite the talk of continuing progress on a new agreement to reduce strategic arms, most officials say that there is little to no likelihood of one being completed before Reagan leaves office. Still, Administration members want to get a new START agreement as far along as possible—or ostensibly so—to leave to the next President to complete. A senior Administration official said to me in a recent interview, "My day would not be spoiled if we have a complete START package to leave at the end of the Administration, with S.D.I. as the outstanding issue." But the Strategic Defense Initiative, or Star Wars, is only one of several remaining issues. Even if the United States and the Soviet Union resolve most of their remaining differences, a START agreement would be far from ready for ratification, and would in fact be something of a phony document. The real difficulty in consummating a START agreement has less to do with the much discussed problems with verification, which are difficult enough, or even with the President's insistence that the United States has the unilateral right to proceed with his dream of having America protected by a space-based defense system, than with fundamental decisions about what our defense policy is which have yet to be made by the Reagan Administration—and probably won't be made before the next President takes over. And all of this is affected by the Administration's end-of-second-term fatigue. There has been no great drive within the Administration for arms control. Getting Senate approval of the intermediate-range-nuclear-forces agreement (I.N.F.), which was finally achieved, Perils of Pauline style, on the eve of the summit, proved more time-consuming and difficult than the Administration had figured on (this difficulty, too, had to do in part with the fatigue).

Secretary of State George Shultz has been distracted—by the Middle East and Panama, among other matters. He recently returned empty-handed from what will probably be his last trip to the Middle East. The Panama debacle was overtaken by the summit; it was probably in hopes of that that the Administration desperately tried to get an agreement with Noriega before the summit (Shultz even delayed his departure), with Administration officials torn over whether it would be more embarrassing to get the rather lenient agreement that the United States had proffered to Noriega, or to not get it. With Bush having taken a step out of Reagan's shadow by saying that the indictments brought against Noriega should not be dropped (for good measure, the Senate adopted a resolution, sponsored by Robert Dole, opposing the dropping of the indictments, by a vote of eighty-six to ten), the internal war within the Administration over whether to drop them went public. (Bush is said by an adviser to have been surprised at all the attention, and praise, his step had attracted.) While Bush and his friend Treasury Secretary James Baker were arguing that the indictments should not be dropped, Shultz and national-security adviser Colin Powell went on television saying that they should. (Their argument within the Administration was that it had already paid the political price for discussing the dropping of the indictments, which weren't of much practical value, and the important thing was to get Noriega out.) The President stuck with the original plan to drop them if that would get Noriega to leave office, and then the Administration was humiliated once again when Noriega rejected the offer. Not content to leave bad enough alone, Assistant Secretary of State Elliott Abrams suggested that perhaps we would try to overthrow Noriega, but we'd already tried that, and he also let it be known that the use of military action was not ruled out (even though Carlucci had already held him off about this earlier). Another idea that has been floating around is to try to get someone to arrest Noriega and take him to a part of Panama under American military jurisdiction—where, presumably, he would be offered the options of leaving Panama or facing trial. (This is the way the United States got Juan Matta Ballesteros, a major Honduran drug dealer, arrested and brought to the United States—causing anti-American riots in Honduras.) More than one Administration official has called the Panama affair "a disaster," something that was got into without much thought as to how, or even why. Powell is said by associates to regret not having got into the thing earlier and stopped it before it got so far along. The White House has been trying to discourage public statements by officials about how soon they expect Noriega to go. Meanwhile, the peace talks between the Contras and the Sandinistas have broken down, with each side blaming the other, and the Administration debating over whether to ask Congress to resume military aid to the Contras. Some officials want to at least tide the Contras over until the next Administration arrives. One Administration official, talking to me recently (even before the military coup in Haiti this week) about the various recent setbacks to its policy in Nicaragua, El Salvador, and Guatemala, and the growing resistance to our large presence in Honduras, said unhappily, "We're back to where we were in 1980." He may have been too optimistic.

The biggest obstacle in the way of a START treaty, according to a number of officials, is the fact that the military can't decide what kind of land-based missile systems it wants as a result of the contemplated fifty-per-cent reduction of each side's warheads. The Joint Chiefs of Staff don't want to be pressed to make such a decision, and no real treaty can go forward until one has been made and the chiefs are on board. Even if the Administration goes for a piece of paper—to have something to show—without having resolved this underlying issue, the Senate would never approve a START treaty until it was resolved. There is also a question as to whether the chiefs would go along with such a gambit. A senior Administration official told me recently, "Where the chiefs are is 'Don't try to pin us down on START until we know what we can plan for.'" The chiefs don't know what they can plan for because basic questions about our military structure have not been resolved by the Administration. One powerful senator says that he finds the current state of defense policy so incoherent that he is about to throw up his hands. The next President, he says, will have to resolve things.

The issues that will have to be resolved before a START agreement can come into being involve pride, politics, and serious philosophical differences about how to structure the best deterrent under a START regime. The Administration and Congress have been fighting for nearly eight years now over the large, ten-warhead MX missile, which the Administration and the Air Force prefer, with a number of powerful members of Congress, including Sam Nunn, preferring a single-warhead mobile missile, the Midgetman. Nunn believes that adherents of S.D.I. within the Administration have resisted the Midgetman because they feel that they have a better chance of selling S.D.I. if the force posture is vulnerable, and that for the same reason the MXs that have been wrung from Congress are based in vulnerable fixed silos. Powell said to me in a recent interview that for now both the MX and the Midgetman will go forward "at some level determined by Congress, and the next Administration will have to make a choice." Just about no one thinks there is the money, not to mention the rationale, for both systems. Powell said, "The Joint Chiefs of Staff would have difficulty going to closure on a START treaty without knowing the nature of a mobile program—if there is a mobile program." Carlucci has proposed placing the MX on railroad cars, which hasn't been met with a lot of enthusiasm on Capitol Hill and is the latest in a long list of bizarre proposals for basing the MX. Nunn says that a trainload of MXs would make "a vulnerable and lucrative target." There are also other unresolved issues between and within the military services over how the reduced number of warheads from a START agreement should be allocated. One observer says that the real problem isn't getting an agreement with the Soviet Union, it's getting one among the services.

Nunn says, "Until we develop a consensus on our ground-force posture and relate that to stability in an arms-control context we're not ready for a START agreement." Some people—Richard Nixon and Henry Kissinger, among others—argue that a START agreement might in fact lead to a strategic imbalance in the Soviet Union's favor. But another school of thought holds that a START agreement wouldn't make much difference one way or another, that it would be largely a symbolic treaty (as is the I.N.F. agreement, which removes only four per cent of the world's nuclear weapons). According to this view, a real difference would come only from a treaty that made still deeper cuts, or a policy that dramatically redesigned both sides' force structures, with single-warhead missiles (not necessarily mobile) replacing multiple independently targeted reëntry vehicles—the MIRVs that Nixon and Kissinger brought upon us in order to buy off the military on an earlier arms-control treaty. (Kissinger later said, "I wish I had thought through the implications of a MIRVed world.") Nunn is among those who would like to see a return to a single-warhead world, and who think that the Soviets might agree (and that such a change would be verifiable). Dukakis, in his recent talk on foreign and defense policy, reiterated his opposition to both a mobile MX and the Midgetman, and made no mention of any other single-warhead missile. His advisers say that he might support a single-warhead missile, but Dukakis himself doesn't say this. As an adviser describes his position, Dukakis would want to get a START agreement first and then decide what to do—decide, in Dukakis's words, "what new weapons systems, if any," we'll need—which is opposite to where the Joint Chiefs, and Nunn, are. Bush supports the proposal to put the MX on railroad cars, and, according to a spokesman, supports the idea of "looking at" a single-warhead system but is "not at this point ready to propose a particular system."

As for S.D.I., various solutions are possible, especially as it becomes increasingly clear (perhaps to all but the President) that the President's concept won't work, and as it has also become clear that Congress won't allow the President to break out of the anti-ballistic-missile (A.B.M.) treaty, or reinterpret it, to test, develop, and deploy a space-based S.D.I. The ambiguous and tortured wording on this subject that both sides agreed to at the Washington summit, last December, is not acceptable to the United States as treaty language, and Powell, representing the President's views, earlier this year shot down an attempt by Shultz and arms negotiator Paul Nitze to negotiate with the Soviets over what testing would be permitted. The Administration is still locked in an internal argument on this point. Moreover, the Administration hasn't decided what kind of defensive system it would like to have. The resolution of this, too, awaits the next President.

The most fascinating by-product of the Moscow summit was the new insights it gave us into Reagan. Not an introspective man, he has been with us for a long time without revealing much about himself. He presents himself as he wants us to see him. The recent books about him tell us more about the passive, uncurious side of him that we had known was also there. Overreliance on those books, though, can throw people off about the canny, determined, even bullheaded Reagan; if he weren't those things as well he wouldn't have been President for eight years. Without those attributes, he would not have dominated the agenda to the extent that he has, the Iran-Contra affair might not have happened, and he might not have ended up in Moscow. Reagan defies convention and makes leaps of imagination—for good or for ill. Of course he oversimplified in Moscow, but his oversimplification allowed him to send powerful messages, as it does here. His pushing for human rights may or may not have been helpful to his (and Gorbachev's) cause, his talk about freedom may or may not have hit its mark, and he was downright embarrassing when he talked about American Indians (saying that "maybe we should not have humored them" by letting them stay on reservations and maybe we should have let them become citizens—which they are—and that "some of them became very wealthy because some of those reservations were overlaying great pools of oil") or when, to ease up on Gorbachev, he attributed human-rights problems to "the bureaucracy." But the large leap of imagination he took, the one that got him to Moscow, endorsing a Soviet leader who is also a visionary, and therefore at risk, might change history.

The revelations came in some seemingly offhand remarks Reagan made in the course of his five days in Moscow. We have known of course that Reagan relates to movies. He gave Gorbachev a copy of "Friendly Persuasion," because, he said, it showed "not just the tragedy of war but the problems of pacifism, the nobility of patriotism, as well as the love of peace." The movie, starring Gary Cooper and about a Quaker family during the Civil War, has an ambiguous moral about the use of force, and must have puzzled Gorbachev and his colleagues as they tried to fathom the meaning of Reagan's gesture. We have also known that he thinks in visual terms, and that his acting skills have been a critical part of his political career. But in Moscow, perhaps out of an awareness that his Presidency is coming to an end, he let us in on how that works. At a meeting with intellectuals and artists, he said, "In looking back, I believe that acting did help prepare me for the work I do now," that it had given him "two indispensable lessons." The first, he said, quoting the Soviet filmmaker Sergei Eisenstein, was "The most important thing is to have the vision. The next is to grasp and hold it. You must see and feel what you are thinking. . . . You must hold and fix it in your memory and senses." He continued, "To grasp and hold a vision, to fix it in your senses, that is the very essence, I believe, of successful leadership." The second, he said, was "You get inside a character, a place, and a moment." At the same event, he explained his evolution from the decrier of the "evil empire" to the friendly tourist in Moscow. He said, "In the movie business, actors often get what we call typecast." He explained, "The studios come to think of you as playing certain kinds of roles, so those are the kinds of roles they give you. And no matter how hard you try, you just can't get them to think of you in any other way." And then he said, "Well, politics is a little like that, too. So I've had a lot of time and reason to think about my role." And back in Washington he told a group of reporters that he felt that his trip was like a Cecil B. De Mille production, and that he had "dropped into a grand historical moment."

IX

The Democratic Party, in the process of redefining itself and with Michael Dukakis as its instrument, left Atlanta with its morale and hopes higher than they had been in more than a decade. At the end of its four-day Convention, which concluded on the high note of Dukakis's successful acceptance speech—largely unexpected and therefore all the better received—the Democrats felt better about their candidate and his chances of winning than they had when they arrived in Atlanta. Dukakis's speech was a good one but not a great one, and his rising to the occasion should not have been such a surprise. All year, he has been highly disciplined, and, with few exceptions, has met the demands of the nominating process—culminating in Atlanta. Though most people didn't know, or forgot, he had given effective speeches before, but the Dukakis people, who work hard, and with some success, at getting people to think what they want them to think (at "spinning"), had so succeeded in lowering expectations of Dukakis's speech that it might have seemed a wonder that he dared show up in the hall at all. The immediate positive commentary on the speech magnified its success. In all, the Convention and his performance in it gave Dukakis size: at the end of it he was of a larger dimension than he was at the beginning. As was to be expected, the path to the tableau of unity at the end was not smooth, with Jesse Jackson (with unintended help from Dukakis) holding unity hostage for as long as he could, and causing the Dukakis camp more grief than it had bargained on.

The Democrats are in a transitional phase, out of redistributive liberalism into they-are-not-sure-what, a transition that is as much a matter of necessity (the budget deficit, the fate of previous, liberal candidates) as of conviction. Dukakis is a transitional figure, also a matter of necessity as much as of conviction, and is trying to avoid any label at all. The transition could be seen in the pro-

214

gram of the Convention, in the debates about the platform, in the new pragmatism, born of a will to win for a change, that took over the Party. Having lost four of the last five elections, three of them by embarrassing landslides, the Democrats have been suffering from something of an inferiority complex, and their desire to win, and to be accepted as adults, served as a suppressor on their usual fratricidal tendencies.

Though, as the polls indicate, Dukakis got a boost from the Convention (he went from being very close to Bush to leads of seventeen points shortly after the Convention), his people, despite their current euphoria, are well aware that a long, tough campaign lies before them. In fact, the "bounce" that Dukakis got from the Convention is about the same as that received by the nominee after the last three Democratic Conventions, and new, post-Convention adherents tend to be the least faithful ones. Because of that, the Dukakis campaign swung right into campaigning, in the hope of solidifying the advantage the Convention had provided. As of now, the race is widely considered "competitive"—that is, it is close enough in enough states to make it possible that either Dukakis or George Bush could win, but this does not rule out a landslide.

Dukakis's choice of Lloyd Bentsen as his running mate was certainly made with the electoral college math in mind (Texas has twenty-nine electoral votes) but also as the result of a process of elimination. Out of a large party, Dukakis's choices fairly quickly dwindled down to a precious few. Bill Bradley, Sam Nunn, and Thomas Foley took themselves out, and before long the Dukakis people were looking at a list that wasn't very long: Senator Bob Graham, of Florida, was too new to the Senate and couldn't be counted on to deliver his state. Lee Hamilton was seen as attractive but of no known electoral strength. John Glenn and Lloyd Bentsen were both tempting, and both had partisans among Dukakis's advisers, but both also presented problems, and there was a school of thought among the Dukakis people that neither could be said to represent "the future." Both men were on the list for more than their potential strength in their home states: both were expected to give the ticket a more conservative hue as Dukakis tried to win over key groups—Democrats who had voted for Reagan, independents, and white males (these groups are not mutually exclusive). But discontent within the Dukakis camp over the possibility of either Glenn or Bentsen momentarily brought the names of Richard Gephardt and Albert Gore into play—and both men were belatedly summoned to Boston—but each brought with him some negative history from the primaries. Gore was the more serious candidate of the two, because of the strong predilection among some of the Dukakis people to go South in their choice, both to pick up whatever states possible and to pin Bush down in an area of his presumed strength.

Dukakis himself has a history of going right at an opponent's base. Moreover, the Dukakis people did not want to "write off" the South. Susan Estrich, Dukakis's campaign manager, told me in Atlanta, "The direction we chose not to go was to concede any area to George Bush and have to win ninety or ninety-five per cent of the rest of the country." Toward the end, Gore was ruled out largely on the ground that his campaign for the nomination showed him not to be mature and seasoned enough. Hamilton remained a possibility until nearly the end, and was supported by those who thought that Dukakis should go for the classiest candidate (Bradley, Nunn, or Foley would have fit in this category) and that such a candidate would wear best. Opinions were vetted among the Dukakis staff, but only a small number of advisers talked to Dukakis himself—who gave few signals of what he was thinking. The process became less tidy and more public as it went along, and Dukakis came under some criticism for teasing Ohio audiences as he campaigned with Glenn during the last week in June; he was therefore more circumspect when, in early July, he campaigned with Bentsen in Texas and along the Arkansas border. (He also campaigned with Hamilton.) Some of the press were also saying that the Vice-Presidential selection process was taking "too long," though it is hard to see how one can be too careful.

Still, the top Dukakis people decided to get the thing over with—they had long since decided to try to get the running mate selected and announced in advance of the Convention, in the hope of becalming the followers of Jesse Jackson, whom Dukakis had no intention of selecting but who would not get out of the way. When, on the night of Monday, July 11th, Dukakis, his wife, Kitty, Paul Brountas (the campaign chairman), Susan Estrich, and Jack Corrigan (the deputy campaign manager) met at the Dukakis home to make the decision, some advisers were not at all happy that the final decision had come down to Glenn and Bentsen. Glenn had financial problems, and there were questions about some dealings by members of Bentsen's family. Glenn's problems were considered the more insuperable, and for this, among other reasons, the choice was Bentsen.

Bentsen is a silky, courtly insider, an intelligent man who says little on the Senate floor, but knows how to work the system. He's more competent than interesting, and runs his office like a business. He is a favorite of business lobbies; labor did not favor him at all—some labor leaders remember a vote that Bentsen cast "wrong" on labor-law reform, in 1977—but it is swallowing him, in the interests of unity and winning. Bentsen is not one for speaking out on national issues, but, as the new chairman of the Senate Finance Committee (he took over at the beginning of last year), he has, as Dukakis keeps pointing out, a considerable legislative record. (This year, he managed the trade bill, and after the President vetoed it, because of its provision to give workers sixty days' notice of plant closings, he managed a separate plant-closings bill, which the President, to the relief of key Republicans, has decided not to veto. A new trade bill has just been passed, and the President has said he'll sign it. Bentsen also managed a bill to provide catastrophic health care, and a welfare-overhaul bill.) But Bentsen is not to be confused with Lyndon Johnson, a noisy wheeler-dealer; he works quietly and is somewhat aloof. Bentsen, unlike Johnson, was born to wealth, and has a patrician manner—but he is also believed by the Dukakis people to have a strong political organization in Texas, which made him attractive. Bentsen has been trying to get on the ticket one way or another for some time. He made a brief and little-remembered run for the Presidency in 1976, and he was a willing public participant in Walter Mondale's Vice-Presidential selection process. The Dukakis team picked him with inconclusive data on whether he could make the difference in Texas, but hoping that he could help the ticket not only there but also in the other "oil patch" states of Louisiana and Oklahoma, all of which have troubled economies, and that he could persuade moderate and conservative Democrats that Dukakis was nothing to fear. (Bentsen and Dukakis have many policy differences, including over aid to the Contras, support of the MX and Midgetman missiles, school prayer, federal funding for abortions, the death penalty, and gun control.) It is instructive that the first two

stops Dukakis and Bentsen made together immediately after the
Convention were in south Texas (where both men showed off
their Spanish) and in Modesto, California, a swing area. (They
also went to North Dakota and Missouri, which have been going
Republican.)

When Dukakis says that he will campaign in all fifty states, and
the Dukakis people say that he means it and that they will challenge
Bush in every state, what they all mean is that they will keep the
challenge broad for a while, see what their options are, and narrow
down the states in October. At that point, the key decisions about
"resources allocation"—the main resources being the candidate's
time and television ads—will be made. The talk of going everywhere is, of course, to serve the purpose of trying to keep the
Bush people off their feed and to force them to spend their own
resources nearly everywhere. Dukakis can be quite determined
about where he wants to go: shortly before the large number of
contests on March 8th, the campaign organization scheduled a
visit to Arkansas. Dukakis said he wanted to go to Idaho (which
was also having a contest on that date), and he went to Idaho
(which he carried). "He hijacked the plane," says Jack Corrigan,
adding, "We present him with a schedule and he changes it. If
he says he wants to go to all fifty states, he'll go to all fifty states."
Tom Kiley, a Dukakis campaign strategist, said to me in Atlanta,
"To an extent never seen before, we're going to run a national
campaign. Mike talks about this not only publicly but also privately
to us. He says, 'I don't want you ruling out any areas.' He thinks
this could be a watershed election—that there could be a regional
realignment. He thinks we can win some Western states that Democrats haven't been winning, and, obviously, this Convention is a
celebration of the South."

The Dukakis plan is to take the Republicans' presumed advantage in the electoral college head on, and the choice of Bentsen
was part of that plan. Another Dukakis adviser says that "the
electoral college nightmare" for the Democrats is the 1976 election, where with a change in a few votes in a few states Jimmy
Carter would have won the popular vote and lost the electoral
college. Therefore, the adviser says, in order to get the necessary
two hundred and seventy votes "you have to keep more than four
hundred electoral votes in competition at all times—a safety margin that is comfortable—rather than follow in the minimalist the-

ory that makes you vulnerable to an all-out assault in one state."
And picking Bentsen was a real thumb in the eye to Bush, who
claims Texas as his home state, and whom Bentsen defeated for
the Senate in 1970. Kiley says, "At the least, Bush will have to
spend three million dollars in Texas he hadn't figured on spending there."

Jesse Jackson's domination of the news in the days leading up to
the Convention, and in its first two days, should not have been a
surprise. Causing attention to himself, and disruption, leading to
concessions by the disrupted, are Jackson specialties. A major
activity of his Operation PUSH (People United to Serve Human-
ity), in Chicago, was demonstrating against businesses until they
gave in and bought Jackson off one way or another. That Jackson's
followers have their own needs, which the Party is showing less
interest in these days, is not in question; but what Jackson was
pushing for just before the Convention had little to do with those
needs. Jackson is very good at creating grievances. The only surprise was that the Dukakis camp handed him one.

  Just hours before Bentsen was chosen, Jackson said publicly
for the first time that he wanted to be the Vice-Presidential nominee. But at the time he said this, at the end of a meeting with
Brountas in Washington, he knew—as he had known all along—
that it was not in the cards. Moreover, Jackson had privately,
among his own advisers, disparaged not only the office of the
Vice-Presidency but also Dukakis. It was understood among Jackson's advisers that, since the end of the primaries, he had been
talking about his interest in the Vice-Presidency as a way of exercising leverage to exact some other things. It was also a way of
keeping attention on himself, and gave him a new cause. But
though a number of people around Jackson knew that his seeking
the Vice-Presidential nomination was a game, his followers did
not. For them it had become—with his encouragement—the test
of whether the racial barrier to a black being on a major-party
ticket could be broken. That Jackson was not seriously seeking
the Vice-Presidential nomination is attested to by the fact that he
never submitted the financial information the Dukakis people had
requested of all potential running mates. In fact, some people
around Jackson, who were in contact with some people around
Dukakis, had agreed on a plan whereby one day Jackson would

emerge from a meeting with Dukakis and announce that he was grateful for receiving the "serious consideration" he had asked for, but that he didn't want the slot. But this didn't fit into Jackson's scheme, and of course it never happened. Jackson was having far more trouble letting go of the attention and excitement of being a candidate than even those close to him had reckoned on. Meanwhile, Jackson led his people to the top of the mountain—encouraging them in the belief that he should be the Vice-Presidential nominee—and had to figure out how to get them down without his losing face.

As the time approached to make the Vice-Presidential selection, the Dukakis people were becoming increasingly irritated not only with Jackson's refusal to concede that he had lost the race for the nomination but also his insistence that he be treated as a sort of co-nominee. By this time, the Dukakis camp had already compromised with Jackson on changes in the rules (cutting the number of super-delegates by more than a third and eliminating "winner take all" features of state contests) and had accepted some of Jackson's platform proposals and was engaged in negotiations on others, and Jackson had been promised a speech in prime time (he had given one in prime time in 1984). But Jackson complained that he hadn't been consulted about the choice of the keynote speaker. He said he wanted to discuss the Vice-Presidency "in detail" with Dukakis, and that his reaction if someone else was picked would depend on who the choice was and how it was explained, and that he and Dukakis had to meet to discuss "the partnership" the two must form to win in November.

About ten days before the Dukakis people chose Bentsen, someone who knows Jackson well said to me, in a different context, "What Jesse reacts most to is not being treated in a way he thinks he should be." This person added, "It can be on little things." So when, on the Tuesday morning after they had settled on Bentsen, the Dukakis people failed to get word to Jackson before he heard it, on arriving in Washington from Cincinnati, from a reporter at the airport, they struck him in a dangerous place. For all their explanations of what went wrong—someone didn't give someone the right phone numbers (this was apparently untrue), they missed him in Cincinnati and he was then airborne—it is clear that if it had been important to Dukakis that he get hold of Jackson he would have got hold of him. (The Secret Service could have been used to relay a message.) It is also clear that Dukakis and his people had no intention of letting Jackson even try to exercise a veto right, or of giving him special treatment when it came to informing those who would not be named. Brountas told me in Atlanta, "Governor Dukakis felt they should all be treated equally." (Both Brountas and Dukakis had told Jackson that neither he nor any other possible running mate would have a say on anyone else.) In Atlanta, various Dukakis people described what they had done wrong as failing to reach Jackson before he heard about Bentsen from a reporter—and nothing more. Brountas, in his meeting in Washington with Jackson, did promise him that he would hear about Dukakis's decision before it was made public, and Jackson gave Brountas numbers where he could be reached. It was also made clear to Jackson that he couldn't be considered if he didn't turn in the requisite financial information, and just after that Jackson said publicly that he wanted to be selected as the running mate. It would also seem that the Dukakis people, for all their efficiency, hadn't made tight plans for informing various aspirants. (Glenn heard about Bentsen on his car radio.) And they clearly didn't think through the consequences of appearing to insult Jackson. Someone close to Jackson says the real problem was that he *was seen* (television cameras were at the airport) hearing about Bentsen from a reporter, and thus felt publicly humiliated. Besides, Jackson did feel that the slight was intentional—and he was probably half right. By the time this happened, even some Jackson advisers thought he was too far out there, making too many demands, and was in danger of being widely seen as overreaching. Now he had an issue, and he used it.

At a press conference he held on Tuesday afternoon, Jackson, restrained but obviously very angry, said, "I'm too controlled, I'm too clear, I'm too mature to be angry" (this sounded like a lesson one or more of his advisers had drilled into him), but he did leave the door open to letting his name be put forward for the Vice-Presidency at the Convention, and said he'd bring about a dozen platform issues to the Convention floor. But Jackson turned his grievance, which was a personal one, into one that had been inflicted on all blacks, and at an N.A.A.C.P. convention that night he made a fiery speech. He ended the speech by shouting, to the cheers and applause of the crowd, "I will never surrender!" and "I may not be on the ticket but I'm qualified!" and, with the crowd joining in, he repeated, "Qualified! Qualified! Qualified!"

The plain truth is that he wasn't, having held no public office or run anything of any size, and not being an especially disciplined person. Jackson may have come in farther back than other runners-up in recent Presidential races, but he didn't choose to play by their rules. All year, Jackson has tried to have it both ways: to be treated as a white candidate would be treated and also to be treated as a special case. He is a protest leader seeking to work within the political system, and the ambivalence of his situation is hard for him as well as others to balance. He pushes at the edges of the system, and sometimes beyond them, and then becomes hurt and angry when it pushes back. Jackson likes to deal in what he calls "creative tension." And he has a special hold on his followers, and he knows it, and he uses it. If his cause turns out at times to have more to do with his personal needs than with their lives, so be it.

And then Dukakis unwittingly played into Jackson's hands further by appearing insensitive about the matter. This was one of those occasions, and an exceptionally unfortunate one, in which Dukakis's back was up. As far as he was concerned, the failure to reach Jackson was just a slip up, no big deal, nothing to apologize for. A speech he gave on Wednesday to the N.A.A.C.P. went over badly: Dukakis seemed not to understand that a large part of his audience (especially after having been whipped up by Jackson) felt hurt and angry, he was grudging and abrupt in his acknowledgment of Jackson, and he seemed not even to know how to talk to blacks. Dukakis has lived a pretty narrow life, centered in the Boston suburb of Brookline, where he grew up and still lives. He has neither travelled nor read widely. (It has been much noted that he once took a book on Swedish land-use planning on a vacation.) His wife has said that she can't recall his ever reading a novel. (Following the Convention, Dukakis did try harder with black audiences.) The most amazing example of his lack of understanding was his saying offhandedly on Wednesday, more than once, that he could understand how the blacks felt because he knew the members of AHEPA, an organization of Greek Americans, would have been disappointed if he had been in the same situation as Jackson.

By this time, and in the next few days, Jackson was complaining that the one-to-one meetings he had been having with Dukakis (there had been four in the latter months of the campaign) had been "superficial," that they needed to talk in depth. These sessions were apparently neither very warm nor productive; Jackson would talk and Dukakis wouldn't respond much—the two men speak different languages. Jackson began voicing aloud his complaints about the dinner that he and his wife had had at the Dukakises' on the Fourth of July: the food didn't suit him, the conversation was unsatisfactory, and when he began to tell Dukakis that he wanted the Vice-Presidential nomination they were interrupted by Dukakis's daughters serving ice cream. (As the Dukakises and the Jacksons later watched the Boston Pops, Jackson publicly had a meal brought to him.) The Dukakis people say that Jackson's reference to the Vice-Presidency was fairly general. (As for food, Kitty Dukakis has said that the menu was checked with Jackson's Chicago office several times.) The Dukakis people had hoped that Jackson would use the Fourth of July dinner as an occasion to take himself out of the running, but Jackson had other thoughts. A number of people who know Jackson, including people close to him, believed that even if he had been called by Dukakis earlier—even before Bentsen was called—Jackson would have found another issue. A black who knows Jackson well said to me at the time, "What this is about is 'stick-up.' Jesse wants a plane. He wants to walk into a meeting with Dukakis and say, 'Stick 'em up.' "

In 1984, Jackson made a fuss until the Mondale campaign—in August—agreed to provide him with a plane and some money to get blacks to register and vote in November. This time, Jackson was disturbed by press accounts that one of the things he wanted was a plane, but it was true. At his direction, negotiations between the Dukakis and Jackson camps over how many platform disagreements would be brought to the Convention floor were suspended. The Dukakis people quickly denied a press account that Dukakis would meet with Jackson in Atlanta. Even after the missed phone call, they were determined to avoid bilateral negotiations in Atlanta between the Jackson staff and the Dukakis staff on anything other than the Convention program and processes, as well as avoid a meeting between the two top men. The Dukakis people wanted no suggestion that they were being held up by

Jackson as Mondale and his people had been at the 1984 Convention, where protracted negotiations had gone on. But after days of phone calls between Bentsen and Jackson (the two men already had a political relationship, and Bentsen had had more experience dealing with coalition politics, and blacks, than Dukakis had), and between Brountas and Jackson, and Dukakis and Jackson, and between other advisers, what the Dukakis people ended up with was protracted negotiations in Atlanta between the two staffs and a meeting there between Jackson and Dukakis.

Jackson, meanwhile, had to begin to turn around, because he had no option but to end up supporting Dukakis by the end of the Convention. At the same time, Jackson had to be able to say to his followers that his protest had not been in vain. So as he rode in his highly publicized bus caravan from Chicago to Atlanta in the days preceding the Convention, he began to send out signals that he could be dealt with, but on his terms. Sounding every bit as if he still considered himself co-nominee, he said he wanted to be part of "the equation," that he wanted a "partnership" with Dukakis "based on shared responsibility," that he wanted "a seat at the table." (He had already begun to say that if he was to be a "vote picker" he wanted to "sit in the big house.") The Dukakis people were having trouble understanding what this was all about. One said to me in Atlanta before the Convention, "We're linear." Brountas said to me in Atlanta, "The reaction to the choice of Bentsen surprised us a little. Reverend Jackson was very serious about the idea that he had earned the right to be asked. Until Monday he hadn't indicated he would accept. Meanwhile, he was talking very enthusiastically, and his people were very disappointed."

Over the weekend before the Convention, Jackson's representatives in Atlanta, meeting with Dukakis advisers, were making a number of demands, including that Jackson have a role in the transition process if Dukakis is elected; that Jackson have full access to Dukakis if he becomes President; that Jackson be a full partner in the choice of the next chairman of the Democratic National Committee (the Jackson representatives took a run at getting Paul Kirk, the current chairman, replaced after the Convention, but the Dukakis people wouldn't have it, saying that Dukakis had made a public commitment to Kirk for the remainder of his term, which ends in January); and that Jackson supporters be given positions in the D.N.C. They were also discussing jobs for Jackson people in the Dukakis campaign. The Dukakis people say that they refused to discuss anything beyond the election. But the two sides did come to terms on a number of things (not all of which have become public): providing Jackson with a plane and a budget (reportedly five million dollars) for the fall campaign, jobs for some of Jackson's people in the campaign, and new positions for Jackson supporters in the D.N.C. (There is developing a tradition of Democratic candidates' yielding Party changes to Jackson that will affect the next election.) Brountas said to me in Atlanta, in the course of that weekend, that it was premature to talk to Jackson about a role in the transition, and that, as for constant access to a President Dukakis, "we didn't get into that. We said that in the course of the campaign there would be consultation and communication at all levels. If we win, the other things follow naturally." The Dukakis people say, credibly, that they had planned all along to bring some Jackson people into the campaign, but they had resisted discussing this before the Convention was over. The price for the missed phone call was new positions in the D.N.C.; the meetings, in Atlanta, past midnight, of the two staffs; and the meeting, on Monday morning, between Jackson and Dukakis. Meanwhile, the big story in Atlanta over the weekend had become: when would Dukakis and Jackson meet? Thus, Jackson continued to dominate the scene, and he played it for all he could. In the end, it did get down to the question that Jackson all year had hated: "What does Jesse want?" Addressing a black church on Sunday, Jackson revealed some important parts of his philosophy: "It's not over until it's over, and then it's not over." He also said, "The race goes to those who hold out." But he was at that point a protest candidate without a great deal to protest about.

After the three-hour breakfast Monday morning, to which Dukakis brought Brountas and Jackson brought Ron Brown, his Convention manager, and which Bentsen later joined, to help with the healing, Jackson, Dukakis, and Bentsen held a jammed press conference at the Hyatt Regency, Dukakis's headquarters hotel. The breakfast was something of an encounter session, at which Dukakis and Jackson spent some time getting things off their chests. The agreement, which Dukakis and his advisers vigorously denied was a "deal," had been worked out beforehand by the

staffs, and from all reports Dukakis firmly refused to discuss anything beyond the election. But Dukakis did say, at the press conference, in the course of praising Jackson, that he was "a great
leader, an inspirational leader, who has inspired millions and millions of people to become a part of American politics—and, we
hope, beginning in January, a part of American government."
Dukakis was deliberately vague about just what had been agreed
upon, and Jackson, who has a very expressive face, looked for
most of the time quite unhappy. At the breakfast, he had told
Dukakis that by "partnership" he had meant being "part of," and
in an interview later that day he said, "In my part of the country,
partnership does not mean lawyers and papers. It means being
friends, sharing the work and sharing the responsibility." Jackson
also said that he had won Dukakis's agreement to seek certain
legislative goals—which Brountas later told reporters were things
Dukakis already backed. Having Bentsen also at the press conference was to head off photos of only Dukakis and Jackson, but
gave rise to charges by Republicans, who had hoped that Jackson
would disrupt the Convention and turn off white voters, that the
Democratic ticket was a "troika." Several Democrats were left wondering how long the truce with Jackson would last. Meanwhile,
the Dukakis campaign had lost a week's time.

There were an uncommon number of parties surrounding the
Convention, in part because Atlantans were intent on being hos-
pitable, in part because everything about Conventions seems to
grow exponentially. Ted Turner, of CNN, threw a bash Sunday
night at which the Dukakises, the Bentsens, and the Jimmy Carters
showed up. Carter used the propinquity of the Convention to
propel his resurrection, and was very much on display. At the
Turner party, Dukakis made some remarks that fell completely
flat. A reception that a Washington law firm had planned to hold
on Monday for Bentsen had to be moved to a larger room because
of the firm's good fortune in its choice of guest of honor.

Some tension remained all week among the various groups that
were simultaneously choreographing the Convention: the Democratic National Committee, some Hollywood producers whom the
D.N.C. had brought in to apply some show-biz know-how and
glitz, and Dukakis people who were trying to tone down the glitz.

By the time the Dukakis people got into it, a number of decisions had already been made, and the Convention hall had been turned into a stage set for television. The ludicrously large podium (in the too small hall) made the speakers look tiny, and the salmon, eggshell, and azure colors, which replaced red, white, and blue because they supposedly looked better on television, made it look as if the Party had been victimized by a decorator. On television, they came across as salmon, eggshell, and azure—next to which the red Jackson placards and the blue Dukakis placards were a welcome sight.

Part of the Dukakis strategy is to have others take Bush on frontally while Dukakis (for as long as possible) remains above all that and discusses "issues." Another part of the strategy is to try to make the election turn on the persons of Bush and Dukakis, on the theory, which is based on poll data, that people will see Bush as the weaker leader. Thus, on Monday night Ann Richards, the keynote speaker, roasted Bush—in her deep Texas accent and with perfect timing. ("Poooor George." Pause. "He can't help it." Pause. "He was born with a silver foot in his mouth.") Calling Bush "George," which came across as a wimp name, was part of ridiculing him, and ridiculing him was part of trying to make him look hapless. The other most memorable line of the Convention was the "Where was George?" refrain that Edward Kennedy got the audience, which was having a whale of a time, to join him as he recited various Reagan Administration mishaps. The Dukakis polling suggests that people are much more concerned about the Iran-Contra affair, and whatever Bush's role in it was, than they are about the Administration's tortuous relationship with the Panamanian leader Manuel Antonio Noriega (who is still in power). The Dukakis people will use the drug issue—arguing that an increase in imports occurred while Bush was chairman of the South Florida Crime Task Force—to point up what they want people to see as Bush's ineffectiveness.

The Dukakis people say, and obviously hope, that the election will turn on domestic issues, and not foreign policy, where Dukakis is vulnerable. (Polls show that people have more confidence in Bush than in Dukakis in handling foreign policy, an advantage the Republicans are determined to exploit.) They say, and obviously hope, that people are uneasy about their economic future despite the continuing recovery, which is now in its sixty-seventh month, and despite the fact that unemployment is lower than it has been since 1974. (The current drought could also be a political burden for the Republicans.) While polls do indicate that there is a substantial amount of economic anxiety, the Administration's economic news continues to be good—especially if one ignores the huge debts the United States has piled up. (The forced decline in the value of the dollar has begun to lower the trade deficit and rising exports have had a boosting effect on the economy, but we still have to borrow huge amounts from abroad.) Interest rates are low; the shadow of inflation is beginning to appear, but most people doubt that the Administration or the Federal Reserve Board would do anything about this until after the election. But the recovery has been uneven, and Bentsen, using a phrase Dukakis has taken to, has described the economy as "Swiss cheese." (The Republicans are currently running a four-million-dollar ad campaign aimed at reminding people how bad things were under Carter.) The Dukakis people know that Bush's attacks on Massachusetts' prison-furlough program and on Dukakis's vetoing a bill requiring that schoolchildren recite the Pledge of Allegiance, and on Dukakis's opposition to the death penalty, did take their toll and caused Dukakis's lead in the polls to shrink, or all but disappear, in the little more than two weeks before the Convention. (Bush calls Dukakis "a card-carrying member of the A.C.L.U.") Some Dukakis advisers say (but not all agree), and hope, that Bush has shot his wad on these issues, having used them so early in the campaign. But the Bush campaign can be expected to run ads on them. This week's flap, which the Bush people (and Reagan) helped stir up, over whether Dukakis had ever seen a psychiatrist—he said flatly that he hadn't—is an omen of the kind of campaign we're in for.

The Dukakis people know that the Bush campaign will rely heavily on the issues of peace and prosperity, which is one reason they hope to keep the question centered on the comparison of the two men—on, as the Dukakis people say, "which man better understands the problems of the average American." (In the course of the Convention, it even appeared that the Iran-Iraq war might end, as Iran agreed to a United Nations resolution calling for peace.) In Atlanta, Susan Estrich said to me, "What we're trying to do here, in addition to reaching out to loyal Democrats, is reach at home the swing Democrats, the Reagan Democrats. So we're focussing on questions people have about their economic future, trying to show that we're people who understand the American dream—about health care, housing, jobs—versus a candidate who doesn't understand those concerns, doesn't speak to or for average Americans." At the Convention and in the campaign, Estrich said, the emphasis would be on Dukakis's own story as an immigrant son (Dukakis never used to talk about this), and on "basic values—family, patriotism, public service, integrity." Not everyone around Dukakis feels that, though he recites lists of needs that must be met, he conveys a feeling that he understands these problems. This, too, could be a result of the fact that he hasn't seen much of life; it also comes from the cool personality. (In any event, they do feel that Dukakis is better at this than Bush is.) Both candidates are talking about change, but Dukakis, inevitably, is talking about more change than Bush can. One Dukakis adviser said to me in Atlanta that he thinks that "in elections people think in large terms about change early and then sober up." He went on, "If in October people say, 'Things could be worse,' it will take all our wits to say convincingly, 'Things can be better without taking great risk.' "

The Dukakis campaign agenda is a decidedly middle-class one. For the time being, at least, the Democrats (with many exceptions, of course) have had it with liberalism, think it is a loser (see the 1984 election), and even try to avoid the word. Dukakis, like many of his contemporaries, describes himself as "progressive." He is in fact part of a generation of Democrats (with exceptions) who would rather not deal in ideology, and offer themselves as pragmatic "doers." This group includes several of Dukakis's contemporary governors, as well as some of the younger members of Congress. One of the governors, Bill Clinton, of Arkansas, was selected by the Dukakis people to give the sole nominating speech (usually there are nominating and seconding speeches), in order to describe Dukakis's credentials to the nation, which barely knew him. But the speech disastrously misfired—it was dense and cerebral as well as overly long, not the sort of speech one gives to a political convention. (The Dukakis people, trying to help Clinton out the next day, said that they had gone over the speech and found it fine—they did say that the first draft, which they worked over, had been even longer and denser, with a great deal about international economics—and that so had Dukakis. This was not promising.) Dukakis is a liberal, but current economic as well as political realities are a deterrent to espousing liberal programs.

Because of that, and because the fight in this election is presumed to be over Democrats who voted for Reagan and over independents—and because the Democratic Party has its own heavy baggage—those parts of the Convention that the Dukakis people could control were as lacking in ideology, and aimed at the middle class, as possible. The Democrats are going after people who live in the suburbs, if not the most affluent ones; they are aiming at middle-income and lower-middle-income workers, blue collar or service jobs, who are presumed to be not very interested in politics, and concerned with immediate matters. A Dukakis adviser says, "You have to communicate to those people more around economic issues and leadership—that defines a Presidential campaign—and less around a checklist of issues." Thus, there was a lot of talk, starting with Ann Richards, about two-income families struggling to make ends meet, worrying about their children's education and about paying for long-term health care for their parents. And there was a great deal of emphasis on "the family," which as the week went on became as syrupy as it was lacking in any real meaning. Democrats had been seen as having turned their back on "family values." Reagan, in 1980, had got there first. So as little as possible was said all week about abortion and homosexuality, and the Democrats, newly tamed, went along. Paul Kirk, after he became chairman, in 1985, had led the way to diminishing the Party's factionalism by abolishing the Party's various constituency-group caucuses. (He was also successful in discouraging interest-group endorsements of candidates.) Polling done for the D.N.C. this year found, nonetheless, that people questioned the Democrats' competence to manage the government again, and so a major goal all week was to show that they could run a Convention. Another burden the Democrats carry, according to the Party's own polling, is that they are seen as having been, when they last held office, naïve on foreign policy as well as unable to manage the economy. This is a major reason the Dukakis campaign places so much emphasis on portraying Dukakis as the competent manager. The Dukakis people hope that their candidate's qualities of steadiness and predictability, his self-assurance will help people over the hurdle of choosing him to manage the economy and,

despite some positions Dukakis has taken and despite his inexperience, foreign policy. (The self-assurance can also come across
as excessive. It can also get in the way of something some Dukakis
advisers feel their candidate still has to do—spend more time
learning about foreign policy. But Dukakis is, by many accounts,
a very stubborn man.) The "unity" that the Democrats struggled
for at the Convention, and that the Dukakis people talked about
so much, had an external as well as internal purpose: to show the
world that the Democrats can at least manage their own affairs.
There was also a great deal of emphasis on Dukakis as the son of
immigrants, a shining example of "the American dream." But the
relevance of Dukakis's own story to that of struggling middle-class
Americans was never quite clear, since it was his parents who had
struggled to achieve, while he was born to relative comfort, and
his parents could afford to send him to Swarthmore and Harvard
Law School. (However, there can be no doubt that Dukakis is an
achiever.)

Tom Kiley said to me in Atlanta, "There is a feeling among
the American people that things have been neglected—invest-
ments we should be making in people, in children." He added
that the two words that get the strongest negative reaction are
"foreign competition"—people feel that we aren't fighting back
—and that this mitigates the Republicans' argument that things
are going well. Irwin (Tubby) Harrison, Dukakis's pollster, said
to me in Atlanta, "The election is coming down to two issues:
though unemployment is low, a great many people feel uncertain
about their economic future; and, despite the talk of 'standing
tall,' that America has receded internationally." Harrison added,
"When you ask what is the greater threat, the Soviet Union or
Japan, it's Japan two to one." As for all the talk about people being
concerned about their children's economic future, Harrison said,
"For most people the future is tomorrow morning—it's a more
immediate concern. They're told about the good economic figures,
but they aren't seeing it in their own lives." Another Dukakis
adviser says, "Bush says that things are going well, that they could
be worse; Dukakis in similarly vague and thematic terms says
things can be better. If that's the debate, we win." The Democrats
will remain vague and thematic, this person said, "because we
have little choice, because of the deficit." Thus, this person said,
the electorate wants to be told that the deficit will be reduced and

that taxes won't be raised—and at the same time that something will be done to solve the problems of education, of child care (a new, hot issue), of housing, and of long-term medical care.

The middle-class agenda, a Dukakis adviser said, is back with a vengeance; before, it was poor who were all the rage. Kiley, for one, explained that this change was the result of eight years of Reaganism, in which middle-class needs weren't met and the "axis of resentment" shifted away from the poor—who were seen as "special interests" indulged by the Democrats (which led to big government)—to the wealthy, who are seen as having been indulged by Reagan. But the Democrats are still competing on Reagan's terms, and those terms include a political consensus that the Democratic Party can't talk very much about the needs of the poor and win the election. Even Tip O'Neill said to reporters at the Convention, "We really got too far off to the left, to be perfectly truthful." Now the Party that had for so long prided itself on championing the cause of blacks is trying to be less identified with blacks, while still retaining their loyalty. This is a difficult exercise, and one that makes a number of white Democrats, including some who advise Dukakis, uncomfortable. Democrats, including Dukakis, try to bridge the divide by talking about "economic opportunity," improvements in education, and, as Dukakis says, "decent and affordable housing for everyone," not specifying the intended beneficiaries. Dukakis talks a lot less than he used to about the homeless, or about hunger. But of course there is no way all these needs can be met for the poor and the middle class, given the budget deficit and given current political realities.

Jesse Jackson is aware of this tension between the Party's constituencies, and has put himself forth as the leader of the "progressive wing" of the Party. (When Bentsen was chosen, Jackson began to say that he represented one wing of the Party and Bentsen another, and "it takes two wings to fly.") Though this situation is felt by many to help Dukakis by making him appear more moderate than he is, the tension within the Party could cause continuing difficulties—including when, if he does, Dukakis has to govern. Jackson has already begun to push at Dukakis, saying last week that he was still unsure of the ticket's commitment to meeting the concerns of his supporters. One of the platform issues Jackson took to the Convention floor (having reached agreement with the

Dukakis people on vague wording on various Jackson proposals calling for more spending for certain programs) revealed the tension behind the unity of the Democratic Party. (The platform remained brief but still had a lot of goodies in it for the Party's interest groups.) Because the Dukakis campaign was loath to have the Party say anything suggesting that taxes might be raised, it opposed and succeeded in defeating Jackson's proposal that taxes be raised on the wealthy. The Dukakis people met their immediate political needs, but it was still strange to see the Democratic Party reject a proposal to raise taxes on the wealthy. Jackson's other proposal that came to vote—that the United States should abjure first use of nuclear weapons—was also defeated, after a debate that became tangled in ideology and some confusion over what the whole thing was about. A third proposal, calling for recognition of a Palestinian state, was debated but not voted upon; this partial consideration of the controversial proposal was the result of a compromise within the Jackson camp, as well as between the Dukakis and Jackson camps.

Jackson's speech to the Convention, while effective and in parts dramatic, was not nearly as electrifying as the one he gave in 1984 ("God is not finished with me yet"), and the audience was not as ecstatic as it was four years ago. Jackson came over forcefully on television, but in the hall it seemed that he was out of gas— intellectually, emotionally, physically. He is so talented a speaker, and has worked up so much material over the years, and he knows so well how to speak from and to the soul, that he could still put together a strong speech that captured many people. But he seemed spent, strayed far from his text, and pieced together a speech composed of a hodgepodge of his greatest hits from the campaign trail. To many people who had not heard him much, this was plenty good enough. After being introduced by his five children, Jackson talked of the importance of finding "common ground," repeating the phrase several times, and praised Dukakis in a constricted kind of way. ("I've watched a good mind fast at work, with steel nerves. . . . I've watched his perspective grow as his environment has expanded. . . . I know his commitment to public service.") He also said, "His foreparents came to America on immigrant ships. My foreparents came to America on slave ships. But whatever the original ships, we're in the same boat tonight." He spoke as he often did in the campaign, about his own early life, making

it sound more wretched than it apparently was, and he spoke
movingly, as he often does, about the poor. Jackson, as he often
is, was part poetry and part demagoguery. And he concluded with
a chant he had been using frequently: "Keep hope alive! Keep
hope alive! Keep hope alive!"

The idea of having Olympia Dukakis, the award-winning actress,
introduce her cousin, the candidate, was to have her get people
past Dukakis's image as a technocrat, to tell people about his roots.
In her short speech, and in the film she had made to accompany
her speech, she was boffo—coming across as a warm, gemütlich
Greek, the sort of person one would love to have as a cousin or
an aunt, and her warmth spread to the image of Michael Dukakis.
(If she loves him so, he must be O.K.) To further the image of
Dukakis as a frugal man who would not waste the taxpayers' money,
Olympia Dukakis, in the film, showed off his twenty-five-year-old
snowblower, saying, "I say Michael gives the word 'frugal' new
dimension."

Dukakis's entry into the hall from one side of the Convention
floor was a stagy attempt to show him as a man of the people.
(Jimmy Carter had done the same thing in 1976.) The audience
was to look for him, as it would a prizefighter. The campaign
considered but rejected as too hokey the theme from "Rocky" to
accompany his entrance. Instead, it used Neil Diamond's "Coming
to America," which has now evolved into the campaign theme
song, because of both its immigrant theme and its pulsating, energetic beat. When Dukakis reached the podium and accepted the
crowd's cheers, there could be no question that he was moved by
the situation, and this feeling penetrated and lifted his speaking
ability. The shake of his large head was familiar, but the glow the
occasion brought to his face seemed new. He had been good at
speaking before, but perhaps not that good—and his rising to the
occasion, his giving off a sense of command, seemed to both relieve
and energize the Convention audience. Until then, its attitude
toward Dukakis had seemed like that of someone entering into
an arranged marriage: everyone says it's the right thing to do but
your heart's not in it. And, for all the cheering that the Convention
audience did for Dukakis—with many of the cheers and chants
seeming orchestrated and somewhat synthetic (the Dukakis campaign kept tight control over the Convention from a trailer parked

just outside)—the cheers didn't seem to come from the gut. The audience seemed happy, but not frenzied, as Convention audiences can become.

Once again, Dukakis, the mechanic, described the race for the Presidency as "a marathon." He described himself as a product of "the American dream," and, with a slight catch in his voice, talked about his parents. He talked, as he had at times in the campaign, about "the next American frontier," and, as he so often had, about "good jobs at good wages." Trying to ward off any unwelcome labels, he said, "This election is not about ideology, it's about competence." This wasn't a great line; "competence" is a clunker of a word, it doesn't lift. Besides, competence can be used for good or ill. There was in fact little in the speech that was memorable. He made a joke about his frugality; Dukakis still isn't long on humor, but he's making more of an effort, and the campaign has two jokesmiths helping out. The speech was upbeat and positive, calling for "a new era of greatness," "the idea of community," and stressing the importance of economic opportunity. He talked a good bit about standards—trying to draw a contrast with the Reagan era. ("It's time to raise our sights.") He talked about lighting "fires of innovation and enterprise from coast to coast," and about making Americans "proud of their government." He got in a few political shots, questioning Bush's role in the Iran-Contra affair, and saying—as Richard Nixon had in 1968—that he would get a new Attorney General. (In fact, by this time Edwin Meese had announced he would resign, saying that the report of the Independent Counsel, which he had received but which remained private until the week of the Convention, had "vindicated" him. When the report was released, it said that Meese had probably broken the law, but would not be prosecuted, on two matters—filing a false tax return understating taxes he owed to the government, and violating federal conflict-of-interest laws, by participating in a Justice Department review of telecommunications policy at a time when he held stock in telephone companies. The report said that there was "insufficient evidence" that Meese had taken bribes or gratuities in the Wedtech scandal, or that he had violated the law against bribing foreign officials, in the case of the Iraqi pipeline. To replace Meese, the President had already selected former Governor Richard Thornburgh, of Pennsylvania.)

Dukakis also went through a long list of expensive things he said should be achieved (and spoke a little Spanish), giving no price or method of payment, of course, evading the question of cost by saying that these things would be "goals" and suggesting that some of these goals would be met by non-government sectors: give people on welfare the training and the child care they need; "invest in our urban neighborhoods"; "revitalize small town and rural America"; "give our farm families a price they can live on"; "decent and affordable housing for every family," and he did talk about ending "the shame of homelessness." He also called for legislation to provide for "basic health insurance for every family in America." He paid tribute to teachers, which appealed to the members of teachers' unions in the audience. He talked little about defense or foreign policy, but he did praise Reagan for having "set the stage for deep cuts in nuclear arms." He said, "We can do a lot more to bring peace to Central America," and also said that this election is "not about overthrowing governments in Central America." (The recent Sandinista crackdown on the opposition in Nicaragua led Republicans and the Administration to promote once more legislation to give military aid to the Contras. The Republicans enjoy the prospect of Bentsen, who has supported such aid, having to decide whether to vote with his Senate record—he is also up for reëlection this year—or with his Presidential candidate. Bentsen has said he would vote for the aid.) Toward the end, Dukakis returned to the theme of family, mentioning Ann Richards' family, Jackson's family, and his own family—coyly saying that he would have a grandchild around the time of the Inauguration. And he ended effectively, coming back to the idea of "marathon," relating it to ancient Greece and the oath that the citizens of Athens took long ago: "We will never bring disgrace to this, our country, by any act of dishonesty or of cowardice. . . . We will transmit this country greater, stronger, prouder and more beautiful than it was transmitted to us."

As Jim Wright, the betroubled House Speaker, who, as chairman of the Convention, presided over the proceedings more than many Democrats would have liked him to but not more than many House members expected him to (there were also four co-chairmen), acted as master of ceremonies, a large number of people were brought onto the podium. First, there was Kitty Dukakis, and then the rest of the Dukakis family; then the Bentsens and their family; then the Jacksons and their family. The Dukakis people had spent hours working out this podium tableau of "unity," and told the Jackson camp point blank that there was to be no opportunity for a "three-shot" of Dukakis, Bentsen, and Jackson. The other Presidential candidates and their wives were announced (Joseph Biden is still recuperating from surgery, and Gary Hart was made to feel unwelcome, and went home early), as were numerous other Party luminaries. Before long, the podium was a mob scene. The people on the podium and in the audience waved little American flags as the balloons and the Mylar confetti fell and the band played "The Stars and Strips Forever." Jackson managed to maneuver so that there was an opportunity for a photograph of the Dukakises, the Bentsens, and the Jacksons, which was on the front page of several papers the next day.

X

The Republican Party left New Orleans hopeful but shaken. George Bush's acceptance speech, like Michael Dukakis's, was widely deemed a great success, and for much the same reason: neither man is an exceptionally gifted orator, and Bush's organization, like Dukakis's, had actively and successfully lowered expectations. Moreover, much of the press, having lavished praise on Dukakis's speech, was inclined to give Bush equal treatment. Too much is made of these speeches: an acceptance speech is a set piece that the candidate has a great deal of time to prepare for, and about which he receives much advice, and he has as sympathetic an audience as he'll ever have. These speeches have little to do with how we see or react to Presidents most of their time in office. Yet it seemed as if the race for the Presidency had been reduced to a song contest. This is a curious standard for judging who should govern us. In any event, Bush's blunder in choosing a mediocrity, Senator Dan Quayle, of Indiana, as his running mate hovered over the Convention Hall on even the final, celebratory Thursday night, and as the Convention ended most people knew that the story was not over. While most of the focus in the last day and a half of the Convention was on whether Quayle had pulled strings to get into the National Guard so as to avoid service in Vietnam, this was a tangent. (It had become clear that his influential publishing family had helped out, but not whether Quayle, a strong supporter of the war, had been given special treatment—about which there is still ambiguity.) The real point was that Bush chose as the person to be next in line for the Presidency a man who not even he argued very strongly was qualified to succeed him. (Bush did not even mention this factor when he announced his choice.) Nor did Bush's top lieutenants, who were gamely and with varying degrees of enthusiasm defending his decision. (As the choice blew up in their faces, almost no one wanted to take credit for it.)

In the last dozen years—after Spiro Agnew and with the exception of the Democrats in 1984—we have come to take the office of the Vice-Presidency seriously; we have become more aware, after successful and unsuccessful assassination attempts, of the possibility that a Vice-President might have to take charge. That Bush, who must be aware of these things, and had several far more qualified people to choose from, chose Quayle, who from the outset presented other serious problems as well, raised unsettling questions about Bush's judgment. It also raised questions about the competence of the people around Bush, because Quayle was chosen by an obviously flawed system. More striking than the fact that the Bush people made mistakes was that they didn't make original mistakes. Everything that was flawed about the decision —the failure to thoroughly check Quayle's background and to thoroughly vent the pros and cons among the political advisers, the choice of someone unknown and untested—had happened before.

As the Republicans gathered in New Orleans over the mid-August weekend before the Convention, the polls had begun to narrow following Dukakis's large gain from his Convention, but Dukakis was still leading (by from seven to seventeen points). Dukakis had not had an especially good couple of weeks. Some of his own people were worried that he had become too reactive, and was saying little, just as Bush had begun to step up his assault. (The worry about the fact that this remained the case well after the Republican Convention has led to a change in the campaign's management.) Bush, with the help of better speechwriters, called Dukakis "the Stealth candidate" (after the bomber that is supposed to be invisible to radar) and called the Democratic platform "the black hole of American politics." Since the Democratic Convention, Republicans, including President Reagan, obviously frustrated by Dukakis's elusiveness, had been jumping on the Democrats for, as they put it, trying to hide the fact that Dukakis is a liberal. (Reagan, in his Saturday radio address after the Democratic Convention, said, "You'll never hear that L-word—liberal—from them.") The Dukakis campaign got tied up for a week over the rumors, fanned by the Bush people, that Dukakis had sought psychiatric help after his brother died and after he lost reëlection to the governorship; Dukakis had got his back up over releasing more medical information (just as he had got his back up over the failure to reach Jesse Jackson to tell him about the Vice-Presidency), and the campaign endured several days of stories about possible mental-health problems (and lurid rumors, also spread by Bush allies) before Dukakis decided to release as much information as previous candidates had, and Reagan, with his inapt remark ("I'm not going to pick on an invalid"), went too far. (A Bush campaign official noted to me that the controversy had forced Dukakis to in effect say, "I'm not crazy.") On August 4th, Dukakis appeared at the Neshoba County Fair, in Philadelphia, Mississippi, an area with a racist history, and did not mention to the virtually all-white crowd the finding nearby of the bodies of three murdered civil-rights workers on that same day twenty-four years ago. (Last week, Jackson said that he wasn't ready to give Dukakis wholehearted support, because the Dukakis campaign had not brought aboard enough of his aides and because Dukakis needed to send "signals of sensitivity" to blacks.) Also in early August, Bush made two strong speeches on foreign and defense policy, to which Dukakis responded by complaining that Bush was being "negative," by bringing up once again the Iran-Contra and Noriega affairs, and by criticizing Bush for not yet having agreed to any debates. A Dukakis defense-policy speech given at New York University shortly before the Republican Convention, which had been billed as a major address, said little.

Bush and his allies in the White House persuaded the President to veto a bill authorizing funds for the military (despite the fact that his Defense Secretary and national-security adviser had approved it); in doing so, Reagan blamed the Democrats for trying to "redirect us only to weakness." Senate Republicans withheld support of a bill, passed by the Senate, authorizing "humanitarian" aid for the Contras—after military aid was rejected—thus setting up the Democrats for accusations that they had "lost" Nicaragua. The surprise action by the Federal Reserve Board in early August raising the discount rate, and thus interest rates, in the face of signs of rising inflation, was ominous for Bush (Dukakis called the increase an "irresponsibility tax" that was the result of "eight years of endless borrowing and spending"); but Bush got a break when the trial of Oliver North was put off until after the election. Bush also made speeches on ethics, indicating he would have higher standards than Reagan, and on child care, making an odd but, to the right wing, ideologically correct proposal to provide every low-income family a thousand-dollar tax credit for child care whether or not both parents work; a Democratic proposal would give Federal funds to the states, to be used for grants to day-care centers or vouchers for parents. Bush's child-care proposal (made before a women's group) was one of three he has made that would undo the tax-reform law passed in 1986—the others would lower the capital-gains tax and restore tax breaks for the oil-and-gas industry. Bush also pledged to a Hispanic group that he would put a Hispanic in his Cabinet, but Reagan was able to get on with this by naming a Hispanic, Lauro Cavazos, Secretary of Education. Reagan also accommodated Bush by reversing himself and allowing the plant-closing measure to become a law. And polling by Bush's campaign indicated that his attacks on Dukakis—suggesting he is soft on crime, short on patriotism, and weak on defense—were working.

The formal announcement, shortly before the Convention, that James Baker would give up his job as Treasury Secretary (to be replaced by another Bush friend, Nicholas Brady) and take over as chairman of the Bush campaign came none too soon for many Republicans, who saw the Bush campaign organization as adrift, faction-ridden, and headless. (The press secretary had already been replaced.) The collegiality of which so much had been made early this year wasn't working. And some key Republicans were not pleased with the pugnacious style of campaign manager Lee Atwater; one told me, "They need adult supervision over there." Whether or not Baker was keen on running the campaign, he had little choice, since Bush is an old, close friend and Baker could have got some of the blame if he stood by while Bush lost. Privately and publicly, Baker told people that it would be very difficult for Bush to win, because the Republicans had been in power for eight years and the Vice-Presidency was a difficult office from which to run for President. (The implication: don't blame Baker if Bush loses.) Baker was expected to impose discipline, provide a smoother presence on television, and be able to talk to Bush as a peer. Bush, the existing campaign structure complained to Baker—and as Baker was to learn anew—could be quite stubborn on political matters, thinking his many years in public life gave him more expertise than his advisers.

Bush is a more complex character than he often appears. He

is dignified and a gentleman, but he is culturally confused: not content to be a Connecticut aristocrat—his striking out for Texas to go into business there was something aristocrats did—he keeps trying to reidentify himself. Thus lately we have been told, frequently, of his affection for pork rinds and country-and-Western music. At an ethnic festival, he puts on a baseball cap and a satin jacket and eagerly samples a great many dishes. (His advisers have tried to persuade him not to wear the hats—as he did earlier this year when he played truck driver.) More than one Republican strategist pointed out to me in New Orleans that Bush has a continuing problem with "body language"—something they think should have been worked on more. One of these strategists said, "Body language is usually more important than content—Reagan's proof of that."

While Bush is by all accounts a considerate man, he also has a peevish, even spiteful, streak; people who supported Robert Dole, or otherwise—and sometimes for a not very big reason—got on Bush's wrong side, are not welcome in the campaign no matter how much they may be needed. (Most candidates have a touch of this, but Bush has a long trail of outcasts.) His family has also thrown its weight around; for example, Bush's brother Jonathan tried (unsuccessfully), with what he said was George's support, to oust New York Republican national committeeman Richard Rosenbaum, who had supported Dole. (On the Convention floor, Rosenbaum told me that Jonathan Bush had called him "and said his brother had sanctioned it, that they wanted the national committeemen to be original Bush supporters.") Bush is a far more determined man than his pleasant and sometimes weak demeanor would suggest: it took Baker some time to persuade Bush to drop out of the race for the nomination in 1980, and his comeback in New Hampshire this year was in some part due to his grit. He can be tough, and even rough, but his awkward attempts at showing machismo throw people off. (At the Convention, Bush said he and Quayle would be "a couple of pit bulls.") Bush is well educated and has had a lot of exposure to the world, but he is, according to people who have worked closely with him, intellectually lazy and undisciplined. He doesn't read much. The depth that we would like to impute to him is apparently not there. Thus, having few strong views of his own and seeming not entirely sure who he is, he has in his various public roles been able to blend into the scenery and adjust his opinions. But, unlike Dukakis, he has a large circle of friends, which includes a number of politicians, in both parties, who feel warmly toward him. For this and related reasons, some Republican strategists argue that Bush ought to agree to many debates with Dukakis, on the theory that the public would end up liking Bush better.

The Bush strategists made what turned out to be their first mistake about the Vice-Presidency when they decided that, since the Convention would otherwise have no suspense, they would hold off the announcement of Bush's running mate until the last morning. While such announcements at Conventions used to be routine, the intensity of the media coverage today (which affects a great many things) made the speculation about a running mate the dominant story to such an extent that it threatened to swallow the Convention. The Bush people encouraged the speculation by dropping hints—so as to build what they termed "the suspense factor." The carefully made plans of Convention managers to get other "messages" through began to go awry. Over the weekend before the Convention, and on its first day, most of the talk in New Orleans, in the hotel lobbies, at the many parties, on television, was about whom Bush might choose. (New Orleans went all out to show people a good time, and its many delights made it a lot of people's favorite Convention city.) Various claimants to the position went through the indignity of selling their wares on the Sunday talk shows (although no one forced them to); by Monday, Dole was publicly complaining about the process ("I don't care for it"). On Saturday, there was a much talked-about story in the New York *Times* saying that Quayle (a late entry) was one of the finalists. We learned later that this had been leaked by Baker in order to head off the choice of Quayle (he apparently thought he was failing to dissuade Bush), on the theory that the idea of Quayle would meet with such opposition that Bush would back off. But it didn't, because almost no one believed that Bush would choose Quayle.

There were, after all, some very estimable alternatives. Robert Dole, who was told by Bush he was his second choice, had the potential of bringing real strength to the ticket, but his unpredictability and sharp tongue made him a risk. (His wife, Elizabeth, was not as serious a possibility, though her name was bandied about by the Bush people, who at one point had put out a very long list of possibilities—a new form of patronage.) Also, it seemed unlikely that Bush would want to spend the next four years in the company of such independent men as Dole and Jack Kemp (who had strong backing on the right), and he evidently felt he had the luxury of choosing not to do so. (Why Dole would want to be Vice-President is another matter; people who know him well say he is bored with being Senate Minority Leader and sees the Vice-Presidency as the route for yet another try for the Presidency.) One Bush adviser says that Dole and Kemp (who aren't particularly fond of each other) cancelled each other out: that if Kemp were picked Dole "would walk," and if Dole were picked the Kemp forces would have been most unhappy. Some people in the Bush high command, and close to it, thought that the strongest choice would be Richard Thornburgh, the former governor of Pennsylvania, who was recently confirmed overwhelmingly as the new Attorney General. Polling by the Bush camp showed that only two possibilities could bring a state into Bush's column: Senator John Danforth, of Missouri, and Thornburgh. (If the polling had indicated that California's Governor George Deukmejian could have brought them his state, the Bush people probably would have tried to talk him out of his reluctance to run for fear of turning the state over to a Democrat.) The other attractions of Thornburgh were that it would be sort of reverse-Bentsen —going at the Democrats in a state they hope to hold—and that Pennsylvania has nearly as many electoral votes as Texas (twenty-five to Texas's twenty-nine). Moreover, Thornburgh represented integrity as well as law and order, a nice contrast with Edwin Meese. (Susan Estrich, Dukakis's campaign manager, most feared that Bush would pick Thornburgh.) According to Bush advisers, Danforth was in the mix until the end, as was Howard Baker.

Bush kept his counsel to an even greater extent than Dukakis had—and this may have been part of the problem. The results of background checks by an attorney, Robert Kimmitt, an associate of James Baker, on the possible running mates went, on Bush's instruction, directly and solely to Bush. The political advisers had no opportunity to spot problems and raise alarums. Bush, trying to draw a contrast with Dukakis, said he knew all the candidates well enough that he didn't have to interview them himself. People who were in on the process say that no one knew whom Bush would choose, and, says one, "I don't think anyone other than George Bush can tell you why somebody didn't make it." Bush's advisers travelling on his plane to New Orleans formed a pool on whom Bush would select. According to two of them, no one guessed Quayle. One adviser said to me, "I can honestly say that no one knew." Another said, "When he told us, the reaction was one of surprise." (In New Orleans, Bush advisers quite noticeably said, "It was the Vice-President's decision.") Though about ten names remained in consideration until the end, everyone figured that Bush had narrowed it to four or five, but, says one Bush adviser, different advisers would have guessed a different four or five.

One apparent finalist, Senator Pete Domenici, of New Mexico, also had the support of some top Republicans; Domenici, who served as chairman of the Budget Committee when the Republicans controlled the Senate, is highly esteemed and, to boot, is the son of Italian immigrants, and a Catholic with eight children. Domenici had supported tax increases and cuts in Social Security payments in order to cut the deficit (as had Dole and a number of other Republicans), but as the New Orleans Convention approached he said that raising taxes may no longer be necessary. Senator Alan Simpson, of Wyoming, who is popular in Washington and a friend of Bush, was under consideration, but he brought no obvious electoral or demographic strength to the ticket—and he has a sharp and tangy tongue. Simpson, who had decided he didn't want the job, made sure he didn't get it by emphasizing, on "Meet the Press," that he supported cuts in entitlement programs, and that taxes would have to be raised, and by saying, on the subject of abortion, "I am pro-choice. . . . Once you flunk that litmus test you're doomed. It's crazy."

Opposition to abortion has become a litmus test for Republican candidates, and conservatives are in firm control of the Party. The platform, conservative in all respects, calls for a constitutional amendment outlawing abortion, and does not make an exception even for when the life of the mother is at stake or in cases of rape or incest, as many Republican politicians do—including Bush, who has changed his mind on the subject several times. The Party's position on some social issues, especially abortion, disturbs some libertarians on the right, but the right-to-lifers have the upper hand. As it happens, the names of possible running mates were run by Representative Newt Gingrich, of Georgia, one of the centurions on the right. When I found Gingrich on the Convention floor on the last night, he told me that his preference had been Kemp or Quayle. He said that he had told the Bush people that Danforth was acceptable to the right-to-lifers but was stylistically more aloof than Quayle, and that Thornburgh would have caused "some disgruntlement," because he hadn't always been correct on abortion. Gingrich told me he said to the Bush people that "either Kemp or Quayle would be the best choices," and that "if for any reason they couldn't pick Kemp, Quayle would be a great choice and would send the right signal to the movement." He said that Phyllis Schlafly and Paul Weyrich (head of the Free Congress Foundation) were delighted with the choice.

Among the reasons hardly anyone thought that Bush would pick Quayle were his reputation as a lightweight, the fact that Indiana is a reliable Republican state (though Bush was behind there as the Convention opened) and has few electoral votes (twelve), and the fact that he comes from a family of great wealth. It was assumed that Bush would vary the ticket, especially since the Dukakis campaign was running at him as being an aristocrat who is out of touch with mainstream Americans. At a bash thrown by the New Orleans *Times-Picayune* on Saturday night, one right-wing activist said he had just heard that the Quayle family trust fund is worth hundreds of millions of dollars—"That will certainly solve our silver-spoon problem," he said. Other reasons most people assumed that Quayle wouldn't be picked were that he was both unknown and untested and hadn't been subject to the merciless scrutiny national candidates must endure. (Republican elders warned Bush against selecting someone untested, especially at such a late date.) Another reason was that whatever the facts were about Quayle's golfing weekend, in 1980, with two fellow House members and the lobbyist Paula Parkinson, who later posed nude in *Playboy*—Quayle had said he had nothing to do with Parkinson, who was another congressman's companion—common sense dictates that you don't, if you can help it, start out a campaign with something you have to explain. (On the last day of the Convention, one right-wing leader speculated glumly that Parkinson would reemerge—as she did the following week, claiming, to *Playboy*, that Quayle had tried to get her to make love to him. Quayle, talking with reporters at his home while he was symbolically throwing out his trash, denounced the story as "totally untrue.")

Bush, obviously, had his own reasons, objective and subjective, for choosing Quayle—picking a running mate is a little like picking a spouse. It is the case that Quayle was championed by Bush's pollster, Robert Teeter, and his media adviser, Roger Ailes. (Quayle was also supported by Craig Fuller, Bush's chief of staff.) In New Orleans, after the selection blew up in the Bush campaign's face, Teeter let it be known that Ailes had been the more enthusiastic Quayle supporter. The selection has also been attributed to Atwater, but Quayle was not among Atwater's top two choices (Kemp and Elizabeth Dole were), and though he did favor the idea of picking someone of a younger generation than Bush, he had in mind someone older than Quayle. Both Teeter and Ailes apparently saw Quayle as a fresh face (in that they were correct), a "baby boomer" who might attract the votes of millions of others born since the Second World War. (Many people had thought that the idea that those of a given generation would vote alike had gone out with Gary Hart and Joseph Biden. And the idea that baby boomers will flock to one of their own is unproven. One of the most successful politicians with this age group is Ronald Reagan.) Moreover, their argument went, Quayle could help in the Midwest and energize the right. (A recent Quayle press conference, in Missouri, was cut off after two and a half minutes when Quayle stumbled over answers to questions about farm programs.) Quayle has an almost uniformly hard conservative voting record—though he did co-sponsor a jobs program with Edward Kennedy. Quayle has voted against civil-rights legislation, and he led the Senate opposition to the plant-closing bill. A number of Republicans in New Orleans, among them some conservatives who backed Kemp, whose politics include reaching out to blue-collar workers and to blacks, thought the ticket would have been stronger if it offered more "inclusiveness." On the Convention floor, a moderate senator said to me, "They need to go out and get some moderates. They need all the help they can get."

Quayle's selection was the media-candidacy theory run amok. In Ailes' view, Quayle's telegenic face would provide an attractive picture, the "visual" of him with Bush would be good. (Much was made of the fact that Quayle had been a client of both Teeter and Ailes, but both men also had other clients on the list of possibles.) Quayle has sometimes been said to resemble Robert Redford. (He doesn't.) Redford, after all, was the star of "The Candidate," a

1972 movie about a handsome son of influential parents who, with the guileful aid of a campaign strategist and ending up talking gibberish, wins election to the Senate. The famous last line of the movie has the victorious candidate saying, "What do we do now?" According to a story in the Washington *Post*, a law-school classmate of Quayle's said that Quayle had been interested in going into politics long before he went to law school; the classmate said they saw the movie together and afterward talked about it for eleven straight hours.

It was some of Bush's reasons (which, of course, can only be inferred), plus the questionable judgment that Bush displayed, that were so troubling. The week before the Convention, one Republican strategist said something to me that turned out to be quite prescient. Bush, this man said, would select someone who would "reaffirm that everything he's done is correct." Thus he would pick someone who would be unto him as he had been unto Reagan: grateful, unquestionably loyal, and even malleable. A good bit of amateur psychology was practiced in New Orleans— but that doesn't make the theories wrong. It was speculated that Bush did indeed want someone like himself, or who could be made like himself—and also someone with whom he would be socially comfortable. Quayle would be no threat. David Keene, who heads the American Conservative Union and worked in Bush's 1980 campaign, said to me in New Orleans, "Quayle's ideology is O.K., but only counts for that much"—he held his thumb and forefinger a quarter-inch apart. He added, "I don't think Bush picked him because he's conservative; I think he picked him for social and cultural reasons." All of the theories notwithstanding, when Bush, on Tuesday afternoon, shortly after his arrival in New Orleans, announced that his choice was Quayle, the general reaction was one of sheer astonishment.

Quayle's début was not auspicious. The announcement scene was strange to begin with, almost certainly because it hadn't been planned that way. Bush was standing in front of the stern-wheeler, the Natchez, that had brought him from the naval air station where he had landed (and seen Reagan off to California), addressing a rally. In an attempt to be informal, he had removed his tie and jacket and stood there in a short-sleeved shirt, which made him look concave. When Quayle was announced, he bounded up on the stage from out of the crowd and, alternately grabbing a startled-looking Bush's arm and jumping up and down and waving his own arms, he shouted a number of vacancies: "Believe me, we will win, because America cannot afford to lose!" Nearly punching Bush in the stomach, Quayle cried, "Let's go get 'em!" (Quayle shouts and waves his arms on the Senate floor as well.) A team selected by the Bush campaign to break in and run the campaign of whomever Bush named was awaiting Quayle. The Dukakis campaign did a similar but less dominating thing for Bentsen, though Bentsen was more seasoned. A Vice-Presidential candidate can be unprepared for the daunting demands and brutal pressures of a national campaign. Quayle was especially unprepared. His team is headed by Stuart Spencer, a shrewd political consultant, who managed Reagan's two campaigns for governor of California and has remained an adviser. He is someone Nancy Reagan calls on in a crisis. (Spencer, one of those who have got on Bush's wrong side, was not welcome in his campaign; James Baker got him for the Vice-Presidential duty.) Spencer had hoped for Domenici; he had his work cut out for him.

Shortly after six-thirty that evening, Baker and Teeter held a press conference at which they made the case for Quayle; the interesting thing was that they felt they had to. Baker, an experienced lawyer and political salesman who is always in command, looked very unconvinced of his case. (On the other hand, Pat Robertson and Gordon Humphrey, a right-wing senator from New Hampshire, who had threatened to lead a walkout from the Convention if an appropriate conservative wasn't picked, had both been on television praising the selection of Quayle.) Baker, looking grim, told the press conference that putting "the first baby boomer on a national ticket" was "a bold stroke." Asked if Bush felt he had picked the person best qualified to succeed him if necessary, Baker—who on one of the Sunday shows had said that the first criterion should be for "someone who is clearly competent to be President of the United States in the event some misfortune befell the President"—replied, "The issue is not who might have been the very best qualified to be President. The issue is getting someone who is extremely well qualified to be President and who might have some other attributes as well."

As soon as a press conference held by Bush and Quayle the following morning was over, both the Bush people and the press knew there were problems. Quayle, looking frightened and nervous, gave evasive and clipped responses to questions about Parkinson and about his service in the National Guard, as well as to questions about his wealth and about the secret funding of the Contras. (Rob Owen, who was North's courier, had worked in Quayle's office in 1982 and 1983, met North at that time, and tried to help the Contras then; this was during the congressional ban on military aid to the Contras.) The Bush people said that Quayle had bumbled on the Guard and Parkinson matters because he had been prepped for different questions on these subjects. This was not reassuring. A number of people there, including Bush people, felt that if Quayle had at least indicated an awareness of the unfairness in the fact that the Vietnam War was largely fought by those who didn't have the money or connections to avoid it, he might have been all right. It was not until later that day that the fact that Quayle had called on his family's connections to get into the Guard came to light—"Calls were made," Quayle said in one network interview that evening—and it became the topic of much of the television coverage that night. The implication was that Quayle had received special treatment—though the facts weren't known. If the Bush people had checked into this further, they might have been better able to deal with the situation.

On Wednesday afternoon, the Bush people hastily put together a press conference at which various senators, some of whom were known not to have too high a regard for Quayle, attested to his value as Bush's running mate. Some senators arrived late and hurriedly, having just been rounded up by the Bush people. It was noticeable that several of them cited as the reason for their enthusiasm the observation that Quayle would be an "enthusiastic" campaigner. (The numerous testimonials gave one the feeling that we were attending Quayle's funeral.) In fact, from virtually the time Quayle was named, senators who praised Quayle publicly said quite different things once the television cameras were gone. Senator William Cohen, of Maine, who had been widely quoted as saying of Quayle's having been chosen, "I'm stunned," said to me on the Convention floor Thursday night, "The question isn't whether he's too young; the question is whether he's young and *wise*." (Quayle is forty-one, but the question raised by a number of people in New Orleans was not about his age but his maturity.) Off the record, a number of senators went further in questioning the choice. John McCain, of Arizona, who as a Navy fighter pilot spent over five years as a P.O.W. in North Vietnam, and whom the Bush campaign made heavy use of during the National Guard flap, privately told people that he and Quayle, both of whom are members of the Armed Services Committee, had attended a defense briefing of Bush, and that he himself had gone home most unimpressed with Quayle's grasp of the subject.

A fair number of rumors were swirling around New Orleans, and on Wednesday night the Bush campaign went into a crisis mode. The high command cancelled Quayle's scheduled television appearances for the next morning and met well into the night, tracking down rumors and deciding what to do. The meetings resumed the next morning. All of this fed the crisis atmosphere, and, in the hyperexcitable Convention setting, people, gathered in hotel lobbies and meeting over lunch, began to not only speculate on whether Quayle would be dropped from the ticket but rehearse what Quayle would say upon taking himself out. ("I do not wish to be a burden to the ticket," etc.) The most dramatic thing that has happened before becomes the expected. The Bush people later said, uniformly, that dropping Quayle "was never seriously considered"—a phrase that is not airtight. They understood, of course, that having to drop him would be a calamity, might end the election then and there. So the better, and chosen, option was to try to tough it out. Who knew? Maybe he could still end up a plus for the ticket—a possibility that could not be ruled out.

The Vice-Presidential speculation and then uproar seriously interfered with the messages the Convention planners hoped to send. (It also diverted attention from Bentsen's financial records, which were released Wednesday. The plan was to release them at a time when attention would be on Bush's running mate, but, because of Quayle, this scheme succeeded beyond the Dukakis and Bentsen people's wildest dreams. Press examination of the records was largely perfunctory. Though it did come out that Bentsen was worth at least ten million dollars—a figure that had once worried the Dukakis and Bentsen people—Quayle's supposed wealth made Bentsen look like a man of modest means.) The Convention planners intended to tear down Dukakis and build up Bush—in that order—and to talk about how much better things have been under Reagan than they were under Carter, and warn of the consequences of electing another Democrat. The goal, said one strategist, "is to drive Dukakis's negatives up and drive George's down." It was to be neither a polite Convention nor a polite campaign. A senior official of the Bush campaign had said to me before the Convention that the purpose of drawing "the contrast" between Bush and Dukakis in the course of the campaign would be to "keep the focus on the other guy—you always want to keep the focus on your opponent." There are plans for tough ads against Dukakis on emotional issues, such as Massachusetts' furlough program (under which a convicted killer escaped and committed rape and robbery). Stuart Spencer said to me in New Orleans, talking about the campaign to come, "It's going to be no prisoners taken—lots of negative advertising, lots of charges by surrogates, and any time there's an opening, take it." Roger Ailes said to me recently, "Dukakis is a mean little guy; he complains that people are mean to him and he gets under and rabbit-punches, knees in the groin. He pulls it off with this weary, arrogant façade—'Oh, they're being so mean to me.'" Warming to his subject, Ailes said, "He's the most vicious, dirty politician in America." One strategist said, "You have to keep the pressure on, like this"—and he made the sign of a knife at the throat. He added, "The Dukakis campaign hasn't been under pressure; they've never been up against a group like this one. Dukakis will have cross-current media coming at him from all sides." An effort would be made to force Dukakis into making a mistake. A strategist also told me that pressure would be brought on Kitty Dukakis, on the theory that she can be high-strung, and therefore vulnerable. The first example of this strategy may have been the charge made last week by Senator Steve Symms, of Idaho, that he had heard that "there are pictures around" showing Kitty Dukakis burning the American flag at a sixties anti-war demonstration. Symms offered no documentation, and Mrs. Dukakis flatly denied that such a thing had taken place.

Convention planners said there would be no "personal attacks," of the sort that the Democratic keynote speaker and Kennedy ("Where was George?") had made; this Convention would stick to the "issues." In their effort to hold the "Reagan Democrats," they would stress the defense issue and certain social issues having to do with patriotism and crime. Much was to be made, at the Convention and in the campaign, of Dukakis's veto of a bill

requiring public-school teachers to lead their students in the Pledge
of Allegiance, and the furlough program. Dukakis asserted after
the Republican Convention that he had vetoed the Pledge bill,
which carried criminal penalties, on the basis of advisory opinions
by the state supreme court and attorney general that it was
unconstitutional—but this is a difficult point to get across in the
midst of a political campaign. (The Bush people were delighted
that Dukakis responded, thus keeping the issue alive, and Bush
seized on Dukakis's explanation to ask, "What is it about the Pledge
of Allegiance that upsets him so much?") The Republican National
Committee sent to every delegate a copy of a *Reader's Digest* article
about Willie Horton, the recipient of the infamous furlough—
who could have been expected to be quite famous by the end of
the Convention but whose name was barely mentioned, though
the furlough program came up often. Historians may wonder
how it was that the Pledge of Allegiance became an election
issue—as of now bidding fair to be the Quemoy and Matsu of
1988. A very precise Convention plan had been drawn up; this
was to be the most scripted Convention ever—down to what delegation leaders were to say during the roll-call vote on the Presidential nomination. (The roll call went awry and lasted until past
12:30 E.D.T.)

Even Reagan's speech, the big event on Monday night, fell a bit
flat. (Reagan was deliberately put on early in the week so as to
get him out of town and give Bush the limelight. The Convention
was deliberately not held in California so as to minimize Reagan's
presence.) One of the problems was the hall, which, in contrast
to the Democrats', was too large. The Superdome, which covers
fifty-two acres and on the outside looks like a large atomic pile
and inside gives one the feeling of being inside a huge mushroom,
is usually used for football; the fabric curtains that walled off the
unused half and the high roof (twenty-seven stories high) soaked
up the sound, and the sound system that was used was unac-
countably faulty, making it difficult to hear in whole sections of
the hall. (The sound system was improved over the week but was
never great.) The size also destroyed any feeling of intimacy.

The other problem with Reagan's speech was that he was simply having one of his off nights. (For all his famous skill as a
communicator, Reagan is uneven.) He talked, in his familiar husky

voice, about the high inflation and interest rates under Jimmy Carter, the taking of hostages at the American Embassy in Teheran, the "malaise" with which Carter will be forever, if mistakenly, branded. (Carter didn't use the term.) He spoke of numerous foreign-policy achievements: the Soviet withdrawal from Afghanistan, the Iran-Iraq ceasefire, the prospect for peace in southern Africa, the I.N.F. treaty. He rang many familiar changes but didn't stir up anything close to the frenzy he had at previous Republican Conventions. He's moving on—becoming irrelevant. He praised Bush, saying that Bush had worked on reduction of paperwork ("And George was there"), and said, "George played a major role in everything we've accomplished in these last eight years." He went on, "So, George, I'm in your corner." And he said, pausing for effect, "Go out there and win one for the Gipper." Sometimes it seems that Reagan does actually think he is George Gipp, the part he played in the movie "Knute Rockne—All American." The line between fantasy and reality is not a firm one in Reagan's mind. And Reagan understands theatre; Bush doesn't—and neither does Dukakis. (Jesse Jackson does.) Reagan's facility at employing myths and symbols is one of the keys to his political success—along with his easygoing persona, which is also partly a creation. He is popular, but less popular than Dwight Eisenhower was at the end of his second term. (Reagan's approval rating has been hovering around fifty per cent.) Moreover, there is a question as to whether Reagan has coattails. He didn't in 1986. Stuart Spencer says that Reagan "has never had coattails, because he's not viewed as a politician."

A drumbeat of Dukakis-bashing emanated from the podium for the next two nights, and though Dukakis offers some real targets, there was a shrillness, and even a demagogy, to the attacks on him—and a repetitiveness that took the edge off. Dukakis's defense policy is fair game, but several Republican speakers, including the usually thoughtful Thomas Kean, the governor of New Jersey and the keynote speaker, went beyond that to question his patriotism. The Democrats had poked fun at Bush, but there was little humor in the Republicans' counterattacks. Republicans are fine folks, but something happens to them in Convention assembled that doesn't bring out their best. The delegates are almost entirely whites and well-off, and there is a whiff of smugness, even intolerance. Moderates, not to mention liberal Republicans, have been largely driven off, and those who still come to Conventions almost uniformly hold their tongue. Orthodoxy is the order of the day.

Representative Henry Hyde, of Illinois, who was put on the Tuesday-night program to offset Kean, who does not toe the line on abortion, said the Democrats are "the party of abortion on demand and every taxpayer is an accessory." Jeane Kirkpatrick, who had roused the Republican Convention in Dallas four years ago with a stinging attack on the Democrats' foreign policy, once again assailed the Carter Administration, and said, "Neither the United States nor the world can afford another learning experience like that." She said the Democrats have a policy of "unilateral concessions and wishful thinking." The "Dukakis Democrats," she said, "do not understand how the prudent use of American power" has helped bring about various foreign-policy successes. She called Dukakis "another very liberal governor with a technocratic style and no foreign-policy experience," and said, "Michael Dukakis doesn't say he will make America vulnerable, but that is the inevitable consequence of unilaterally cancelling our major weapons systems." She added, "Michael Dukakis simply doesn't take the need for defense seriously." (Actually, Kirkpatrick, who had supported Dole, and George Bush are not overly fond of each other.) Kirkpatrick's speech didn't go over as well as the one four years ago—in part because of the hall, and in part because much of the material was tired. And the New Orleans Convention lacked the hyperbolic nationalism of the one in Dallas, where America's victories in the recent summer Olympics inspired the frequent chanting of "U.S.A.! U.S.A.!"

Once Kean, who but for the abortion issue could be a major figure in the Party, got past the requisite attacks, he gave a thoughtful speech. (Kean, pointing out that the Democratic Convention décor had substituted vaguer colors for the traditional red, white, and blue, said, "I believe Americans, Democrat and Republican alike, have no use for pastel patriotism." He also said, "What does the name of Dukakis sound to you like?" To which the audience shouted, "More Taxes!") Kean who practices what he calls "the politics of inclusion," and won reëlection in 1985 by appealing to blacks as well as whites (getting sixty per cent of the black vote), talked about the need for "freedom from racism, freedom from poor schools," and said, "The simple truth is that there are no spare Americans." He went on, "To those who are ill-schooled, ill-trained, or ill-housed we must reach out . . . because it is the right thing to do." He continued, "We will search out bigotry and racism—we will drag it into the sunshine of understanding and make it wither and die." Kean is what Bush might have been if ambition hadn't confused him.

Pat Robertson, who followed Kean, gave a thumping, moralizing, and somewhat zany speech. Robertson, who for a brief moment earlier this year had thrown a fright into the Republicans, had been almost forgotten. But his strange smile and chuckle brought it all back. And Robertson and the intense evangelical following he built are not going to go away. In his speech, Robertson, shouting the whole time, attacked the French Revolution and AIDS victims ("Disease carriers are protected and the healthy are placed at great risk"), and said, "Michael Dukakis will pack the federal courts with A.C.L.U. radicals." Like Bush, Robertson called Dukakis "a card-carrying member of the A.C.L.U." (The crowd booed.) Robertson played all the emotional keys: school prayer, abortion, big government.

The only speaker who really caught the attention of the audience on Tuesday night was Gerald Ford (who got on after prime time). Ford said, "This year's Democratic ticket is a tax increase on its way to happen." Demonstrating indignation at Kennedy's taunt, a lively Ford went through Bush's career, getting the crowd to join him in the chant "George was there!" Ford said, to cheers, "I'll be damned if I will stand by and let anyone with a smirk and a sneer discredit the honor, service, accountability, and competence of George Bush." And, like other speakers, he made Jackson part of the Democratic ticket—and threw back at Dukakis his saying, in his acceptance speech, "This election is not about ideology, it's about competence." Ford said, "If the *three* Democratic standard-bearers in this campaign think it is about competence, let any one of them, or all three of them put together, top the demonstrated competence of George Bush."

The Democrats having put on a big display about family at their Convention, the Republicans were determined to top them. The Republicans had started family as a theme, and they weren't about to cede it to the Democrats. At the same time, Bush's image-makers clearly decided that it would warm up his image if he were seen with his large, handsome, and obviously loving family—and it did. But the Republicans overdid it. Bush, who said that he had previously tried to shelter his family from public life and keep it as an "oasis," was constantly talking about and parading his family before the cameras. Four of his five children, and his Mexican-American daughter-in-law, all spoke for him during the roll-call vote. (The daughter-in-law also seconded his nomination, in Spanish and English—in an attempt to offset Dukakis.) One of Bush's half-Mexican grandchildren led the Pledge to the flag one night. Bush was seen on a screen at the Convention and on television watching the roll call with his grandchildren crawling about him. Perhaps now that it has been established that both Dukakis and Bush have loving families, we can set that matter aside and get on with other things. (Reagan, of course, does not have a particularly close family.)

Robert Dole, though disappointed, gamely praised Quayle in his speech to the Convention Wednesday night and formally nominated him the next night. In his Wednesday-night speech, Dole blasted Dukakis as "one of those liberals who is embarrassed by America's strength," and attacked what he called "Dukak-eyed" ideas. Senator Phil Gramm, of Texas, who is moving into a position of leadership of the Republican right, and who nominated Bush, emphasized a key theme of the Convention. Attacking the "amnesia merchants of the Atlanta Convention," who want us to forget how bad things were under Carter, he said, "So help us God we are not going to allow them to do that to America again." During Carter's Presidency, said Gramm, who stirred up the hall, "the American flag drooped in shame." Asking a series of rhetorical questions, to which the audience responded with the expected "No!," Gramm said, "Is there anybody here who doubts that a President Dukakis would cut defense and wimp America and endanger peace?" Gramm slammed Dukakis for opposing the mandatory sentencing and the death penalty for drug dealers and vetoing the mandatory Pledge of Allegiance. "The competition of vision and ideas can never end until all the world is free, including . . . the Soviet Union itself." Gramm also praised Bush's record. His speech was followed by a flag-waving demonstration, at which the Republicans specialize—despite the Democrats' effort to catch up.

Following Dole's speech Thursday night nominating Quayle, the seconding speech was given by Indiana's senior senator, Richard Lugar. Lugar, the ranking Republican on the Foreign Relations Committee, is a highly esteemed man, and his standing there, also gamely, only served to underline the question of why Bush had picked Quayle instead. (Quayle is more dynamic, but one wouldn't think that's the top criterion for the man "a heartbeat away." Bentsen certainly isn't dynamic.) The Convention floor Thursday night was awash in speculation about Quayle's fate: he was still on the ticket, but no one could be sure what was coming next. Since the Bush people had missed the National Guard problem, there was reason to wonder what else was out there. A bit earlier, Newt Gingrich had said, on CNN, "All of us are clearly a little anxiety-ridden." On the floor, Gingrich said to me, "Quayle will be seen as a baby boomer—in an off-the-wall way, this controversy is an example." (As Gingrich and I spoke, the hall was darkened while "Taps" was played, to honor the war dead.) Delegation leaders had been primed by Convention managers to say that when Quayle joined the Guard there was a fifteen-per-cent vacancy in his unit—a "fact" they left behind them in New Orleans—and to suggest that criticism of Quayle's joining the Guard was impugning the honor of millions who had served in it. Quayle's brief acceptance speech was a series of banalities that did little to ease concern about his depth or maturity. But the delegates, egged on by Bush floor managers in gold baseball caps, cheered him noisily. Young demonstrators who had been brought in snaked though the hall and added to the noise, on cue. ("Quayle! Quayle! Quayle! Quayle!") Delegates to National Conventions have become automatons—compliant extras in a television production. When Quayle said, "I served six years in the National Guard, and, like millions of Americans who have served in the Guard and who serve today—and I am proud of that," there was another little floor demonstration, and the gold caps led the cheer "U.S.A.! U.S.A.! U.S.A.!" This cheer was repeated when Quayle, still shouting, said, of Indianans, "But, most important, we love our country."

Bush's speech was preceded by a brief film (it was kept short in hopes of getting it on the air) that began and ended with Bush playing with his grandchildren. The film also showed pictures of Bush being shot down in the Second World War. And there seemed some cognitive dissonance when the film showed Reagan being shot and the narrator said, "George Bush knows what it means to be a heartbeat away from the Presidency." Bush, coming on-stage, looked handsome in his blue suit, and he smiled his crooked smile as another demonstration was mounted. (It had to last at least as long as the one for Dukakis did.) Speaking strongly but slowly (thus keeping his voice low), Bush said, "There are a lot of great stories in politics about the underdog winning—and this is going to be one of them." He gracefully spelled out the transition he was making from loyal Vice-President to candidate for Presi-dent. Exaggerating a bit, he said that "the differences between the two candidates are as deep and wide as they ever have been," and he spelled out some differences as he sees them. He said, "My opponent's view of the world sees a long slow decline for our country. . . . But America is not in decline." Alluding to Dukakis's acceptance speech, Bush said, "Some say this isn't an election about ideology, it's an election about competence," adding, "Well, it's nice of them to want to play on our field." He went on, hitting Dukakis's line where it was vulnerable, "But this election isn't only about competence, for competence is a narrow ideal. . . . Com-petence is the creed of the technocrat who makes sure the gears mesh but doesn't for a second understand the magic of the ma-chine." Referring to a term Bentsen and then Dukakis have used, Bush said, "They call it a Swiss-cheese economy," and, subtly work-ing Jackson in, he said, to the delight of the audience, "Well, that's the way it may look to the three blind mice." And he added, "When they were in charge, it was all holes and no cheese." He cited various economic gains under Reagan, following each with "And I'm not going to let them take it away from you." But he also acknowledged that things could be better, and promised to create thirty million jobs in the next eight years (an extraordinary figure his advisers later backed off of). He dwelt for a while on the Reagan Administration's foreign-policy successes, and said "a pru-dent skepticism is in order" toward the Soviet Union. (Bush has been more cautious than Reagan.)

The speech was clearly aimed at, among other things, the "gen-der gap" (the fact that more women prefer Dukakis): Bush made no mention of aid to the Contras and made only a slight reference to S.D.I. He said, "I want a kinder and gentler nation." It was not clear what he meant—though Bush was putting himself forth as a gentle man—or whether he was intending to draw a contrast with Reagan; and other parts of his speech were raw partisanship and divisive. (Some of his self-description—saying "I may not be the most eloquent," that "I may sometimes be a little awkward" —was embarrassing; he ought to stop discussing himself and let people discover him for themselves.) The speech was a skillfully and beautifully written one, by Peggy Noonan, who wrote some of Reagan's most effective speeches; but some of the lyrical writing didn't seem to fit Bush—it seemed like clothes tailored for another man. So much artifice goes into these speeches that it is difficult to know to what extent they actually come from the candidate. Bush went down the list of emotional ("hot button") issues, pointing out his differences with Dukakis—over school prayer, the death penalty, gun control (he framed the issue as "Should free men and women have the right to own a gun to protect their home?"), and Massachusetts' furlough program, and vowed that he will never raise taxes. For Reagan's tough-guy challenge to Congress, "Make my day," Bush substituted "Read my lips." (There was no mention of the budget deficit.) The lines about guns and taxes sent members of the New Hampshire delegation (where I was watching Bush's speech) to their feet, but most of the cheering during the speech was being done by the young people who had been imported into the hall. Bush pledged to improve education, seek a drug-free America, bring the disabled into the mainstream, stop ocean dumping, and "put incentives back into the domestic energy industry." As he listed these things he sounded decisive, like an executive. He spoke strongly about the need for ethics in government, and said, "I hope to stand for a new harmony, a greater tolerance." He concluded, "I will keep America moving forward, always forward—for a better America, for an endless enduring dream and a thousand points of light. That is my mission. And I will complete it." And he closed by asking everyone to stand and pledge allegiance to the flag (for the second time that night). This was not in his prepared text. Bush has learned a little shamelessness from Reagan.

In the days following the Convention, the Bush people tried, with some success, to turn the National Guard issue against the press. This is an old trick. Quayle's appearances before veterans' organizations were a predictable success (but when he got off on other subjects he was shaky). Bush, seeming liberated, was a spirited campaigner, comparing Quayle favorably to those who had gone to Canada, torn up their draft cards, or burned the American flag—and keeping up the attack on Dukakis. Dukakis began to respond only two days ago (about Iran-Contra); meanwhile, amid worry over the direction things were taking, a decision was made to bring back John Sasso, Dukakis's former campaign manager, who resigned last fall over the Biden flap, as vice-chairman of the campaign. Polls taken shortly after the Convention showed Bush ahead, which was cause for thought among the Bush people— and also the Dukakis people—over how much farther ahead Bush might have been had he chosen a different running mate.

XI

This most dismal of Presidential campaigns, which has now gone
through its first phase, leading up to the debate Sunday night,
has set a new low in modern campaigning and left us with the
question of whether after the election is over, either man will be
able to govern. At this point, it is hard to see how either candidate
can be an effective leader—will be able to build and hold enough
public support to take the country through a difficult passage.
Oddly, we have two candidates for the Presidency neither of whom
comes off as a natural politician, yet a President must be a good
politician to be successful. Both of them got nominated by utilizing
smart tactics and superior resources, and by the failings of their
competitors, but these things fall short of what is required of a
national leader. Neither candidate is very spontaneous or very
interesting. The public's lack of any real enthusiasm for either
one of them is nearly palpable, and unless this changes neither
one will take office with much wind at his back. The shifting polls
mainly reflect a lack of strong support for either man—of an
unprecedented scale. Without strong public support, even at the
outset, the next President will have difficulty setting the agenda,
dealing with Congress, or bringing coherence to now jumbled,
even chaotic, economic and defense policies. The Reagan legacy
will not be an enviable inheritance, but it's not surprising that
neither candidate is talking very much about hard choices that
will have to be made. It's generally assumed that there's little to
gain from that. The particularly low and mean nature of this
campaign (which also should not have come as a surprise) is attributable to the cynical—and thus far effective—strategy of the
Bush campaign. Michael Dukakis is no pushover—he can play
rough, and has done his share of distorting Bush's record—but
George Bush's nearly unrelenting onslaught, distorting and de-
magoguing Dukakis's record (a record that does have its vulner-

abilities), will, if it works, have further debased the coin of Presidential elections. Just as Reagan's 1984 election showed that a candidate can get away with being sequestered—offered to the public only via well-staged scenes—and saying little, the Bush campaign, if it is successful, and if it stays on its present course, as Bush's pleased advisers say it's going to, will have also established that just about anything goes. If Dukakis is defeated, it will be for other reasons as well, some of them exogenous factors having to do with neither candidate, and some having to do with his own failings as a candidate. But conclusions will be drawn about what seems to work. There are no ground rules for Presidential elections; we know that there will be attacks and exaggerations and distortions, but we more or less trust the candidates and the people around them to keep things within bounds. It is impossible to draw the line in the abstract, but we can tell when the line has been crossed. A backlash is always possible, but if there is to be one the opponent has to be an effective and likable enough candidate to be the beneficiary—a standard that Dukakis has yet to meet.

The biggest surprise thus far has been the change in Bush as a candidate—something the Dukakis campaign certainly hadn't reckoned on. The tentative, frantic, and often awkward Bush has been replaced by a forceful, aggressive, and only sometimes awkward Bush. His aides say that this all came about when Reagan departed from New Orleans, that Bush had planned all along to hold back until he was officially the leader of his party. But this is too pat. Clearly, if Bush had been capable of being a better candidate before, he would have been one. Clearly, the difference comes from a discipline that has been imposed on him by his friend and campaign chairman James Baker—who can talk to Bush in a way no one else can—and by Bush's continuous training by Roger Ailes, his media adviser. In the primaries Ailes had been somewhat—but far from completely—successful at getting Bush to speak slowly, thus keeping his voice at a lower register and his thoughts under some control. But now a more compliant Bush seldom strays from his prepared text—it's when he does that he can get in trouble (as when he recently said, "I stand for anti-bigotry, anti-Semitism, anti-racism"). Bush's mangling of thoughts or words when on his own bespeaks a certain sloppiness of thought processes, or some sort of short-circuiting that goes on in his head. (His advancing, on September 7th, the date of Pearl Harbor by three months was by itself no big thing, but it was part of a strange pattern.) Baker is well aware of the importance of discipline, knows that a careless statement ("we tried to kick a little ass last night") can become a defining event, and he has made it clear to Bush that if he wants to win he must stick to the program. Bush is kept as inaccessible to the press as possible—which is almost entirely —to ward off any stray embarrassing remarks by the man who wants to be President of the United States. Bush's success as a reincarnated candidate and his obvious new confidence are circular: the better he does, the more confident he feels, and the better he does, and so on. A combination of Ailes' coaching and the new confidence have improved Bush's body language—the flapping of the arms and the wiggling of the body are much reduced (but not gone). Ailes has tried to keep Bush from allowing his eyes to dart around nervously. He even looks larger. "Ailes is a genius," one Bush adviser says.

But this leaves us with the question of who is George Bush. What we see is a nearly totally packaged candidate following a script. And his willingness to follow the particular script he has been given also raises the question of what, if anything, is at his core. The Bush people say that their polling shows that Bush's attacks on Dukakis for vetoing a bill that required teachers to lead students in the Pledge of Allegiance have worked, and that the combination of the Pledge issue and attacks on certain positions that Dukakis has taken on crime has been very effective in undermining Dukakis, in getting across a picture of Dukakis as a Massachusetts liberal. "Liberal" has become a term of opprobrium in politics because it is associated with big government (which is presumed not to work, though the evidence, like the results of various programs, is mixed), high taxes, social engineering (though conservatives have their own forms of this), leftism in foreign policy—and also the civil-rights revolution. Reagan was able to capture and capitalize on the reaction against all these things— and Bush is seeking to follow his footsteps in this as in other respects. The plain fact is that Dukakis *is* a Massachusetts liberal, who took a number of positions in the sixties and seventies (when he was in the state legislature and in his first term as governor) that fit the tenor of his state and the times. Some he has taken more recently. He also believes in the efficacy of government programs, in governmental activism, though he has tried to devise programs that don't incur a great deal of government spending. (But he doesn't always get this across.) When the Bush people say that a politician of another stripe would have signed the Pledge bill even if, as Dukakis says, the state attorney general and a state-supreme-court advisory opinion said it was unconstitutional, and would have let it be tested in the courts, they have a point—if not a very uplifting one. For good or for ill, Dukakis is pretty stiff-necked as politicians go. (As the Bush people say, James Thompson, Governor of Illinois, and a Republican, signed a bill requiring schoolchildren to recite the Pledge.) Dukakis has supported the nuclear freeze, and he supported a proposal to exempt young men from Massachusetts from going to Vietnam. (The then governor of Massachusetts, a Republican, signed it.) Bush said on Labor Day, with intended innuendo, "I wouldn't be surprised if he thinks a naval exercise is something you find in Jane Fonda's workout book." Yet one of the ironies is that other, more liberal, Massachusetts politicians have resented Dukakis for not playing any significant role in the civil-rights or anti-Vietnam War movements. In the course of the nineteen-seventies, in part as a reaction to some of the actions of the antiwar movement, social conservatism became a strong political force: Jimmy Carter ran on conservative social values, and Ronald Reagan made them a touchstone of his Presidential campaign. The Bush people argue that conservative social values are still the prevailing ones in this country, and they have set out to systematically show that Bush is closer to a majority of the people on these issues than Dukakis is. Bush, in Boston yesterday to accept the endorsement of the Boston Police Patrolmen's Association (which has frequently supported Republicans), summed it up: the endorsement, he said, underscores "the fundamental differences that I have with my opponent on questions of values and how to treat the criminals. And when it comes to these questions, my opponent is simply out of the American mainstream." (Dukakis countered with a rally with police and other law-enforcement officials from Massachusetts and elsewhere, including Bush's adopted home state of Texas.)

The Bush campaign is not offering rational discourse on these issues but instead is playing to atavistic feelings. As demagogic as Bush and his surrogates have been on the Pledge issue—asking why Dukakis doesn't want schoolchildren to say the Pledge of Allegiance, suggesting that he is the less patriotic candidate—polls show that the public has overwhelmingly gone along. But the real point of raising the Pledge issue is to place Dukakis far to the left on the ideological spectrum. The Bush people figure that any time a Dukakis surrogate talks about the Pledge as a constitutional, freedom-of-speech issue—as Dukakis did in late August—the Bush side wins. A Bush aide said to me recently, "They just don't get it. They shouldn't make legalistic arguments. You can't escape the common sense of it, which is, 'Let's be for kids saying the Pledge rather than against it.'" Bush's success with the Pledge issue has turned this into the most flag-bedecked campaign ever. Both candidates stand in front of very many flags, or very big flags, and their audiences are given little flags to wave. Bush topped off the flag contest by making visits to Findlay, Ohio, known as Flag City, and, a few days ago, visiting a flag factory in New Jersey. Most of the flags that are waved at political rallies are imported from Taiwan. Campaign workers scratch the "Made in Taiwan" imprint off the handles. By the end of this election, the flag could mean less, not more.

The Bush people feel that they have made their point about the Pledge (they shamed the Democratic-controlled House of Representatives into reciting the Pledge every morning) but that there remains much to be milked out of some crime issues. Next, the Bush people say, they will drive home the issue of the Massachusetts furlough plan, which allowed weekend furloughs for first-degree murderers ineligible for parole. (Other states and the federal government have furlough plans, but none go that far, and Massachusetts' has been changed.) Willie Horton, who committed rape and robbery while on such a furlough, is about to become famous. (Bush has told audiences, incorrectly, that he also committed murder while on furlough.) One Bush strategist said to me recently, "Every woman in this country will know what Willie Horton looks like before this election is over." (Horton, who is black, has a somewhat menacing visage.) The furlough issue is mentioned in a Bush ad about crime, and the Bush campaign is considering whether to use Horton's picture in an ad. (It does appear in an ad run by an "independent" group, the National Security Political Action Committee, on some nationwide cable networks. The Bush campaign says it has nothing to do with this

group, but that doesn't mean that it minds the ads.) The Bush
campaign has already been running ads in California, Ohio, and
Texas on Dukakis's crime record. (The Dukakis campaign is running one that argues that Dukakis has been tough on crime.) In
Texas, the Republican Party has mailed a brochure to some three
hundred thousand conservative—or "swing"—Democrats which
has a picture of children with their hand on their heart and says,
"Here are the words Dukakis doesn't want your child to have to
say: I Pledge Allegiance to the Flag . . ." and which also points
out that Dukakis opposes the death penalty and supports gun
control. Recently, Bush, after being criticized for the McCarthy-
esque undertone in his saying that Dukakis is "a card-carrying
member of the A.C.L.U.," pointed out that Dukakis had said in
the course of the Iowa caucus contest, "I'm a card-carrying member of the American Civil Liberties Union." During a recent Bush
visit to Philadelphia, Senator Arlen Specter, Republican of Pennsylvania and a former district attorney of Philadelphia, told reporters, "There's nothing wrong with belonging to the A.C.L.U."
But the Bush people will not pass up what they think is good
material.

The Bush campaign organization functions with great discipline.
A theme is decided upon and stayed with for days. (The idea had
been for a theme a week, but outside events, or Dukakis speeches,
sometimes call for a change.) Some Bush people say that the Dukakis campaign makes a mistake in changing subjects daily. (It
used to change subjects within a given day but recently has started
to stay on a topic for a day, and sometimes for more than a day.)
The data-driven Bush campaign each night measures the impact
of a particular Bush sally and decides when a point has been made
or needs reinforcement. (The Dukakis campaign measures sen-
timent every night, but is not as efficient at getting the results
smack into the campaign.) The Bush campaign also has a great
advantage in being composed at the top of people who are running
their third campaign together, and some have worked together
longer than that. The Dukakis campaign doesn't come close to
matching the Bush campaign in experience in general elections.
Much the same group that brought us the two Reagan campaigns
is directing Bush—minus Michael Deaver, the former close aide
to the Reagans who was sentenced this week for perjury in con-

nection with his lobbying activities after he left the White House. (He received a hundred-thousand-dollar fine and was sentenced to three years' probation and was required to perform community service.) But the Bush campaign officials have absorbed everything Deaver taught them about backdrops and camera angles, and it places at least as much emphasis as Reagan's did on the picture that will be presented on the television news programs. This election has come to be as dependent on the image as music video—and about as deep. Thoughtful speeches are still occasionally given (mainly by Dukakis), but there is limited payoff. They receive little coverage on the news programs. If there is an attack line in the speech, that is what will make the news. More than ever, it seems, the contest for who will govern us for the next four years has come down to one over "sound bites" and pictures.

The arrival in August of Baker as the chairman of the Bush campaign has given it a discipline it had been lacking, and set its tone. Lee Atwater, the campaign manager, is well known for his combative approach, his willingness to do things that others might balk at, and Baker has backed him. The Bush campaign, through its "negative research" on Dukakis, found the Pledge veto last spring, and Bush advisers say that when it was mentioned to Bush in a meeting late last spring he recognized it as a good issue, and that when Bush started to talk about the Pledge and the furlough he began to do better in the polls. But these issues were controversial with the Bush camp and didn't come into heavy use until the Republican Convention. An associate of Atwater's said to me recently, "Prior to Baker, every time Lee wanted to toss a grenade others in the campaign would say it wasn't a real issue, it didn't have a life to it, it didn't fit with our themes of peace and prosperity, that the press would bang us on it—no one was particularly encouraging. Baker is much more offensive-oriented, and no one will try to go around him to the Vice-President, the way others did to Lee before." When Baker officially came to the campaign (he had, of course, been in close touch with it all along), he believed that the Pledge, crime, and gun-control issues had a lot of juice left in them and could be used very effectively in ads.

The Bush people believe that they have hit upon a formula for making negative campaigning acceptable: from time to time, Bush will give a "positive" speech, or within a speech attacking Dukakis he will say something about what he is for This way, when criticized for negative campaigning they say that it is "comparative," and point to the "positive" things Bush has said. (The subtlety seems to have been lost on, among others, Barry Goldwater, who, in the course of introducing Dan Quayle at an event in Arizona this week, said, "I want you to go back and tell George Bush to start talking about the issues.") Thus, every once in a while Bush will repeat his acceptance-speech line about wanting a "kinder and gentler nation," or give a little inspirational speech. After touring the flag factory, Bush, standing in front of an enormous flag, said, "What's the end purpose of this economic growth? Is it just to be rich? What a shallow ambition." (The previous day, Dukakis had criticized Bush for offering "a warmed-over call to selfishness." Bush had said that Dukakis had "pursued a strategy of dividing Americans" by class and region. Actually, the Dukakis people had hoped to make more of the class issue than they have.) Bush also said he was "haunted" by the thought of children who grow up "amidst the violence and horror" of the inner cities. He also said that "flag sales are doing well and America is doing well." The previous week he had said that flag sales had dropped under Carter and increased under Reagan.

Baker's propensity for cutting losses was on display when, in early September, he forced the resignation of Frederic Malek as deputy chairman of the Republican National Committee. Malek was one of those odd personnel choices that Bush makes on occasion (Quayle): despite the fact that Malek was well known as Nixon's "hatchet man" when he served as his personnel director, and despite the fact that he had no real training for the job, Bush picked him to run the Republican Convention. This was among other things another example of Bush's vindictiveness: two experienced Republicans who had run previous Conventions were ruled out because they had supported Robert Dole for the Republican nomination. Following a report, on Sunday, September 11th, in the Washington *Post*, that Malek had, at Nixon's request, made a count of the number of Jews at the Bureau of Labor Statistics, which had been disagreeing with Nixon's rosy economic reports, Baker got Malek to resign at once rather than become a political liability. (Malek told the New York *Times* that weekend that he had also made a list of their names. Two B.L.S. officials were removed from their jobs, but Malek said that he had had nothing to do with that.) Bush, who apparently didn't get the point, called Malek "a most honorable man." (The Bush campaign also had to get rid of seven members of its advisory coalition of ethnics because of past, or even recent, alleged anti-Semitic activities.)

By running the kind of campaign he did, Bush succeeded in driving up Dukakis's "negatives"—measured by the number of poll respondents who say they view a candidate unfavorably— and his own down, to the point where the two men were about even on this score going into the first debate. (The Dukakis people used to set great store by Bush's high negatives.) Unhappily for the Dukakis campaign, Bush had managed not only to erase Dukakis's substantial lead of earlier this summer (much of which was caused by Dukakis's success at the Democratic Convention) but to maintain most of his own post-Convention lead by campaigning continuously following the Convention (all but one day between the Convention and Labor Day), and started out on Labor Day slightly ahead. The Dukakis people had hoped to start out at least even. (Dukakis's lead in the summer wasn't really as strong as the seventeen-point difference between him and Bush suggested: half the respondents, when asked what they really liked about Dukakis, couldn't say.) In early September, Lee Atwater told me that he'd always thought that "three things would come into focus after Labor Day that would help us." These were, he said, that the issues of peace and prosperity would come onto the agenda to a greater extent, that Reagan would enjoy a rise in popularity, and that the Republicans' base in the electoral college would firm up —that the states which had been voting Republican in recent elections would return to the Republican fold. To a greater or lesser extent, all of these things have happened. Some (but not all) Southern states, which seemed up for grabs when Dukakis was ahead earlier this summer, are back in the Republican column, and Bush is comfortably ahead in Florida. Quietly, the Dukakis people have decided to not allocate further resources to Florida, Alabama, Mississippi, South Carolina, and Virginia. Bush is slightly ahead in Texas and Ohio, while California and most of the other industrial states are close, as is Missouri. (The candidates' itineraries give clues as to which states are close.) The candidates are also about even in Washington and Oregon—and the Dukakis camp thinks it is ahead in the usually Republican Montana and Colorado. The Bush camp has sent a barrage of advertising at California, Texas, and Ohio in the hope of locking up all three states early, but the strategy has not been completely successful as yet. But the Dukakis people had managed to arrest their candidate's slide by mid-September, and, going into the debate, Bush has not put the election away.

Another line of attack the Bush campaign intends to pursue —despite Bush's own vulnerabilities on the subject—is the environment. Bush's approach to this issue in early September was a model of the form his campaign has developed. First, standing on the shore of Lake Erie, he gave a "positive" speech, declaring himself an environmentalist, and saying that he would go further than the Reagan Administration to protect the environment. This wouldn't take much. (Actually, Bush had said many of the same things before, in May, but that speech had received little attention.) The next day, Bush went boating in Boston Harbor and assailed Dukakis for his inaction in cleaning it up (Dukakis was vulnerable on this point), and on the following day Bush appeared on the New Jersey coast and said that Dukakis had proposed dumping sewage from Massachusetts off New Jersey. (To demonstrate the threat to sea life, Bush held up a crab, which bit him.) What with the washing up of hospital waste on Eastern coasts, and signs that the long-predicted "greenhouse effect" (the warming of the earth's temperature as a result of the trapping of heat by gases created by fossil fuels) is coming to pass—this summer's drought is taken as a sign—environmental issues are back on the map. But, while both candidates talk about the environment, neither of them has proposed the hard measures that many people feel need to be taken: among other things a far stricter fuel-efficiency standard for automobiles, and a gasoline tax. (This would also help reduce the budget and trade deficits.) Dukakis has assailed Bush for taking contradictory positions on offshore drilling in California—an important issue in that state—and for attempting in the early years of the Reagan Administration to reduce certain environmental regulations; he has also been highly critical of the Reagan Administration's environmental record. But the Bush people say that Dukakis is also vulnerable on the filling in of wetlands for development projects in Massachusetts, and one Bush aide says, "Mark my words. By the end of the election, we're going to take the environmental issue away from him."

Using distorted statistics, Bush has attacked Dukakis's record in Massachusetts, which is neither as good as Dukakis says it is nor as bad as Bush says it is. Dukakis has run into fiscal difficulties this year and in a Cromwellian move this fall tried, without success, to keep the rambunctious state legislature from meeting before the election. (The state senate is in session.) Dukakis may have said that "this election is not about ideology, it's about competence," but Bush is trying to paint him as an ideologue and raise questions about his competence. To keep the upper hand on the questions of peace and prosperity Bush has kept up the attack on Dukakis on defense issues, charging, incorrectly, that Dukakis opposes every new weapons system, and warning of the perils of allowing the Democrats to once again manage the economy. The Bush campaign arranged for Bush to be seen witnessing the destruction of the first American missile under the treaty to reduce intermediate-range nuclear missiles (I.N.F.), in Karnack, Texas, following which, Bush, in Tyler, with cowgirls arrayed behind him, said that Dukakis would give away strategic-weapons systems "and he asks for nothing in return." While Dukakis has opposed both a mobile MX system and the Midgetman, a mobile single-warhead missile, Bush goes too far. He says that Dukakis "has opposed every new weapons system since the slingshot." He has described himself as "on the American side" of certain issues, leaving the listener to draw the obvious conclusion.

Both candidates are, of course, trying to define the economy in terms that best suit their own purposes. And each one has points on his side: Bush can point to a rise in the median family income (ten per cent) since 1981; Dukakis can say that that rise has largely been caused by women entering the work force to produce two-earner families in order to make ends meet. Bush can point to the drop in interest rates and inflation under Reagan; Dukakis can point to the slow growth of earnings in those years. Bush often points to the fact that seventeen million new jobs have been created under Reagan, but the growth in jobs on an annual basis was greater under Carter than it has been under Reagan. He has said, "Expansions don't die from old age, they die from bad policies." One set of poll figures the Dukakis people watch is the percentage of people who think the country is on the right track or the wrong track economically. It was with uneasiness that the

Dukakis people saw the result—right track—going very much in Bush's favor this fall.

The Bush people are obviously nervous about Quayle—who gives them much to be nervous about. Various polls and focus-group interviews indicate that people are uneasy about Bush's selection of Quayle as his running mate. (A recent *Wall Street Journal*/NBC News poll found that by more than three to two voters said that Bush had made a "bad choice," and by more than two to one they said that Lloyd Bentsen would make a better President.) In Quayle's campaigning, his inexperience and uncertainty, as well as his immaturity, keep peeking around the figure his assigned managers are trying to make him be—and sometimes they come into full view. When he departs from his script, it is usually disastrous. An attempt to show his defense "expertise" by allowing him to speak from note cards was not at all successful (among other things, he cites one of Tom Clancy's best-selling military-adventure novels as a basis for his defense positions), and he got himself into an awful mess when, at one of his very few press conferences, he tried to answer a question about the Holocaust. He said, "It was an obscene period in our nation's history," and, when called on for that, said, "Not our nation's but in World War II. I mean we all lived in this century. I didn't live in this century but in this century's history." Throughout this exchange, Quayle looked rattled and terrified. Quayle's assigned role is to take on Dukakis, but the way he does so is often sophomoric. (He said Dukakis had lost his "top naval adviser. His rubber ducky drowned in the bathtub.") Though the National Guard issue has gone away, questions about Quayle's past continue to surface. (His financial report indicated that he was not likely to directly inherit a share of the assets of his family's large trust. But he could inherit large sums from his relatives.) On September 9th, the Cleveland *Plain Dealer* reported that he had got into the Indiana University Law School, after first being rejected because of low college grades, under a program that was designed to help minorities and economically disadvantaged students. (For some reason, Quayle's college and law-school records have not been released.) Quayle has taken to comparing himself to such late bloomers as Franklin Delano Roosevelt and Winston Churchill.

* * *

Neither Dukakis nor his campaign organization was prepared for what came at them following the Republican Convention. The new Bush took them, like almost everyone else, by surprise; they had been counting on the awkward misspeaker, the Yalie who would ask a waitress at a truck stop for "just a splash" of coffee and could come off as a weakling. (A big premise of the Dukakis campaign had been that Dukakis would come off the stronger of the two men.) Like a number of others, they had thought that such issues as the Pledge and the furlough program were played out and would be seen as irrelevant to a Presidential campaign. As the Bush people had figured, Dukakis and his campaign were unprepared for the rigors of a general election—and certainly for the kind of all-out onslaught that the Bush people would make. There is a great deal of difference between a nomination contest and a general-election contest, and few who have not gone through a general election are prepared for it: the demands are far greater and the pressures far more brutal. Even the logistical requirements are of a different order. Holding an event in the wrong kind of hall, or failing to seal off an event to hecklers—both of these things happened to the Dukakis campaign in the first days of the fall campaign—can ruin the story a campaign had hoped to get on that night's television news. A misstatement on the part of the candidate becomes a very big thing. The Dukakis campaign started out the general election with very few people who had been through a general election before—up and down the ranks. Even John Sasso, whom Dukakis brought back in just before Labor Day, to try to arrest his slide in the polls and get his campaign on an even keel, has worked in only one general-election campaign —that of Geraldine Ferraro four years ago.

The largest problem the Dukakis campaign faced as the fall campaign began was the candidate himself. In the two weeks following the Republican Convention, and for much of the time in September, leading up to the debate, Dukakis behaved very strangely. In August, at his insistence, he was spending time in western Massachusetts, as he does each year. (As it happens, he may have needed to spend time there, because some Massachusetts polls showed Bush nearly tied with Dukakis in the state.) During the August period, we frequently saw Dukakis standing before a blue curtain (in contrast to the interesting pictures of Bush), and he was available to the press nearly every day, often responding to inquiries about one or another of Bush's charges—and the response, usually a defensive one, would be the Dukakis story on the evening news. Dukakis, of course, should have understood this—that controlling the agenda is a principal goal in Presidential politics—and kept to the subject he wanted to talk about, if he had any. To the surprise of the Bush people, among others, what thrusts he made at Bush were often lame. And sometimes they misfired. It was during this time that Dukakis offered his constitutionally based rebuttal to Bush on the Pledge of Allegiance—an action that all his aides deny having had anything to do with. It is now accepted as a given that in the course of a political campaign there is no point in basing an argument on the Constitution. On the Saturday before Labor Day, we saw Dukakis, obviously on the defensive, appearing at Ellis Island with his wife and his mother, and, with the Statue of Liberty in the background, leading the crowd in the Pledge of Allegiance. (The Dukakis campaign had wanted to start out Labor Day at Ellis Island, but the Bush people had already booked it for Quayle. On Labor Day, Quayle toured Ellis Island and, at the Statue of Liberty, explained to the crowd the Pledge of Allegiance and, referring to Dukakis's veto, said that the "mind-set that would impede the daily recitation of the Pledge of Allegiance is the same mind-set that could well sterilize public education of its proper role as a transmitter of the values and standards upon which we must rely, and which have been central throughout our history.") Dukakis's charge, in Texas in early September, that Bush's attacks on him about the Pledge smacked of McCarthyism was considered by many—including the Bush people—as too "élitist" to be widely understood. A great many people wondered why Dukakis didn't haul off and let Bush have it in a way that everyone would understand for questioning his patriotism. This gets back to Dukakis's instincts. For a man who has been in politics for some time, he shows a curious lack of political instinct—of spontaneity, of knowing just what to do at the right moment, of feel. A President must have feel—but it's not clear that either candidate for President has it. (Lloyd Bentsen, Dukakis's running mate, has feel, and has turned out to be a very competent campaigner. But that won't have made much difference if Dukakis loses Texas—as the Bush people predict he will.)

For much of this period, Dukakis has looked glum, even grim.

He rarely smiles, and definitely has not looked as if he were having a good time. Campaigns are gruelling, but the candidate must show a certain joie de vivre, zest for the game; if he doesn't, he's not likely to attract a strong following, or go over very well as President. The visage that Dukakis has largely been showing on our television screens (try watching with the sound off) has not been one that would be very welcome night after night for four years. Aides say that this grim expression stemmed from the fact that Dukakis was tired, that he had been overscheduled. While the latter is apparently true (his schedule, which had been far more demanding than Bush's, has been cut back), one wonders. Dukakis, after all, has been telling us all year that he is the marathon runner, the one who will pace himself until he prevails— and during the primaries he seemed such a man. Several of Dukakis's traits that seem to be putting many people off now were apparent all along: his lack of humor, his arrogance (the any-fool-knows-this expression); there had seemed something grim about him all along; and it was clear some time ago that there was a question of how well he would wear—whether before or after the election. Even if Dukakis has been tired, or unhappy about the political fix he was in in early September, one wonders about his lack of discipline—he seemed either uninterested in even trying to pretend he was enjoying himself, or unable to do so. Politicians, like other performers, often feel a lot worse than they let on, but they do what they have to. We want zest in our politicians: Harry S. Truman showed zest; even the aging Reagan shows zest in most of his public performances. From time to time in the primaries (and certainly in his acceptance speech), Dukakis has shown some zest. Dukakis's advisers—at least those who can talk to him this way—have implored him to smile when he is before the cameras. He has held two or three rallies where he turned in a strong and cheerful performance, but those have been the exception. One Dukakis adviser says, "There's nothing about his mood that a turnaround in the polls won't change." But how would he react, before or after the election, if things went badly for him again?

In early September, Dukakis was aware that he was stumbling around. Rarely a good listener, he wasn't very interested in the advice his campaign people had for him. And the campaign people were worried about the situation. A Dukakis adviser said to me in early September, "He's so lifeless. I would almost say he's a quitter if I didn't know better." In the primaries, he had at least run as an optimist, and though he was still uttering an optimistic line from time to time, his demeanor did not bespeak optimism. In an appearance at a fund-raiser in New York on September 8th, he succeeded in depressing a large percentage of the crowd by talking glumly about the difficult days of the campaign ("There will be good days and not so good days; there will be good polls and not so good polls"), and in Washington the following week he left a large dinner gathering of Democrats in lower spirits than before his brief appearance. It's a strange thing when a candidate doesn't understand that he is supposed to—or can't—rally the troops. Dukakis's own understanding that he was in serious trouble was what led him to bring back John Sasso as vice-chairman of his campaign. There was widespread relief within the campaign about Sasso's return, because everyone understood that he could talk to the candidate, to whom he is very close, in a way that no one else could.

Since Sasso's return, the candidate's performance has begun to improve—but there is still a long way to go. Quite a bit of overhauling of the campaign's support structure has gone on: more experienced advance people, schedulers, speechwriters, and people who could deal with issues were brought in. (Among the new speechwriters is Theodore Sorensen, who wrote for John F. Kennedy.) Like Bush when Baker took over, Dukakis felt less compelled to involve himself in the details of the campaign, and as he grew more confident of the support structure beneath him he began to improve as a candidate. But many of his appearances were still flat. Sasso felt that if Dukakis's downward slide weren't halted he could be behind by large double digits in October, and then it would be impossible to get his message out, because the topic would be how badly he was doing and why wasn't he doing better and so on. Sasso also had a blunt meeting in New York in early September with Jesse Jackson, who had been less than helpful to Dukakis, and since then Jackson's advice has been solicited more, and he has begun to bestir himself on Dukakis's behalf. (He has cut spots for black-oriented radio stations and made appearances for Dukakis and the Democratic Party's voter-registration drive.)

In order to shore up Dukakis's candidacy, an effort was made to present him in more interesting settings (with as few "press availabilities" as possible), and give a series of substantive speeches that would both get him off the defensive and flesh out his message. This was also an attempt to portray Dukakis as substantive —in contrast to Bush. The attempt to rival the Bush people at offering interesting pictures for television backfired, of course, in the now famous episode of Dukakis riding around in a tank. (This followed a foreign-policy speech, but took most of the attention away from what he had to say.) In the tank, Dukakis looked as a Presidential candidate never should—ridiculous. The large helmet on his large head (but small body) and his droopy face made him look like Snoopy. The campaign sent him into Yellowstone National Park to view the damage from the extensive fires that had been raging there, but Dukakis had nothing to say. He spoke to some of the people who had been fighting the fire for weeks, but avoided taking a position on the controversial question of whether the National Park Service had erred in sticking for some time to its policy of letting naturally occurring fires burn.

To "inoculate" Dukakis against further charges that he was unschooled in foreign policy or "weak" on defense, his campaign arranged for him to give speeches on these subjects three days in a row, starting at the beginning of the second week in September. The speeches dealt with the United States' role in the world, with relations with the Soviet Union, and with defense policy. To the distress of some Dukakis advisers, a fair percentage of the first speech was an attack on Bush (for failing in his assignments to deal with terrorism and drugs)—which got much of the attention on the news programs. It also contained a dig at Bush's choice of Quayle, whom Dukakis chooses to call by his formal name: "I want a real war against drugs; his answer to drug kingpins like Noriega is J. Danforth Quayle." (Bush has said he would put his Vice-President in charge of the anti-drug policy, as he had been.) He also said, as he has before, that he might attack terrorists' base camps—something even the Reagan Administration considered too risky, with the exception of Libya. In his second speech, Dukakis criticized Bush for not—unlike himself and Reagan—seeing in Mikhail Gorbachev an opportunity for a new relationship with the Soviet Union. (Bush has expressed more skepticism.) Some of his proposals seemed more thought through than others, but again his attacks on Bush and Quayle—plus the picture of him riding in the tank—were what made the news. The third speech, given at Georgetown University, repeated, with slightly more emphasis, Dukakis's support of the Stealth bomber and the Trident II D5 sea-based missile and his support of a new cruise missile—to counteract Bush's charge that he opposes all new weapons systems. Echoing the views of Sam Nunn, one of the authorities on defense Dukakis had met with before the speech, he criticized the idea of basing MX missiles on railroad cars as being strategically unsound—rather than, as before, too costly. This time, he bowed toward the "strategic concept" of the Midgetman missile (which is favored by Nunn and House Armed Services Committee chairman Les Aspin) but continued to criticize it as too costly. For some reason, Dukakis won't come out for a new single-warhead land-based missile (not necessarily mobile) favored by many Democrats, though his aides have said he might favor such a weapon. Nor will he attach his name to the very interesting proposal—proffered by Nunn, among others—to move the world away from multiple-warhead missiles to single-warhead ones, which could provide more stability. In his Georgetown speech, Dukakis once again championed some costly new conventional-warfare weapons. (His espousal of more spending on conventional defense has always seemed a bit of protective coloration, a camouflage of his opposition to a number of strategic weapons. His proposal to place more emphasis on conventional and less on strategic weaponry makes a number of serious defense experts—and a lot of Europeans—nervous.) In not offering any proposal to deal with the land-based leg of the strategic triad (but, his aides point out, at least conceding that something may have to be done about it), Dukakis was in the same position as Bush, who supports both the MX and the Midgetman but concedes that there won't be the money for both. In his speech, Dukakis also backed away from his sudden embrace of S.D.I. the week before, in the course of a press conference following a speech on defense. Dukakis's statements then were inconsistent with what he had said before and with each other. He also made no mention in his Georgetown speech of a ban on flight-testing of missiles, which he has said he supports—but which could prevent the development of new missiles. The major problem with Dukakis's speech at Georgetown was that he had to give it at all. By the time he did, he was on the defensive on the subject of defense, and the thick of a general-election campaign is a hard place to get complicated thoughts across. Dukakis has paid a price for his predilection for assuming that he knows more than he does and his supreme confidence in himself as a quick study. He should have had the defense subject buttoned down a long time ago.

The greatest effort on the part of the Dukakis campaign in recent weeks has been on trying to sharpen and flesh out Dukakis's central theme: that he is the candidate who best understands the needs and concerns of the middle class, and the one best qualified to deal with them. It's a complicated message, because it requires convincing people that they are not as well off as Bush says they are, and playing to their anxieties about the future without being the candidate of "doom and gloom." The Dukakis campaign has gone at this in various ways. In late August, it tried out the theme of "Bring prosperity home"—but one problem with that was that it accepted that Reagan had created prosperity. The idea was to work on people's concern that America is losing its economic primacy to Japan, that our economy is dependent on foreign investment, and that jobs have been going overseas. At one point, Dukakis elaborated on his mantra of "good jobs at good wages" by adding, "in the good old U.S.A."—but that didn't bring down the house, either. He has talked about what his campaign calls "the middle-class squeeze," but it's a complicated (for campaigns) concept. In the past couple of weeks, there has been an accelerated and disciplined effort to show Dukakis as the candidate talking about programs that would help the middle class (the poor, who are out of fashion these days, get a few crumbs), portray him as the candidate of change, as the person best qualified to handle the next period of people's lives—and draw the contrast with Bush. (Bush has countered with coming out for a day-care program, endorsing the idea of parental leave, and supporting an increase in the minimum wage—but he has as yet spent little time on these subjects. Dukakis has endorsed a Democratic bill, pending in Congress, to require companies to give parents unpaid time off in cases of birth or serious illness of a child. He has also endorsed an increase in the minimum wage and "the concept of" a Democratic-sponsored day-care bill pending in Congress.) The model, says a Dukakis adviser, was this past Tuesday, the day Bush visited the flag factory, when Dukakis unveiled a universal-health-care program and also said, "Mr. Bush, don't you think it's time you came out from behind that flag and told us what you intend to do to provide basic health care for thirty-seven million of our fellow-citizens?" The program, modelled on one Dukakis had started in Massachusetts, which required employers to provide health insurance for their employees, was a little wobbly, as was a college student-loan program he had offered two weeks earlier, but they succeeded in portraying Dukakis as offering concrete proposals. (Dukakis made other health proposals that same week.) In featuring these programs, the Dukakis people were trying to force a change in the agenda—get it off of Bush's issues and onto Dukakis's. At the same time, there has been more focus on hitting back at Bush right away—as with the rival police supporters. Plans are in the works to go at Bush even harder after the debate—in Dukakis's appearances and in the campaign's advertising. Dukakis plans to hit at Bush on Noriega, and to go at him for casting the tiebreaking vote in the Senate, in 1985, in favor of a Republican-sponsored budget proposal that would have, among other things, reduced the cost-of-living allowances under Social Security. Bush's was a responsible vote for a real attempt to lower the budget deficit—but Reagan later pulled the rug out from under the Senate Republicans by walking away from the Social Security cuts, which he had originally supported. Dukakis has frequently singled out programs that would have been cut in the Republican proposal and slammed at Bush for voting for the cuts. This is somewhat unfair (though a common Democratic practice)—and won't encourage politicians to cast brave votes in the future. There is also to be more emphasis in the coming period on the theme that America is losing its competitive edge—Dukakis began to move toward this in the past week, in a speech in Little Rock, Arkansas (though he didn't mention Japan specifically). The Little Rock speech was his most effective one yet in describing himself as the champion of the middle class, and it had familiar Sorensen touches ("unless we can get this country moving again"), and optimism. But the speech received only a brief mention on that night's network-news programs.

A big challenge the Dukakis camp faces going into the first debate is that polling indicates that people know little about him, that—not surprisingly—they find him vague. It will take some time for the picture of him as offering proposals to sink in, if it does, but movement in the polls since Labor Day also suggests that what Dukakis has been doing has helped him. Much of what people knew about Dukakis is what Bush has said about him. Therefore there was the big effort to lay out programs, and there will be a big effort, in the debate and afterward, to present Dukakis in a more favorable light—to get people to like him more and have confidence in him. The Dukakis campaign's internal polls, like the public ones, have shown the race tightening again. A couple of weeks ago, the Dukakis campaign had its candidate behind Bush by twelve points and dropping—now it has him only four points behind, though some Dukakis people think the real difference is more like six points. (This is similar to what public polls are showing.) So Dukakis, who is a very determined man, has another shot at this election, but also a large challenge.

XII

September 29
Sunday night's debate was very much a reflection of the two candidates' campaigns, but it also offered people a sense of the two men. Deprived of a script, Bush was at times confused and squeaky; Dukakis was only partly successful in his effort to project a warmer image. Though both men were on the surface polite—barely—the nasty undertone of the campaign was present on the stage. The debate, sponsored by the Commission on Presidential Debates, a group representing the two parties, and held at Wake Forest University, in Winston-Salem, and the first of two between the candidates (Bentsen and Quayle will meet next week), came off as more of a debate than the format, employing a panel of journalists to ask the questions, might have led to. (The format, and that there will be only two debates and that the debates are being held during the Olympics and the culmination of the baseball season, were all the handiwork of Baker, who bested Dukakis's campaign chairman, Paul Brountas, on just about every issue concerning the debates. Baker had the advantage of being able to at least appear not to care whether there were any debates at all, but still most people think he outnegotiated Brountas.) Debates have played too large a role in Presidential elections: the buildup is tremendous (like everything else, it grows from election to election), the campaigns come to a virtual halt before them, and judgments about who "won" (which shouldn't be made at all) are often based on highly superficial criteria. (For example, Reagan's prepared one-liner to Carter, "There you go again.") Perhaps if there were more of them, any one of them would not carry so much weight. One of the concessions Baker won was that the second, and last, debate would occur more than three weeks before the election (so that a slip by Bush would not be too large a factor on Election Day); though Baker did this out of concern for his own man, it's also better for the country.

283

Perhaps because news commentators recognized the distortions that one-liners had been allowed to cause in the past, and because the one-liners this time were so obviously contrived, the commentary after the debate refrained from placing much emphasis on them. Bush had more of them, and since there had been so much talk before the debate about how Roger Ailes would supply Bush with one-liners—as he had during the primaries—they were seen for what they were. Among Bush's were "I had hoped that this would have been a little friendlier evening. I'd wanted to hitchhike a ride home in his tank with him" and "That answer was about as clear as Boston Harbor." (Bush preceded this one by saying, "Is this the time to unleash our one-liners?") Dukakis, for his part, referring to Bush's budget proposals, said, "If he keeps this up, he's going to be the Joe Isuzu of American politics."

Fortunately, there was little judging of who had "won" on the part of the commentators immediately afterward—in part because there was no obvious "winner" and in part because of wise restraint. (ABC, to its discredit, did an instant poll.) The two candidates actually did debate a number of the issues of the campaign and if they broke little new ground (a debate is no place to take big risks) they offered the viewer a pretty full *tour d'horizon* of the campaign thus far. Though pressed to do so, neither man offered a realistic plan for reducing the deficit. (Bush failed to rebut a Dukakis suggestion that he would cut Social Security.) Dukakis talked a lot about programs he is offering and programs he sponsored in Massachusetts, while Bush continued to try to paint Dukakis as a big-spending liberal whose "values" (a word Bush used a lot) place him "out there on, out of the mainstream." Bush asked, "Do we want this country to go that far left?" Bush brought up Dukakis's membership in the A.C.L.U., pointing out that it wants to get rid of the ratings system for movies ("I don't want my ten-year-old grandchild to go into an X-rated movie") and remove the tax exemption of religious institutions (Bush mentioned only the Catholic church). At this point, Bush said, "I think I'm more in touch with the mainstream of America." There was nothing subtle about his approach. He also, defensively, brought up the Pledge issue, saying he was not questioning Dukakis's patriotism, and Dukakis, of course, was ready. (Bush must have known he would be.) This time, Dukakis replied more along the lines many people thought he should have all along: "Of course the Vice-President's questioning my patriotism. . . . And I resent it." And he went on to talk about his immigrant parents, who "taught me that this was the greatest country in the world. I'm in public service because I love this country." This had obviously been rehearsed —it seemed that almost everything was—and Dukakis appeared indignant, but not impassioned, about the point. He then went on to offer a cheap shot of his own, pointing out that Bush has presided over the Senate for the past seven and a half years and "he's never once suggested that a session of the Senate begin with the Pledge of Allegiance." (A number of people, including some in the Dukakis camp, question whether Dukakis's emphasis on being the son of immigrants is completely helpful; they suggest —and some data back them up—that a lot of people resent and fear waves of immigrants; and there is also some simple prejudice against ethnics.) Bush also, inevitably, brought up Willie Horton (though a great many people don't yet know who he is, and Bush didn't identify him), and said, "I am not going to furlough men like Willie Horton, and"—and this caught one's attention—"I would meet with the victims of his last escapade, the rape and the brutalization of the family down there in Maryland." (The Bush campaign has considered such a meeting.)

Bush also made reference a few times to the expression "a thousand points of light," which had sounded good (if like Reagan) in his acceptance speech, though its meaning was unclear. By the time Bush got done with the debate, the thousand points of light stood for help for the homeless, for help for inner-city children, and for private schools and private church schools helping with education. Asked about having said that he was "haunted" by the lives of inner-city children, Bush denied that the Reagan Administration had cut programs that would help them—and said that he favored the program that provides nutrition and medical help to pregnant women and young children (the Reagan Administration made several attempts to cut the program, which is estimated to serve only half the women and children who need it). Dukakis hit Bush on the Administration's attempts to cut programs, and added, "Being haunted, a thousand points of light— I don't know what that means. I know what strong political leadership is."

Dukakis was on the offensive for most of the debate and was

clearly the better debater—quicker on his feet. He was, as usual, composed and controlled. While aggressive, he stayed just this side of unpleasant (which he had been in some of the debates during the primaries), but his persona still was not entirely pleasing. Still, his being there at all, going toe to toe with the Vice-President (whom, in a levelling move, he called "George" from time to time), had to help him, give him more authority. The first debate usually helps the challenger in this respect. (Bush, for his part, said of Dukakis, "Wouldn't it be nice to be the ice man so you never make a mistake?" He was trying to be like Reagan— the nice guy who may not always get things right, but, shucks.) Dukakis went at Bush hard about Noriega (in this case somewhat unfairly) and the Iran-Contra affair—using these issues to question Bush's credentials and his judgment. The Bush people had gone to great lengths to play down Bush's debating abilities, though Bush had done rather well in the primaries—better than he did Sunday night. He was not as shrill and herky-jerky as he had been against Geraldine Ferraro four years ago, but he was frequently struggling with words and sentences, and at one point lost his place and couldn't improvise. One could see him struggling to get out the thoughts and sentences his advisers had stuffed into him. Bush came off as the warmer man—because he is. One could almost see the effort Dukakis made, at times successfully, to come across as warmer (though his occasional smiles seemed forced) and a man of more feeling than he usually seems to be—and on occasion he lapsed into the dry didact. (He was decked out in a better suit than usual, with firm shoulder pads for a change.) When he was asked about his "passionless, technocratic" style, Dukakis replied, with some—but not a great deal of—feeling, "I care deeply about people, all people," and then he went on to list the kinds of people he cares about (the ones who don't yet benefit from his programs). If he has to describe his passion, to assert that he has it, he has a problem.

Both men were on thin ice on defense policy. Dukakis recited his list of weapons that he is for, and came out flatly against the MX and the Midgetman, and made no mention of any need to modernize land-based nuclear forces. He lapsed into his old litany about the Reagan Administration, and Bush, wanting to "spend billions and billions on Star Wars"—a system that he said "makes no sense at all." Bush responded by asking rhetorically why Dukakis, who did say again that he would spend a billion dollars on research for S.D.I., is "willing to spend a dime on something that you consider a fantasy and a fraud." Bush denied that he has been inconsistent about whether he wanted to deploy S.D.I. (he has been), and said, "When it is deployable, I will deploy it." But Bush got mixed up when he was talking about land-based missiles. Acknowledging that "tough choices" would have to be made, he said, "We are going to make some changes and some tough choices before we go to deployment on the Midgetman missile or on the Minuteman [another land-based missile], whatever it is. We're going to have to, the MX, MX, we're going to have to do that." Realizing that he was in trouble, Bush—alluding to a joke that has been going around about his having advanced the date of Pearl Harbor by three months and the fact that the debate was on September 25th—paused and said, "It's Christmas. It's Christmas." The joke had it that Bush had pulled out of the September 25th debate because he wanted to be with his family on Christmas. Viewers who did not know the joke must have been puzzled by Bush's behavior. And, asked what weapons systems he would cut, he replied by naming three that had already been dropped. (In a debate in the primaries, Bush had been confused about the terms of the I.N.F. treaty.) Especially for a man of his experience, Bush is curiously uninformed. Bush also became rattled in answering a question about Quayle: meaning to say that there were three people in the race who understand defense issues, he said, "There are three people on our ticket that are knowledgeable in the race, knowledgeable in defense, and Dan Quayle is one of them." Bush indignantly chided Dukakis for calling Quayle "J. Danforth Quayle," tried to say that Quayle had been named for a family friend who had been killed in the Second World War—but Bush didn't get the line right, and it wasn't clear what he was talking about.

Bush's closing statement was not outstanding: he meandered through a list of areas the two candidates disagree on, saying, "I am the change," and said, "In the final analysis, a person goes into that voting booth, they're going to say, 'Who has the values I believe in? Who has the experience that we trust?' " And, in what seemed to be a sly reminder of the rumors about Dukakis's mental health that the Bush people had fanned in August, Bush asked, "Who has the integrity and the stability to get the job done?" And he answered his question, "I am that man." Dukakis's closing repeated familiar lines about his being a product of the American dream, and a sequence that he had developed in the primaries about "the best America": "The best America doesn't hide, we compete. The best America doesn't waste, we invest. The best America doesn't leave some of its citizens behind, we bring everybody along. And the best America is not behind us. The best America is yet to come."

Not everybody in the Dukakis camp thinks this is a great litany, though it is at least optimistic, and there was within some disappointment that Dukakis had not, as it had been planned that he would, talked about himself in terms of the themes that he and his campaign have worked so hard to develop—about himself as the candidate of the average American, and about the need to fight to regain America's primacy on the world's economic stage. There was a feeling that he had been too much programs and not enough warmth. Within the Bush camp, it was understood that the Vice-President had not been at his best, and that he needed to talk more about programs of concern to middle-class Americans—which Dukakis was talking about. But, of course, each camp insisted that its man had done splendidly.

On the day after the debate, both sides declared victory and sent their candidates out to establish and perpetuate "momentum" from the debate. At the same time, they took steps to limit some of the damage to their man in the debate. Baker, in a sign that he thought the matter was important, met with reporters that morning and said that Bush concluded after meeting with his staff that he didn't think women should be treated as criminals if they received an illegal abortion. Bush had been asked during the debate about penalties and replied, "I haven't sorted out the penalties, but I do know that I oppose abortion and I favor adoption," to which Dukakis had responded, "Well, I think what the Vice-President is saying is that he's prepared to brand a woman a criminal for making this decision." In the course of that same day the Dukakis camp decided that it had a problem with the A.C.L.U. matter, to which Dukakis had not responded the night before (his answer had dealt only with the Pledge). One reason it decided that it had this problem was that when Dukakis appeared at a rally in Cleveland, John Glenn told reporters that Dukakis had this problem. So in the course of the day the Dukakis campaign put out a statement listing issues on which Dukakis disagreed with the A.C.L.U.—including, it said, ending the tax-exempt status of the Catholic church, opposing child-pornography laws, and removing the words "under God" from the Pledge of Allegiance. (This had been added by Congress in 1954.) It also listed issues on which the A.C.L.U had opposed Dukakis's action as Governor. At a rally in New Jersey that night, Dukakis also cited some of these issues and said, of Bush's suggestion that Dukakis agrees with every A.C.L.U. position, "That's nonsense and he knows it." (His rebuttal was deliberately held until after the news programs so that it wouldn't be the Dukakis story.) He listed some of the issues on which he disagrees and said—referring to the A.C.L.U.'s defense of Oliver North's right against self-incrimination—"and I certainly don't support Oliver North."

At a rally in Jackson, Tennessee, that day, Bush—who was appearing with Quayle for the first time since just after the Republican Convention—once again attacked the Democrats' economic record, referred to "big spenders" and "big taxers" out of Massachusetts, and said, "We must never turn our defense over to a liberal governor or a liberal Congress." In the course of an extended football metaphor, Bush said of the Democrats, "They were the fumble and we are the recovery," and, with Quayle by his side, he said, "We cannot gamble with inexperience in that Oval Office." Dukakis, at the Cleveland rally, argued that he was the one in the mainstream and suggested that Bush favored "raiding the Social Security trust fund" in order to reduce the deficit, and took the crowd (which did not seem very worked up) through a litany of issues on which Dukakis charged that Bush had said "Not one word." Among these was health insurance for those who do not have coverage. (Bush had said something vague about allowing people to "buy into" Medicaid.) Dukakis said of Bush, "He sees no challenges, he offers no solutions, and he will lead America nowhere as President of the United States."

Bush followed the next day with a proposal for a tax break for low- and middle-income people who put up to a thousand dollars a year into a special savings account; the Bush and Dukakis people differed over how much this would be worth to the saver, but in any event it wouldn't be very much. (A Bush adviser said that for someone in the twenty-eight-per-cent tax bracket the yield after ten years would be a hundred and forty-five dollars.) The

Dukakis camp, which estimated that the saving for that same person over five years would be under twenty dollars, was delighted that Bush gave it an opening, and swung into attack, ridiculing Bush for having said that his proposal would help people "become better able to afford a home, pay for college, or start a business." (On Wednesday, Dukakis held up a twenty-dollar bill as he mocked the proposal.) The Dukakis people felt that Bush was reacting to them—the Bush camp, of course, says that the proposal was in the works for a long time—and also that, for the first time, Bush was on their turf, not talking about Dukakis the liberal. In Illinois on Tuesday, Dukakis, becoming more upbeat and aggressive at last, moved closer to the populist tone his advisers had been seeking, and talked about international economic competition. As the week went on, Bush returned to hitting Dukakis as a liberal, who would appoint liberal judges, and said Dukakis's tax-collection plan would have the I.R.S. harassing people. Dukakis went at Bush on the environment and ethics, calling the Reagan Administration's record a "Hall of Shame." John Sasso says that Dukakis has now "laid the foundation" for his message—but the Dukakis camp knows that the message still needs sharpening. The Dukakis people say, and obviously hope, that the Bush message is thin—is made up, as Sasso puts it, "of manufactured issues." The Bush people think otherwise, and plan variations on their themes. By mid-week following the debate, the Dukakis camp's polling had its man still behind by several points—and the Bush camp had its candidate slightly ahead. We're in for some more weeks of slugging.

XIII

As the Presidential election entered its final weeks, the Dukakis campaign believed that its candidate had little time left to do something that would give his candidacy a liftoff, and the Bush campaign worked to nail down a victory that was still just eluding it. Dukakis's creditable performance in the first Presidential debate hadn't given his candidacy the boost his people felt it needed, nor had Lloyd Bentsen's wipeout of Dan Quayle in the Vice-Presidential debate—though the latter did help. Many people think, rightly or wrongly, that tomorrow night's debate will settle the thing. As Dukakis continued to struggle to find his voice, to give his candidacy some overarching theme and purpose—and as his advisers and supporters continued to wait for him to do something exciting—Bush continued to campaign as the man who wants "a kinder and gentler nation" but is also ready to smear his opponent and play on people's fears. Neither man has worked his way into the hearts of the American people—and a great many voters remain undecided. But one of them will have to try to lead the nation after this.

Neither the Dukakis nor the Bush camp was satisfied with where it stood at the beginning of October. Though Dukakis and his people believed he had "won" the first debate—and most polls bore this out—he was unable to capitalize on his victory. The problem was that poll after poll—including the Dukakis camp's own polls—showed that people didn't like him. His frosty, arrogant-seeming manner put people off. Bush may have mangled a number of things he was trying to say, but he came across as the nicer guy—which he essentially is. (But the kind of campaign he has lent himself to raises serious questions about him.) The Bush people had hoped to have the election, for all intents and purposes, put away by early October—to convince the press and the public that it was over—but Dukakis was still standing. Though he was behind by small margins in the national matchups, and though a number of the states, particularly in the South and the West, that usually go Republican were beginning to fall into place for Bush, giving him an electoral-college advantage, almost all the big states remained up for grabs. The electoral college is weighted in favor of the small states, and the old Democratic base in the industrial states is no longer reliable. The Dukakis people knew that they had to tighten the race soon, that his candidacy had to "accelerate," or any chance of victory would get beyond their reach.

Dukakis was up against four problems: Bush, through a combination of unrelenting attacks and smears, had succeeded in painting him to many people as a woolly liberal out of touch with the mainstream; Dukakis's attacks on Bush lacked punch; his positive message was still vague; and people didn't much like him. Obviously, some of these problems were easier to deal with than others. In early October, he began to sharpen his attacks on Bush, saying, in a speech at Northwestern University, that he had "failed" his "missions" to deal with drugs, terrorism, trade relations with Japan, the banking system, and deregulation. Trying to get people to again think of Bush as weak—a perception that Bush, by his rough campaign and improved style, had done much to overcome—Dukakis said, "If Mr. Bush couldn't stand up to the Ayatollah, if he couldn't stand up to Noriega, if he couldn't stand up to Japan, if he couldn't stand up to the special interests, why should anyone believe he'll stand up for the economic future of this country?" But Dukakis's argument, like others he makes, was a bit recondite—requiring the processing of a fair amount of information—as opposed to reaching people at a gut level, which Bush, for better or for worse, does. Dukakis also tried to walk the line between saying that things can be better and appearing to "downgrade" America—a charge that Republicans have developed against Democrats when they say that things can be better. Pointing to the decline in the United States' share of the world market for such things as color televisions and telephones, Dukakis said, "Cite these facts and George Bush will say you're downgrading America. . . . My friends, if we disregard these facts, we endanger America." In any event, few people heard much—or any—of Dukakis's speech, because the networks gave it little coverage. (CBS gave it none.) Dukakis, moreover, isn't big on repetition; he seems to believe that once he's made a point it's been made, whereas the Bush campaign understands that politics requires repetition—lots of it.

Also in early October, Dukakis began to refine his "positive" message, and he and his campaign settled on the theme "The best America is yet to come." Dukakis had been saying this before, and repeated it in his closing statement in the first Presidential debate. It was settled on in part because it expressed optimism, goals, standards, and even a little nationalism (Dukakis also says, "We can make America number one again"), and in part because the Dukakis people hadn't been able to come up with anything else. They hadn't found a sharp way to communicate the idea of the "middle-class squeeze" Dukakis was addressing himself to, and hoped that through his programmatic proposals people would see that he has ideas for helping the middle class. But the programs, as some Dukakis people realize, while giving the messenger some validity, can't substitute for people's having confidence in the messenger, and a large sense of where he wants to take the country. The Dukakis people continued to rely on enough people's deciding in the end that they are not satisfied with their economic situation or prospects and that they want change. This has been, in fact, Dukakis's only hope. The Dukakis camp's optimism of last summer that it would be no big problem to paint Bush as out of touch with mainstream America has been delivered a double whammy—by Bush. Also, there are some things that Dukakis won't do. He has resisted being the populist some around him would like—in part because he isn't a populist. Though he has partially yielded to entreaties to make economic nationalism a major theme, he has been unwilling to go as far in the direction of xenophobia as some of his advisers would like.

In Hartford, on October 3rd, Dukakis set forth his domestic message more sharply and coherently than before, contrasting his proposals to Bush's and saying that Bush "doesn't understand" the concerns of the middle class: "He says everything's fine, not to worry. But ask yourself this: Could your children buy the house they grew up in? Can they finance a college education without mountains of debt when they graduate? Is your family really getting ahead—or is it just running in place or even falling behind?" He said, "Mr. Bush offers complacency, I offer change." He talked about America's losing its competitive edge in the classroom, the workplace, and in the world economy, saying, "I want us to take charge of our future—to make America the best that it can be." He said that the national debt and foreign debt had led to foreign investment in our plants, our land, and our bonds, and that "unless we can take charge of our future our children will be unable to enjoy the same standard of living as their parents, and they'll have to deal with burdens of debt and decline that we're putting on their shoulders." That our debts have made us increasingly dependent on foreign capital to finance them is true enough, but the amount of foreign investment in our industries has not been so great—especially as compared with United States investment abroad—or as threatening as some political rhetoric suggests. And he continued, "That's what this election is all about. Will we look to the past and be satisfied with what some of us now have, or will we look toward a future of opportunity and hope, not just for some of our citizens but for all Americans—in every part of this country?" At least, that's what Dukakis would like the election to be about. As it happened, Dukakis's speech received no mention on the three major television networks, for he gave it on the same day the space shuttle Discovery returned to earth—with Bush on hand at Edwards Air Force Base, in California, to greet the astronauts—and a hostage was released by his captors in Lebanon.

Outside events have been breaking well for Bush. The shuttle flight, nearly three years after the explosion of the Challenger, was invested with much emotion, anxiety, and pride, and was widely hailed as a national triumph. The release of the hostage —an Indian national who holds a United States residence permit and had been held along with three others who had been teaching at Beirut University College—seemed an affirmation of the possibility that Americans still held hostage in Lebanon (there are nine of them) might be released before the election. With the cessation of the Iran-Iraq war, the United States announced that it would begin to withdraw some ships from the Persian Gulf, and at the same time Iran sought to repair relations with Western nations. United States government officials say they are not certain how much leverage Iran has on the various groups holding hostages, and officials have denied any involvement in negotiating the release of the hostages, but, for obvious reasons, they are having trouble being believed. Bush is also benefitting from the fact that Reagan's popularity has been rising—in part as he becomes a nostalgic figure—reaching about sixty per cent, an unusually high figure, and one he had not enjoyed since just before the Iran-Contra scandal broke, in November, 1986. Reagan is campaigning hard for Bush, especially among "Reagan Democrats." Reagan often appears before young people, with whom he does far better than Quayle.

To try to pull Bush back, diminish the distance between the two candidates, the Dukakis campaign went in for heavy advertising in early October, making a big investment in ads in which actors depicted Bush managers cynically talking about packaging their candidate, and which concluded with the announcer saying, "They'd like to sell you a package. Wouldn't you rather choose a President?" The Dukakis people say their research shows that a significant number of people see Bush as a packaged candidate. But the ads have met with a great deal of criticism by political observers who argue, with some validity, that they are too complicated, that it is difficult to figure out even whose ad it is. The Bush campaign has outgunned the Dukakis campaign on ads; it took the Dukakis people some time to organize a group of commercial and political advertisers to come up with ads (in this it was seeking to emulate the "Tuesday Team" that produced ads for Reagan's 1984 campaign), and meanwhile the Bush campaign, which entrusted the responsibility for ads to Roger Ailes, Bush's media adviser, was on the air with unanswered ads attacking Dukakis on such things as crime and his delay in cleaning up Boston Harbor. Also, the Bush ads each made a simple point, and they were in synch with what Bush was saying, so that his "paid media" and "free media" reinforced each other (which is how it should be), while for much of the time Dukakis's ads were off by themselves and lacked focus—as the Dukakis campaign itself did. Following the Vice-Presidential debate, the Dukakis campaign also ran ads attacking Bush for working to weaken environmental regulations and for other lapses on the subject of the environment, and for casting a tie-breaking vote in the Senate to cut Social Security benefits. And it ran two tough anti-Quayle ads: one had the handlers discussing whether it was too late to dump Quayle, and the other showed an empty desk chair in the Oval Office and pointed out that one in five Vice-Presidents has had to take over as President. Bush's ads, reflecting the split personality of his campaign, show him playing with his grandchildren or have him saying in his acceptance speech, "I want a kinder and gentler nation," and also go at Dukakis hard about crime, the environment, and his raising taxes in Massachusetts. A Bush ad on the furlough program, showing prisoners going through a revolving door, is very powerful, if misleading in its facts.

Making Dukakis more likable was perhaps the hardest task of all. He is what he is, at least publicly. Because of television, and as a result of Reagan, whether we like a President or not has taken on more importance. Neither Lyndon Johnson nor Richard Nixon was a particularly lovable figure: it was enough that they appeared competent to do the job. But now we seem to want more than competence, or than even a combination of competence, decency, and high intelligence: we want to have a nice time with our President, enjoy his presence in our living rooms, have a very long and pleasant date with him. Dukakis does have qualities that make him hard to take at times, and efforts to mask them or to divert our attention from them will be ultimately futile. His advisers do their best to loosen him up, but it's a struggle: when possible, they have him campaign in rolled-up shirtsleeves, and they feel, rightly, that he comes across warmer when his wife or one of their daughters is around. Ads projecting a warmer Dukakis are ready for after the second Presidential debate, and Dukakis has already begun accepting numerous opportunities to appear in television interviews (opportunities that Bush had turned down) and try to be more relaxed and warmer, and, cutting through the campaign flak, tell people who he is and what he believes in.

By running such an aggressive campaign—one that is likely to be emulated, if it works—Bush has shucked the "wimp" appellation (which had bothered him quite a bit). The term was never quite fair, but it did bespeak a certain weakness in him—a weakness that, beneath the bluster, is still apparent. A man who will do just about anything his advisers suggest is not a particularly strong one. Bush's aides let it be known from time to time that he insists that his accusations be accurate—even though they often aren't—and that he is troubled by, say, making such an issue of Dukakis's membership in the American Civil Liberties Union. Of course, all he has to do is stop. Two days before the second Presidential debate, Bush, in an interview with the New York *Times*, expressed concern that he was being criticized for running such a negative campaign, and some of his advisers told the *Times* that he didn't really like to be negative. These things do not convey strength; Bush doesn't have to say anything he doesn't want to. Bush is the same person he has been all along—a pleasant guy with some real weaknesses who lacks definition—but his playing the bully seems to have led much, perhaps most, of the public to see him as a mensch. Though people say they don't like negative campaigns, they often work. Bush has even developed an odd and seemingly unnatural body gesture: riding in an open car or standing on a platform accepting the plaudits of the crowd, he flings his arms up and out so that they form a V, making him look like an overage cheerleader.

The Bush campaign has continued its stratagem of mixing positive proposals with the negative attacks in order to fend off criticism for the particularly nasty campaign it has been running, to appeal to independent voters, and to make sure that Dukakis isn't the only one offering enticements to the middle class. At the same time that he offered his proposals, Bush attacked "liberal programs," saying, accurately, that "taking hard-won money from the middle class" and putting it in programs for the poor "caused more resentment than closeness." Several of his proposals are vague, and one of them, a $3.9 billion mélange of programs for children, Bush didn't even bother to outline himself; a fact sheet was distributed to reporters. Another, called YES, for Youth Engaged in Service to America, offered in early October (there was a spate of Bush proposals around then), proposed the spending of a hundred million dollars to encourage public service in the ghettos by high-school children. (A number of Dukakis people were not at all happy that Bush got to this sort of proposal before they did.) Bush's chief of staff, Craig Fuller, told reporters that day that Bush "was uncomfortable with a perception forming that this is a campaign that was not talking about issues as much, because he has been talking about issues." In offering the proposal, Bush said that this was what he meant by the phrase "a thousand points of light." (On another occasion, Bush admitted that when he first saw it in the draft of his acceptance speech he was as baffled as everyone else.) Shortly after his appearance, in Sacramento, in which he made the YES proposal, Bush appeared at a rally in Riverside and attacked Dukakis for being weak on crime.

* * *

It was widely understood that a great deal rode on Quayle's performance in the Vice-Presidential debate, in Omaha on October 5th. Dukakis had been making an issue of him, but if he performed adequately the issue could be gone, even if that didn't make him any more qualified for the Vice-Presidency. There was some real concern within the Dukakis camp that Quayle would indeed do adequately and that his youth and vigor would stand in helpful contrast to Bentsen. Both camps went through the usual nonsense of "lowering expectations," and a great deal of suspense was allowed to build once again over a ninety-minute event—a single event that could therefore play a large role in determining the Presidency.

The two most surprising things about the Vice-Presidential debate were that Bentsen was as good as he was and that Quayle was as bad as he was. Bentsen had campaigned competently and surefootedly, but in the debate he showed a command and an assurance as well as an apparent ease that made him the best of the four candidates in these events thus far. Though he clearly was prepared to make certain points, he appeared far less scripted and more natural than any of the other contenders; unlike the others, he conveyed wisdom. Quayle's performance was astonishing—especially given the fact that he has some of the best trainers in the country. But these trainers either permitted or could not prevent Quayle's looking wooden and frightened—like a young man hesitantly reciting his lessons and knowing little else. Quayle had been an effective enough debater in the past, and what could have been expected was that he would come on vigorous (but not too vigorous), assertive, and showing a certain youthful charm. But the pressure of the situation obviously got to him—or he was overcoached—and there were precious few moments in which he appeared the slightest bit relaxed or natural. Bentsen, in sharp contrast, seemed relaxed and natural almost throughout, and though he is no dynamo, and his creased face makes him look older than he is (sixty-seven), he came across as a man we could feel comfortable with in a crisis—which is, of course, the whole point in thinking about potential Vice-Presidents. Quayle looks even younger than he is (forty-one); there is a vacuousness to his pale-blue eyes that adds to the impression of his insubstantiality.

Quayle's flubbing three questions about what he would do should he have to take over the Presidency was symptomatic. He clearly hadn't been prepared for this question, so he persistently gave an answer to one that he had: a recitation of his qualifications—his twelve years in Congress, his service on the Senate Armed Services Committee and the Budget Committee, his sponsorship of a jobs-training bill. He had already given this answer to the opening question—dropping such ten-dollar words as "telemetry" and "encryption" to show his knowledge, but putting the words in no context. Throughout the debate, in fact, Quayle was asserting his qualifications without offering substantive proof of them. The first time he was asked what he would do if he had to take over, he quite hesitantly said he would pray, for himself and for the country, and assemble the President's advisers—and then went on to the twelve years in Congress. The second time, he said, "I don't believe that it's proper for me to get into the specifics of a hypothetical situation like that"—and returned once again to his twelve years in Congress. He also said that he had met with Prime Minister Margaret Thatcher of Great Britain, and Chancellor Helmut Kohl of Germany: "I know them. They know me." (Quayle met each of them once, for only a few minutes.) The third time he was asked the question, he talked again about his qualifications and also said that he would know the President's top advisers and his Cabinet officers "on a firsthand basis" and would call them in and talk to them. These exchanges were painful to behold, and his inability to think up some form of the right answer—call in the Joint Chiefs of Staff, reassure the allies, speak to the American people, perhaps address a joint session of Congress—was baffling.

Of course, Quayle's most painful moment was caused by Bentsen's picking him up on that part of his third answer in which, as he had been doing on the campaign trail, he asserted that he has had as much experience as John Kennedy had when he sought the Presidency. (Bush's top advisers had put forth this argument at the Republican Convention.) As soon as Bentsen gave his withering response, one knew that this would be the most memorable moment of the debate, the one that would be replayed often, and Bentsen delivered his lines with perfect timing. The effectiveness was in the way it was done: Bentsen's saying, more in sorrow, slowly, "Senator, I served with Jack Kennedy." (Pause.) "I knew

Jack Kennedy." (Pause.) "Jack Kennedy was a friend of mine." (Longer pause.) "Senator, you're no Jack Kennedy." As Bentsen started to go ahead with what he would do if he had to take over as President, an obviously wounded Quayle said stiffly, and with what seemed more petulance than anger, "That was really un-called for, Senator." So Bentsen levelled him again, with elegant phrasing: "You're the one that was making the comparison, Sen-ator. . . . I did not think the comparison was well taken." ("Petu-lant" is a word that a senator who likes Quayle uses to describe him. This person also says that Quayle is more given to argument than compromise, and is known to give Republican colleagues who try to work out compromises a hard time.)

Quayle did his share of attacking Dukakis, saying whenever possible that Dukakis is a liberal, one who would raise taxes and is opposed to the death penalty. (He referred to him as "Tax-Hike Mike.") Quayle suggested that Dukakis might impose "an-other Jimmy Carter grain embargo." (Dukakis has said he wouldn't.) With obvious predetermination, he got in digs at Dukakis by tak-ing digs at supporters of Dukakis and Bentsen in the hall. Quayle answered a question about what experience in his life had shaped his political philosophy by telling of his grandmother's saying to him, "You can do anything you want to if you just set your mind to it and go to work," and then, though the hall seemed silent, said, "Now, the Dukakis supporters sneer at that because it's com-mon sense. They sneer at common sense advice, Midwestern ad-vice from a grandmother to a grandson." He also took a shot at the press, calling himself "the most investigated person ever to seek public office."

Bentsen tried to set the terms of the debate at the outset, saying, "This debate tonight is not about the qualifications for the Vice-Presidency; the debate is whether or not Dan Quayle and Lloyd Bentsen are qualified to be President of the United States." He dealt with questions about his differences with Dukakis—over Contra aid, gun control, the death penalty—by evading them and proceeding to discuss the things that he and Dukakis agree on. He painted Quayle as a right-winger who had opposed child-nutrition programs and money for childhood immunizations and had tried to undermine the I.N.F. agreement. (Quayle had pushed for what many considered a treaty-killing amendment.) Bentsen seemed least at ease when he was defending Dukakis's record, getting out statistics and facts he had been instructed in. But he had scope, talking with authority about the trade imbalance, the national debt, the economic challenges this country is facing. Unlike Quayle—and to a greater extent than Dukakis or Bush—he looked at home with what he was saying. He was better at pushing some of Dukakis's themes than Dukakis had been: he said that as we come to depend on foreigners to help us finance our debt "we lose some of our economic independence for the future," and "You know, if you let me write two hundred billion dollars' worth of hot checks every year I could give you an illusion of prosperity, too."

Following the debate, the Bush camp showed several signs of concern. The next day, Bush himself did not mention Quayle until he was pressed to do so by reporters. (He said that Quayle had done "an outstanding job.") Reagan used a "photo opportunity" at the White House to say that Bentsen's line about Kennedy was "a cheap shot." The night before, Lee Atwater, Bush's campaign manager, who is not known for his delicacy, had called it "a cheap shot." When Reagan is called upon for such duty, it is a clear indication of worry. Also on the day after the debate, Bush's campaign chairman, James Baker, said on CNN, "When you think about what might have happened, we have to be pretty happy." Robert Teeter, Bush's pollster, told reporters that though he had conducted a focus-group test during the debate he hadn't yet had time "to pick through the numbers." Public polls were saying that by margins of nearly two to one people thought that Bentsen had "won" the debate.

While Bush was having as little as possible to do with his running mate, an unaccustomedly joyful Dukakis appeared with Bentsen at a rally in Lone Star, Texas. Dukakis, obviously happy about the events of the night before, said that the choice of the running mate is "the first national-security decision." He said, "You have to choose somebody who is ready to step into the Oval Office at a moment's notice and who knows what to do when he gets there." Dukakis and his people thought that the Vice-Presidential debate was a break for them, and they wanted to ride it for all it was worth. They went on the air the day after the debate with their negative ads about Quayle. Dukakis, as he had before, tried to turn it into a question about himself and Bush: "This is the first

Presidential decision that George Bush and I had to make. Judge us by how we made it and who we chose." But this, too, is a relatively complicated point. Dukakis and Bentsen were appearing in a hard-hit area in East Texas; about five thousand workers had been laid off by the Lone Star Steel plant in the last few years. The Dukakis people feel that what chance the Dukakis-Bentsen ticket has in Texas—at that point it was behind by some ten to twelve points—depends on how people feel about the difficult time the state, like other oil-patch states, has been through. With the end of the Iran-Iraq war and new struggles within OPEC, the price of oil had dropped substantially, to about thirteen dollars a barrel, the lowest in over two years. And the drop in oil prices, with its consequent effects on the Texas economy, plus deregulation, had led to the failure of nearly a hundred banks in Texas this year thus far—more than half the total for the United States. However, some reports have it that things are looking up in Texas, and the Bush campaign has done an effective job in painting Dukakis to Texans as a man who is soft on crime and supports gun control. The Dukakis camp has started to run its own, defensive gun-control ad in Texas, saying that Dukakis supports the right of hunters to own guns. His advisers wanted it to also say that he favored the right of homeowners to possess guns, but Dukakis rejected that.

Bentsen's principal assignment had been to help the ticket carry Texas, but now he was in the unexpected position of being the star of the campaign. Suddenly, he was hot. His rallies had an excitement to them that neither of the Presidential candidates had been able to generate authentically. The emergence of this improbable star said some telling things about this election, and about how we choose candidates. Bentsen's new glory came not because he had got off his now-famous line about Kennedy; it came about because he was the most—in fact, the only—authentic figure in the race. What people were responding to was that for the first time this fall they had seen a genuine, whole person, someone at ease with himself and his knowledge. His dignity was most welcome in a campaign where there had been little of it. But not only had Bentsen fallen quite short when he made a brief try for the Presidential nomination, in 1976, but there is little likelihood that he ever could have won the nomination. Had he begun the long march, starting in Iowa, he would have been dismissed as too old, too unexciting, and too conservative. The "Presiden-tialness" that people are responding to in him, as they do, or might, in the case of other national figures, does not necessarily lend itself to nomination demands. This is not to say that no one with dignity and bearing and a certain stature and broad scope could make it, but people like that tend not to try, or don't do very well if they do. And the demands of the nomination process claw at what dignity and Presidentialness a person might have. Bentsen undoubtedly would have been rejected as too conservative by the liberal activists in the Democratic Party, who have their own litmus tests, and tend to dominate in the nomination process. (Jimmy Carter won because the liberal vote was divided among other candidates.) Bentsen's voting record—supporting school prayer and Contra aid, opposing federal financing of abortions, being generally pro-business—made him only just tolerable to the Party when Dukakis selected him. Following the Vice-Presidential de-bate, Bentsen, whose campaign had been limited largely to Texas and the South and Southwest, and centered on appearances on local television, was sent into such key states as New Jersey and Pennsylvania, and he held large rallies.

Quayle, meanwhile, was relegated to the byways of the country he had been travelling before, mostly appearing before friendly audiences—though he was in Detroit on Columbus Day. In his appearance there, Quayle, after saying he felt that the question of what he would do if he had to assume the Presidency was "totally inappropriate," because it was hypothetical, gave his response as to what he would do under various circumstances. Quayle's dec-laration of self-liberation from his "handlers," the week after the Vice-Presidential debate, was the most interesting thing he has done, but there is a question of how much there was to it. He had become understandably fed up with the stories about him as the creature of his handlers (who hadn't done very well by him for the debate), as well as angry with stories quoting Bush advisers as less than thrilled with him, and conceding that he is a drag on the ticket. (Polls show that Bush does better when he alone is measured against Dukakis than when the Bush-Quayle ticket is measured against the Dukakis-Bentsen ticket. People in charge of winning California for Bush have told the Bush campaign to keep Quayle out of the state.) On Tuesday, Quayle told reporters trav-elling with him in southwest Ohio, "I got tired of all the bad publicity. I decided it couldn't get any worse and I was going to take over. . . . I'm the handler." A number of people were skeptical, and thought this was Quayle's handlers' latest trick. Quayle's doings remain under the strict control of the Bush campaign, and he remains largely inaccessible to the press.

As promised, the Bush campaign went all out on the furlough issue in October. On the day after the Vice-Presidential debate, Bush, in Texas, appearing, as he was to do often in coming days, with law-enforcement officials, launched a new assault on Dukakis on the issue of crime, attacking him for opposing the death penalty and mandatory sentences for drug dealers, calling him one of the "liberal theorists" who had forgotten that law enforcement's "first priority" is "to protect the safety of our neighborhoods and law-abiding citizens." (Bush also met with a group of victims of crime.) He also said that he would set up a new section in the Justice Department to deal with street gangs and would spend an additional billion dollars over the next four years on building federal prisons. Bush did not say where this money would come from, just as he hasn't in offering his other programs; he remains firm ("Read my lips") in saying he will not increase taxes. (Also in Texas on the day after the debate, he reiterated his support for tax breaks for the oil-and-gas industry, saying, as he does of his proposal to lower capital-gains taxes, that the proposal would pay for itself. Things didn't work out that way after Reagan's tax cut was enacted.)

But Bush's biggest ammunition following the Vice-Presidential debate was aimed at Massachusetts' furlough program. He described in gruesome detail the events that occurred when Willie Horton, whom the Bush people have made the most famous furloughee in America, raped and brutalized a Maryland couple. Horton had escaped while on his tenth furlough and committed his new crime in April, 1987. On the day Horton was caught, in Maryland, a moratorium was placed on furloughs for convicted murderers who are not eligible for parole. It was this category of furloughs that set Massachusetts apart—under a law instituted when Francis Sargent, a Republican, was governor, and continued under Edward King, the conservative Democrat who defeated Dukakis at the end of his first term. Earlier this year, Dukakis, under pressure, signed a law eliminating furloughs for first-degree murderers. (Two murders were committed by people furloughed while Reagan was governor of California, and the federal government regularly furloughs convicted drug dealers, one of whom in 1987 committed rape and murder.) Bush said that Dukakis had given a "generous vacation" to fifty-nine criminals convicted of violent crime who escaped while on furlough (this is not correct), and said, "Clint Eastwood's answer to violent crime is 'Go ahead. Make my day.' My opponent's answer is slightly different. His motto is 'Go ahead. Have a nice weekend.' " Bush said that Dukakis had shown "an astounding lack of sensitivity, a lack of human compassion" toward victims of crime and their families.

Last Friday, the day after Bush launched his new attack on the furlough program, in what we are supposed to believe was a coincidence, the Maryland couple, Clifford and Angela Barnes, began a four-state tour, beginning with California and Texas, to speak about their experience and criticize Dukakis for never apologizing to them. The tour was sponsored by an "independent," Los Angeles-based group that backs Bush. The same group also sponsored a radio ad in which Clifford Barnes recounts his grim experience. That evening, it became apparent what Bush advisers might have meant when they told me not long ago that before the campaign was over the American people—one adviser talked in terms of American women—would know what Willie Horton looks like. Two networks ran a picture of Horton, who was now in the news. (His picture was already running on some cable networks, in an ad sponsored by another "independent" group.) The furlough issue, like the crime issue as a whole, conveys a subliminal message about race as the Bush people are well aware. A Bush aide says, with some satisfaction, that Dukakis's negatives with white voters are so high as to be insuperable. Some Democrats think their party is still suffering from the backlash to the civil-rights revolution.

Finally, Dukakis, who had taken most of Bush's attacks lying down, responded, and did it effectively. On Saturday, Dukakis spoke at Bates College, in Maine, from which both of his parents had graduated. Pointing out that his own family had been victims of crime—his elder brother had been killed by a hit-and-run driver, and his father, then a seventy-seven-year-old doctor, had been robbed, tied up, and left in his office late one afternoon—Dukakis said, "I don't need any lectures from Mr. Bush on crime-fighting or on the sensitivity or compassion we must extend to the victims of crime." He continued, "Unlike Mr. Bush, who will not take responsibility for anything, I, as a chief executive, took full responsibility for that tragic Horton case and acted to change that policy—and Mr. Bush knows it. So let's look at the facts and stop this shameless playing of politics with the tragedy of crime." Dukakis advisers were pleased that Dukakis had finally got over the hump of talking about his own family's experience, and thought this response so strong that he should have continued to give it —but Dukakis wanted to get on to other subjects.

On Monday, Dukakis and his wife, Kitty, marched up Fifth Avenue in the Columbus Day parade, and Dukakis also offered a program to help the middle class purchase housing. Appearing in Levittown, he pointed out that the grown children of people who had bought homes there when the houses were first built, shortly after the Second World War, could not themselves afford to buy them, and that some had to live with their parents. On Tuesday, Dukakis, speaking at Tufts University, in Massachusetts (both candidates were winding down their schedules in order to prepare for the next debate), promised to "make America number one in science education" and "the technologies of the future," saying he would set up partnerships of the federal government, the business community, and the states to accomplish these things. At Tufts, Dukakis also sounded more protectionist than usual, but still didn't go as far as some of his advisers wanted.

On the same day, Bush, appearing in Seattle (en route to Los Angeles, where the debate is to be held), took Dukakis on for his talk of economic nationalism, saying, "There have always been those who would prey upon people's fear of change." He continued, "Frankly, I've been surprised at my opponent's recent turn to protectionist demagoguery. I don't think he really believes it —he ran against this so-called 'economic nationalism' in the primaries." Bush said, "My opponent desperately needs an issue, and he's willing to scare people to find it" (he had a point), and said that Dukakis was like the members of the Know-Nothing Party of the nineteenth century, which played upon fear of foreigners and Catholics. Bush, as part of his effort to offset the impression of him as a creature of privilege, called for strict law enforcement against inside traders and other white-collar criminals. He said, "They may not carry guns and they may wear fancy suits, but they are a real danger to society, and they should be hit with the maximum penalties of the law."

On the eve of the second debate, Democrats, including some in the Dukakis camp, are fairly pessimistic about the outcome of the election—though few will say now that they think Dukakis has no chance. They know that Dukakis has still not developed a compelling economic message, or given people a strong enough reason to turn out the incumbents when times don't seem very bad. Dukakis could get away without having much of a message in the primaries, but now he can't. Though there are more than three weeks remaining before the voting, and Bush has only a slight lead over Dukakis in the polls—of three to six points, with most polls putting it at three—most close observers feel that Dukakis can't win under the current circumstances. Though the undecided vote has dropped, a substantial part of each candidate's support remains "soft." By some estimates, a third of the electorate is still uncertain. Dukakis has recouped his lead in California and Washington, and Bush's advantage in Ohio and Missouri has been slipping. But the arithmetic of the electoral college is continuing to swing in Bush's direction, and though most of the big states are still too close to call, Dukakis has far the greater burden in getting to the necessary two hundred and seventy votes. The networks have broadcast electoral-college analyses this week that make the election all but over, but though the result may be similar to the one they are predicting, they are getting ahead of the story. And some of their predictions on how various states will do rest as of now on shaky data and assumptions. We seem to have an obsession with "knowing" how an election will turn out, which gets in the way of just watching it happen—and can affect what happens. Some Democrats gave up on Dukakis a while ago, and the optimism at the end of the Convention in Atlanta is gone. It is to be remembered that a Dukakis victory is not in the true interest of certain Democrats—future candidates for President, for example, or important members of Congress, who are more important if the opposition party holds the White House—though of course these people can't say such a thing out loud. Some Democrats, remembering the Carter Presidency unhappily, aren't keen on carrying water for another unpopular President, which is what they fear Dukakis would be. Many Democrats who have been waiting for eight years to return to the government are glumly concluding that they'll have to wait longer. The Bush people talk optimistically and feel that victory is within their grasp— but that they haven't quite reached it. What Dukakis has to do in the debate is not necessarily, as several analysts—and also the Bush people—are saying, something dramatic; he has to come off with a strong enough performance to make the contest more truly competitive than it is now, more near to even, and give his candidacy propulsion into the final stretch. His people know that if he doesn't do this he probably can't win.

XIV

Whatever Dukakis needed to do in the debate to give his candidacy a lift, to accelerate it, didn't happen. There is something very puzzling about Dukakis: there have been times in the course of this year when it seemed that he would be an upbeat, can-do, enthusiastic, and optimistic candidate, a person who couldn't wait to get in there and roll up his sleeves and make things happen. That's the kind of governor he has been, but these are not usually the things he projects. An adviser says that Dukakis wanted to run that kind of campaign but could see, in the face of the Bush attacks, that it wasn't working. Some advisers think Dukakis was thrown off by the nature of the Bush campaign, and that this is where the zest went. (But they aren't really sure where it went.) In any event, Dukakis didn't have the presence, the command-ingness, to surmount the Bush attacks. Dukakis aides say that he rejected an all-out negative campaign against Bush (and they are not sure that such a campaign would have worked, either). It may well be that Dukakis simply doesn't have the dimension to com-mand a national stage. Dukakis has not yet become a national figure in the sense of someone who speaks to and reaches the nation at large. The explanation may lie in his experience: to become governor of Massachusetts (or of most states) one does not need to command a large following, offer a compelling vision, be a strong leader. A Presidential candidate without a compelling message or a particularly engaging public persona has formid-able problems getting through. Dukakis had never run a big campaign. It is enough—when running for the office of gov-ernor, or in it—to meet with people in small groups and be reasonably competent. There are exceptions, but good gover-nors don't necessarily make good national leaders; these days, governors are mostly managers. Dukakis's concept of the Pres-idency also seems to be based in his experience as a governor:

he speaks of it as calling groups into a room, forming "coalitions" and "partnerships"—not as leading the country through establishing a relationship with the people and moving them. (It is not yet established whether Bush will be able to move people.) The nomination contest did not require that Dukakis be of national dimension; the only time he has seemed to be was when he gave his acceptance speech in Atlanta. But that turned out to be an exception.

In the debate, Dukakis seemed flat and at times almost disengaged. He was clearly trying to come across as warmer and less snappish than he did in the first debate, and he succeeded, but this wasn't enough. (The warmth was mostly a technical matter of looking into the camera more softly. The half smile was unconvincing.) The Dukakis camp's goal was to deal with the problems that Bush's "favorable" ratings are higher than Dukakis's and that a relatively high percentage of people say they still don't know much about Dukakis. It wanted to avoid a repetition of the first debate, in which Dukakis seemed to win on points but hurt himself with his sharp and pedantic manner. The Dukakis people talk as if there is a conflict between the candidate's trying to be more likable and being tough on Bush, but, of course, that's not necessarily the case. Yet it seems to be so for Dukakis, who is not very deft with the knife. His advisers loaded him up for the debate with self-deprecatory remarks, which weren't used, and other keys to a more pleasing personality. But they were trying to make him something he isn't, and it didn't work. They were playing Bush's game. In trying not to be "mean," Dukakis was blah. He may have had so many goals in his head that he froze. He was stiff in manner and prone to recitations—of lists of things he would do, of what he had done. Dukakis, like many other liberals, is a process-oriented man: he thinks process and loves process, he enjoys dealing in policy. But this is not enough for a national leader—it does not move people. He spoke in the debate—several times—of the need to make "tough choices," but that won't win over masses of voters. Nothing was more telling in this respect than Dukakis's choosing to observe a ground rule of the debate (obviously imposed by the Bush people) that neither candidate could challenge the other to a third debate—after Bush responded to a question about whether there should be another debate by flatly ruling out another one. After the debate, at a rally and out of the national eye, Dukakis called for a third debate. Bush may not have all the attributes of a leader, either, but he has managed during some of this fall campaign to look like one. Dukakis's narrow-gaugedness, his minimalist world experience, shows. Bush is not a particularly deep or thoughtful man, but he has been around and has a range of experiences to call upon to offer himself as someone who knows and has seen a lot. Dukakis is back to lacking size (this has nothing to do with his relatively short height); the one time he showed size was in his acceptance speech. Some politicians show size the moment they enter a room (Ronald Reagan, Mario Cuomo, Jesse Jackson). There is something so contained about Dukakis that he offers little to connect with. (John Kennedy was contained, but he conveyed an energy of belief and was eloquent—and of course he had charm, and a keen sense of humor.)

A big problem for Dukakis in this and the first debate, as well as in his campaign, is that he lacked a theme. He was supposed to talk about "making America number one again," and all that, but he didn't, and anyway it isn't much of a theme. When the debate ended, it didn't seem that Dukakis had said or done anything that would lead millions of undecided voters to conclude that he was their man—much less cause great numbers of people who had been inclined to vote for Bush to change their mind. Dukakis seems to lack imagination—thus he let a number of opportunities to say something interesting go by. He seemed incapable of spontaneity. He didn't even bring up Bush's use of the furlough plan and give the strong response he had given at Bates College. This was a great disappointment to his advisers. Moreover, the issue on which Bush has done the greatest damage to him is crime. Dukakis is correct when he claims, as he did in the debate, that Massachusetts has had "the biggest drop in crime of any industrial state"—but it doesn't seem to do him much good. Dukakis did talk about the furlough and his family's experiences the next day in California, but this was a little late. Dukakis's mechanistic answer to the first debate question, a deliberately shocking (and tasteless) one about whether, if his wife were raped and murdered, he would support the death penalty, was much pointed to afterward as symptomatic of Dukakis's stiffness and lack of emotion. ("No, I don't," he replied, and went on to make his routine points about the death penalty.) Dukakis advisers think that he was aware that he had blown it with this response, and he wasn't able to recover in the rest of the debate. Asked about the fact that people don't find him likable enough—a question that had been anticipated—Dukakis blew the opportunity to say something interesting (or "likable"), by saying pretty seriously, "I think I'm a reasonably likable guy . . . but I'm also a serious guy. I think the Presidency of the United States is a very serious office." Though he had been prepared to do so, he didn't take much opportunity to try to respond to the issues Bush has used, successfully, to paint him as a leftish politician out of the mainstream—he didn't begin to express the kind of moral outrage that might make people think again about what Bush had been saying, and see Dukakis as a man of strength. Dukakis has let Bush win the strength contest by default.

Bush's performance in the second debate was substantially better than in the first one—in fact, his best performance of the year. Bush was far more relaxed and coherent than in the earlier debate (the two are undoubtedly connected); though he mangled a few sentences, he came across as confident, in command, and a very pleasant fellow. It's odd that the same man can give such different performances. He joshed with the panel and abjured obviously rehearsed one-liners. (Dukakis did neither.) Roger Ailes says that Bush went through less intense preparation for the second debate, and that he and Bush did a lot of kidding around on the day of the debate. Ailes says, "I felt if he went in relaxed, he'd do better." Bush was told about the problems with his performance in the first debate, and resolved to do better. His advisers have said all year that he rises to the occasion, and, says one, as he gets closer to the Presidency he becomes more Presidential.

Clearly defensive about criticism of the kind of campaign he has been running, Bush was far less harsh and far more positive than before—though he still got in sly digs at Dukakis, and used the word "liberal" as often as possible. Dukakis, defensively, chided him for using "labels"—to no avail. He had been prepared with material to take the "liberal" issue on more aggressively, but didn't use it. In being defensive about the label, he seemed to accept Bush's premise that it's a terrible thing to be a liberal. Though Bush has changed his views on a number of things, he came across as someone who believed firmly what he was saying. He drew the differences between himself and Dukakis without being shrill about it. Whenever he could, he went to what has been working for him in his campaign—depicting himself as more in touch with mainstream America's values than Dukakis is. (He also used the word "values" a lot.) He took as many opportunities as possible to point out that he, unlike Dukakis, favors the death penalty, that Dukakis had supported the nuclear freeze, and to charge that Dukakis advocates "unilateral cuts" in arms. Bush accomplished enough in the debate, and Dukakis didn't.

Dukakis tried to deal with the new, more moderate George Bush by saying several times, "I don't know which George Bush I'm debating," and pointing out differences between what Bush is now saying and actions he took or positions he supported as Vice-President. Dukakis was right that Bush, as head of the regulatory-relief task force, tried to dismantle certain environmental regulations, but because Congress overrode some of these actions Bush was able to claim progress in these areas. Dukakis was correct that Bush, in casting a vote to freeze Social Security cost-of-living allowances for a year, had voted to "cut" Social Security benefits, but Bush was right that Dukakis had supported that idea in the National Governors' Association—both were supporting a large deficit-reduction proposal—and also that Democrats always demagogue this issue "just about this time of year." Both men continued to avoid specifying anything politically difficult they would do to reduce the budget deficit, and both seemed to rule out making any cuts in entitlement programs. Dukakis left himself open to criticism by failing to say what he would do to modernize the ground-based missile system, but he seems not to want a new system, despite what his advisers say, and mentioned often his intention to cut certain defense spending. For the first time in a while, he went back to his criticism of the Administration's policy in Nicaragua as a "failed policy" and a "fiasco." Neither he nor Bush has talked about the Contra-aid issue very much, for parallel reasons: both Bush's position in favor of supporting the Contras and Dukakis's position against it carry political risk. Contra aid is unpopular, but some of Dukakis's political advisers say that his position reinforces the picture of a liberal. Dukakis's mention of the Nicaragua issue in the debate was a reversion to type. (Congress has approved twenty-seven million dollars in "humanitarian" aid to the Contras, but the Administration has given up trying to get more military assistance.)

Bush took every opportunity he could to stress the themes of

peace and prosperity, and to associate himself with Reagan. Dukakis took his best shot at arguing that it is time for change, saying,
"I don't think we can be satisfied when we're spending a hundred
and fifty billion dollars a year on interest alone on the national
debt—much of it going to foreign bankers. Or when twenty-five
per cent of our high-school students are dropping out of school,
or when we have two and a half million of our fellow-citizens—
a third of them veterans—who are homeless and living on streets
and in doorways in this country, or when Mr. Bush's prescription
for our economic future is another tax giveaway to the rich. We
can do better than that." (The trade deficit widened substantially
that day, but Dukakis didn't mention it.) But what he said was not
convincing enough. Bush made his best case for staying with his
party, and with the man who had served under Reagan. He also
took note of the fact that big things are happening in the Soviet
Union. The recent upheaval in the Kremlin, giving Mikhail Gorbachev more power, and the clear signs that Gorbachev and his
allies believe that the Soviet Union must turn to radical economic reform, at the cost of foreign adventures, or even pure
Communism—plus the increasing cracks in Eastern Europe—
present the next President with important challenges and will
require great wisdom. Neither man is very convincing about having thought these things through.

In his closing, Bush crisply and firmly went through his differences with Dukakis—on taxes, the death penalty. He said he
"would appoint judges that have a little more sympathy for the
victims of crime and a little less for the criminals." (In the debate
Bush had said that he would not appoint liberals who "legislate
from the bench" to the Supreme Court—three Justices are in their
eighties—and defended Robert Bork. Dukakis and his people
thought this gave them an opening, and Dukakis talked about
Bork the next day, but whether this will sway millions is questionable.) Despite its importance, Dukakis has said little about the
Supreme Court, because the Court issue suggests the issues of
crime and civil liberties—that's what Bush is saying when he vows
not to appoint liberals to the bench—and both issues are political
losers with the socially conservative middle-class voters Dukakis is
trying to win over. Bush said, "This election is about big things,"
and he is right. The candidates may not be talking about big things
very much, but the next President will have to play a big part on

the world's unpredictable stage, and deal with difficult economic and other domestic issues. Bush, in his closing, hit all the important notes: having placed himself as more against crime and taxes than Dukakis, he insisted that he does want "a kinder and gentler nation," and said that he wants "to invest in our children" and supports child care. (The child-care proposal, along with others that Bush has said he is for—parental leave and a higher minimum wage—have all died in Congress.) He aligned himself with Reagan: "I ask you to consider the experience I have had in working with a President who has revolutionized the situation around the world. America stands tall again." He said that he would like to be able to tell his grandchildren that as President he had achieved a ban on chemical and biological weapons. And he closed by paraphrasing Lincoln, as Reagan often does, calling America "the last best hope of man on earth." It was a very effective closing, which Dukakis hadn't come close to matching.

Following the debate, Dukakis and his people, though they knew that the prospects were now very bleak, had to struggle to keep the nation from concluding that the election was over, and Bush and his people had to ward off overconfidence—or the appearance of overconfidence. With polls indicating that people felt by two-to-one margins that Bush had "won" the debate, and with the gap between Bush and Dukakis in the national polls widening, this was difficult. Over the weekend, the Los Angeles *Times* and CBS gave Bush leads of ten and eleven points respectively, and on Monday the NBC/*Wall Street Journal* poll put Bush ahead by a whopping seventeen points. Even the Bush people said that this was excessive. Both camps' polling showed Bush comfortably ahead, and the only question was how much of this was a temporary phenomenon—a reaction to the debate and also the subsequent coverage that said Dukakis had blown his last big opportunity. The television coverage of the campaign inevitably reflected the polls, with the pieces about Dukakis framed by comments about the trouble he was in. This phenomenon, which the Dukakis people had been trying to stave off, makes it more difficult than ever for the candidate to get his message across—if he has one. Dukakis campaigned spiritedly in California and Texas on Friday and Saturday—saying several things his advisers wish he had said in the debate—and on Sunday, before an audience of supporters in

Faneuil Hall, in Boston, he sharpened his message further. The rally at Faneuil Hall was designed to pick up Dukakis's spirits as much as those of his supporters. Dukakis's advisers said that in this closing phase of the campaign he would talk more about values, comparing his own to Bush's—offering himself as the candidate more likely to stand up for the average American, and Bush as the one who favors the wealthy. Saying some of the things he had been supposed to say in the debate, he portrayed himself as someone who accepts responsibility, and Bush as the man who sat through seventeen meetings on the question of arms sales to Iran and didn't object, and who won't accept responsibility for Noriega's being on the United States' payroll after it was known he was a drug dealer.

None of these themes were new, of course, but, the Dukakis people said, they would be put more sharply—and they were. This leaves the question of why they hadn't been put more sharply before. Or whether it matters. What Dukakis said or failed to say in his campaign is only part of his problem; the other part— probably the larger one—has been Bush's ability to paint Dukakis as a liberal, out of touch with the mainstream. Yet Dukakis, by his slowness to react, or even to see the peril in what Bush was doing to him, became an accomplice in Bush's strategy. A few people around Dukakis saw some time ago that Dukakis was vulnerable on the defense and crime issues, but generally the campaign underestimated the potency of the issues of the Pledge of Allegiance and the furlough program, just as it had underestimated Bush (almost everyone did) as a Presidential candidate. Dukakis was dismissive of these issues long after people around him saw that they were trouble.

This is not the first time we have seen a Presidential candidate begin to find his voice at the end, as he seemed to be going down the tubes—and wondered why it had taken so long. At Faneuil Hall, Dukakis said, "I may not express my feelings as eloquently as some. But does anyone doubt what I would have said if I was in the room when they made those decisions to sell arms to the Ayatollah, to put Noriega on the payroll, to veto civil rights and women's rights, or to choose people like Dan Quayle and Ed Meese and James Watt and Robert Bork? I would have said three simple words: 'This is wrong.' That's the test of leadership; that's the test of passion and principle; and that's the issue in this election." He also said, "I want to be President of the United States not because it's the next rung on the ladder but because it's the way to act on my values. And I mean the commitments of a lifetime, not labels and buzzwords that score well in the polls." But these were still complicated points, made a little late. Dukakis was appealing to reason, while the opposition was reaching people's emotions, through symbols. He delineated more sharply his differences with Bush on relief for the average American—pointing to, among other things, Bush's proposal for a cut in the capital-gains tax and his savings plan for the middle class, which would yield little. "Accountability is the essence of democracy," Dukakis said. "I've taken responsibility for my mistakes. But Mr. Bush takes responsibility for nothing." Though there was a certain eloquence to what Dukakis said, and also some poignance, more than this would be needed to turn the election around—and the Dukakis people knew it.

Early this week, Dukakis went on to Ohio, Michigan, and Illinois, giving a variation of the Boston speech and emphasizing his empathy for working Americans. He said, "The difference between George Bush and me boils down to this: George Bush wants to help the people who already have it made. I want to make every American a full shareholder in the American dream." To try to show a warmer, more human Dukakis, he appeared not only before crowds but also in small settings—a café, a bowling alley—and he was back to playing "Happy Days Are Here Again" on the trumpet. On Tuesday, in Michigan, Dukakis appeared before more lively crowds than usual, and was himself more lively than usual; the behavior of a candidate and his crowd are symbiotic. Continuing to portray Bush as the candidate of the rich —some of his aides had wanted him to do more of this before— Dukakis told working people, "I'm on your side," and pledged to get rid of the trade deficit and advocated more training programs. And, running as an acknowledged underdog, he hammered Bush for the kind of campaign he has been running: "He's got the flags and the balloons but no convictions and no ideas and no plans." On the same day, Bentsen, in California, began to hammer at the Bush campaign, calling it "a carnival sideshow of nonsense and negativism."

Over the weekend, stories out of Boston indicated that the Dukakis camp had settled on a strategy of trying to carve an

electoral-college victory out of seventeen states that remained relatively competitive, but this was not really a strategy. Toward the
end of a campaign, candidates always narrow down the number
of states they focus on—Bush is doing the same thing, and the
two men are focussing on essentially the same states. The Dukakis
pretense of a fifty-state campaign was abandoned some time
ago—as the Dukakis people had said last summer that it would
be—though not before Kitty Dukakis travelled to Alaska and Hawaii. The strategy, to the extent that it can be called one, was to
try, through a sharpened message and a heavy use of ads and
appearances on television programs, to narrow the Bush lead back
to low single digits so as to try to make the race competitive again.
In fact, part of the strategy involves going to states where Dukakis
has very little chance now—Georgia and Louisiana as well as Texas
at the end of this week—in order to negate the idea that Dukakis
has written off entire regions. What Dukakis says in Texas, where
the ticket is way behind, will be heard in the rest of the country
—if it is covered on television at all. New Dukakis ads have him
talking directly and sincerely into the camera about America's loss
of competitive edge and about parents' concerns about their children. Yesterday, in Illinois, Dukakis held up and decried as "garbage" literature that had been distributed by the state Republican
Party (the state Parties are doing a lot of Bush's dirty work), which
mentions the Horton case, and says, "All the murderers and rap-
ists and drug pushers and child molesters in Massachusetts vote
for Michael Dukakis." Many local politicians had been telling Dukakis that he had to answer Bush's attacks more effectively. (In
the jittery stock-market atmosphere, a year after the crash, stocks
dropped sharply yesterday because of a rumor, which was untrue,
that the Washington *Post* was about to publish a politically damaging story about Bush's personal life.) An ABC poll, released
yesterday and showing a Bush lead of seven points, is considered
too narrow by even the Dukakis people, who are quite realistic
about the probable fate of their candidate and are only hoping
now that the likely defeat will not be of embarrassing proportions.
(Both camps think that Bush is leading by nine or ten points.)
Today, Dukakis said, "Above all, the truth should matter a lot in
a Presidential campaign, because we learned during Watergate
that it matters a lot in the Oval Office."

The Bush campaign, meanwhile, is proceeding according to

plan—it has always had more careful planning than the Dukakis campaign—and this week Bush is attacking Dukakis on the subjects of defense and foreign policy. On Monday, he appeared at a Martin-Marietta plant outside Denver and hit Dukakis for not saying how he would modernize the land-based part of the strategic triad and for calling the Strategic Defense Initiative "a fantasy." A Bush aide acknowledges that if elected Bush, who has avoided the question, will have to make a decision about which land-based system to pursue. On Tuesday, Bush appeared at Westminster College, in Fulton, Missouri, where forty-two years ago Winston Churchill first spoke of the "Iron Curtain," and he said that the turmoil in the Soviet Union and Eastern Europe was the result of Reagan's policy of "peace through strength" (though obviously internal problems had much to do with it). Bush delivered the speech in a thoughtful manner and did not mention Dukakis—and also did not say how he would deal with the new situation. He said that what exists now is "a rusting curtain," and, "It would be far too simple, even dangerous, to conclude . . . that Soviet foreign policy is driven exclusively by economic weakness." Yesterday, Bush called on Dukakis to join in a bipartisan agreement that United States troops not be withdrawn from Europe, but Dukakis had never suggested that they be. Today, Bush appeared in New York, where he was endorsed by the Patrolmen's Benevolent Association, the nation's largest municipal police union, and championed the death penalty and attacked the furlough program. An "independent" committee is now running an ad showing the Barnes couple. In the ad, Clifford Barnes says, "For twelve hours, we were beaten, slashed, and terrorized. My wife, Angie, was brutally raped." He also said, "When his liberal experiment failed, Dukakis simply looked away." The Bush campaign has begun to run new ads about Dukakis and defense, one of them showing the famous scene of Dukakis riding in a tank, and listing weapons Dukakis has opposed. The list is incorrect and misleading in several respects. The other ad shows a nuclear explosion and a picture of Bush greeting Gorbachev, and says, "This is no time for uncertainty or weakness." The Bush people feel that the theme of "peace through strength," of Reagan's having brought respect to America through an arms buildup, is a winner (whatever the facts), and they are right. They have successfully presented Bush as someone who offers continuity and change: as one who will continue all that was good about the Reagan period but will also do more for the middle class and for children, and for the environment, and as someone ready to build on Reagan's arms-control successes. It's a potent package, and at the same time the Bush campaign has successfully painted Dukakis—as some Dukakis advisers had feared he would—as representing risky change. The Bush people are concentrating fiercely on not making any mistakes now that victory is near, and on running as hard as if they were behind. Atwater says, "That's the best way to keep a lead." As was planned all along, Bush will concentrate on the big states that remain relatively close—the industrial states in the Midwest, Missouri, and California, plus Texas (even though Bush is ahead in Texas by about fifteen points), New Jersey, Washington, and Oregon. (It is also making some effort in New York and Pennsylvania, which should be relatively friendly to Dukakis, in part to make Dukakis use more resources there.) These are the states most elections get down to in the end. Roger Stone, a political consultant who is running the Bush campaign in California, says that "a very important strategic decision was made this week about California." He had proposed, he said, and James Baker had approved, "that our TV ads should remain offensive—some people say 'negative,' I say 'offensive'—that we should keep pounding the furlough, the death penalty, and mandatory sentencing, that it was not time to go for a 'kinder and gentler' strategy, as it were." Stone says that the same decision has been made for Texas, which is being run for Bush by Charles Black, a business partner of his, whereas other states will see a mixture of ads. So, in the final weeks, the Bush campaign will continue to run negative as well as positive ads and will go after Dukakis on taxes and the economy, and on crime. The last week, the Bush people say, is to feature a recapitulation of all the issues Bush has used against Dukakis, in a combination of benign persuasion and whatever amount of attack is necessary.

XV

As George Bush now assembles his own Administration, the long struggle he went through to get where he is recedes in our national memory. The dew is on him, as it always is, for however long, on our new Presidents. By now, his victory, which was a solid one in terms of the numbers, is largely seen as inevitable and the campaign as a minor set of events on his way to the White House. All but lost are the probable lasting effects of the election and the surprisingly strong (and little noticed at the time) showing that Michael Dukakis made—strong enough to cause the Bush camp considerable concern toward the end and a fair amount of tension on Election Day. The interesting thing is that Dukakis came close at all. Bush seemed to have everything going for him this fall: a popular President campaigning hard for him, sufficient prosperity, a world in which there were no apparent immediate threats to the nation, a pleasant personality, a background that at least suggested familiarity with national and international affairs, a campaign team that was long on experience and highly disciplined, and a willingness to do whatever was necessary to win. His nomination had been sealed a lot earlier than his opponent's had, and, unlike his opponent, he had a clear path to his Convention. At the same time, the Democrats' longtime advantage of a substantial lead in the number of people who considered themselves Democrats had been effectively erased.

Yet Bush's being written off earlier as an ineffectual candidate in bad political shape was not unconnected with reality; last summer, his own people had felt that they faced daunting obstacles, and even they hadn't foreseen Bush's metamorphosis (with a little help from his advisers) into a strong, disciplined campaigner. In July, when Bush and his close friend James Baker, who was to become his campaign chairman, went on a fishing trip to Wyoming, Baker told him they had a very, very steep hill to climb.

After the Democratic Convention, Dukakis was seventeen points ahead. Bush was seen as Reagan's loyal Vice-President and little else, and even Baker was not sure whether Bush could overcome the negative views of him once he slipped the yoke of simply being Vice-President, as he did when he saw Reagan off in New Orleans. Bush certainly had all the desire that is required of someone trying to become President—and Dukakis apparently didn't. Bush had been trying to become President for more than ten years, had run for the nomination once before and as the Vice-Presidential candidate twice. Against him was a rookie who was way beyond his depth in Presidential politics, backed up by a campaign that was short on Presidential-campaign experience and riven by internal feuding—a man with a personality that was destined to not wear well and with obviously thin knowledge about foreign-policy and defense matters, and who seemed for stretches of time this fall to have doubts about what he had got himself into, and to be unhappy, even depressed, about what he was going through.

The rookie factor is much underestimated in Presidential politics. It is no accident that since John Kennedy all our elected Presidents but Jimmy Carter had been around the track before. They had run for the Presidential nomination, for the Vice-Presidency, or the Presidency. According to someone who would know, Dukakis hadn't even paid much attention to national politics before he ran for the Presidency. He had been content to be governor of Massachusetts, which had been his goal in life. He enjoyed the work, and the comfortable pattern of going home to have dinner with his family every night. Unlike most people who run for the Presidency, he had not had a consuming desire to be President; he was talked into making the race by John Sasso, his closest associate, and by his wife (whom Sasso also worked on), and, with good reason, viewed the possibility of his even being the nominee as a very long shot. Other people with greater stature and more national experience were in the race at that point. All of a sudden, he had to acquire the desire to be President—and, an adviser says, by the time he got to the Democratic Convention he did. But as the fall election approached he was stumbling around, unable to find a coherent rationale for his candidacy, rejecting a lot of advice—good and bad—and insisting on running the race his way. What some aides are now willing to refer to as his "depression" in August was caused, as one adviser puts it, by his sudden realization that he didn't know how to run for the Presidency. When he finally found his voice, at the end, and became the happy warrior, it was too late. Too many mistakes had been made and too much time had been lost. His persona had indeed become a liability. That he was able to come as close as he did bespeaks real weaknesses in the Bush candidacy.

The Presidential campaign of 1988 did something new to our Presidential elections. A degradation occurred which we may have to live with for a long time. The Bush campaign broke the mold of modern Presidential politics. Negative campaigning of a new order of magnitude has now come to Presidential politics. And it worked. Future candidates may not feel the need to run the kind of campaign Bush and his people did, for the Bush strategy was born of Bush's own considerable weaknesses going into the fall campaign, and future targets of such a campaign will undoubtedly be more adept than Dukakis was at handling such attacks. Whether Bush could have won without it, or whether Dukakis could have won under any circumstances, we can never know—though there is no end of theories on these questions. After each election, we enter the land of unprovable hypotheses. What we do know is that attack campaigning has now "risen" from state politics to Presidential politics, and that the moral many will draw from this year (at both the state and the Presidential levels) is that the way to win is to go on the offensive against your opponent early, distort positions to whatever degree you can get away with, play upon people's fears and prejudices—and never let up. It used to be a rule of thumb that a candidate must set forth his own proposals before attacking his opponent, and when Bush started to attack Dukakis in June, on such matters as the Pledge of Allegiance, the death penalty, the A.C.L.U., and the Massachusetts furlough program, it was widely said, even by some Bush advisers, that this was a mistake, that Bush should instead be laying out his positive agenda. (Bush campaign officials had tested these issues with focus groups at the end of May and found them promising.) Though, as the campaign went on, Bush interspersed the attacks with proposals, his people showed a skittishness from time to time about his lack of a clear positive agenda. There is also evidence that their campaign tactics began to backfire toward the end. The moral that future tacticians might draw from this is not that such a campaign should not be run but that it should be run better.

In an era of declining standards, especially in television, which dominates our culture, it should be no surprise that our political life, which is symbiotic with television, has been affected. A shorter attention span, the demand for instant gratification, schlock, and even a form of violence, have all spilled over into politics. The importance of television in Presidential campaigns has been understood for some time, but something new happened this year. Political advertising on television reached new levels in negativeness—in amount and degree. The Bush camp has a point when it complains that the Dukakis campaign also ran negative ads—but they weren't as effective as Bush's were, nor did they engage in the same amount of distortion. A higher proportion of the Presidential campaigns' budgets was spent on ads, and a higher proportion of those ads were negative. (A similar dynamic was going on in Senate races. Ed Lazarus, who was the pollster for Ohio Democratic Senator Howard Metzenbaum, who successfully fought off a challenger who tried to play rough, said, "The fact that everyone spends more money on television changes the way voters make their decisions about the candidates, and how smartly you spend that money changes the way that candidate comes across to the voters. The issues mean less and less and the ads mean more and more.") There was no dearth of money for the Presidential candidates to spend on television. In addition to the $46.1 million in funds each received through the public-financing system, and the $8.3 million each national party can spend, each camp raised at least twenty million dollars in "soft money"—large contributions by individuals, corporations, and unions which cannot legally be donated to the candidates but can go to the national party, or state parties, for "party building" activities. Soft money, which the Republicans first used in a big way in 1980, has made a mockery of the public-financing system, which was supposed to reduce the role of big contributors.

Television coverage of the campaign also slipped some notches. The sound bites were shorter than before, and an even greater emphasis was placed on the visual impact of what the candidate was doing and the setting in which he was doing it, and an even lesser one on what he was saying. Roger Ailes, Bush's media adviser, has been quoted as saying that the three things that will get coverage in a Presidential campaign are gaffes, attacks, and good visuals, and that his campaign tried to avoid the gaffes and provide the attacks and the visuals. Susan Estrich, Dukakis's campaign manager, says, "You didn't make the evening news unless you attacked your opponent, responded to your opponent, or laid out a new program." Among Ronald Reagan's legacies will be the way politics is covered: visuals count for much more than they used to. An aide to one of the campaigns says that if an event didn't have a good visual the television people covering it would consider that bad campaigning, or even wouldn't cover it. Some television reporters and producers took it upon themselves to suggest better lighting or a different setting; with a speech laying out a program, they would demand that the program be boiled down to four points with four bullets, and say that otherwise they wouldn't be able to put it on the air. A good sound bite was also required— to be pointed out to the reporters and producers in advance—in order to get an appearance on the air. There is no reward for thought: thought doesn't make a good picture. Another Reagan legacy is the importance of likability as a factor in choosing our President. Reagan has taught a generation of people what is important in politics and what to like in a candidate.

Michael Dukakis's defeat was largely self-inflicted. Much blame has been laid on his staff, and while some of that blame may be valid he is the one who chose the staff and who did not insist that more experienced people be brought aboard. Unlike Bush, Dukakis played a strong, detailed role in his campaign. Some combination of his stubbornness, arrogance, and inexperience led him to think he knew more about running a Presidential campaign than he did—until it was too late. He has never been good at taking advice. It is not unusual for the staff of a man who has won the nomination to regard itself as up to the job of running the general-election campaign, and to be loath to bring other experienced people in. Unlike the Republicans, the Democratic Party is not long on people with experience in winning general elections, and even those involved in a losing campaign who might have learned something are usually shut out by the next nominee's group. Grudges carried by the Presidential candidate and his staff from the primaries can—and this year did—end up shutting out some talented people.

But more was wrong than the mechanics of Dukakis's campaign: Dukakis was simply not up to it. Even some people who had supported him felt at the end that it was just as well that he had lost. All along, there was reason to question whether he could be a successful President. His arrogance and humorlessness raised the question right away—or should have—of whether he would wear well. His lack of commandingness, his peculiar inability to step up to the big ones—the second debate, an hour-and-a-half interview on "Nightline"—raised questions about whether he was large enough for the job. His publicly displayed moodiness raised questions about his inner stamina—something he had told us often he had in abundance. Some people who have known Dukakis a long time think that somewhere along the way he lost his nerve.

After months of searching for a theme, he finally found one in "I'm on your side," which he began to use shortly after the second debate, in mid-October. Dukakis, according to the people around him, knew that he had done badly in that debate and had probably blown his last chance to win the election. He hadn't felt particularly well on the day of the debate, and too many people had told him to do and be too many things, and at a crucial moment he gave one of his flat performances. Dukakis was going into a freefall in the polls following the second debate, and the "I'm on your side" message was designed to win over core Democrats, whose support should have already been cemented; it was not seen as a message for winning a majority of all the voters, but if it worked as it should maybe something would turn up. As a campaign strategist explained it, "No one thought it would get us fifty-one per cent of the votes; you can't get fifty-one per cent in this economy with that message, but you could get to forty-six and hope for a break, maybe a Bush mistake."

When John Sasso returned to the Dukakis campaign on the day before Labor Day, he talked to Dukakis about the possibility of using the "I'm on your side" theme, and, Sasso says, though Dukakis sort of liked the idea, he wasn't ready to go with it, and the campaign had already invested a lot in the theme of "Bring prosperity home" and talk of the "middle-class squeeze." (Among the problems with the "Bring prosperity home" theme was that the trade deficit, which the Democrats had been able to use to advantage in 1986, was dropping.) Moreover, other staff members argued that "I'm on your side" wasn't an encompassing enough theme for winning the election. As the Dukakis campaign next turned to "The best America is yet to come," there was still a sense within the campaign that a strong enough message hadn't yet been found. Dukakis, who had been themeless in the primaries, sat through endless, enervating discussions of what his theme should be for winning the Presidency. The theme "I'm on your side" had the elements of populism and class conflict—an implied challenge to Bush as a creature of privilege—that a number of Dukakis advisers thought should be major components of his campaign. But only rarely, toward the end, did Dukakis engage in the kind of sarcasm that can punch home an attack on class. (Dukakis continued to eschew the anti-Japanese xenophobia that some of his advisers were urging. His campaign organization in Ohio finally put on the air an ad with the Japanese flag; several state organizations, frustrated with the Boston headquarters' indecision over ads, or refusal to approve sharp ads, went out and made their own.)

When Sasso returned, there were many things to be done to belatedly get the campaign in shape for the fall, and the candidate was dispirited and directionless, and had lost confidence in his staff, which in turn was unable to get through to him. Sasso is one of the very few people Dukakis has ever taken advice from —and it wasn't easy for even Sasso (who sometimes had to throw fits) to get him to listen. A side effect of Sasso's coming in was that many campaign aides stopped what they were doing until they got new directions from him. There were considerable tensions between Sasso and Estrich, each of whom also had loyalists within the campaign. Lines of authority remained unclear. In early September, Dukakis's "negatives" were in the forties— up from about twenty-five just before the Democratic Convention, and eighteen just after it—thanks to Bush's attacks and Dukakis's failure to deal with them.

Dukakis went into the final three weeks of the campaign, after the second debate, in a very weak condition. Effective as the new theme may have been—it was effective enough that Bush coöpted it at the end—Dukakis had to convince people that a man who had been painted (with help from himself) as weak on crime, patriotism, and defense was on the side of the average American. The very shifting of messages was costly—it takes a great deal of time and effort to establish a theme. A number of Republican strategists say that Dukakis would have been far better off using "I'm on your side" early and sticking with it. Sasso now agrees with them.

Everyone is an expert on how Dukakis should have handled Bush's attacks, but at least one Democratic politician who was himself the target of attacks some years ago says that it is a lot easier to know what to do if you're not the person who is being attacked, that he himself was paralyzed. And not everyone counselled Dukakis that he should respond to the attacks: Mario Cuomo admitted in late October that in his advice to Dukakis he had underestimated the power of the attacks. Around the same time, Dukakis said, "Maybe, with the benefit of hindsight, I should have tried to respond sooner"—but he still passed up several good opportunities to do so. Though Massachusetts politics are not gentle, Dukakis had never encountered anything like this before. Though he had from time to time in the past engaged in some tough tactics, he really does believe, as he kept saying, that campaigns should be positive. He felt, an adviser says, that in laying out his programs on health and college education and housing he was running the kind of issue-oriented, substantive campaign that people keep saying they want. But maybe they didn't want it from him. Dukakis, for better or worse, is a good-governmenter. By instinct, he is more reformer than roughhouse politician, more Brookline than Boston, and he was in some ways a political naïf. He had functioned in an essentially one-party situation, and had done nothing that could have prepared him for a big, bruising campaign for the Presidency. In August, when he was being urged by his staff and others to fight back, he stubbornly resisted, arguing that he wanted to run a positive campaign, and that he was not well known enough and did not have enough of a programmatic base to go against Bush. (A biographical ad his campaign had been running in August was dropped when polling indicated that a lot of people aren't keen on immigrants.) Dukakis argued that if he started responding to Bush's attacks nothing else would get through to the voters. For all anyone knows, he might have been right—but this would not have ruled out a swipe or two that might have caused Bush to back off. (Dukakis was also concerned about something else: that the Biden-tape incident made him vulnerable to the charge of being a negative campaigner.) The Bush people were surprised that Dukakis's responses to Bush's charges were so lame.

When people say that Dukakis should have responded to Bush, they are actually talking about various things. To some, it means that he should have met the attacks head on, to others that he should have carried his own attacks to Bush, tried to put more of the focus on Bush. In June, Dukakis's advisers had tested with focus groups the crime issues that Bush was to use against him so effectively, and knew that these issues, in particular the furlough program, could be a big problem—especially since Dukakis had resisted changing the program after Willie Horton brutalized the Maryland couple. Tom Kiley, a Dukakis campaign strategist, says, "We saw it to be potentially more damaging than any other thing we tested." Dukakis's most effective response to the furlough issue—that his own father, at the age of seventy-seven, had been tied up and robbed and his own brother had been killed by a hit-and-run driver and he didn't need any lectures from Bush on how victims of crime and their families feel—had been twice put in his acceptance speech at the Democratic Convention, and twice Dukakis took it out. (He didn't give this response at all until shortly before the second debate, and then neglected to give it, as planned, in the debate.) His aides unanimously thought it was imperative that Dukakis deal with the issue before the Republican Convention, where much would undoubtedly be made of it, and made specific proposals, but Dukakis refused. (One proposal was that Dukakis go to North Carolina, where an ad that an "independent" group was to run on the furlough issue was being tested, and denounce the ad. The thought was also that the scene would be captured for a Dukakis ad.) An adviser says, "His view was the one a lot of us had in May—that the contest was one of character and leadership, and he held the cards." Dukakis gave no effective response on the Pledge issue until the end of the Labor Day week (when he called Bush's charges "garbage" and McCarthy-like), and then he didn't say anything more about it until the first debate, when he said that he resented Bush's questioning his patriotism. By then, Bush had moved off the flag issue, having pushed it a bit too far with his visit to the flag factory in New Jersey in late September. At the same time that some were telling Dukakis to respond to Bush, others were saying that to do so would put the campaign on Bush's turf. In the end, he never built an effective case against Bush—though a number of his advisers believed there was one to be built. Dukakis would say to his advisers, "No one cares what I think about George Bush."

Dukakis, an adviser says, didn't understand the difference between governing and campaigning; in governing, one puts out positive messages and proposals; in governing, one doesn't have to keep repeating oneself. (Dukakis felt that after he had given the response on the furlough program he didn't need to repeat it.) There was nothing in his experience to tell him that negative campaigning—of the sort and on the scale that Bush was doing —would catch on; he didn't understand value attacks. His life— being a law student, a process-oriented governor, a teacher at the Kennedy School—had been the life of reason. He thought that negative campaigning had to do with attacking the other person's proposals, or record, but not his values; he didn't comprehend the importance of symbols, and neither did many of the people around him. Moreover, one adviser says, virtually no one around Dukakis believed that Bush could get away with running such a negative campaign all fall. (Had he had a more effective opponent, he might not have.)

In August, Dukakis's staff proposed that he carry the campaign to Bush, and begin attacking Bush right after the Republican Convention, just as Reagan had begun attacking Walter Mondale right after the 1984 Democratic Convention, to keep him from building a head of steam. But Dukakis's mind was on Massachusetts, and he insisted on taking his annual tour of the western part of the state, and was dispirited by polls showing Bush pulling nearly even with him in his own state. Richard Wirthlin, Reagan's pollster, who also advised the Bush campaign, says, "It's my guess that the Willie Horton/crime/Pledge attacks would have had less than half the impact they did had Dukakis in the early phase taken his own message to people." He goes on, "A campaign has to respond to an attack—sometimes the response is to turn it back against your opponent, sometimes it's another issue, sometimes it's taking some other part of that issue that is more favorable and driving it back to your opponent's face. The Dukakis people never understood that, and Dukakis talked about these issues in a desultory way. It was like watching a campaign respond in slow motion." Lee Atwater, Bush's campaign manager, told colleagues that

Dukakis should have begun his populist campaign of the last couple of weeks of the election much earlier, probably at the Democratic Convention. Atwater said, "If I ever got seventeen points on top of somebody, I'd get on top of him and keep swinging so that he doesn't get going. By the time he did it, he was too much on the defensive. If they'd come out of the Convention with that and kept going, we'd have been hard pressed to come back."

Lloyd Bentsen says that he told Dukakis shortly after the Republican Convention that the attacks on him "were not just outrageous but they were having an effect." Dukakis, Bentsen says, "was incredulous that they would have any effect at all." He adds, "If you don't answer it, it becomes part of your image. You have to answer these things." Bentsen (who is careful to speak well of Dukakis) says that Dukakis could have responded to the attacks (preferably with ads) and still offered his positive program. Bentsen (whom some Dukakis advisers urged to intercede with their candidate) says he tried to persuade Dukakis "early, a few times" but "didn't persist after a while."

In August and September, Dukakis continually rejected attack ads because they didn't have his positive message in them. He rejected whole scripts, or demanded changes in scripts. He also removed biting sound bites from speeches, and refused to discuss it with his advisers. He argued that any ad attacking Bush had to have his alternative in it. He would ask, "Where's Michael Dukakis in that ad?" He believed that he had a big sell job to do, which was true enough, and he didn't understand the degree to which, in the meantime, Bush's attacks were undermining him. Sometimes the Presidential candidate, enveloped in an entourage, exhaustedly hurtling from city to city and event to event, is the least informed person about what is going on. To Dukakis, the sell job was the offering of programs, and he was happy when a four-point program, with bullets, got on television. He didn't approve all-out negative ads until mid-October, when he realized that nothing else was working.

When, toward the end of the campaign, Dukakis started attacking Bush's attacks, his campaign began to move. By making an issue of the attacks—holding up Republican state-party leaflets that made all sorts of wild charges and dealt in the worst sort of innuendo, and calling them "garbage," and cutting ads attacking Bush's ads as "lies" and "distortions"—Dukakis was able to persuade people that Bush was running the more negative campaign. One Dukakis ad had him snapping off a television set that was playing a misleading Bush ad about his defense positions—and saying to the camera, "I'm fed up." People went from thinking that both campaigns were equally negative to thinking that Bush was running the more negative one. The problem was that Dukakis's negatives remained high nonetheless. The theory behind the attack on the attacks was to get people to stop and take another look at Dukakis, to suggest that he hadn't been able to get his message through because of all the flak. Bush's people were sufficiently concerned with the attack on the attacks that for a couple of days he and his surrogates responded by defending, however tenuously, Bush's attacks. But when people did look at Dukakis again too many still found him wanting. And Bush never let up.

Without question, the issue that was hurting Dukakis the most was the furlough program, along with his opposition to the death penalty and his veto of mandatory sentencing of drug dealers. The Bush campaign drove these issues very hard, especially in California, Texas (where Dukakis's favoring gun control also hurt), and Ohio. Willie Horton had become famous, as the Bush people had said he would, thanks to the work of a supposedly "independent" group—people in the Bush campaign knew all there is to know about the various ways in which an "independent" group can be made helpful to a Presidential campaign. Before it even ran, one Bush campaign official read me the text of the "independent" group's ad featuring Clifford Barnes, one of Horton's victims. The same group's ad with Horton's picture became confused in a lot of people's minds with an ad made by the Bush campaign on the furlough program, which showed prisoners going through a revolving door and was misleading about how many murderers had escaped, and some Bush campaign officials, including Ailes, expressed hurt at the very idea that they would have made the Horton ad. But the Bush campaign never asked the "independent" group to stop running it. The Bush people also expressed indignation that they were charged with playing on racism, but, of course, that is exactly what they were doing. (Atwater said to me in all seriousness that he wished Horton was white. Last June, Atwater told a Republican Unity meeting, "By the time this election is over, Willie Horton will be a household name;" in July, he talked to the press about "a fellow named

Willie Horton who for all I know may end up being Dukakis's running mate.") This was not a new thing for Republican Presidential campaigns—Richard Nixon had his "Southern strategy," and Reagan, in Mississippi, in his first appearance after his 1980 nominating Convention, spoke with approbation of "states' rights"—but never had the appeal to racism been so blatant and so raw. Finally, in late October, the Dukakis people went with their own ad, about a convicted drug dealer who had escaped while on a federal furlough and raped and murdered a pregnant mother of two. The murderer, whose picture was shown in the ad, was a Hispanic, and the Dukakis people were aware that it had its own element of racism. (At the suggestion of some Hispanic congressmen who previewed the ad, the man's name was deleted.) The Dukakis people insisted that the point of the ad was to show the Bush campaign's "hypocrisy," but it did nothing to cleanse the atmosphere.

Dukakis was never able to make much of the Iran-Contra scandal, because Reagan had become more popular, and most people had made up their minds about it. Perhaps a more skillful candidate could have more effectively raised questions about Bush's role in it, but this would have entailed a general attack on Bush's character (on other matters as well), which Dukakis ruled out. He harped on the subject of Noriega but was trying to make a connection between Noriega and the nation's drug problem which wasn't realistic or convincing. Neither the Iran-Contra scandal nor Noriega (whom the Reagan Administration is still trying to get out of office) presented the kind of immediate threat to the voters that Willie Horton did. In the final days, Dukakis attacked a comment by Bush that he would consider the foreign-policy implications before retaliating against countries that send illegal drugs to the United States. But Dukakis was engaging in demagoguery; he himself said he would not retaliate against Mexico. Polling for both camps indicated that foreign policy didn't count for much in the minds of the voters, because of the relative stability of the times and the warm relationship Reagan had established with Mikhail Gorbachev. Dukakis also had to be careful about Reagan: it was the accepted view within his camp that taking on the popular President would only cause problems. Thus, when, at the end of July, he said, on the topic of ethics within the Reagan Administration, "The fish rots from the head down," there was consternation within his staff, and Dukakis seemed to realize that he had made a tactical mistake. Neither he nor his advisers wanted to stir up the wrath of Reagan, who could be a dangerous opponent. (It was four days after that that, in the midst of the rumors about Dukakis's mental health—which were in part fanned by the Bush people—Reagan said, "I'm not going to pick on an invalid.") Amid the general mishandling of the defense issue by both Dukakis and his advisers—Dukakis hadn't taken the time to learn enough about it, and he didn't make serious speeches about it until September (whereupon he rode in a tank), because his advisers were divided over whether he should give speeches on the subject, which some argued was Bush's issue—the Dukakis people also managed to miss out on making an issue of the Pentagon procurement scandal. One of his advisers said Dukakis should be "positive" about defense.

Though Dukakis began to draw large and enthusiastic crowds in late October, it was hard to know what to make of this at first. Mondale had drawn large and enthusiastic crowds at the end, and was buried in a landslide. In part, Dukakis's reception had to do with Democrats "coming home," but also involved was the mystical relationship that can develop between a politician and his audience—each feeding the other's enthusiasm and satisfaction. Dukakis had at last come to understand the importance of repetition, and as the race came down to the wire audiences were anticipating his lines, shouting them to him. Appearing in a sports shirt, sleeves rolled up, Dukakis had suddenly become the fiery populist (which he really isn't). He no longer used a teleprompter, which comes between a politician and his audience. But there was a certain antique quality to his populism—he talked about Republicans "popping the champagne corks in their penthouses," and about "Easy Street" versus "Main Street." One Democratic strategist said, "That's how Boston liberals think populists think." And Dukakis was still undisciplined about sticking with his message. He interwove, and interrupted, his "I'm on your side" message with distractions: Watergate, and, in an appeal to women, abortion.

But the most surprising thing Dukakis did, after months of nearly imploring Bush not to use "labels," was to call himself a liberal. By this time, Bush (and Reagan) had turned the word into such a term of opprobrium—with Dukakis colluding by shrinking from the term and allowing Bush to define it—that his owning up to it at that point seemed both astonishing and incompetent. Dukakis's trying to substitute "competence" for "ideology" had given him a very tempting glass chin. The famous line in his acceptance speech grew out of staff concern that if the election was fought on the battleground of ideology Dukakis would lose. So both camps understood this. In fact, this was the first election in which ideology did count for something. Polling done for the Republican National Committee and the Bush campaign by Wirthlin indicated that in this election, for the first time, "liberal" carried a negative connotation and "conservative" a positive one. (In 1980, Wirthlin's analysis did not find ideology to be a factor in the vote.)

All sorts of theories were applied to the consideration of why Dukakis suddenly adopted the liberal mantle on Sunday, October 30th, as he embarked on a daylong whistle-stop tour of California's Central Valley—of what complicated strategy was involved. Speaking from the back of the train, Dukakis said, "I am a liberal in the tradition of Franklin Roosevelt and Harry Truman and John Kennedy." In fact, it was an accident. Dukakis had been discussing with some top aides the idea of reaching out to Democrats by saying that he was a *Democrat* in the *tradition* of Franklin Roosevelt, Harry Truman, and John Kennedy. (And he was, as he said, annoyed that three days earlier Reagan had said, in Missouri, that if Harry Truman were alive today he would be a Republican.) On Saturday, Dukakis had taped a MacNeil/Lehrer interview, to be aired on Monday, in which he said the exact same thing he said the next day in California, but his aides didn't think this was any big deal and didn't consider the possibility that he'd do it again. When Dukakis did do it again, in full view of the world, they were astonished. When he finished speaking, Dukakis sheepishly asked them, "Did I screw up?" The aides decided there was nothing to do at that point but to try to convince the press that the mistake was actually a strategy. They tried to give the impression that there was something they knew from their polling that made this a smart move. And so Dukakis repeated the "liberal" line as he proceeded on his train trip. When he dropped the line in his first appearance the next morning, some reporters told his aides they would say that he was running away from the liberal label again and that his using it the day before had been a mistake. So at his second stop on Monday Dukakis repeated it.

In the closing two weeks of the campaign, the Dukakis people tried also to convince the press that Dukakis had a real shot at winning. Sasso, who joined the road tour for the last couple of weeks, is a very persuasive man, and he succeeded in persuading much of the press that this was possible. He also persuaded Dukakis, and it was this that gave Dukakis the burst of energy and drive he put into the extraordinarily long days of campaigning toward the end—going forty-eight hours straight, back and forth across the country twice, in the last two days—and made him a far better candidate than he had been all fall. Also, if a candidate is "surging," it makes for a better story, and so there was a certain amount of hype—as there often is—in the news stories about the underdog's chances in the closing days. Sasso was aware that Dukakis's chances of winning were remote indeed, but he felt that there was no point in doing what Mondale's aides had done—tell the candidate two weeks before the end that there was no hope. And for both Dukakis and Sasso other things were at stake besides winning: personal pride and dignity were involved; they wanted to do better than previous Democratic losers had (Mondale had lost forty-nine states, and Jimmy Carter had lost forty-four); they wanted to show that the Democrats were on the way back.

But, no matter how much Dukakis had improved, the impressions that had been formed about him—on the basis of his own performance and the job that had been done on him by the Bush campaign—were not easily overcome, and so his negatives remained very high. Bush was winning the contest over who was seen as the stronger leader. Dukakis's performance was still uneven. At rallies, most of the time he turned in a strong performance, connecting with the crowds as never before. He showed a relaxedness, a sense of timing, and even humor; he even showed that he has a natural smile. He made a large number of appearances on television interview and news programs (neither candidate went on the Sunday interview shows)—to get the exposure and try to demonstrate that he wasn't the left-wing weirdo that Bush had made him out to be, and also to draw the contrast with Bush, who had been wrapped in cotton batting and inaccessible to the press. The hope was to smoke Bush out—that he might accept the challenge to speak in less protected circumstances, and make a mistake. Bush (who said, "It seemed like he appeared on every television show except 'Wheel of Fortune.' You see, he was afraid that Vanna might turn over the 'L' word") did respond by appearing on some morning interview shows and on NBC's Nightly News, but though he had difficulty answering questions about his plans to reduce the deficit, he didn't do anything that gave Dukakis a break. (Bush's vague proposal to balance the budget over four years through a "flexible freeze" and no new taxes doesn't stand up to scrutiny.)

Dukakis, in his appearance on "Nightline" for an hour and a half, with an audience of fourteen million—Bush had turned down an invitation to be on the same program—was strangely listless and passive; he took Ted Koppel's aggressive questioning (which at times amounted to lecturing) meekly. The picture was of a small, unhappy man sitting tightly in a big chair. He made no compelling case for himself. He continued to show naïveté in foreign policy—saying, among other things, that former Central American leaders could have got Noriega out of office—but he was given so little chance of winning that little notice was taken of what he said. His aides said he was extremely tired and had been too heavily scheduled before this appearance. But Presidential candidates don't have the luxury of caving in during key performances. An adviser said to me afterward, with some frustration, "I can't explain it, just as I can't explain the second debate."

Dukakis was still having trouble connecting with blacks. He didn't try very often, since his priority was winning back "Reagan Democrats," and his campaign was with difficulty trying to hold on to the black vote without appearing too sympathetic toward blacks. The Democratic Party's identification with the civil-rights movement complicates life for its Presidential candidates, what with the collapse of the old civil-rights coalition of labor and blacks as the demands of blacks began to be seen as a threat to working-class whites. And the plain fact is that there is a great deal of racial prejudice in this country. Thus, neither party was making much of a case to blacks, who were at best stiffed by the Reagan Administration, at the same time that, according to one study, the gap between the income of whites and blacks is widening. With the Republicans stirring the pot of racial prejudice, and with Jesse Jackson, a polarizer, in the role of the most prominent black Democrat (the Dukakis campaign ignored suggestions that it place other black leaders front and center as well), the Democratic ticket was caught in ugly crosscurrents. (The Dukakis camp at first encouraged some people to charge that Bush was running a "racist" campaign but then backed off, on the theory that this wouldn't win them the support of certain voters.) Dukakis had had little experience with blacks (Massachusetts is less than four per cent black), and had little feel for how to talk to them. His standoffish style didn't move them, and he seemed to have little idea of what might be on their minds or what they had been through. As he tried to clap to the music in a black church in Harlem, in late October, his timing was off and he was never in the music. Six days before the election, he appeared at a black high school in Philadelphia and managed to deflate an audience that had just been pumped up by Jackson. Jackson, smarting from criticism for making little effort to help the ticket, was now travelling around the country, on a plane supplied by the Democratic National Committee, but his enthusiasm for Dukakis was within bounds. Like other prominent Democrats, Jackson stood to gain more from a Dukakis defeat than from a victory. One thing several Democrats (including some who may well run next time) feel they've learned from this year is that the black vote in the primaries should not be ceded to Jackson, as it was this year, thus giving Jackson great power at the Convention. (But he managed to have power over Mondale, who had challenged him for the support of blacks.)

George Bush's campaign for the Presidency was premised on the Republican Party's presumed advantage in the electoral college and on the strategy of keeping control of the agenda—a very big item in the minds of Bush's strategists. James Baker sets great store by controlling both the agenda and the candidate; he was the architect of Reagan's content-free, risk-averting 1984 campaign, and headed virtually the same team then. In the cases of both Reagan and Bush, the campaign team feared letting the candidate out very much on his own, speaking for himself. With Reagan, the worry was that he would engage in rambling detours (as he did in the first debate with Mondale) or display his tentative grip on the facts. With Bush, the concern was that what came to be called his "silly" factor—his propensity for saying odd things —would be on display. There was a certain, perhaps unconscious, condescension in the way Bush's people praised him publicly for "rising to the occasion" when he had to—in his acceptance speech, in the second debate.

The concerted attacks on Dukakis were, of course, a means of keeping the attention off Bush—this is the main reason Bush was never allowed to let up. Toward the end, at a fund-raiser at Bob Hope's home, Bush said, "It's going to be a kinder, gentler finish for this campaign," and the next day he was attacking Dukakis again. Bush, after all, had very high negatives—in the forties—in the early summer, a number that was considered by many to be mortally high (at the time that Dukakis's negatives were in the twenties). Lee Atwater has been working for many years on a doctoral thesis on the danger of high negatives to candidates; he has said that a candidate can't survive negatives above the thirties. A Bush campaign aide who does not wish to be quoted by name said to me after the election, "We always recognized the maxim that if you have high negatives the only way to beat him is to get his negatives higher than yours."

Robert Teeter, Bush's pollster and a major strategist in the campaign, says that the Bush campaign had four imperatives: develop the perception of Bush as a figure in his own right; control the agenda; make sure people saw that there were important differences between Bush and Dukakis, despite Dukakis's attempts to smooth them over; and, because of Bush's high negatives and Dukakis's low ones, "get Bush's down and Dukakis's up." Teeter says, "Everything we did was in line with those objectives." These imperatives were drawn up on the basis of certain givens: that it is hard to elect a party to a third term (so Bush ran on the premise "Don't let them take it away," just as Truman had, and just as Margaret Thatcher did in seeking her third term as Prime Minister); that the Vice-Presidency does have a political undertow; that the conditions of peace and prosperity would work in Bush's favor; that Bush was a known and accepted figure—a major-league player and not a rookie—and Dukakis had too far to go in establishing himself in too short a period of time; that there were things in Dukakis's record that made him vulnerable; and that for the first time in ten years the country was not focussed almost exclusively on economic and foreign-policy issues but was also concerned with such issues as drugs, education, crime, the homeless, and the environment. The very lack of "big picture" issues may have allowed more room for the issues of Dukakis's record. The Bush people felt that if they could draw the comparison between Bush and Dukakis, Bush would be seen to be where the majority of the country was.

Part of the strategy was to have Bush give a speech on the "second level" issues—the environment, and so on—in a well-chosen setting, with a "positive" speech, followed by a speech drawing the "comparison" with Dukakis. Teeter says, "But that wasn't our main concern, which was to convince the press that we were talking issues this fall. We didn't get enough credit for it." The Bush people were defensive all along in the face of criticism of their negative campaigning, and two Sundays before the election Baker, appearing on "Face the Nation," introduced to the world a brand-new, three-hundred-and-forty-seven-page booklet, called "Leadership on the Issues," which supposedly comprised the policy proposals Bush had made in the course of the campaign but also contained speeches Bush had given, including one he made in Nigeria in 1985. By this time, there was much talk about whether Bush, if he won, would have a "mandate" to govern—other than to say the Pledge of Allegiance and not let Willie Horton out of jail. The criticism came not just from Democrats or journalists; a number of Republicans were critical of the campaign Bush was running, and concerned that he was not laying out a program for governing.

Baker himself became defensive about the kind of campaign he was overseeing. Though people tended to attribute the dirty business to Atwater, who has specialized in rough tactics and also cultivates the image of a political terror, anyone who understood how the Bush campaign worked knew that nothing of any significance occurred without Baker's approval. Baker, who favored going at Dukakis hard, undoubtedly understood the weaknesses of his own candidate. Five days before the election, Baker gave a speech to the National Press Club in which he defended the Bush campaign as having made more positive proposals than the news stories had portrayed. He charged, as he had before, and as other Bush supporters had, that the Democrats had started it, at the Convention in Atlanta, with "three days of non-stop ridicule—the most vicious form of personal attack." But surely Baker knows the difference between ridicule, on the one hand, and distortion and smears—questioning an opponent's patriotism, suggesting there is something subversive about belonging to the A.C.L.U.—on the other. Besides, Baker had his chronology wrong, as he must have known. Bush had launched his attacks on Dukakis—on the Pledge, the furlough, the death penalty, national defense, and taxes—in June. Atwater says that it was Bush's three-week "blitz" on these issues that enabled him to nearly close the gap in the polls just before the Democratic Convention.

At times, the Bush campaign seemed caught short by Dukakis's laying out programs for the middle class—and improvised. (Bush's program for subsidized savings, which would amount to a pittance, for buying a house, putting a child through college, or starting a business, disappeared quickly after being mocked by Dukakis.) Fortunately for Bush, Dukakis was not good enough at convincing enough people that he would make a change for the better in their lives with little cost to the federal government. Dukakis's creativity in devising such programs for Massachusetts was one of his strong selling points for the nomination. The Bush people also succeeded, as a campaign official had told me they would, in taking the environment issue away from Dukakis. Though Dukakis was vulnerable on the matter of delaying the cleanup of Boston Harbor, he had the support of most environmental groups, while Bush was saddled with the poor environmental record of the Reagan Administration, and had himself worked to weaken environmental regulations. A misleading ad about Boston Harbor (including a misleading "radiation hazard" sign) was given heavy duty by the Bush campaign, especially in the environmentally sensitive states of California and New Jersey (as was one about Dukakis's proposal a few years back to dump Massachusetts sewage off New Jersey) —and the Dukakis campaign never caught up. The Boston Harbor ad had originally been designed as an "inoculation" ad, to protect Bush from being too vulnerable on the environment (just as Bush's trip to Boston Harbor had been a preëmptive strike—to which the Dukakis campaign failed to respond effectively), and to take the battle to Dukakis before he took it to Bush. By the end of the campaign, Dukakis was rated (in Republican polling) only two points more of an environmentalist than Bush.

In pushing the "hot button" issues, the Bush campaign was playing on the same social cleavages—over crime, the flag, and race—that Nixon and Reagan had. It successfully played on people's fears, and made Dukakis, not Bush, the issue. It was completely aware of what it was doing in making a black man who had raped a white woman a prominent feature of the election. In late October, Baker disavowed a leaflet, circulated by the Maryland Republican chairman, showing pictures of Dukakis and Horton and saying, "You, your spouse, your children, your parents, and your friends can have the opportunity to receive a visit from someone like Willie Horton if Mike Dukakis becomes President." It seemed Baker had no choice, but Bush, asked about the leaflet during his interview with Tom Brokaw, on NBC, didn't disavow it. Both Bush and Baker went on to express indignation over a mailing by the California Democratic Party that spoke of "emerging hard evidence of the infiltration of the Bush-Quayle campaign by pro-Nazi activists." (Five days before the election, the chairman of Latvians for Bush resigned in the wake of allegations that he had belonged to the Latvian Legion, which was a unit of the S.S. This followed the resignation of seven others who were alleged to have been involved in pro-Nazi or anti-Semitic activities. Some of these people still serve on the Republican National Committee's Ethnic Heritage Committee.) The Dukakis campaign said it stood by the mailing.

The Bush campaign had made a conscious decision to start emphasizing the furlough issue if Bush "lost" the first debate—otherwise, the issue would not have been featured until later. But since the "spin" on that debate, as Baker saw it, "spun against us," Horton, as part of an onslaught on law and order, was turned to earlier. There is, of course, very little that the federal government has to do with crime, which is essentially a state and local matter, but, according to the polls, crime and drugs were the issues that most voters were concerned about. (Under questioning, Baker finally said toward the end of the campaign that Bush didn't approve of the federal government's furlough program and would review it if he became President.) From the outset, the Bush campaign had stressed the crime issue in California—the state with the most electoral votes, which remained close to the end. Roger Stone, who ran the Bush effort in California, says that the important thing in California was that "we never departed from our game plan—even after the euphoria of the second debate." In fact, the Bush campaign not only kept up the negative television ads but bought what Stone describes as "saturation radio" on the furlough issue and on Dukakis's opposition to the death penalty.

(Stone says that the death penalty was at least as strong an issue against Dukakis as the furlough program.) A hitch occurred in California very shortly before the election, when Sheila Tate, Bush's press secretary, explained the cancellation of a stop at Fresno, where in September Bush had been met by dancing people dressed up as raisins, by saying that Bush had said he didn't "want to see those damn dancing raisins again." Stone says, "That cost us a couple of points." The Bush campaign made heavy use of radio as well as television in several states. In Texas, it ran radio ads about crime, school prayer, the Pledge, and defense issues. The National Rifle Association also advertised heavily against Dukakis.

Bush landed on Dukakis's claim to competence whenever he could. On the Wednesday before the election, the Boston *Herald*, a Murdoch tabloid, ran a screaming headline, "WHAT A MESS!"— referring to a state government overdraft of nearly two hundred million dollars. Dukakis in fact had been having fiscal problems in Massachusetts for several months, a matter that worried him and his campaign advisers. On the same day, the federal government announced that the national unemployment rate was 5.3 per cent, the lowest rate in fourteen years. The latest growth rate, 2.2 per cent, announced October 26th, was the smallest quarterly gain in two years, and the third quarter of slower growth than last year. But increasingly people were telling pollsters that they felt the economy was on the right track, or that they were optimistic about their economic future, and they increasingly indicated that though they wanted change, they didn't want much change. Yet, ironically, according to Robert Teeter, the economy never turned out to be a good offensive issue against Dukakis— because the economy seemed so good to so many people. Teeter says, "When we pressed him about how good the economy was, we didn't gain much." When I asked Teeter whether Bush could have won without the attacks, he replied, "I doubt it." He added, "You never know that. It's a terrific debating point, but there is no answer."

The Bush campaign was constantly calibrating the attacks, deciding when to start or stop emphasizing the various issues Bush was using against Dukakis. Atwater, however, said to me shortly before the election, "I always felt like they were going to be salient issues to the end, because with Reagan Democrats and populist voters those issues would play right through." Others saw these issues as tactical ones—which took hold and went on longer than anticipated, because of the way Dukakis dealt with them, or didn't deal with them. Some campaign officials were aware that the visit to the flag factory had been, as one put it, "a flag too far," and the Pledge issue was rarely heard about again. The Bush campaign never ran an ad about the Pledge; it didn't have to, because so much was made of the issue in the "free media." The Bush people did have an ad about the Pledge "in the can," which some aides wanted to use earlier in the fall but Baker opposed using, on the ground that they had exhausted the issue and were in danger of its coming around to bite them; they fully expected to have another run at the issue at the end, but didn't get to it, and then at the very end, when they saw that Dukakis was closing fast on them, it was too late to get the ad on. (The furlough ad, however, was recycled toward the end.) Teeter, who was continually polling on the impact of issues, says that the times of greatest gains by Bush—whether he was catching up or moving ahead—tended to be when the Bush campaign was focussed on national defense, which reinforced the impression of Dukakis as a liberal, or on the crime/criminal-justice issues. Polling by Wirthlin for the R.N.C. and the Bush campaign in early October showed that three-fourths of the people questioned had heard, seen, or read about the furlough issue, and that of those who knew about it fifty-nine per cent believed that what Bush was saying was true. This told the Bush people that it was worth trying to bring the issue to the attention of the one-fourth who did not know of it. Wirthlin's polling also found that the Pledge issue wasn't affecting voters' attitudes to anywhere near the extent the furlough issue was— which may be the real reason the issue of the Pledge was allowed to fade. The polling also showed that shortly before the election thirty per cent more people identified the phrase "soft on crime" with Dukakis than with Bush—and that only one per cent more identified Dukakis with the phrase "I'm on your side" than they did Bush. In the case of likely voters, Bush was ahead by two points in being seen as on their side. Wirthlin says, "The point is, that was Dukakis's best theme. But if people believe that a candidate is soft on crime, he's not on their side."

Reagan's role in the 1988 election was of incalculable value to Bush. For one thing, Bush was basking in the glow of Reagan's successes, taking credit for being part of the team that was seen by many as having restored America's morale, rebuilt its defenses (the buildup started under Jimmy Carter), tamed inflation, and brought down interest rates. The myths and symbols Reagan had manipulated so well were a gift to Bush. Reagan's failures and embarrassments seemed to fade in people's memories as the year went on, and as he became a nostalgic figure about to leave the scene. (And Bush's opponent was unable to make strong issues of them.) The other way that Reagan helped was in giving his all-out support to Bush. The Reagan White House coöperated with the Bush campaign to an unprecedented extent—in having the President sign or veto bills as deemed helpful to Bush, in making appointments, in putting off unpleasant business until after the election. Following the election, the President pocket vetoed an ethics bill that during the campaign Bush had said he supported; the Justice Department filed a brief asking the Supreme Court to overturn the Roe v. Wade decision on abortion; the Administration moved to make it more difficult for people to appeal decisions affecting their Social Security or welfare benefits; the Labor Department removed the forty-five-year ban on employees in certain industries working at home—unions oppose the change, on the ground that they can't enforce wage and hour laws; the Agriculture Department announced foreclosure on eighty thousand farmers who were delinquent on government loans. Also after the election, Reagan said he wouldn't pardon Oliver North, but at the same time he may have made a trial impossible by refusing to release certain classified documents.

Reagan campaigned hard for Bush and virtually turned the election into a referendum on himself. He told one audience, "I feel a little like I'm on the ballot this year." Though Reagan hadn't been able to be of enough help to Senate candidates he had campaigned for in 1986, the transference to Bush was a more direct one, and of great value. Reagan often appeared before audiences of college students, who were very enthusiastic about him (far more enthusiastic than they were about Bush's young running mate, Dan Quayle). That Reagan is the only President most young people have been aware of has implications for our political future. Reagan does best by far in the approval ratings among those seventeen to twenty years old. He mocked Dukakis's identifying himself with Harry Truman and Franklin Roosevelt, and called him a liberal in the tradition of Jimmy Carter and Walter Mondale (whose names Dukakis had studiously not invoked). At one stop, Reagan said, "If he's Harry Truman, I'm Roger Rabbit." Some Republican strategists question whether Bush would have won California but for Reagan's effort for him there. The Bush camp's polling showed that wherever Reagan went Bush got a substantial boost. So Reagan was brought to San Diego at the close of the campaign, a move that Stone thinks gained the ticket a couple of points. In his final campaign appearance, Reagan was true to form, saying things no other politician could get away with. He said, "If my name isn't on your ballot tomorrow, something more important is: a principle, a legacy." He concluded, "So if I could ask you one last time, tomorrow, when the mountains greet the dawn, will you go out there and win one for the Gipper?"

Quayle remained relegated to the boonies, where he was to cause as little attention to himself as possible. Bush hadn't appeared with him since the day after the first debate, in late Sep' tember. He was kept off any serious talk shows. Quayle did cause attention to himself over some pronouncements on abortion, on which he takes an even firmer position than Bush does. When an eleven-year-old girl from *Children's Express*, a news service run by young people, asked whether she should be denied an abortion if she became pregnant by her father, Quayle said yes. (Bush would permit abortions in the case of rape or incest or when the life of the mother is at stake.) Later, when Quayle was asked by the press what his position would be if Willie Horton had got the woman pregnant, he appeared to make an exception for rape. Getting into a muddled discussion of gynecological procedures, he said the woman should immediately be given a "D. and C.," which he called "a perfectly normal procedure that I would not put into the category of abortion." In reality, a D. and C. isn't performed until later, after the egg has been implanted, and it is, of course, a form of abortion.

In the final weeks of the election, the Bush campaign did everything it could to keep the pressure on Dukakis, and continued its effort to deny him any chance of an electoral-college victory. Baker says that the first priorities after he became chairman of the Bush campaign, in mid-August, were to keep the Republican base in the South and the West, and to lock up Texas, Ohio, and New

Jersey. There were five supposedly Republican states that were causing trouble—Arkansas, South Dakota, Montana, Colorado, and New Mexico—and they had to be worked on, with candidate appearances and media buys, for most of the campaign. (All these states ended up going for Bush.) A lot of effort was put into Texas, in which Bush was far ahead most of the time, and Ohio and New Jersey were virtually carpet bombed with Bush appearances and advertising—and so, for insurance, was Michigan. Bentsen worked Texas hard, and defended Dukakis ("Do you think I'd serve on any ticket with a fella who'd take my shotgun from me?"), but Texas has become alien territory for a Northern liberal, a culture that could not absorb a man like Dukakis. His failure to carry Texas inevitably caused second-guessing of his choosing Bentsen (despite the fact that Bentsen remained the star of the election), and suggestions that he should have gone with John Glenn, who might have helped him carry Ohio. (But Dukakis would have gone with Glenn had his advisers not told him he couldn't, because of some financial questions.)

The Bush camp's strategy of making sure that Bush carried more than the Republicans' base states plus Ohio, Texas, and New Jersey would have yielded them two hundred and seventy-three electoral votes, more than the necessary two hundred and seventy. (Republicans generally win New Jersey, which tends to be less Democratic and less unionized than other Northern states.) Teeter says, "We didn't want to need an inside straight. If you're aiming for two hundred and seventy electoral votes, you should target three hundred and fifty. If you could carry Texas, Ohio, and New Jersey, you could win by carrying California, or Illinois, or Michigan—any one of those pulled the rug out from under Dukakis." Teeter, who is from Michigan, in a decision he says was partly based on the fact that Michigan is less Democratic than it used to be, and partly arbitrary, picked his state as the one to deal the fatal blow to Dukakis.

Toward the end of the campaign, the Bush camp's strategy was, as one official put it, "to shadow the guy—don't let him do anything in the clear—be where he is, get on the air with paid media where he is." So Bush's plane often landed in a state shortly after Dukakis's had left—they were both concentrating on the close states; Bush appeared on television programs; and Bush said, "I'm on your side." The Bush people were conscious of the fact that Dukakis had succeeded in making the case that theirs was the dirtier campaign, and got reports that people were becoming convinced that Dukakis had ended the furlough program. (Thus the Bush surrogates defended the Bush ads, and the furlough ad was recycled.) But the real thing that worried the Bush camp was that all of a sudden Dukakis seemed to be closing on Bush.

The first sighting of what was referred to as a "surge" by Dukakis came toward the end of the week before the week before the election—around October 27th. In the Bush camp's tracking poll (a poll that is taken nightly, to catch changes quickly), Bush's lead went down from about ten points to six. (A close figure nationally had more serious implications, because Bush was so far ahead in a number of states, including Florida and Texas, which meant that California and the large industrial states were closer.) The Dukakis camp didn't pick up such a change in the national numbers but did notice that the race had become close in some key states. But then, according to the Bush camp's polling, the "surge" stopped after two days. And then, toward the end of the following week, very shortly before the election, both camps' polls showed Dukakis starting to gain ground again. Teeter says, "What we couldn't know was whether this was a return to normal, because our leads had been so large, or whether we were in a real decline."
The Dukakis camp realized how much it was up against. It had taken Dukakis ten days after the second debate to recoup the loss as a result of that debate. But he was still about ten points behind—and ten points was a large gap with two weeks left. And shortly after that, the Dukakis poll showed him behind by fifteen points. As Irwin (Tubby) Harrison, Dukakis's pollster, and some other advisers saw it, unless Dukakis was within five points, or even fewer, of Bush by the last week, he couldn't win. On the Friday before the election, both the Dukakis and Bush camps had Bush ahead by eight points. But Dukakis still thought he would win (Sasso was careful in talking to him about numbers), and his campaign still wanted him to finish as strongly as possible—and campaigns as well as candidates can get caught up in the excitement and talk themselves into thinking all sorts of things are possible. The Dukakis campaign had built an elaborate field organization—whose value was questioned by several within the

campaign—for getting out the vote, which, it was thought, might count for a point or two. The two camps were considering the various combinations of states that could make it impossible for Dukakis to win, or perhaps give him a far-outside chance of winning. The Bush people figured that if their man won two of the three states of Ohio, Illinois, and Michigan, Dukakis couldn't win. Bush had been ahead in Ohio by double digits for some time. (At one point, the figure dropped to six.) Texas was well beyond Dukakis's reach. On the Friday before the election, Teeter told me, "The advantage we have now is if any one of a dozen things happens we will win, and for him to win, all of a dozen things have to happen." But no one was taking any chances, and, besides, campaign aides get paid to worry.

As the two weary candidates were slugging it out in the final days, both camps were making last minute scheduling decisions. Bush began to make ominous slips of the tongue, so his schedule was kept as limited as possible. Bush's campaign, reflecting the bifurcation in Bush's own campaigning, ran both attack ads and gauzy positive ads—the granddaughter in the striped dress running into his arms had become a familiar sight. Dukakis made ads in which he looked straight into the camera to tell voters who he was and that he cared about their concerns—but it was a little late for that. Bush, aware of the question of what sort of mandate he could take from this election, said he would have "a mainstream mandate." He said that Dukakis had "socialistic" ideas and was a danger on foreign policy. But while Dukakis, going on optimism and adrenaline and drawing some of his energy from the crowds, became a better and better campaigner, Bush seemed to be getting stale. He had nothing new to say. (But he did have Arnold Schwarzenegger campaigning with him for a day in Ohio and Illinois.) Many of his appearances were before ready-made high-school audiences, which, with their bands, could be counted on to provide the requisite noise. In his final appearance, in Ohio, Bush gave some of his positive arguments for why he should be President and also did a summation of all his arguments against Dukakis. He said, "We need people who are going to have a little more concern for the victims of crime and a little less concern for the criminals themselves." (Bush had been taking around with him and showing off the shield of a policeman who had been killed by drug dealers, and indicating that Dukakis did not feel compassion toward the families of victims of crime. Someone who once worked for Bush says this is the kind of thing he used to think Bush would not do.) Bush listed some things he was for—more spending for the Head Start program; a program for college-tuition savings bonds; more protection of the environment (but against gun control)—and said, "I'm here to talk about the great bright future for an America at work and a world at peace." He said, "Do not go back to where we were in 1980 with the tired tax-and-spend policies that failed us." Looking good and speaking slowly and with strength, chopping the air with his hand (but keeping his eyes glued to his note cards)—and aware that he was about to win the Presidency—he said, "I never felt better in my life. That adrenaline is flowing. The family's together. The country is coming in behind our candidacy, and I want to win this election." He concluded, "I am on your side of the great divide. The mainstream family values are what we need to keep emphasizing."

On the Sunday before the election, Harrison's polling had Dukakis behind (accurately, as it turned out) by eight points. Yet some Dukakis people still entertained the possibility that Dukakis could win—that with very low turnout the field organization could be of great advantage. Just before the election, the public polls (of which there had been too many too often) were showing Dukakis behind by anywhere from five to twelve points—which suggests the degree to which we should rely on them. But the numbers were very tight in several of the big states. At the same time, the Bush people were watching Bush's lead drop from seven or eight points to five or six points. Then, on the morning of the election, November 8th, they got a considerable scare when Teeter's overnight polling showed Bush ahead by only three points. By this time, Bush had been engaged in conversations with his advisers about his plans for the transition, but the low margin over Dukakis put at least a temporary halt to that. The figure made the Bush people particularly nervous because they knew they had a big margin in the Southern states. That afternoon's exit polls taken by the networks were also indicating that it was very close in many of the big states. (The results of these polls are not supposed to be public until the polls are closed in each of the states, but there are ways of finding them out.) Everyone knew that it was only by some extremely remote set of circumstances that Dukakis could win, and the Bush people still thought they would win—but didn't spend a very relaxing day. It was when CBS, at 8 P.M., called Michigan for Bush that both the Bush people and the Dukakis people knew it was over.

Though Bush ended up winning by a margin of eight points (54–46), and an electoral vote of four hundred and twenty-six to a hundred and twelve, a number of states were indeed close. Bush won Illinois, Pennsylvania, Maryland, and Vermont by 51–49, and he won California, Missouri, and New Mexico by 52–48. Connecticut, Montana, and South Dakota were won by Bush by 53–47. Democrats took some comfort from the fact that Dukakis had won ten states (New York, Massachusetts, Rhode Island, West Virginia, Wisconsin, Minnesota, Iowa, Washington, Oregon, Hawaii) as well as the District of Columbia, and that they had picked up one Senate seat. (Bentsen easily won reëlection to his Senate seat.) Bush was the first President since Kennedy to be elected at the same time the opposing party made gains in both the House and the Senate. (The Democrats also picked up one governorship.) Some analyses say that people deliberately divide their vote between the two parties in order to keep both the President and Congress in check, but that is overintellectualizing their act. They deal with the choices they're handed. The vote for senator and representative is a much more personal one than the one for President—voters are more familiar with Senate candidates, who may have been working the state (as senator or not) for years, and House members have become self-perpetuating all-service outfits, using the tools of their office to guarantee reëlection and wiring their districts and seeing to their constituents' every need. The interest groups tend to favor the known incumbent with their financial contributions. (So, in keeping with the patterns of recent years, 98.5 per cent of those House members who stood for reëlection were reëlected.) Turnout, at fifty per cent, was the lowest since 1924, and more people than ever before told pollsters that they were unhappy about this Presidential campaign, and the candidates. While it is fashionable every four years to complain about the Presidential campaign, this time it was different, and for real.

While the Democrats' showing in the Presidential race was an improvement over the last two elections, and some Democrats took comfort in Dukakis's victories, and near-victories, in the West, the results showed that the Party still has a problem at the Presidential level. Bush won the white vote in all regions of the country, most heavily in the South. Despite all the difficulties, Dukakis won eighty-eight per cent of the black vote. Dukakis won back some of the blue-collar voters who had gone for Reagan, giving him fifty-one per cent of their vote, a two-point lead over Bush. (In 1984, Reagan had won them 55–45.) Among Democrats there are as many analyses of what went wrong as there are long-held points of view; people bring to the analysis what they already thought. A number of Democratic politicians think Dukakis could have won the election if he had run a better campaign; many think another Democrat could have won; others think that there is no way a Northern liberal, especially a Northeastern liberal, can win in the foreseeable future—but all these are unprovable hypotheses. Ideas have already been floated about how to rejigger the nominating process once again. Some possible candidates for 1992 (Joseph Biden, Richard Gephardt, Bill Bradley, and Jesse Jackson) got themseves to Iowa this fall.

At a press conference the morning after the election, Bush was subdued, and acknowledged that he was still absorbing what had happened to him. Dukakis, at his press conference later that day, was gracious. He had already gone back to the Massachusetts statehouse to resume his work as governor; he has some repair work to do in his own state. But it seemed that the enormity of the loss had not yet sunk in on him. With the election over, Bush began to actually define himself. Though he was a successful Presidential candidate, even several Republican analysts believed he had never become a good Presidential candidate—one who has a clear sense of where he wants to take the country, and gets that across.

Since the election, Bush has acquired "winnerness," the mysterious process by which he changes in our eyes as well as his own. Winning the Presidency does wonders for a man's confidence, and Bush is enjoying the line of credit that is given to all new Presidents. In the days since the election, he has shown more confidence and self-possession than he ever has before in his various public roles. His appointments are watched with great interest and are invested with meaning that may or may not be there. His announcement, on the morning after the election, of his choice

of Baker as Secretary of State was no surprise—somehow everyone knew that Baker wanted the job, and clearly Bush owed his
longtime friend a great deal. His choice of New Hampshire Governor John Sununu as chief of staff, announced on November
17th, was something else: Sununu had certainly helped rescue
Bush in New Hampshire, and had spent much of the campaign
attacking Dukakis (about whom he seemed to have an obsession).
But Sununu is by most accounts, including those of his fellow-
governors, an abrasive, difficult man, which can be something of
a problem in a chief of staff, who has many dealings with Congress.
(This choice could not have pleased Robert Dole, whose candidacy
effectively ended in New Hampshire, and who remains bitter
toward Bush—notwithstanding the smiling lunch they had together following the election.) Bush has taken several conciliatory
steps—including a meeting with Dukakis—but the Democrats in
Congress know that they won on their own, and they will not fear
Bush the way they feared Reagan, because they do not view Bush
as having Reagan's ability to tap strong public support by taking
to the airwaves. Some of them resent the campaign that Bush ran,
and may remember it at an opportune moment; a few, for the
same reason, say they don't plan to make life completely easy for
Baker. These feelings may wear off over time, but Bush can't be
sure of that. Bush's installation of Atwater as chairman of the
Republican National Committee was a sign that hardball politics
is now enshrined at the highest level. The talk of Bush's desire to
put "fresh faces" throughout the Administration, despite his asking some Cabinet officers to stay on, means that he intends to
build his own political power base within the government, and to
try to secure his reëlection.[2] His personnel choices suggest that
we will continue to see the two sides of Bush we saw throughout
his fall campaign: the "kinder and gentler" Bush and the rough
and ruthless Bush. We will still be finding out how his inner compass works.

He faces a series of daunting problems. The drop in the stock
market and the dollar in the days immediately after his election
bespoke a lack of confidence in his ability to reduce the budget

[2]By year's end, Bush had chosen a largely moderate group, with prior government experience, for his cabinet. He also sought to deal with certain political
exigencies by including Jack Kemp and Elizabeth Dole.

deficit—as by law he must. It also bespoke the irrationality of the markets, because he was the same man, with the same program, after the election as he was the day before it. His "read my lips" vow to not raise taxes had been with us for quite a while. Many people are waiting to see when, not whether, Bush eventually breaks that vow, but if he does a price could be even deeper cynicism among the electorate. Our national savings rate has decreased dramatically in recent years—we have been living beyond our means and borrowing from abroad to finance our spending spree. As a result, the usual growth in our standard of living and in productivity is seriously threatened. And the willingness of others to keep financing our profligacy may not be infinite. (The decline in the value of the dollar over the past three years is a signal.) Interest rates have already risen since the election. The Pentagon's budget requires some hard decisions, since it is now committed to producing more weapons than can possibly be paid for even if the budget is allowed to grow at the pace of inflation. Life in the inner cities, which Bush said in the campaign he was "haunted" by, won't be much affected by his proposal to send better-off high-school youngsters into them as volunteers to help out. Inner-city schools are a disaster. The education level of this country is an embarrassment. Despite the posturing drug bill passed by Congress this fall, no one has a handle on what to do about the drug culture. Corporate debt, fuelled by manic takeovers, is rising at what many feel is an alarming rate; it will take many tens of billions of dollars to bail out the savings-and-loan industry. Fixing the safety, environmental, and management problems at the plants that make nuclear-weapons material—for some reason, the longstanding problems didn't come to light until this fall— will be very costly. Unknown challenges lie overseas. The continuing Third World–debt problem, the spread of nuclear weapons and of the capability for producing chemical weapons on the part of a number of countries (including Libya) are just some of the things to be considered.

After a long struggle, to which he gave a lot and for which he paid a price, George Bush has realized his life's dream of becoming President. Now he has to govern.

INDEX